ENCYCLOPEDIA OF SPORTS PARENTING

Advance praise

"Student athletes experience many personally defining moments on the playing field, as well as in the classroom. While only a few will go on to professional careers as athletes, most of us find the lessons from our athletic experiences are among the most important. Dan Doyle has done a remarkable job in developing his *Encyclopedia of Sports Parenting*—and, in doing so, has done a remarkable service to us all. Dan's vision for the kind of experience students should have through sport comes through with great clarity in this impressive compendium. And that vision is one that will lead to better experience and outcomes for our students, our schools, our communities and our nation."
　　　　　　　　　　　　　　　　　　　—Senator George J. Mitchell

"Dan Doyle's *Encyclopedia of Sports Parenting* is brilliant, and serves a real need in the athletics community. It is, by far, the most comprehensive book that I have seen on this important topic. Youth sports have changed dramatically over the years. Unfortunately, one of the worst trends has been the move to specialization and year round training in one sport for young athletes. With this has come a dramatic increase in the involvement of parents in the athletic careers of their sons and daughters. Dan lays out very clearly the proper role that parents should play in their children's careers. It is a must read, not only for parents, but also for athletes, coaches and administrators."
　　　　　　　　—Mark Murphy, Athletic Director, Northwestern University;
　　　former captain, Washington Redskins Super Bowl Championship Team.

"The book contains more wisdom about parenting, not just sports parenting, than I've ever seen in one place. It is the work of a lifetime of coaching, teaching and writing, and could very well change for the better how the country thinks about youth sports. Dan Doyle is a clear writer and thinker, and the book is something every parent of a scholar/athlete - that's what Doyle wants them to be - ought to read."　　　　　—Tom Condon, The Hartford Courant

"Dan Doyle's *Encyclopedia of Sports Parenting* is brilliant—a remarkable and long-needed gift, not only for moms and dads, but for any adult who has the great good fortune to nurture a child through sports. The writing style embraces clarity, wit and style, and the message is a combination of philosophy and practicality, reality and compassion, honesty and honor. This volume is by far the most comprehensive gathering of advice for parents of youngsters who participate in sports that has ever been compiled."

—Acclaimed novelist, Mary-Ann Tirone-Smith.

"Dan Doyle has given parents a great gift. He has shared his enormous wisdom borne of his experiences as a parent, teacher, coach, and scholar to a subject that touches virtually every family in America. The clarity of his thinking is liberating to this parent who has struggled in his own roles of parent, teacher and coach. Dan's gift is much more than a book about parenting and athletics. It is a book about values, about being an effective parent and helping our children become people of character. If parents across this great Nation committed to his notion of honorable competition, we would be giving our children a great gift, one that would serve them well throughout their lives."   —Dr. Lee Levison, Headmaster, Collegiate School, New York City

"Wow! *Encyclopedia of Sports Parenting* is truly the bible for sports parents of athletes of all ages. The college recruiting section is by far the most in-depth and best ever written on this subject. I plan to highly recommend this book to parents of my recruits—and parents in general. As a parent of two teenage boys as well as being a college coach for the past 30 years, I really appreciate that a long awaited book has been written which will have a positive and profound impact on the sports culture."

—Dave Hixon, Head Men's Basketball Coach, Amherst College

"As a pediatrician, my role is to guide parents in promoting their children's optimal growth and development. The *Encyclopedia of Sports Parenting* is an extraordinarily comprehensive resource that informs both parents and child health providers, alike. This remarkable text addresses virtually all aspects of youth sports through a unique combination of insightful observations, expert opinions, informative anecdotes, and research findings. Dan Doyle offers guidance on nurturing in our children such desirable qualities as integrity, a strong work ethic, mental toughness, self-discipline and self-control, self-reliance and self-esteem, teamwork, leadership, organizational skills, 'competitive self restraint,' willpower, trust, and delayed gratification. These rich recommendations have profound implications that extend beyond sports and also serve as a superb handbook on effective parenting."

—Paul H. Dworkin, MD,
Professor and Chair of the Department of Pediatrics,
University of Connecticut School of Medicine,
Physician-in-Chief, Connecticut Children's Medical Center,
Hartford, Connecticut

(continued on page 473)

ENCYCLOPEDIA OF
SPORTS
PARENTING

DAN DOYLE

WITH

DEBORAH DOERMANN BURCH

Kingston, Rhode Island

Published by Hall of Fame Press

Copyright © 2008 by Dan Doyle

First Edition

LIBRARY OF CONGRESS

CATALOGING IN PUBLICATION DATA

Doyle, Dan, 1949-
Encyclopedia of sports parenting

p. cm.

C.I.P. available upon request
ISBN: 978-09776240-1-0

Printed in the United States of America
Distributed in North America by Moyer Bell
549 Old North Road, Kingston, Rhode Island 02881,
401-783-5480, www.moyerbellbooks.com and
in the United Kingdom, Eire, and Europe by
Gazelle Book Services Ltd.,
White Cross Mills, High Town,
Lancaster LA1 1RN England,
1-44-1524-68765, www.gazellebooks.co.uk

To my sports parents,
the late Marie Doyle and the late Daniel E. Doyle, Sr.,
and to my sports uncle, the late Matthew P. O'Regan
—with great love and gratitude.

CONTENTS

CONTENTS

When the first draft was complete, I contacted a group of highly respected individuals to ask that they read the text and, if comfortable with what they read, offer a testimonial. I am grateful to all of those whose quotes and generous testimonials appear in this book.

Toward the conclusion of the project, I called upon a group of distinguished professionals with a particular interest in sports parenting to serve as "final readers." Elizabeth Abbott, Rick Boyages, Suzanne Coffey, Jerry Creamer, Suzi D'Annolfo, my sons Andy and Matt, Sue Francis McCarthy, Meg McCrudden, Linda Pearson, Art Quirk, Jeanmarie Shea, Jim Skiff, Jere Smith, Rod Steier, Bob Stiepock, Erica Wheeler and Julie Zyla all did a magnificent job, as did seven wonderful Institute for International Sport interns— Chanel Benjamin, Andrea Cortes, Lauren Hylton, Tyler Norsworthy, Caitlin Rogers, Chris Shea and Anna Uehara.

Encyclopedia of Sports Parenting was originally to be published by Warner Books. Several years into the writing, it became apparent that the *Encyclopedia* was a far more extensive project than either side had originally anticipated, one that would take several more years to complete. During this period, the Institute for International Sport decided to form a publishing company, Hall of Fame Press, that would publish two to three sport-themed books per year. Warner Books, and my fine editor at WB, Rick Wolff, were gracious in allowing me to move the *Encyclopedia* series over to Hall of Fame Press, a move that will benefit the work of the Institute for International Sport.

A special thanks to my Institute Board of Trustees, chaired by Russ Hogg, for allowing me the time to complete the project and to Institute supporters and dear friends Chuck Feeney, Bob Carothers, Wally Halas, Ray Handlan, Alan Hassenfeld, Congressman Patrick Kennedy, Bill Lynch, Attorney General Patrick Lynch (RI), Joe MarcAurele, Speaker Bill Murphy (RI), Senator Jack Reed, Senator Jack Revens, Nick Tomassetti, Bob Weygand and my brother Mike.

Finally, I owe a *great* debt of gratitude to my family. My wife Kathy and our children Danny, Matt, Andy, Meg, Carrie and Julie could not have been more supportive during the process. At every step, my family members were eager to look at chapters and offer invaluable insights. They also selflessly gave me space to complete the project, and I am *extremely* grateful for their support.

Why the Title?

I chose the title "The Encyclopedia of Sports Parenting" because my objective with this three-volume series is to carefully address issues essential to developing a comprehensive sports parenting and coaching philosophy. While I do not employ the A-Z format of most encyclopedias, the series, which will include a Volume II of *The Encyclopedia of Sports Parenting* and *The Master Coach Manual*, scrupulously follows *The American Heritage Dictionary* definition of encyclopedia, *i.e., a comprehensive work covering numerous aspects of a particular field.*

In this case, the field is sports parenting!

About Volume II

Volume II (scheduled for publication in 2009) will provide in-depth commentary on additional issues faced by sports parents, commentary which will also be useful for the further development of a comprehensive sports parenting philosophy. Topics addressed in Volume II will include:

Specialization

The Single Parent

Specialty Academies

Time Profiles of Serious Athletes

The Athlete Who Competes in an Individual Sport

The Gifted Athlete

The Passionate Child (who is excessively passionate about sports)

The Shy, Timid Child

The Sensitive Child

The Big Child

The Use of Performance Enhancing Drugs

Sports Psychology & Maximizing Performance

The Long Odds of Obtaining a College Scholarship or Professional
    Contract

Parenting Your College Athlete

Should Your High School or College Athlete Transfer?

Prep School — An Option Worth Considering

Should Your Child Repeat a Grade for Sports Reasons?

The Middle School Years

Bullying

The Risks of Hazing

Dealing with Heckling & Trash Talking

Getting Over the Devastating Error

Physical Courage versus Mental Courage

The Five-Step Sportsmanship Program

Sportsmanship, Self-Control & Non-Violence

Don't Let Your Son be too Macho: Thumos versus Arête

Employing Aristotle's Golden Mean in Your Sports Parenting

How to Deal with "The Politics of Sports"

Coaching Young Athletes from Different Cultures

Hiring a Personal Trainer/Personal Coach

Renaissance Education

Expressing Creativity Through Sports

When Sports Get in the Way of Religious Services

Enriching Domestic Sports Travel

Enriching Foreign Sports Travel (and Hosting a Foreign Team)

Obesity

The Fan Behavior Code at Athletic Contests

Sports Parenting and Racial Issues

Using a Love of Sports to Cultivate a Love of Reading

About *The Master Coach Manual*

The objective of *The Master Coach Manual* (scheduled for publication in 2009) is to raise the standard of coaching and enhance the impact of coaches on society. *Encyclopedia of Sports Parenting* surveys make strikingly clear that coaches—for better or worse—exert a profound effect on the viewpoints, actions and habits of their players. The hundreds of interviews we have conducted with coaches confirm that few have a clearly developed philosophy on issues such as violence, sportsmanship, gamesmanship, character development and intellectual development—including the development of critical thinking skills. Among other objectives, *The Master Coach Manual* will help coaches develop a coherent philosophy which they can impart to their student-athletes—a philosophy that encompasses the recognition that sport, at its best, can contribute to a positive and civil society.

The Master Coach Manual will include commentary on topics such as:

The Criteria to Become a Master Coach

The Societal Objectives of a Master Coach

ENCYCLOPEDIA OF SPORTS PARENTING

SECTION I

DEVELOPING A SPORTS PARENTING PHILOSOPHY

Chapter 1

THE GOOD AND BAD THINGS ABOUT SPORTS

"To the art of working well a civilized race would add the art of playing well."
—Philosopher George Santayana

In 1968, my wonderful coach at Worcester Academy, Dee Rowe, selected me to play on a New England prep school all-star team that toured Europe during spring vacation. The trip took place during the height of the Vietnam conflict and for the first time since World War II, many Europeans treated Americans not as welcome visitors, but as intruders. Our team felt this disfavor in the form of boos during games. We were even confronted with a picket line!

Coach Rowe seized on the harsh reaction to make the tour not merely about games, but also about education beyond the court. He arranged a series of post-game receptions where we met and spoke with our opponents and others in the community, many of whom expressed strong anti-American sentiments. Despite some philosophical differences, it was obvious to me that my teammates and I could develop friendships with individuals against whom we competed and with whom we conversed.

I came away from the experience with a better understanding of Vietnam and a clear recognition that our common interest in sports had brought us together for the spirited discussions. On many occasions since 1968, I have watched sports serve not only as a medium to unite people from diverse backgrounds, but as a proving ground which can profoundly influence personal qualities such as integrity and self-discipline.

To be sure, sports can have a negative, even dark side, that will be addressed head-on in this book. To help you develop a prudent and disciplined sports parenting philosophy, I begin with a list of the many good, if not extraordinary, qualities of sports, followed by a list of its shortcomings.

Good Things About Sports

"All of those people pushing and protesting to let me play showed that sports has a way to change a whole lot of things."
— The first African-American player
to compete in the Sugar Bowl, Bobby Grier

1. Sports can help a child develop a work ethic and a mental toughness, both of which can be useful in later life.

2. Sports can offer repeated opportunities for a child to practice and improve the skills of self-discipline and self-control.

3. Sports participation in childhood can set the stage for a life of physical fitness.

4. Sports can teach a child about fair play, which can serve as an ethical framework throughout life.

5. Sports can encourage the development of self-reliance and self-respect.

6. Sports, as much as any activity, can teach a child about teamwork.

7. Sports can offer varied and increasingly difficult challenges as a child advances in age and skill.

8. Sports can provide a venue for observing and then practicing good leadership skills.

9. Sports can teach a child to listen to and follow directions.

10. Sports can teach a child to face adversity, live with it, and sometimes even conquer it.

11. Sports can teach a child how to win with grace and lose with dignity.

12. Sports can provide a child with a sense of earned accomplishment.

13. Sports can teach a child about human diversity. For many of us, sports was our introduction to diversity.

14. Sports can encourage a child to develop organizational skills.

15. Sports can channel a child's competitive spirit in a healthy direction.

16. Sports can help a child learn to focus amidst distractions, a skill transferable to non-sport learning.

17. Sports can produce utter joy.

18. Sports can teach a child constructive methods for dealing with mistakes, and nurture a resolve to do better the next time.

19. Sports can foster a sense of belonging by offering a child a place on a team and even new friends.

20. Sports can help a child cultivate "competitive self-restraint," a term you will read throughout this book.

21. Sports can be a basis for wonderful conversations, trips, reunions, laughter and, most importantly, close relationships.

22. Sports can offer a healthy alternative to idle time, especially for youngsters from at-risk neighborhoods.

23. Sports is the "official headquarters" of positive mentoring in our society, notably by the thousands of firm, fair and caring coaches who work with children.

24. Team sports provide a child with the opportunity to focus on something bigger than oneself.

25. Sports can strengthen the bonds between parents and children, and it can help bridge a generational gap.

26. Sports can create powerful and lifelong bonds among young athletes and between young athletes and their coaches.

27. Sports can serve as a source of personal, family and community vitality.

28. Sports can teach a child about the importance of preparation.

29. Sports can help a child learn the value of setting goals, and develop the perseverance to attain the goals.

30. Sports can help a child learn to deal with different types of authority, from the coach, to the captain, to the referee.

31. Sports can help a child learn to deal maturely with unpleasant people and situations.

32. Sports can help a child learn how to manage a passion.

33. Sports can help a child learn that it is okay to resist peer pressure.

34. Sports can help a child learn to build trust, particularly with teammates.

35. Sports can help a child learn the value of delayed gratification.

36. And, at its best, sports can help us believe that anything is possible!

Yet Not All is Good

As a youngster playing sports in Worcester, Massachusetts, it was common to hear a well-meaning coach say, "If you're a success on the court, you'll be a success in life."

This is not necessarily true!

Several years ago, I helped a journalist friend prepare a list of a region's best athletes of the 20th century. I enjoyed the process, and actually ended up sending my friend 96 names. I recently pulled out my list, and reviewed it with an eye toward what these 96 successful athletes had done with their lives.

While some on the list enjoyed successful careers and/or personal lives, a surprising number struggled mightily in one or both areas. "I peaked at 18, and after that it was all downhill," confided one former star player.

For those unable to transfer athletic excellence to other undertakings, there seemed to be a revealing common denominator: their success as young athletes had given them a false, even delusional sense of self-importance. For many, athletic success was accompanied by the passivity and even complicity of parents, coaches or teachers who permitted the young stars to take short-cuts and neglect their academic and character development.

When parents encourage balance and perspective, sports can have a wonderful impact on a child. Without such balance and perspective, sports can produce detrimental, sometimes devastating consequences.

Bad Things About Sports

"In all important respects, the man who has nothing but his physical power to sell, has nothing to sell which is worth anyone's money to buy."
—Author Norman Wiener

1. Sports can encourage a child to focus so intently on becoming a star that the child neglects other essential areas of life.

2. Sports offer the most common avenue to adolescent acclaim, a fleeting journey that will end soon—and often abruptly.

3. Sports can cause a child to fall into a pattern of rationalizing unacceptable behavior. A good example is the athlete who becomes so competitive that he will do anything to win, convincing himself that the ends justify the means.

4. A few sports foster a culture of violence. Such a misguided culture too often spills over into barbaric acts in and out of competition, and also produces a copycat reaction among some impressionable young athletes.

5. Sports can produce an unhealthy level of stress in a child, particularly a child who is pushed to excel and who feels a failure with every loss.

6. Sports can produce irrational, boorish behavior among parents and athletes.

7. Sports can produce many athletes who are negative role models.

8. Sports can produce many coaches who are negative role models.

9. Sports can produce many parents who are negative role models, especially those who overvalue athletic achievement.

10. Sports, even team sports, can promote selfish behavior.

11. Dreams of sports glory can induce some parents to completely lose perspective of the really important things in their child's life, especially that the athlete is a child.

12. Sports can chip away at a child's self-esteem. A child who falls short of athletic goals or who perceives that one is valued only for athletic ability may lack a sense of value and self-worth off the field.

13. The desire to win can lead some young athletes to turn to harmful, illegal substances.

14. Sports can be so time-consuming that it leaves some athletes with little time for studies or social life.

15. Sports can be a distraction from serious academic pursuit. At the highest level of intercollegiate competition, colleges are producing magnificent athletes who, in many cases, are ill-equipped to engage in any meaningful life's work.

16. From blaming referees for poor calls to listening to those who say, "you are being treated unfairly," sports can be a haven for excuses.

17. Sports can allow many who are physically gifted to behave like arrogant bullies.

18. Sports can allow many who are physically gifted to underestimate the real meaning of hard work.

19. The link between sports stardom and arrested development is far too common.

20. The "trample the opponent" philosophy espoused by some coaches and

parents sends the wrong message about the core value of empathy.

21. When sports are more important to the parent than the child, it can create distance and resentment, particularly when a child's performance does not live up to parental hopes and expectations.

22. Burnout or injuries from sports can lead to neglect of physical fitness.

23. Finally, sports can teach a child that it is acceptable to cheat or take shortcuts to win, especially if coaches and parents turn a blind eye toward such practices. Gamesmanship tactics such as "orchestrated chatter" in youth league baseball to distract the batter, or flopping in basketball, when a defensive player fakes an offensive foul by falling to the floor, are frequently encouraged by coaches and parents, and employed by young athletes. Acceptance of these tactics fosters a belief that such behaviors are not only acceptable but admirable; to win at any cost is okay.

How can there be so many good and bad things about sports? There are a number of reasons, but they all relate to the fact that sports have an unusual, almost unique capacity to evoke powerful emotions and desires within many of us. When these feelings are channeled in the right direction, sports can be a productive, even ennobling experience. Yet, when strong desires and emotions are allowed to follow an obsessive course, the end product will likely include one or more of the bad consequences discussed.

As a sports parent, you must be prepared to cultivate the positive qualities and firmly confront the negative possibilities. Your job is to maintain your own balanced attitude, while encouraging your youngster to pursue a healthy and balanced approach to school, sports and character development.

This book will provide you with specific strategies on how to accomplish these objectives.

A Guiding Principle

"Be courageously temperate and temperately courageous."
—Aristotle

A good and simple concept to follow, in sports parenting and other facets of life, is Aristotle's Golden Mean—finding that balance or "golden mean" between deficiency and excess.

Chapter 2

A VALUES-BASED SPORTS PARENTING PHILOSOPHY

"Day by day, what you choose, what you think and what you do is who you become."
—Greek Philosopher, Heraclitus

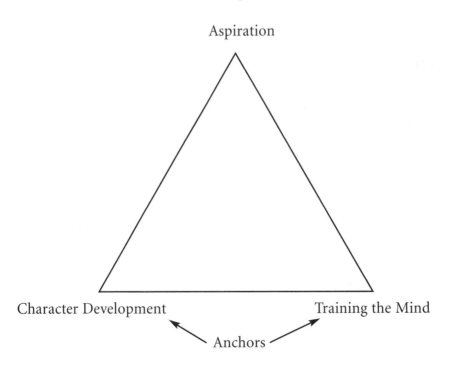

Aspiration

Character Development   Training the Mind

Anchors

The Anchor/Aspiration Approach to Child Rearing

"Slight not what's near through aiming at what's far."
—Greek Playright, Euripides (455 BC)

My anchor/aspiration approach to child rearing is simple. It proposes that aspirational goals such as excellence in sports or the arts are wonderful —they ennoble our lives. But the aspirations must be fortified by two anchors —character development and training the mind—or serious problems can develop. The two anchors provide the critical foundational support; they are the building blocks upon which a child's development rests. The top athlete or flutist deficient in one of the two anchor categories will face serious problems. The top athlete or flutist deficient in both anchor categories will face very serious problems.

In sports, *acclaim often precedes maturity*, and this is why if your child decides to pursue excellence in an extra-curricular activity, it is important for you to monitor your child's development of the two anchor traits. The intense, highly focused specialist is at risk of neglecting one or both of these critical areas. The fast train of athletic success and entitlement thrusts many athletes into a corrosive cycle of neglecting appropriate character and/or academic development.

The Late Earl Woods

In 1995, just before Tiger Woods won the U.S. Amateur championship in Newport, Rhode Island, I had a conversation with Tiger's dad, the late Earl Woods. I found Mr. Woods to be a wonderful man—full of wisdom and perspective, and deeply committed to the well-being of his son. I also discovered two important sports parenting qualities shared by Earl Woods and his wife, Katilda.

- Neither Mr. nor Mrs. Woods pushed Tiger to golf greatness. As Mr. Woods explained, it was Tiger's passion, not that of his parents, that was the driving force behind Tiger's success. (A point Tiger has confirmed on many occasions).
- At the core of the Woods' parenting philosophy was a consistent focus on character development and training the mind.

Just as Earl and Katilda Woods did so well with their son, vigilant parents of sports specialists should send the following message: "We want you to pursue your dream, but whenever we see neglect in your studies or character, the ball (or club or flute) will be taken away." The objective is not to suppress a child's desire to excel but rather to support the desire by making sure that the two anchors are safely moored. Failure to demand consistent effort toward achieving proficiency in the anchor qualities is very detrimental to a youngster's long-term development. Aspirational sports goals should never be mistaken as substitutes for, or interchangeable with, the anchor values.

SUCCESS AND ACADEMIC RIGOR

Our surveys of successful career people who played sports in their youth make an obvious but important point: Many told us that their love of sports did not detract from the anchor qualities of training the mind and character development. While the athletic accomplishments of these highly successful adults covered a wide span, most fell into the "average athlete" category. The majority, however, seemed to recognize the limits of sports, and the boundless opportunities associated with academic rigor and good character.

Eleven Important Values to be Learned from Sports

Because sports are so engaging, they offer a good vehicle for teaching strong lessons to children. Many of the following values come under the umbrella of good sportsmanship which, broadly defined, emphasizes honesty, fair play, winning and losing gracefully, and respectful treatment of all players, officials, coaches and spectators. Parents should help their child develop and practice a sound, values-based sports philosophy, the tenets of which are useful in all facets of life.

Throughout your child's sports career, teach and reinforce the following values—and begin early!

1. Balance and Perspective
2. Honesty/Good Sportsmanship
3. Self-Reliance/Responsibility
4. Self-Control/Non-Violence
5. Hard Work/Perseverance
6. Respect
7. Empathy
8. Teamwork/Unselfishness
9. Tolerance
10. Moral Courage
11. Physical Fitness

2

Level I — Elementary/Youth League Players

Which values you teach, and when, will depend upon the age of your athlete. Athletes of elementary school age, who play on a school or youth league team, should be taught the following values and their fine points.

Value I — Balance and Perspective

"She has been blessed with a gift of maturity and perspective, something that many athletes learn only much later in life, if ever. Somebody raised her right."
—*New York Times* on Olympic Skater, Michelle Kwan

Parents must help their child establish a balanced, reasonably structured lifestyle which demands good character and academic proficiency, and thus encourages a child to choose extracurricular/recreational activities such as sports, music or the arts. Parents should not allow sports to become so time and labor intensive that schoolwork suffers. Parents should not allow sports to gain such importance that an athlete only feels valued for her sports performance or for winning.

Six Points Regarding Perspective

Be sure your young athlete understands that:

1. Schoolwork, good character and good behavior come first, and sports are a complementary and beneficial extracurricular activity.

2. The joy and satisfaction of participating in healthy, fair and challenging competition—and the benefits of physical fitness—are among the most important reasons to play a sport.

3. You are proud of your player's hard work and effort, whatever the final score!

4. Winning is a worthy goal, but it is not the only objective of sports.

5. Losing is as much a part of sports as winning, and it is important for an athlete to learn from both—and learn how to handle both with grace.

6. A sports career will probably take up a very, very small percentage of your whole life.

Parents need to continually reinforce a balanced point of view about where sports fall within the overall context of childhood learning and development, as well as a balanced attitude toward the sport itself.

Value II — Honesty and Good Sportsmanship

Emphasize the following:
- Always play by the rules *and* the spirit of the rules, even when no one is looking.
- Never cheat to gain unfair advantage.
- Never go along with others who cheat or play dirty.
- Honesty and fair play extend to unsupervised games and activities. In unsupervised play, it is the athlete who must deal fairly with line calls, fouls, and playing time issues.

Why is good sportsmanship so important? For two very simple reasons: First, it is the right thing to do, and second, no fair minded person likes a cheater. Institute for International Sport surveys of young athletes found that among the most common reasons that athletes did not like or respect opponents or teammates was because they used unethical means to win.[1]

Encourage your child to talk to you about any questions regarding what is right and wrong. Also, encourage your maturing player to discuss such issues with the coach!

Value III — Self-Reliance/Responsibility

Parents who want their child to develop self-reliant, responsible behavior must allow their athlete the freedom to learn how to deal with problems without constant parental intervention. Firm rules and guidance on issues such as good sportsmanship and self-control are okay. Parental micro-management regarding issues such as playing time, playing position and coaching strategy is not okay.

Intrusive parenting stifles a child's growing self-reliance.

Seven Self-Reliance Points

Encourage your player to do the following:
1. Plan ahead and practice time management skills for completing homework both before and after sports activities.

2. Gather equipment, uniform, water, etc. before a game without constant parental reminders.

3. Employ self-discipline to practice and improve skills during free time.

4. Engage in "free play" and "pick up" games in which players learn how to stand up for their rights, negotiate and compromise.

5. Learn to deal with directions, discipline, and criticism from coaches, as

well as frustrating issues with teammates. Your job is to advise, not act on behalf of your child. Parental intervention in coach/team activities is rarely appropriate or necessary unless there are health, ethical, abuse or sportsmanship problems.

6. Learn to deal with disappointing play by increasing resolve rather than by making excuses.

7. Discuss problems and problem-solving strategies with you, and then try to follow through independently. This is a key goal in the self-reliance journey!

Value IV - Self-Control/Non-Violence

Young athletes need to understand that sports involve physical activities which result in accidental, incidental, i.e., "part of the game," or sometimes intentional physical contact. Explain that the rules for each sport clarify which types of physical contact are permitted and which types are not. *The player's job at all times is to maintain self-control in response to any physical or verbal harassment, contact or fouls.*

- If you are accidentally or intentionally hit, tripped or hurt, *do not hit back, retaliate or argue with other players.* Step away, and let the officials and coaches handle the problem.
- Avoid confrontational posturing, eye contact or verbal barbs while stepping away; in an emotional situation any of these behaviors can provoke a fight.
- Contact by you that is intended to hurt someone, illegally stop or impede a player, or retaliate and get revenge, is never acceptable.
- Practice the "Don't punch back, play harder" credo. When bumped or fouled, your job is to return to the game and focus on playing harder.
- In discussions with your young athlete, make known your objection to profanity, trash talking and baiting officials. Make it clear that these behaviors are unacceptable during or after a game. Explain that fighting, during and after sports competitions, has resulted in severe, sometimes permanent injuries, and even death.
- Explain that self-control often leads to better and more consistent performance — *and surely leads to a better quality of life.*

When using sport as a vehicle to teach self-control and non-violence, *parents must not tolerate* low-grade aggressive tactics such as elbowing, shoving or tripping, which can escalate dirty play or promote fighting.

Your *unambiguous* parental message should be: "No fighting, dirty play or retaliation of any sort, regardless of whether you think the coaches and officials are watching." To reinforce your message, you must establish clear consequences for any violations.

And, by the way, it is *always* important for parent spectators to model self-control! Bad parental game behavior is a source of great stress and embarrassment for children. It can also provoke copycat behavior in a child. Parents do not have the right to take the joy of sport away from a child by their lack of self-control.

A QUESTION TO POSE TO YOUR CHILD!

Billy Lee Long, who coordinates Institute for International Sport activities in the Pacific Rim, is as fine an example of the "honorable competitor" as I have ever observed. As a boy in Australia in the late-50s, Billy was among a small, select group of fledgling tennis players trained by the great Australian coach Harry Hopman. Others in this select group included the likes of Rod Laver, Roy Emerson, and Billy's best friend, Kenny Fletcher, who went on to win 14 Grand Slam doubles titles.

Billy himself had a sparkling career in professional tennis, followed by an equally successful business career. As he approaches age 70, he is an inspiring combination of fitness, intellect, goodwill and serenity.

Based on my admiration for his perspectives on sport and life, I asked Billy about how his parents raised him. I was particularly interested in any specific lessons he recalled as being vital to his success in life, and his present state of equanimity.

Billy responded, "When I was a little boy, my dad, who was our town's best athlete, was firm but gentle. During those times in my youth when I was confronted with some type of challenge or disappointment, my dad would ask me, 'how are you going to persevere?' He would then help by providing me pointers on how to persevere in the face of the particular challenge, but would always leave it up to me to take it from there.

"I am not sure there is a more important question and ensuing discussion that a parent can raise and talk about with a child."

By the way, that remarkable sports parent from Australia, Billy Lee Long, Sr., is 97 as of this writing, and still playing three rounds of golf a week!

Value V — Hard Work/Perseverance

Sports can be very useful in encouraging a youngster's striving spirit. Explain to your player that hard work and extra practice will bring improvement and make a player more valuable to the team. Youngsters will no doubt enjoy their activity more if they work to do their best and improve their skills. At an early age, begin to teach your player about setting goals and developing the resolve and work habits to pursue such goals, even when disappointed. *A wonderful aspect of sports' success is that it often involves hard work and delayed gratification.* Impress upon your child that when success comes after a long period of hard work, it can be even more rewarding than immediate gratification.

Alas, the value of delayed gratification has been lost on many contemporary parents.

Value VI — Respect

"Premature ideas of independence, too little
repressed by parents, beget a spirit of insubordination."
— Thomas Jefferson

Children should be taught to treat everyone with respect. In sports, this encompasses teammates, opponents, coaches, officials and spectators. Tell your child that, "you should never say or do anything that is rude or could hurt another person's feelings or body." No doubt, your child has heard, seen, or been victimized by teasing. Ask her how she would feel if she were being teased for striking out or making a bad kick.

In addition to treating everyone with respect, players should be taught how to earn respect for themselves and their teams through good sportsmanship, hard work and skill development.

Some players go into a competition loudly stating they are going to "get some respect" from another team or player. This is a serious misuse of the word. There is a difference between trying to force respect and earning respect. "Getting some respect" may be a good motivational slogan for a team that wants to gear up for a game, but genuine and enduring respect is a by-product of effort, skill and honorable play.

Value VII — Empathy

Helping your player to understand the feelings of others will be a major step toward your child's maturity. Tell your young athlete:

2

- Winners should never be loud, boastful or taunt the losers.
- A player should never tease or make fun of a less skilled player.
- A teammate who makes a mistake does not need criticism, and usually appreciates encouragement. Make a habit of saying something nice to someone who is less skilled, has lost, or has made a mistake.
- Before you do or say something that could hurt someone, think about how you would feel if you were the other person.
- If you see someone being teased or humiliated, ask yourself:
  - How would I feel if I were that player?
  - Is there anything I can do to help this person?

Value VIII — Teamwork/Unselfishness

Athletes who engage in team sports should be taught that the team comes first—period! Teams work best when everyone plays unselfishly and puts team goals ahead of individual statistics. *If you expect your child to place team goals above personal goals, you must consistently demonstrate your unselfish commitment to the team.* Remember, what is best for the team may not always feel like it's fair, or best, for individual players.

Value IX — Tolerance

Many youngsters go into sports having had no contact with people from other backgrounds. Sports can teach athletes how to feel at ease with people of different races, religions and socio-economic groups.

Take advantage of team sports to make the following points to your athlete:

- It is wrong to be intolerant of people who are different, whether because of dress, skin color, hairstyle, accent, point of view, religion or ethnicity.
- Sports can help you feel more comfortable working with people from all kinds of backgrounds.
- Treat all people the way you would like to be treated, with respect and good sportsmanship.
- When athletes strive toward common goals, there is a good chance that mutual respect and friendship will develop.
- The intense level of emotions generated, and the desire to achieve victory, help players forget personal differences.
- If you are mistreated because you are different, do not respond in a nasty way. Rather, stand up for your rights by maintaining your self-

2

control, displaying dignity, and doing your best.
- People who set a good example by treating everyone courteously and with respect encourage good behavior in others.

Value X — Moral Courage

Moral courage is standing up for what is right, especially when it is not easy or popular. Studies on bullying show that it is often a popular "star" player or student who belittles or bullies others. Tell your youngster:
- Never "go along" with those who single out teammates for harassment or teasing.
- Try to have the courage to speak up when you see another teammate being teased or picked on. Such courage is a quality that can be improved upon over time, and beginning the practice is the vital first step.
- Bullies lose much of their power if they are ignored or verbally confronted, especially by a group.
- Competing in unsupervised games may demand that a player exhibit moral courage by making honest calls of fouls or other infractions.

VALUING THE WHOLE CHILD

Sports should not gain such importance that the young player only feels valued for athletic excellence or winning.

Throughout this book, you will read about the perils of those parents who make young athletes feel worthwhile only if they win. I caution against this for many reasons, including:
- If your child is a skilled athlete, it is likely that most of the feedback received from friends, teammates and even adults relates to the child's sports performance.
- If your child is a *highly* skilled athlete, virtually all of the feedback received will be about sports performance.

This is precisely why you must balance the gale force of sports with consistent attention to the two anchors of character development and training the mind!

Value XI — Physical Fitness

Early in your youngster's life, explain and regularly emphasize the many benefits which result from being physically fit. Tell your player, "Staying physically fit will help you feel better, look better, think better, play better and probably be healthier for the rest of your life."

It is the parent's job to make sure their child receives adequate sleep and eats properly. *Remind your young athlete that sleep and diet strongly influence one's ability to properly perform.*

Levels II & III — Middle School and High School Athletes

In middle school and high school sports, parents should reinforce the values taught to their youth league player. Older athletes must also learn about making more complex choices, such as those involved in gamesmanship and even substance abuse.

Gamesmanship

"The method or art of winning a game or contest by means of unsportsmanlike behavior or other conduct which does not actually break the rules." —The New Book of Knowledge

Rules of sports make a clear distinction between which acts are and are not permitted. Since rules cannot anticipate every behavior or misbehavior, there are some activities which may not specifically violate the rules, but which clearly violate the spirit of the rules. *Gamesmanship tactics include dubious conduct, methods or techniques used to gain advantage or win, but which may not be clearly addressed in the rules of the sport.*

As a parent, your three steps are:

- Explain the meaning of gamesmanship to your child.
- Explain that you believe that gamesmanship tactics should not be used because they violate the spirit of the rules and establish a pattern of taking shortcuts to win.
- Tell your player, "When in doubt about whether to use what might be a questionable tactic, it is probably best to wait and discuss it with me or the coach."

Examples of gamesmanship include:
- A defensive basketball player "flopping" to convince a referee that he picked up a charge.
- A golfer intentionally casting a shadow over the line of a putt.
- A tennis player intentionally stalling between points to throw off an opponent's rhythm.

2

- A batter who, on a full pitch count, pretends there is dirt in an eye and steps out of the batter's box hoping to disrupt the pitcher's concentration.
- A football player who fakes an injury to stop the clock.

Gamesmanship practices are at the core of many sportsmanship/ethical problems in sport and, indeed, in life. Help your child understand the many gray areas in which maneuvering is possible, and firmly teach your player that such tactics are unacceptable. If the coach allows or encourages gamesmanship techniques, tell the coach that you object.

THE "CIRCLE OF CONCERN" EXERCISE

When lecturing to high school and college students (and parents!) I often ask them to do the following:

Draw a circle

- Write down within the circle those groups you really care about, like your family, your personal friends and your teammates.
- Now, confidentially place outside the circle one or more groups you don't really care about. (This step generally causes some to hold back, but with gentle prodding most will agree to confidentially write down one or more groups.)

I then point out following:

- At-risk male youth in gangs accord their fellow gang members considerations such as civility, respect and loyalty. The same is true with many of those who associate with other negative groups/forces in our society.
- When gang members step outside of their very small circle of concern, they care little about those outside the circle and often do horrible things to them. It is as if those outside the circle are somehow not human.

My final step in the exercise is to encourage the audience to always try to widen their circle of concern to include those with whom they may have little in common. I tell them that, "the wider our circles, the better the chances for a civil and just society." I also point out that a problem with some coaches is that they foster within their teams a "small circle approach."

I strongly urge you to engage your child — and yourself — in this exercise.

Respect

Whenever you feel the time is right, teach your young athlete that the word competition comes from the Latin word "competere," which means to strive together, not against each other. Respect is an important part of this concept. Impress upon your young athlete that the honorable competitor respects opponents and, when an opponent tries hard and plays fairly, one often ends up both respecting and admiring the opponent. If a coach teaches your child to dislike or hate opponents, this is the wrong lesson, and you should strongly object.

Empathy

"Understanding so intimate that the feelings, thoughts and motives of one are readily comprehended by another." — The New Book of Knowledge

Many athletes receive confusing signals from parents and coaches about empathy, particularly in the treatment of opponents. It is appropriate to give 100% effort, yet such effort need not preclude treating opponents with respect and decency. Parents must encourage this practice! Young adolescents have highly sensitive feelings. For this reason, it is essential that you emphasize that other athletes may be just as sensitive. *Make it clear that empathy is often at the core of moral decision-making—and is clearly at the core of a moral society.*

Make the following sports-related points to your child:
- Most middle school and high school players have invested a lot of time, energy and heart in their sport, and they should be treated with consideration, whether on the bench or on a losing team.
- The pursuit of individual or team excellence does not require that you show no compassion or empathy for other players.
- Discerning players do not condone the practice of running up the score in a game already won.
- After the game, always treat your opponent with civility and respect.

Some athletes and coaches believe that empathy toward opponents gets in the way of winning. Yet many of the greatest coaches and players are empathetic people who are discerning enough to respect the boundaries of fierce competition.

One benefit of a loss or disappointing performance is to help a child understand how others feel when they lose—and why empathy is so important.

Make the following life-related points to your child:
- An empathetic person is one who can look at the world through the eyes of others.

- Empathy is an essential ingredient to fixing and maintaining relationships.
- A child who learns empathy will have a richer life than one who fails to cultivate this vital character trait.

The pursuit of excellence in sports does not have to conflict with empathy or compassion. You have a right to object if your child's coach encourages, or fails to discourage, behaviors that demonstrate a lack of consideration for the feelings of others.

Self-Control and Non-Violence

Help older players understand that losing self-control and/or resorting to physical and verbal aggression are not intended parts of the game, and have negative consequences, including:

- A loss of focus.
- Less likelihood of achieving one's short-term and long-term sports goals.
- A loss of self-respect and the respect of others.
- Possible physical injuries.
- Feelings of ill will.
- Disruption of a team's focus and equilibrium.

Tell your child to anticipate the possibility of dirty or violent play, and to react with self-control. Remind your athlete of the importance of quickly disengaging without confrontational eye contact, or a contentious verbal response, and to employ the "don't punch back, play harder" credo.

Tolerance and Moral Courage

Since one of sports' most important societal contributions is fostering respect for diversity, encourage your young athlete to show a personal disapproval of bigotry. "If you see examples of bigotry, let the offender know that you are offended by such actions," is your message.

Reinforce this message by telling your child what Max Lerner wrote in 1949, *"If we practice racism then it is racism that we teach."*

Drugs/Dishonesty/Moral Courage

In addition to gamesmanship tactics, new opportunities for dishonesty may tempt your middle or high school athlete. Steroids and other performance enhancing drugs are easily obtained, and for a player desperate to make the starting line-up, improve speed, size, or win games, the temptation may be great! Sports psychologist Dr. John Sullivan points to several alarming studies of elite athletes. These studies found that more than half of the surveyed athletes have used performance enhancing drugs to win, even knowing the likelihood of serious and permanent health risks.[2]

Carefully explain that the use of such drugs is not only a form of cheating, but almost guarantees short-term and/or long-term bodily harm. Victory without honor, or victory at the expense of one's health, are not desirable outcomes for any athlete. Use of performance enhancing drugs is wrong for many reasons, including the fact that those who use drugs often corrupt others — *forcing them to consider drug use in order to keep up. Refusing to use drugs, even when teammates or coaches exert subtle or not so subtle pressure to do so, requires moral courage.*

Parental Passivity and Silent Complicity

"All that is necessary for evil to triumph is for good people to do nothing."
— Political philosopher, Edmund Burke

Parents should punish their children for unsportsmanlike conduct, whether officials do or not. Parents who fail to discipline a young athlete often rationalize their failure with excuses such as the umpires are unfair or the other team plays dirty. Dads and Moms must let their athlete know that misconduct will result in home discipline. Parents who ignore problems send the message that misconduct is acceptable.

If you fail to actively and consistently teach your child the right values, you are by default leaving your child open to learning the wrong values. Harmful values include a win at any cost mentality, outright cheating, arrogance, selfishness, acts of aggression, and taking shortcuts to get ahead.

Parental Tenacity

An essential quality for winning athletes is the tenacity to expend the effort needed down the stretch. A winning parent must also display a consistency and tenacity in helping their child develop strong positive values. Tenacious parents summon their inner strength and resolve to do what is right for the child in spite of fatigue, or protest from the child. Just as tenacity separates good athletes from great athletes, it separates good parents from great parents.

An Important Question!

Why would any parent neglect to help their child learn and practice the strong positive values addressed in this chapter?

My Sports Values Scorecard

"Value – a principle, standard or quality considered worthwhile or desirable."
— The New Book of Knowledge Dictionary

The Sports Values Scorecard (*found on page 26*) is designed to help parents look beyond the team record or individual statistics of a young athlete, and to consider whether the sports experience is fostering positive values. The scorecard can be used as a seasonal and long-term reference for parents to track key attributes and values which they hope sports will help nurture in their young athlete. These qualities do not develop without consistent, balanced guidance from parents. Coaches change from season-to-season and also from sport-to-sport, so it is up to parents to be clear about what they expect from their child.

As you review the scorecard's list of behaviors, attitudes and developing values, consider your player's strengths and weaknesses. Use the checklist to help pinpoint where your athlete might need explanations, discussion and guidance from you. For example, a confident, extroverted and skilled player might find it easy to slip into selfish play and to criticize less advanced players. When you witness or hear about good or bad behaviors, whether they are your child's or those of a teammate, use them as a lead-in for discussions about why you encourage or discourage such behaviors.

Share the scorecard with coaches to help them emphasize the beneficial values and qualities that can be developed through sports. Encourage athletic administrators to incorporate the qualities addressed in the scorecard into school and league athletic programs.

Epilogue

Shortly after I completed the draft of this chapter, my son Matt exited a fitness club in Chicago. It was an early August evening on an allegedly safe street, and Matt was but weeks away from entering the JD/MBA program at Northwestern University.

Four youths, reared in a subculture that glorifies violence, decided that their self-gratification for that evening would be to play one of the most barbaric "games" ever conceived. "Pick em out, knock em out" involves a group of thugs targeting an unsuspecting person and beating that person into a state of unconsciousness. Playing this vile game requires only cowardice and a complete lack of respect for human life.

On this evening, August 11, 2005, these four dispossessed young men exited a train in downtown Chicago and, moments later, decided on my son as their mark. Without Matt ever seeing them, they swooped down on him, beat him, and when he was down, kicked him repeatedly to the head.

Matt was unconscious for nine days, and remained hospitalized with severe traumatic brain injury for the better part of three months. During this period, Matt underwent three major brain surgeries and fought off such side effects as pancreatitis and pneumonia. While he still suffers from seizures, Matt has made a courageous and miraculous recovery. Matt is currently enrolled as a student in the Northwestern JD/MBA program.

In learning a great deal about these four boys, I discovered that three of them had a strong interest in sports. At his sentencing, one of the young men even spoke of his desire to play college football. My research made it clear to me that despite whatever parental deficiencies existed, had one strong, firm and fair coach entered the lives of these four boys and spread the unambiguous message of fair play, self-restraint, respect for others and commitment to non-violence, they might have spared Matt, our family and society from their act of savagery.

Matt and my family have done our best to forgive the four boys, hopefully putting into practice our belief that our world needs more cycle breakers than revenge seekers. We have offered to help the four boys if they show a commitment to becoming productive citizens.

While the incident still burns inside of me, and probably always will, it has increased my personal resolve to combat violence—and to use sports as an agent of change.

As a result of the attack on Matt, the Institute for International Sport has developed a sports-related non-violence program. The program involves our working with at-risk male youth ages 12-18, and training coaches who work with young men in this category. (For information on this program, other details on Matt Doyle, and a series of poems that I wrote when Matt was hospitalized, visit (*www.internationalsport.com/nv*).

2

MY SPORTS VALUES SCORECARD

"Values are those by which a life can be lived, which can form a people that produces great deeds and thoughts."

— American philosopher and essayist, Allan Bloom

Name of Athlete: _____

Year: _____

Sport: _____

Season: [Summer] [Fall] [Winter] [Spring]

Value	Needs to Learn	Making Progress	Regularly Demonstrates
1. Balance and Perspective	☐	☐	☐
2. Honesty/Good Sportsmanship	☐	☐	☐
3. Self-Reliance/Responsibility	☐	☐	☐
4. Self-Control/Non-Violence	☐	☐	☐
5. Hard Work/Perseverance	☐	☐	☐
6. Respectful, Courteous Behavior	☐	☐	☐
7. Empathy	☐	☐	☐
8. Teamwork/Unselfish Play	☐	☐	☐
9. Tolerance	☐	☐	☐
10. Moral Courage	☐	☐	☐
11. Physical Fitness	☐	☐	☐

Chapter 3

CLARIFYING THE IMPACT OF THE SPORTS EXPERIENCE

"The secret of the world is the tie between person and event.
Person makes event and event makes person."
— American Poet, Ralph Waldo Emerson

One person might vehemently state that, "The only value of sports participation is fun and exercise"; another might state with equal certainty that, "Sports participation can produce lifelong lessons in teamwork and fair play."

The benefits derived from sports are highly subjective and variable, and often relate to the participant's level of interest and commitment. These levels may shift at different ages, or a child might approach one sport as "fun" and another as "serious." I see the impact of sports falling into four broad categories. Each category has value!

The Four Categories of Impact From the Sports Experience

Category I. Recreational, Social and Fitness

Many people seek no more than fun, friends and good exercise, and derive these benefits from their recreational sports pursuits.

Category II. Educational

Category II encompasses those benefits derived from Category I, along with instructional benefits such as:

- Learning the value of teamwork.
- Learning self-control.
- Working with people from diverse backgrounds.
- Learning fair play and sportsmanship.
- Learning the skills required to achieve proficiency.
- Setting goals.
- Undergoing the process of delayed gratification.
- Dealing with losses.
- Learning to manage time and energy.
- Exposure to new people and places through sports travel.
- Observing leadership qualities.

Category III. Becoming an Honorable Competitor

Category III encompasses those benefits derived from Categories I & II, and goes a step further. In Category III, an athlete makes a philosophical commitment to practice fair play and honorable competition in and out of sports. The Honorable Competitor aims higher than merely "playing by the rules;" the Honorable Competitor tries to achieve a mindset of "competitive self-restraint," and employs a credo of "don't punch back, play harder." Many adults who played sports in high school or college have found this approach to be beneficial throughout their adult lives.

Category IV. Practicing a Fit-for-Life Philosophy

"Health is the vital principle of bliss, and exercise of health."
—Scottish playwright, James Thomson

Category IV encompasses those benefits derived from one or more of the first three categories, and involves a person practicing a fit-for-life philosophy throughout adulthood. Our surveys further reveal that Category IV "fit-for-life" adults hail from all three of the initial categories.

Building the Foundation for a Category IV
Experience for Your Child!

One of *the* most important sports parenting goals has nothing to do with trophies or press clippings. This particular goal involves setting the stage for a Category IV fit-for-life experience for your child. While the results of this process will not take actual shape until your child's "official" playing days are over, you must begin the process early—and be vigilant in your reinforcement of its long-term value.

A Major Finding

Research has long made clear the extraordinary benefits of a regular exercise regimen for adults in terms of health, appearance and overall quality of life. Recent research takes a giant step forward by proposing that exercise can actually help make one smarter! The research suggests that exercise, particularly vigorous exercise, "plays a key role in the human brain, not only growing new nerve cells but also causing older nerve cells to form dense, intraconnected webs that make the brain run faster and more efficiently."[3]

The direct connection between a fit body and a fit mind is at the core of our work at the Institute for International Sport. For my part, I work out every day and honestly feel that I have as much energy as at any time in my adult life. I began to preach the benefits of physical fitness to our six children in their early youth, and continue to do so now that they have reached adulthood.

On this vitally important matter—and parental opportunity—think of your Category IV fit-for-life parenting objective taking shape in two phases.

Phase I
The "Under Your Roof" Phase

When your children, including your college-aged children, are under your direct care and supervision, you should cultivate and reinforce their commitment to remain physically fit through adulthood. During the years your youngster is participating in athletics, regularly discuss the many immediate and long-term benefits of maintaining physical fitness. Point out that fitness leads to:
- Better physical health and a fit appearance.
- Increased self-confidence and a better self-image.
- Better mental health, clear thinking and "joy of living."

Here are four discussion tips to help you with this important objective:
1. Make your child aware that their ultimate sports goal should be to "stay fit throughout your adult life." You may emphasize—and periodically repeat—the following message: "My gift to you is to make you aware of

the many extraordinary benefits of being physically fit throughout life. Your gift to me as an adult will be to stay physically fit."

2. Prior to each discussion, make sure to check the Web for the latest research, which can serve as the basis for stimulating conversation.

3. Be prepared to discuss — and counter — the most common objection to adult exercise: "I'm too busy." Your message is, "I want you to remember that you should never be too busy as an adult to exercise. *You must think of exercise in the same vein as eating and sleeping — as a daily requisite of a positive, productive, healthy and full life.*"

4. Tell your child, "Not only will a regular fitness regimen produce benefits such as physical health and self-confidence, but if you stay fit when you get older, it will probably have the same effect as building a savings account. In this case, your 'annuity' could well be a decade or more of good 'quality of life' — something you will greatly appreciate as you get older."

Treatment of Injuries

Many of our surveyed former athletes made clear that an all-too common hurdle to the fit-for-life objective is a nagging sports injury that had not been properly treated in their youth. During the "under your roof" phase, you play a *vital* role in making sure that any injuries your child suffers receive proper attention and are not neglected to the point that they will cause your child problems through adulthood.

Balance

It is important for your athlete to maintain balance in sports activities. Too much intense activity and pressure can lead to physical injury, burnout, and even quitting. Our surveys confirm that the burnout from athletic excess in childhood sports is a major roadblock to lifelong fitness.

Phase II

Adult Offspring — Your Transition to "Counselor of Wisdom!"

"A sound mind in a sound body is a short,
but full description of a happy state in this world."
— British philosopher, John Locke

Contrary to the position of some "experts," your parenting does not end when your child reaches adulthood. Rather, it simply moves—hopefully seamlessly—from the duties of regular supervision to the far less time-consuming yet equally important "counselor of wisdom" phase. Depending upon the issue, your counsel will vary in its force and frequency. On the matter of fitness, here are three tips:

1. There is a distinct difference between nagging and civil, caring counsel. If you see your adult offspring neglecting fitness, it is not only your right but your obligation to engage your offspring in discussion about this important issue.

2. Keep an eye on new research about exercise and share this information with your offspring.

3. Continue with your exercise regimen, so that your encouragement is rooted in your good example.

A Good Insurance Policy

A good way to help ensure that your child will take your "fit philosophy" lessons to heart is to be a model. This can be difficult for a variety of reasons, including, for some, past injuries that preclude regular exercise. Yet for most parents, a fit-for-life philosophy is well within reach; if not strenuous exercise, then at the very least, regular walking. If you have fallen out of shape, it is important to get back into shape—not only for you but for your child.

The Payoff

The ultimate payoff for your great efforts will be your child someday saying to you: "I attribute my health and positive state of mind to my love of fitness. I attribute all of this to my parents."

A Special Group

Our surveys of former college athletes reveal that one inspiring group, women who played sports before Title IX, was the most serious about maintaining "fitness" throughout life. One of these athletes told us, "Our teams received little recognition or publicity. We played because we loved our sport and enjoyed the benefits of being physically active."

Sports as a Positive Use of Idle Time

"Understanding human needs is half the job of meeting them."
—American politician, Adlai Stevenson

One of sports' most valuable qualities is that it can provide a positive alternative to idle time. My work with at-risk youth has convinced me that many children who find little love or educational support at home are well served by a rigorous sports schedule. Any reasonable adult would much prefer to see a young person choose a full schedule of sports activity than engage in some of the alternative choices that are harmful, if not illegal.

I once heard a high school coach from a well-heeled suburban town criticize a fellow league coach at an urban school with a high drug and crime rate. "The guy thinks football 365 days a year, and is always pushing his kids. There should be more to life," was the suburban coach's salvo.

Yet when I looked into the urban coach's track record, I found that his demands, which might have been extreme in other situations, had literally saved many of his players from the temptations of the street. "The school attendance, grades and graduation rate of the football players have all dramatically improved since his arrival," the principal said.

All of us must be mindful that the circumstances of some children may dictate a sports regimen that might, on the surface, seem excessive, until one carefully examines the alternatives. Out of practical necessity, the sports recipe for a child living in an at-risk neighborhood may need to be more extreme. In this case, if the sports regimen is "values based" and helps this child achieve a Category II (educational) or a Category III (becoming an Honorable Competitor) experience—and lays the groundwork for a Category IV (fit-for-life experience)—the impact is *very* positive.

Last Point

If your athlete is an intense competitor, point out that maintaining life-long fitness may or may not involve actual competition. It depends upon one's adult choice of activities, which could range from zealous training for a triathlon to walking purely for enjoyment and fitness. Whatever the sport's category your child engages in as a youth, encourage fitness for life as a long-term objective.

Finally, consider my short verse on this vital matter:

Frank Galasso

Abiding Purpose

A parent's gift
To sensitize
The lasting worth
Of exercise
"For if your aim
is living whole
you must make fitness
your lifelong goal."

Chapter 4

DO WE LEARN MORE FROM WINNING OR LOSING?

"Life is a succession of lessons which must be lived to be understood."
—American Poet, Ralph Waldo Emerson

When I ask high school and college students whether they learn more from winning or losing, most respond that they learn more from losing. As the discussions evolve, so does the understanding that no athlete experiences one without the other, and that valuable lessons are to be found in both winning and losing.

The Value of Winning

"Rapid motion through space elates one."
—Irish Author, James Joyce

For many competitors, it is the moment of victory that spurs them. During competition, every sense is at a high pitch. When victory is secured, the rushing adrenaline is replaced by feelings of euphoria and utter contentment. One surveyed athlete wrote: "I have not found such joy in any other part of my life."

For a young athlete, there is value to experiencing "the feeling"—a powerful combination of contentment, pride and accomplishment upon winning. This wonderfully unique feeling is often the result of, and reward for, considerable effort and hard work. As a parent, your objective is not to allow the allure of winning to become so important that it supercedes doing what is right. One of sports' most lamentable qualities is that many young athletes are allowed, if not encouraged, to let their desire to win run roughshod over honorable competition.

In helping your child build an ethical code which encompasses the development of the many positive values that should go hand-in-hand with sports, you must consistently make clear that winning never overrides fair play.

Let's look at some requirements for winning, for there are lessons associated with such achievement.

At the youth league level, winning is often related to natural talent and/or size. The athletic success of the fleet, well-coordinated 5'10", 165 pound 12-year-old has little to do with hard work! While some athletes move up the competitive ladder and succeed because of their physical gifts, many others—perhaps the majority—succeed not merely because of natural talent, but because of some or all of the following qualities:

The 13 Admirable Qualities of Successful Athletes

1. A desire to learn.
2. A mastery of the fundamentals.
3. A mastery of advanced skills.
4. Proper execution of the plays.
5. The ability and maturity to listen to, and learn from, instructions and constructive criticism.
6. Self-discipline and self-control.
7. Goal setting.
8. The hard work and willpower to achieve the goals.
9. The resiliency and perseverance to rebound from defeat.
10. The ability and maturity to engage in self-analysis and re-setting of goals.
11. An unselfish commitment to teamwork.
12. The ability to focus and perform under pressure.
13. The tenacity to expend the extra effort needed down the stretch.

The Aftermath of Winning

The winner, especially one whose success is based on competing honorably, may experience the following benefits:

- The winner will justifiably feel good about the accomplishment.
- Winning will often produce a sense of self-confidence. Your job is to make sure this attitude is reflected through quiet and admirable self-assurance, as opposed to arrogance, which some misinterpret as self-confidence.
- The winner will often feel not just a bond, but a genuine love for those players and coaches who took the journey, overcame the obstacles, and shared in the success. Though not a sportsman, English cleric Charles Kaleb Colton understood this concept when he wrote in 1825: "The firmest friendships have been formed in mutual adversity, as iron is most strongly united by the fiercest flame."

4

THE ESSENTIAL QUALITY OF TENACITY

Just as the tenacity to expend the extra effort needed down the stretch is vital for athletic success, so, too, is tenacity a vital quality for sports parenting success.

Winning sports parents are so committed to the well-being of their child that they do as great athletes do in the fourth period of a tough game: they summon their inner strength and resolve to do what is right for the child, consistently overcoming rationalizations such as fatigue or protest from the child.

This quality of tenacity often separates good athletes from great athletes, and good parents from great parents!

A Point of Caution

"No meaningful success is achievable without meeting true resistance."
— *New York Times* sports columnist, Harvey Araton

A gifted athlete who is easily winning competitions may need stiffer competition. A young athlete learns little when achievement is gained without facing any real obstacles.

The Value of Losing

"Be a doer, not a stewer." — Senator Bob Dole

Facing failure and disappointment can be an essential learning experience for a young person. Our research of successful people demonstrated that they learned how to turn early disappointments into a resolve to achieve. At its best, the sports experience can help a youngster learn and practice methods for effectively dealing with failure and disappointment, a quality many successful people have mastered.

Consider what two winners say about losing:

- "Success is not built on success. It's built on failure. It's built on frustration. Sometimes it's built on catastrophe."—Sumner Redstone, CEO of Viacom.

- In acclaimed novelist Pat Conroy's *My Losing Season*, his wonderful non-fiction book about his senior year as a point guard at The Citadel, Conroy wrote, "The great secret of athletics is that you can learn more from losing than winning."

Six Reasons Why Losing in Sports Can Help a Young Person Become a Winner in Life

1. Losing forces a player to analyze and make playing adjustments so as not to repeat mistakes.

2. Losing may help a player develop empathy for the losses or mistakes of others.

3. When faced with disappointment, an athlete learns to develop resiliency and mental toughness. Psychiatrist Dr. Richard Davidson points out that, "Stressful events give us practice at bouncing back from unpleasant emotions. They are like an exercise to strengthen our 'happiness muscles,' or a vaccination against melancholy."[4]

4. Losing may help a player become more introspective. As Pat Conroy wrote, "Losing can help you consider those deeper stirrings that move beneath."

5. The athlete who has faced defeat will appreciate success even more.

6. Losing can create a resolve to work harder and do better in future undertakings.

One of the things that came out of our surveys of successful people is that the loser or modestly successful athlete often finds within a desire to excel in future pursuits, and an awareness that there is plenty of time to reach goals. "I knew I had the rest of my life to turn my disappointing sports career into success in new avenues to which I was better suited," wrote one of our surveyed respondents.

In *My Losing Season*, Conroy wrote, "After our losing season, we went out and led our lives, and our losing season inspired every one of us to strive for complete and successful lives."

Remind your player that:

- Many successful adults had losing records as athletes!
- Many successful former athletes have losing records as adults!!

A LEGEND'S FORESIGHT

In 1965, Jackie Robinson worked as a TV analyst for ABC at the Little League World Series, in which a Windsor Locks (CT) team defeated a team from Ontario, Canada for the championship. An innocent remark by Robinson about the noble effort of the Canadian team prompted a surprising response from a Connecticut resident, who wrote a letter to the *Hartford Courant* complaining about Robinson's "biased reporting."

Not one to back away from a debate, Jackie Robinson wrote a letter of response to the *Courant*, in which he stated: "When I said the Canadians had nothing to be ashamed of, I meant it. They conducted themselves well. They gave a superior team a tough battle, and certainly deserve credit for their play.

"I implied nothing that the gentleman read into my remarks. I am certainly no expert in announcing, but try to call them as I see them.

"The writer reminds me of the parent I feel puts too much emphasis on winning, when we should be instilling in our youngsters the importance of being good losers as well."

Jackie Robinson was ahead of his time in a number of ways.

4

Responding to Losses and Mistakes

Many successful athletes have mastered the art of effectively responding to losses and disappointments. Successful people view failure as feedback. They deal with it, learn from it and move forward.

Parents can help their young athlete learn to deal with losses and mistakes by conveying appropriately balanced attitudes toward both winning and losing. Be sure to show as much pride in your player's effort as in the wins!

If your athlete has already developed poor responses to losing or disappointment, try to teach and regularly remind your youngster about the following points:

1. All sports involve mistakes and losses, and successful athletes must learn to deal with the strong emotions brought about by losing.

2. Successful athletes acknowledge and accept their disappointment, and then redirect their energy into learning from their mistakes.

3. Successful athletes do not mope about their mistakes! *They have learned how to quickly return to normal.*

4. Learning from mistakes and losses includes maintaining a positive attitude and:

- Analyzing whether the loss/error was due to something the athlete did or failed to do.
- Understanding that some bad plays are due to chance, timing or actions of a teammate or opposing player.
- Understanding that most games involve dozens of mistakes. "Basketball is a game of mistakes," was the way Hall of Famer Bob Cousy once described his sport.
- Refocusing on improving individual skills, teamwork and execution— all of which may help prevent future errors.

Remember, as parents you must set the tone and encourage your youngster to practice the steps necessary to respond constructively to the emotional swings of losing and disappointment.

A Balanced Perspective

"Perspective: the relationship of aspects of a subject to each other and to a whole."
—The New Book of Knowledge Dictionary

It is important to let your child know that you share her joy in winning and empathize with her disappointment upon losing, but that you will never be disappointed if she puts forth effort and plays honorably and within the rules of the game! When your athlete enjoys success, your job is to promote pride in the effort and point out the results obtained through her hard work. After a loss, your job is to help your athlete learn from it. When parents make it clear that they most value their athlete's participation, integrity, and effort, not the win/loss record or star status, emotional balance will come more easily following both winning and losing.

Bob Knight makes the salient point that, "You can win and still not succeed, still not achieve what you should. And you can lose without really failing at all." Help your player learn not to become intoxicated by success or defeated by failure, and understand that the difference between victory and defeat is sometimes measured in inches, milliseconds or just luck.

Finally, I offer two short poems that address elements of victory and defeat:

Frank Galasso

4

Lessons from Defeat

As the clock winds down
Reality screams
There'll be no happy ending
To pre-game dreams.

Fleeting depression
Is aided along
By time's intercession
And an ode of the strong:

"For winners in life
No loss breaks their pace
They analyze and learn
Then get back in the race."

Frank Galasso

Winning

The big game
Ends
In victory
Offspring of
Noble effort
Of team, body and mind
A man of wealth
Could never buy
This feeling
This joy
So gloriously one of a kind.

SECTION II

PARENT / COACH ISSUES

Chapter 5

YOUR EXPECTATIONS OF THE COACH AND THE COACH'S EXPECTATIONS OF YOU!

"Blessed is he who expects nothing, for he shall never be disappointed."
—English Poet, Alexander Pope

Mr. Pope's view notwithstanding, a sports parent should have basic expectations of the coach, and the coach should have basic expectations of the parent. Expectations on both sides may vary depending upon a child's age and the level of competition.

What to Expect From a Youth League Coach

1. Exemplary conduct, which includes:

   - Teaching without screaming or bullying.
   - Exercising self-restraint and tactfulness with all persons involved in or watching the game.

2. A genuine interest in the welfare of children, and a desire to make the team experience worthwhile.

3. The head coach, though not necessarily the assistant coach, should have a basic, but not necessarily a textbook knowledge of the sport. Remember, this is a volunteer.

4. The head coach and the assistant coach should learn how to teach the

core fundamentals of the sport and possess a willingness to learn more about the sport. Since effort is a bedrock principle of sport, you should expect it of the youth league coach just as the coach should expect it of your child.

5. Fun, purposeful practice sessions which include positive reinforcement and a block of time devoted to fundamentals.

6. Good sportsmanship. If sports is to reach its potential as a positive force in society, it follows that a youth league coach should be committed to good sportsmanship and fair play.

7. A clear set of team rules and consequences, emphasizing no bullying on or off the field.

8. Fairness toward all players. Remember, on the matter of playing time, what is fair in an equal time recreation league may not be what is fair on a highly competitive travel team.

9. A team first philosophy that teaches:

   • The good of the team supercedes the desires of the individual.
   • Treat everyone with respect, including other players with whom your athlete has little in common.

10. A reasonable approach to scheduling practices, team meetings and games—one that is consistent and planned well in advance.

11. Injuries/safety. The coach and the league should have a well-defined policy for dealing with injuries, which should include each parent submitting a medical form that details the child's medical background and parent and physician contact numbers. It is unreasonable to expect a trainer to be present at every game due to costs. Medical forms, well-stocked first aid kits (have an athletic trainer recommend what should be in the kit), and readily accessible phones to call 911 should be available. It is also a wise league policy to require CPR and first aid training for coaches.

12. A team roster with names, addresses, phone numbers, email addresses and a notification system for schedule changes.

What to Hope For From a Youth League Coach

1. A more than basic knowledge of the sport, including real proficiency in teaching the fundamentals of the sport.

2. Someone who cares enough to discipline the child when appropriate. In other words, if Johnny cusses out the umpire and the coach benches him, you should be grateful that the coach cares enough about Johnny to take

appropriate action. Remember, it is often easier to look the other way than to do what is right for the child.

3. A rapport with players that transcends the games.

4. The knowledge and willingness to tell the child and parents what the child needs to do to improve. This input should include suggested drills which make it easier for Dad or Mom to say, "Let's go out to the field to work on what the coach has recommended."

5. Someone who will take the teachable moment from a win or loss and transform it into a valuable life lesson.

6. Someone who exudes a love of the sport and thus helps your child learn to love the sport.

7. A coach who treats your child the way he wants his own child to be treated.

8. A sense of humor.

"THE 90% PARENT"

"But enough of me. Let's talk about you. What do you think of me?!"
—Ed Koch

Most parents understand that their child is one of many attending camp or playing on a team, and their expectations for time and attention are tailored appropriately. However, there are other parents, particularly those of young children, who are extreme in their demands. I call them "90% parents," because they demand a disproportionate amount of the coach's, camp counselor's or teacher's time and attention for themselves and their child.

There are likely to be three unfortunate results from the behavior of "90 percenters."

1. Humiliation—children of "90 percenters" may be embarrassed by the attention seeking, micro-managing behavior of their parents.

2. Intrusive parenting prevents a child from learning to deal with team/camp issues, and the child fails to become self-reliant.

3. Other parents, coaches and teammates often resent the demands of "90 percenters." Children of "90 percenters" may even experience backlash.

Whether your child is on a team or in camp, your expectations need to be fair and considerate of the needs of the other players, parents, coaches and counselors.

What The Youth League Coach
Should Expect From Parents

1. Realistic, open-minded expectations for their child and team.

2. Not to expect one's child to always start or be the star.

3. Your effort to assure your child's on-time participation in all practices and games.

4. Your exemplary conduct toward all parties involved in your child's sport.

5. Advance notice when your child must miss a practice or game, unless due to sudden illness or emergency.

6. Your commitment to the team concept.

7. Your assistance with volunteer tasks such as drinks and snacks.

8. A hands-off attitude toward your child's playing time, position and team strategy.

9. Your commitment not to "hover" over your child during games or practices.

Signing Up For A "No Cut" Youth League

When you register your child for a "no cut" youth league, you need to be aware of the following points:

1. **Fully enrolled with waiting lists.** Many "no cut" youth leagues have a maximum number of youngsters they can accommodate, and a registration deadline. This is not an arbitrary arrangement. It is based on available space, and a suitable amount of time to place players on teams, assign coaches, send out the notifications, and start the season on time. You need to:

    • Take the responsibility to research the registration deadlines, rather than expect that the information will simply come your way.

    • Understand that missing the deadline may put your child on a waiting list, and accept your responsibility for being late.

2. **Roster Size.** Most team sports have determined optimal roster sizes. In setting team sizes, league officials are aware that too many players may negatively affect the playing time and teaching environment for all participants, including your child.

3. **Adding Teams for Late Registrants.** This may seem like a viable alternative to you, but remember this involves the need for additional practice and game space, uniforms, equipment, coaches, referees and schedule changes.

4. **Two Suggestions!**

- Volunteer your time, for this will probably ensure your child's place on a team.
- Mark your calendar to contact the league officials or local recreation office to learn the application procedure and deadline. Most leagues need at least two or three months to get organized.

Although many leagues use town facilities, your child's participation is not a birthright, but a privilege. Most administrators are trying to include as many players as conditions permit. Work with them!

What to Expect From a High School or College Coach

Here are additional expectations for coaches at this level:

1. Professional behavior.

2. A commitment to good conduct, good sportsmanship and the principles of honorable competition both on and off the field.

3. A clear explanation to all team members of the negative ramifications for the athlete, team, school and family whenever a team member misbehaves.

4. A strong knowledge of the sport, which encompasses expertise in X's and O's, scouting and breaking down films.

5. A clear policy of no drug or alcohol use, including precise information addressing the physical and psychological consequences and team penalties for use of such substances.

6. A desire to learn more; the best coaches I know are always trying to learn.

7. A truly supportive position regarding academic requirements, especially leading up to and during exams.

8. A commitment never to risk an athlete's health or to play an injured youngster who is not medically cleared by a sports medicine expert.

9. Relationships with highly qualified sports medicine physicians and rehabilitation specialists.

10. A commitment to develop a team-first attitude.

11. A high school coach who assists with college counseling, is willing to contact college coaches and offers sound advice on non-school play, including AAU/Club and travel teams.

12. A college coach who assists with job recommendations—both summer and career.

13. A college coach whose program graduates a high percentage of its players.

What to Hope for From a High School or College Coach

1. A coach who truly values and regularly monitors the education of the players.

2. An experienced, enthusiastic and respected coach, or an enthusiastic young coach with superior knowledge of the sport.

3. A coach who maintains regular contact with players after graduation.

4. A coach who is well-read and who enjoys conversing with players about non-sports issues.

5. A program whose former players take an interest in the present players, visit, and sometimes mentor undergraduates.

6. A high school coach with excellent college contacts for those players who wish to pursue college sports.

7. A college coach who not only writes recommendations but assists players in the job market through contacts with alumni or other professionals.

8. A coach who assigns readings and tests athletes on the facts and consequences of using recreational drugs, performance enhancing drugs, and alcohol.

9. A coach your young athlete considers to be an invaluable mentor.

What High School and College Coaches
Should Expect From Parents

1. Those previously listed expectations of youth league coaches which remain relevant at the high school and college level.

2. An understanding that some of the most important lessons derived from the high school and college varsity athletic experience will be from losses and other disappointments.

3. Your "hands off" relationship on issues of playing time, position and strategy.

Playing for "The Taskmaster"

Any period during which a youngster plays for a "taskmaster" coach may not be one of complete harmony. An effective coach demands much from athletes and stretches them beyond their comfort zone. At times, this may be stressful for both you and your young athlete, but a coach who cares enough to enforce the rules can make this "coming of age process" a valuable growth experience for a high school or college athlete.

The Influence of Winning and Losing
on Coach–Player Relationships

Like it or not, the relationship between athletes and coaches is often influenced by winning and losing. Over the years, it has been interesting to observe teams whose players demonstrated greatly differing reactions to the same coach, based upon the success or failure of the team. A successful team exalts the coach while a losing team often blames the coach for its failure. Same coach, same system, dramatically different reactions! Look beyond winning and losing and consider whether the coach fosters effort, teamwork, integrity and grace in both victory and defeat.

5

A Legend's Message

Several years ago, I joined 29 other individuals at a two-day "think tank" in Arizona to discuss the state of sports in America. It was an eclectic group of sports enthusiasts, ranging from actor Tom Selleck to broadcaster Bob Costas. During the two-day gathering, I had the good fortune of conversing with the oldest and wisest participant. When our discussion turned to the impact of the firm and fair coach in a young person's life, the revered sage leaned forward and made the following comment: "If a parent expects perfection in their child's coach, the parent—and the child—are sure to be disappointed, because no coach is perfect. If you contact every man who played for me or the parents of those men who played for me—I'm certain that most would say good things about me and their overall experience in our program. Yet a few would say just the opposite, and the same is true with every coach who has done it for any length of time."

The bearer of this message was John Wooden.

An Interesting Survey Result

As you reflect on the strengths and shortcomings of your child's coach, consider how surveyed high school and college athletes responded to our question: "Of all the educators who have entered your life since kindergarten, has a coach been one of the most important to you?"

- Ninety-four percent of the high school athletes surveyed responded yes.
- Ninety-three percent of the college athletes surveyed responded yes.[4]

It is common for athletes to look back at a coach as the educator who most profoundly influenced their lives.

Finally, my verse in tribute to the best of coaches:

5

Frank Galasso

5

The Principled Coach

A staple of sport
The four-square coach
Who reaches a child
With an honest approach.

Her guiding reproof
So quick to convey
"My job is to keep you
From going astray."

His nuggets of wisdom
You never outgrow
He journeys to milieus
Even parents can't go.

Her lessons of life
Add might to the soul
Ennobling young lives
Their unparalleled role.

Chapter 6

DEALING WITH THE COACH

"The coach is first of all a teacher."
—UCLA Basketball Coaching Legend, John Wooden

In our survey of coaches with 10 or more years experience at the high school or college level, opinions on parental involvement in sports were clear. Eighty-four percent stated that parental interaction is "far more frequent now than it was ten years ago," and 71% stated that such interaction "often crosses over into interference."[5] Coaches made it strikingly clear that the biggest change in their job has been the extent to which parental "helpfulness" has slipped into parental "intrusiveness." These coaches are not referring to the average parent, but rather to the favor seeking, overly protective or adversarial parent who has difficulty simply allowing their child to join a team and play by the rules. Some parents are always on the lookout for any slight or injustice, and ready to support their child's complaint without further investigation.

Most of these coaches said they have no objection to parental contact, as long as it is handled in a responsible manner. One basketball coach wrote, "When parents call with information that helps me do a better job with their daughter, I like it. What I don't like, and what may drive me from coaching, are the parents whose sole objective is for their daughter to get more shots at the basket or playing time, with no regard for my job of being fair to all 12 players. . .and the interests of the team."

Before offering guidelines for interaction with the coach, let me begin with a hardball reality: When your child signs up for a team, neither of you are taking up membership in a participatory democracy! In sports, individual rights become secondary to the good of the team.

Key Objectives

Key objectives of sports participation include allowing your child to experience the benefits of delayed gratification, and to practice and grow in self-reliance and problem solving skills. My advice on parent interactions with coaches is based on the assumption that young athletes should deal with most coach/team issues. This includes youth leaguers!

Since recommendations in this chapter are intended to help youngsters develop self-reliance, parents should work at practicing a hands-off philosophy, unless contacting the coach is related to information gathering, ethical issues or health and safety.

A Question to Consider

How many well-adjusted adults do you know who were raised by micromanaging parents who tried to make everything perfect for their child?

Dealing with Volunteers

If you are contacting a volunteer coach or league official, bear in mind that most volunteers believe they are "giving back." This good feeling is often at the core of volunteerism. Indeed, many volunteers may not be receptive to criticism, feeling it is not part of the "job description."

The fact that they are volunteers does not absolve them from accepting constructive feedback. Any reasonable volunteer coach should be receptive to input from a parent, as long as it is made in the spirit of politely providing information to help the coach do a better job with the child, not favor the child.

If you decide to approach a volunteer coach or administrator with a complaint or with constructive feedback, remember that:
- Volunteers should be judged more benignly than professionals.
- Volunteers may, understandably, have less tolerance for criticism than a professional paid to take the heat.
- *You* must be the diplomat. That's right! It is up to you to handle difficult situations with diplomacy— even if the volunteer does not return your tactfulness.

Dealing with the Youth League Coach on Scheduling Matters

When your child commits to a team, the games, practices and meetings may interfere with your schedule. At the youth league level, it is perfectly acceptable for you to contact the coach prior to the season to request general information about practice, game and meeting schedules. You should not seek to adjust the schedule (Remember, this is not a democracy!). Your call is to seek information, and the coach should be cooperative.

Once you know the schedule, if a normal family commitment, such as a weekly religious service, prevents your child from attending regularly scheduled practices or games, you must assess whether playing on the team is worthwhile for your child. Also consider that your child's frequent absence is unfair to the other team members, and that your player might be taking a spot from a youngster who can attend most practices and games.

A child who signs up takes on a responsibility to the team. For any important family commitments such as weddings or vacations, you are obligated to inform the coach well in advance, or as soon as you are aware of a game/practice which must be missed. The coach needs such information for planning and player rotation.

A youth league coach should be flexible when given advance notice of a family commitment. One coach wrote, "I do not object to vacations or weddings—I object to late notice or last minute 'whims.'"

How Youth Leagues Can Help

Parents and children benefit when a youth league adopts reasonable policies to accommodate family needs. Here are two examples:

1. Because of a limited number of fields, a 16-team youth soccer league schedules two practices per week for each team. To accommodate family schedules, the league allows parents to request that their child play for a team that practices on specific days/nights.

   A league official explained, "We retain the right to refuse the request, and we cannot always comply with all requests. But we have found that by offering families this option, it makes play possible for some youngsters who would otherwise be unable to play."

2. The same league entertains requests from parents to put two friends on the same team to help a child feel more comfortable, or place two players together for carpooling.

   "Sometimes parents ask for three or more youngsters to be on the same team, and we do not honor those requests...two is our limit on special requests," continued the league official. "We also refuse the request if the two youngsters happen to be such superior players that they would upset the competitive balance of the league. We are on watch for attempts to 'stack teams.'

"In general, we try to accommodate requests that help a child feel more comfortable or help a family with transportation and scheduling requirements."

If your child's league has this type of cooperative policy, you should not take advantage of the league's goodwill by requesting a special option when you, or your child, do not really need it. This includes unfair requests for three or more friends to team up.

What if the Schedule Changes?

Game and practice schedules may change due to weather, league or facility issues, or coaching decisions. If a change interferes with an important family commitment, you have the right to tell the coach that your child must miss a practice or game. Remember, for your player to miss a game, the family commitment should be an important one.

If you take this step, it remains the responsibility of you or your child to inform the coach of your decision, not simply allow your youngster to skip the game or practice with no communication.

What About Playoff or Championship Games?

Your child's team is in the playoffs the same week as your long-awaited beach vacation! Such games, if unanticipated, may result in difficult family choices. It is right for a family to want to take a vacation, as it is right for a youngster to want to play in the championship game. To avoid being faced with this dilemma, in your preseason discussion with the coach about scheduling, find out about post-season tournament possibilities—dates and locations—for the league championship and all-star team activities.

Let's look closely at this issue.

At the youth league level, if your child's team advances to the playoffs or league championship, missing a game should take place only under extreme circumstances. The simple reason, especially if the youngster is integral to the team's success, is that the other players and coaching staff are depending on your child. Do not plan a family vacation based upon the assumption that your child's team will not make the playoffs or your child will not be asked to play on an All-Star team, even if your child is a long-shot.

In making your decision, be aware that these "big games" do not come along often. For a child, competing in a playoff or championship game can be one of the highlights of youth. You should not be dismissive of the meaning of such a game to your child, and your extra effort is not out of balance, it is proper. However inconvenient, arrangements should be made to get players to the game or tournament, and fulfill their responsibility to the team. This may mean that you have to drive the 150 miles back from vacation, allow the child to stay with a teammate's family, or make some other unusual accommodation to get your child to the game.

High School and College Scheduling

At the high school or college varsity level, the scheduling of practices, games and meetings is a whole different situation. We are talking about a more serious commitment, and once your child reaches this level, your obligation is not to schedule a vacation or even a wedding that will conflict with a game that was scheduled well in advance. The coach's obligation is to provide the game schedule as soon as possible to assist your planning.

On the matter of missing a practice, while there should be more flexibility for important family obligations, the decision still rests with the coach. Obviously, unexpected emergencies, like a death in the family, fall into a separate category.

You should also understand that a high school or college coach is not usually in a position to make firm, long-term practice schedules, because the needs of the team can dramatically change over the course of the season. If the team plays poorly on a Friday night and the coach schedules a Saturday morning practice at 8 A.M., or if the coach schedules hockey or basketball practice over the holiday season, you should be prepared to be inconvenienced.

Contacting The Coach

Your child is on the team and all is not bliss. The child is playing right field and batting ninth, instead of what is obvious to you — that the child should be at shortstop and hitting third. You want to buy the coach a one-way ticket on Greyhound, or at least suggest another avocation.

Yours is not an uncommon plight, but you cannot call or meet with the coach every time you disagree with a decision. If you frequently feel that your child is being cheated out of a starting position, adequate playing time, or an All-Star team slot, you are probably mistaken and lack objectivity.

Guiding Principle

Sports parenting would take a quantum leap forward if parents adhered to the following principle: O*n matters of your child's playing time, position and team strategy, bite your tongue; when a coach crosses the line on ethical, professional, sportsmanship or health and safety issues, open your mouth!*

When Not to Intervene

1. **Do not** contact the coach during a game unless your child is attempting to play while too sick or injured to safely do so.

2. **Do not** contact the coach during the season to question strategy. In the unlikely event the coach seeks your opinion, feel free to offer advice! Even if you know, or think you know more about the sport than the coach, it is important to recognize that matters of strategy fall within the coach's domain, not yours.

3. **Do not** contact the coach during the season to discuss your child's playing time, unless the coach is in violation of the league's rule on playing time. You should not expect the youth league coach to play your child more than the time required by the league, or more than what is in the best interests of the team. Some recreational youth leagues wisely require minimum playing time, while highly competitive travel teams/leagues usually do not. At any level, it is good practice for your athlete to take responsibility for asking the coach, "What can I do to earn more playing time?" This is an athlete-coach and not a parent-coach discussion.

4. **Do not** try to convince the coach to change your child's playing position during the season. Again, it is your athlete's responsibility, not yours, to ask the coach to try a new position in practice and/or games.

5. **Do not** try to persuade a coach or league committee that your player's statistics merit a spot on an All-Star team. There are many intangibles involved in such selections, and these selections are not your decision.

Parental interference in these areas is at the core of many sports parenting problems and troubled coach-parent and coach-player relationships. A prep school headmaster told me of a parent who poisoned his son's attitude and willingness to play his role on the team by sending the coach long, denigrating letters with strategy and playing time demands. The selfish dad prevented the boy from contributing to the team and deriving the benefits of team play.

On the surface, these guidelines may seem a bit rigid. However, in the overwhelming majority of cases, following them will help you reach your objective of raising a good, self-reliant child, not to mention preventing you from intervening in a way that might prove embarrassing to both you and your young athlete.

The Shy/Timid Child

If your child expresses reluctance to approach the coach about issues such as playing time or position, you can encourage your athlete by:

- Role-playing with the child, with you taking on the role of the coach. A role-playing conversation can help the child get over her fear of approaching the coach.
- Suggesting a letter! A good way for a child to organize thoughts is by writing a polite letter to the coach asking for a phone call or meeting to discuss whatever issue concerns the child. The process of writing a letter and presenting it to the coach is a helpful practice. You may ask the child to read the letter to you and make suggestions to help clarify the point.

Playing Out of Position

A frequent point of contention between parents, their athletes, and the coach, relates to playing a position which the parents or player do not believe best fits the athlete's size, skills, or preference. Unless there are medical issues involved, a youth leaguer should not worry about her playing position during a short season. There will be many seasons ahead.

Keep in mind the following points:

1. It is a player's responsibility to ask a coach to try out a different position. Taking on this responsibility is a valuable learning experience for a young athlete.

2. If your youngster is reluctant to ask a coach, try role-playing with you as the coach.

3. When possible, coaches may allow players to learn and practice at different positions, but this is the coach's prerogative.

4. Competency at any position requires practice and teamwork. It can be difficult for a baseball player to become proficient if his position is constantly rotated among too many players. Six athletes wanting to play first base cannot be accommodated.

5. Remind an unhappy player that his job is to do the best he can in his assigned position.

6. On multi-year teams, such as a Little League or a high school team, coaches may properly play older, more experienced players in key positions, and younger players will have to earn their chance to play a favored position. (Remember the value of delayed gratification!)

7. Players who want to work at learning a new position, or improve skills at several positions, can take the following steps:
   - Practice on their own.
   - Attend sports camps where, prior to enrollment, the director agrees to instruct and play an athlete at a specific position.
   - Work with a coach or personal trainer who teaches specific positions and skills.

The Value of the Multi-Position Player

In most instances, you should not be concerned if the youth league coach is playing your child at different positions. A player who can effectively compete at more than one position is invaluable to a team, and the coach may be paving the way for your child to become such an athlete. Trying new positions may also result in your child finding the one that is most comfortable. So, if Molly is moved from third base to shortstop—relax!

Finding a Way

As a teenager, I once attended a camp at which legendary Boston Celtics coach Arnold "Red" Auerbach spoke. I recall one of his principal points: *If you want to be good, you'll find a way.*

Remember, Coach Auerbach was not addressing parents, he was addressing a group of high school basketball players, challenging us to be resourceful. Since that time, it has often occurred to me that one of sports' prevailing strengths is to dish up a challenge—like the 6'5" high school junior basketball player faces in learning to play guard—and afford the youngster (not you) the opportunity to develop his own solution.

Do not underestimate the value of such a challenge, or the ingenuity that many youngsters will display in meeting the challenge. It might be affixing a broomstick to a chair in the backyard to increase the arc of a shot, or working a part-time job to save enough money to attend a summer baseball camp to learn a new position. As Red Auerbach preached to our eager ears, countless athletes have found their way, and the effort alone is a valuable experience.

You can offer guidance to your high school athlete, but encourage your athlete to develop a solution.

When Contacting the Coach is Okay

The 24-Hour Rule

If you decide to contact the coach while you are upset, you must employ the "24-hour rule": *make yourself put the phone down and wait 24 hours*. It is amazing what a good night's sleep and further reflection will do for your composure, not to mention the success of your call. Remember, your mature approach is a key to the call producing positive results.

It is acceptable to contact the coach for the following nine reasons:

1. If you have information the coach needs to do a better job with your child. This includes any relevant academic, medical, and home information that will help the coach better work with your young athlete.

2. Your athlete may seek improvement tips from the coach, and you may want to discuss the tips so you understand how to help your child.

3. You need information from a coach regarding team rules, off-season play, camp recommendations or college sports options.

4. When the coach is acting in an unprofessional manner which you believe penalizes or harms a player's relationship with the coach and/or team. An example of unprofessional behavior is when a coach gossips about one team member to another team member and the other players hear about it.

5. If you feel the coach is employing unethical strategies or poor sportsmanship, not only should you react, it is your obligation to do so. At any level, you may feel more comfortable going over the coach's head to a league official or athletic director to register your complaint. People are placed in leadership positions to deal with such issues in a competent and discrete manner, so do not hesitate to ask if you want your complaint kept confidential.

6. When the time commitment demanded by team activities is so extreme that it interferes with academic pursuits.

7. When providing advance notice that a practice or game must be missed.

8. Use of profanity. At the youth league level, employing the "24-hour rule," you should call the coach and say, "Listen, in the heat of the moment, I know that all of us can lose it a bit. But I'm trying to keep my child from using profanity. Would you please help me by not using it in front of the team?"

A coach's use of profanity will make a child think that such behavior is acceptable and, at the youth league level, you have every right to make known your objections. If the coach continues to use profanity, call a league official and make your point in no uncertain terms. At the high school and college levels you should not call unless profanity is regularly and abusively directed at specific players. By this age, it is time for the child to be able to filter good and bad—to learn the meaning of discernment.

9. When you feel your young athlete is too sick or too injured to play. As your child advances up the competitive ladder, you and your young athlete are likely to face decisions on whether to play when your child is in pain, sick or injured. Dr. Kevin Speer, an orthopedic surgeon in private practice in Raleigh, North Carolina, and former head of the Sports Medicine Department at Duke University Medical Center, offers this guiding principle: "Don't be macho. If pain continues for more than one week, obtain a medical assessment of the condition to determine whether the pain is 'safe' or 'unsafe' pain. Once diagnosed, the physician will let you know whether your child is able to safely return to play." Dr. Speer cautions that "many coaches do not seek proper information from a medical expert when a child is first hurt. Many coaches and athletic trainers are too fixated on getting the child back into action—before the child is ready."

When dealing with issues which may be emotional or contentious, such as items 4-9 on the above list, you should make your communications:
- Unemotional, fairly stated and succinct.
- Free from aggressive attacks on the behavior of coaches, parents or athletes.

Suggestion: A respectful, clearly written, unemotional note can help avoid overreaction and allow both parties time to carefully consider the issue.

Verbal Abuse

At the youth league level, a coach has the right to be firm with a young athlete and, on occasion, use a raised voice to motivate, discipline or demand an attitude adjustment. From high school varsity on up, verbal abuse is often in the ear of the beholder. There is a gym language that is allowable in that context which should not be used outside of the gym. Our focus groups with high school and college varsity athletes made it clear that there was little or no objection to the raised voice, as long as it is not the only mode of delivery.

In assessing whether or not a coach is being verbally abusive, consider the following points:

- The age of the athlete. Appropriate verbal demands and chastisements by a college coach might be totally inappropriate in a youth league setting.

- A coach who appears to rely on humiliating, demeaning comments may be crossing the line into verbal abuse. Your objective is to distinguish between the long-term benefits many athletes derive from playing for a tough coach, and when a coach goes from tough to abusive.

- Profanity should never be used at the youth league or middle school level.

- A worthy ideal subscribed to by a number of high school and college teams, and one you may wish to encourage in your community, is the National Sportsmanship Day "No Swear Zone."

(See National Sportsmanship Day– *www.internationalsport.com/nsd*).

Parental Courting of the Coach — An Offensive Foul

When your child is a member of a youth league team on which every player gets equal time and no league standings are kept, developing a relationship with the coach is appropriate.

But when your young athlete joins a more competitive team where the coach is charged with making objective decisions about playing time or whether your child is batting first or ninth, you must refrain from buddying up to the coach.

Interesting feedback from our high school and college coach focus groups included their near unanimous displeasure with parents who try to ingratiate themselves with the coach.

"I must make my decisions in the best interests of the team," wrote one high school coach. "Do I want my parents to be friendly? Absolutely. Supportive? Of course. But when their child is playing for me, I expect the parent to maintain a respectful distance and in no way try to influence me. In fact, any coach who cares about fairness on the team should be offended by such actions.

"Do I want to develop a closer relationship with them after their son graduates? I may, and in many cases, I have."

The line here is clear, and if you consider crossing it, think how you would feel if a coach was being successfully courted by another parent, and your child's playing time was reduced.

Also be aware of an unfortunate but human reaction that several coaches expressed: when a parent tries to curry favor, it makes it much more difficult for a coach to be objective about a child.

Your job is to let the coaches do theirs—with no attempt at undue influence from you!

No Press Conferences or Lawsuits

There have been some highly publicized situations in which perceived "unfairness" to a child athlete has led parents to "go public." Parents have sought publicity and filed lawsuits against coaches and leagues for cutting or benching a child, or for keeping a child off an all-star team.

Any "victory" was, at best, Pyrrhic and embarrassing to the child. Such actions lead to long-term antagonism on all sides.

Seldom, if ever, do a child's sports woes merit complaints to the media or legal redress. There are more appropriate channels to handle such disappointment. As I repeatedly suggest in this book, learning to constructively deal with disappointment is one of sports' most valuable lessons.

Booster Clubs

Booster Clubs are often helpful in providing sports teams with funds not allocated in the school or athletic budget. Many of these clubs are prudently administered and produce worthwhile results. Some do not.

An example of Booster culpability is the parent whose volunteerism or contribution of money results in the misguided notion that the return on investment should be special consideration for the Booster's child. Unfortunately, while this type of "donation" may cause a few misguided coaches and administrators to afford a child special consideration, it inevitably produces feelings of favoritism as well as animosity among the child's teammates.

In your sports parenting, as well as your "boostering," may I point out the obvious: do not expect your support to buy special privileges!

Chapter 7

SHOULD YOU COACH YOUR CHILD?

"For kids, often there is pride, but also anxiety when their parents coach them."
—Executive Director of the Positive Coaching
Alliance at Stanford University, Jim Thompson

In considering the question, "Should you coach your child?" I surveyed 24 youth leagues in a variety of sports throughout the country. Every league drew at least 90% of its volunteer coaches from parents, and nine leagues reported that 100% of the coaches were parents. One league president told me that "51 of our 52 coaches are parents of the players."

"And what about coach number 52?" I asked.

"A grandparent!" replied the president.

In every case, the league official with whom I spoke said that without the help of volunteer parents it would be impossible to recruit a sufficient number of coaches. Therefore, a partial answer to "Should you coach your child?" is you may have no choice!

Should You Coach Another Team?

Some people involved in youth sports propose that rather than coaching your child's team you should coach a different team in the league. There are two problems with this suggestion:

• Most coaches volunteer in order to be involved in their child's activity.

- There are likely to be schedule conflicts such as the inability to attend your child's games and transportation problems to and from your child's games.

Head or Assistant Coach?

If the idea of becoming a head coach is too intimidating, here are five reasons you may wish to start as an assistant:

1. If fortunate, you will get the chance to work under and learn from a knowledgeable head coach.

2. An assistant may not have to make game-related decisions such as starting lineups or substitutions, but often focuses on the role of teacher—the person at practice with the gratifying task of working with the players on fundamental skills.

3. Being an assistant further removes you from the possibility of being seen as one who plays favorites.

4. It might lessen any pressure or initial discomfort your child feels.

5. Some people simply function better in the role of assistant.

If you really want to help, and if you do not mind being in the "number 2" spot, consider this option. It can be a very meaningful one for you, your child and the team.

The "Should You Coach Your Child?" Test

If you decide to coach your child's team, you must recognize that even when you are trying to be objective, others may perceive favoritism in your decisions—especially if you are the head coach. You must also recognize that many parents, perhaps even you, have blinders on when it comes to judging the ability of a child, transforming, in the mind's eye, son Peter into Pelé. When you assume the responsibility of coaching a team of eager young children with hopes of athletic achievement, your first commitment must be to fairness.

Understanding that a child's first coach often makes a lasting impression on the youngster, before you run out to buy your whistle and clipboard, take this important test:

1. Are you committed to never acting with outright or intentional favoritism toward your own child?

2. Are you willing to set aside your ego when dealing with your child's performance? Some coaches worry about other people judging them based

on their child's performance, and are often harder on their own child than on others.

3. If your athlete is involved in close calls such as who bats clean-up, who swims the gun lap, or who makes the all-star team, are you willing to seek the honest opinion of your assistant and/or fellow coaches before rendering your decision?

4. After you have received this input, if it is still a close call, are you willing to choose another child so there is no hint of favoritism? If your child is clearly better and others agree with this assessment, choose your child— do not penalize a player simply because she is your child. According to Jim Thompson of the Positive Coaching Alliance, "Most people believe that coaches tend to favor their own kids, but it can cut both ways. I have observed some coaches who are so concerned about fairness that they are unfair to their child."

5. Are you willing to put in the time to do the job properly?

6. Are you committed to fostering a love of the sport?

7. Are you committed to maintaining your self-control with umpires and referees?

8. If you lack expertise, are you willing to try to learn as much as possible about the sport?

9. Are you prepared to put the needs of the players ahead of your personal goals?

10. Are you prepared to *calmly* handle criticism, complaints and parental demands even if they seem unwarranted?

11. Are you prepared to teach *and* demonstrate principles of good sportsmanship to your players?

12. Can you refrain from giving too many directives to your young athlete? Thompson cautions parents who coach their child not to give "continuous unsolicited advice, because the child may feel like a fire hose is being directed at him. This is a time when less is more."

13. Finally, are you willing to listen to your child's feelings about you becoming the coach?

Admittedly, this is a difficult test. But for those of you who have honestly answered "yes" to each question, do not worry that your name is not Mike Krzyzewski or Joe Paterno—you have the perfect attitude to do the job.

If you did not answer "yes" to all 13 questions and you wish to coach, you must try to change your thinking. Consider these facts:

- Your deportment during this period will long be remembered by your child.

- You will not be the coach forever and, at some point, your child will have to deal with an "objective" coach.

- If you hand your child the starting position or all-star berth, it may delay your child's undertaking of hard work and skill development central to the value of sport. Learning to deal with delayed gratification is a gift of the sports experience.

- Favoring your child might allow the youngster to develop an unrealistic idea of his ability in that sport.

- Offering your child undeserved advantages might, or at least should, diminish your youngster's satisfaction. I am aware that some players are every bit as delusional as their parents about their playing ability. However, I strongly believe favoritism is shortsighted and counterproductive.

- When favoritism is obvious, a child's camaraderie with teammates often suffers. I know instances where youth league teammates verbally and sometimes physically abused the "favored child" when the parent/coach was not looking.

At some point, maybe years later, your child may not appreciate, and may even resent, your favoritism.

You Decide to Coach

Coaching will present a wonderful opportunity to demonstrate fairness to your child. Handled correctly, your unbiased approach may produce some unhappy moments which only later result in your youngster's admiration for your integrity. If you deny your child a starting berth or an all-star selection, as long as your decisions are fair and even-handed, the long-term results will help your child learn to handle disappointment.

I have watched many parents favor their children and have never seen it produce meaningful long-term benefits, or strengthen parent/child respect in a healthy way. On the other hand, I have observed instances when a child's respect increases because the parent/coach was principled in handling issues related to coaching their child.

One of my Bates College basketball teammates was coached by his father in high school. The dad did not start my teammate until his senior year, even though he was an excellent player. I clearly remember my teammate telling me how much he wanted to start as a high school junior, but his dad was adamant that starting a senior was the fair decision. Evident in this conversation was the admiration the boy had for his father's principled decision, and an appreciation for the lesson his father taught him. In spite of not starting as a high school junior, the boy ended up having a fine college career!

When it came time to coach my children, I remembered this lesson.

What! Dad Wants to Coach!???

When a child of youth league age first learns that mom or dad will be the team coach, the youngster's initial reaction might be: "Dad's the coach—cool."

There are, however, other possible reactions, including two that are fairly common:

- "Great, because I'll get special treatment and play whatever position I want."
- "Terrible, because this will be *soooooo* embarrassing."

If your child expresses anxiety, it does not necessarily mean the experience will turn out poorly for either of you. In many cases, anxiety is temporary. If your child's embarrassment, anxiety and self-consciousness about your role as coach are too intense, it may be best for you to factor these feelings into your decision making.

The Preseason Discussion

To deal with any preconceived notions, concerns or misconceptions your child might have, begin your coaching odyssey with a preseason discussion. You might want to include the following points:

- You are coaching because the league needs coaches and other volunteer help.
- In areas in which you are not an expert you will make an effort to learn.
- You are coaching to try and help all team members have a good sports experience.
- It is very important for coaches to be fair. You could tell your player, "As the coach, I'm going to be fair, and you will get no special privileges. If you start, it will be because you have earned it, and if you don't, it will be because other players on the team have earned starting positions. As your coach and parent, I will work with you to improve your skills if this is your goal. I'm going to be fair because I love you; my being fair is going to be good for everyone, especially you."

Conversely, if you show favoritism it sends the message, "Whether or not you've earned it, I'll step in and give you a starting position." Your favoritism violates a core principle of fair play.

My Debut as a Youth League Coach

My own youth league coaching debut occurred one snowy Saturday morning. The local YMCA had organized a basketball league and two of my sons, Matt and Andy, ages seven and five at that time, decided to join. As we were heading to the car, a sudden realization struck with the force of a slam-dunk.

"Dad, what time does the game start?" asked Andy.

"Ten," I replied.

"Ten?" asked Matt with alarm in is voice. "But, Dad, that's when *Jabberjaw* is on!"

I somehow convinced the two unhappy hoopers that *Jabberjaw* could be sidelined that day. Thirty minutes later, with only seven players on the roster, I decided to make my two boys, both fans of the Boston Celtics, my super subs.

"Matt, you're John Havlicek, and Andy, you're Kevin McHale," referring to two legendary sixth men of the Celtics.

Matt, in particular, seemed surprisingly eager to take on this role, for a reason I soon discovered. Three or four minutes into the game, I looked down the bench and found only Andrew, sitting contently with his thumb in his mouth (a first in my coaching career!). There was no sign of Matt, so I asked Andy where his brother was. Not wishing to remove his thumb from his mouth, Andy motioned silently towards the lobby.

I walked out into the lobby to find Matthew Doyle sipping on a Coke and watching *Jabberjaw* on the lobby television. Fortunately, the cartoon ended just before the beginning of the second half, and Matt was happy to rejoin the team!

In preparing you for the improbable events that you are likely to face in your first youth league game, remember these points:

- Revel in the excitement.
- Be enthusiastic.
- Don't expect your team to run the man-to-man offense with Duke-like precision.

And finally, be aware that some of your players will judge the success of the game not by your coaching, or even the outcome—but by the quality of the post-game snacks!

Chapter 8

WHEN YOU COACH YOUR CHILD

"I'm not sure whether I'd rather be managing or testing bulletproof vests."
—Former New York Yankees Manager, Joe Torre

Your First Game

In order to prepare you for this adventure, think about a first-time American visitor to London trying to cross the street in Piccadilly Circus with no traffic lights and a horde of onrushing cars approaching from the wrong direction! Bear in mind that the first-time visitor can step back on the curb; you and your eight-year-old players have no such option.

Along with your clipboard and chewing gum, be sure to bring your patience and your sense of humor.

Love of Playing

For youth league players, there is no greater gift than a coach who combines fairness with an enthusiastic attitude, the ability and commitment to teach the fundamental skills of the sport, and the desire to foster a love of the sport.

There is an undeniable correlation between competency and improvement in a sport and enjoyment of the sport. This does not mean a youngster must be highly skilled to have fun, but placing an emphasis on the early learning of proper fundamental skills will enhance skills and enjoyment.

Since you have decided to become a youth league coach, it is vital to do the preliminary work necessary to teach the proper fundamentals of your sport, for this will help your players enjoy the sport, improve at it and continue to play it.

Thirteen Positive Steps You Can Take!

Even if you have never played the game, here are some things you can do to become a fine coach!

1. Your first step is to research how the best coaches in your sport function. This means observing experienced youth league, high school or college coaches to learn how they teach fundamentals and run practices. *Attending the practice of a master coach can be most instructive.*

2. There are numerous sport specific DVDs and books about teaching fundamental skills that are relatively inexpensive and accessible. Suggest to your youth league that they invest a modest sum from the league's treasury to purchase DVDs and books for a "coaches library."

3. Sport specific websites offer free information, as do many fine organizations such as "The Positive Coaching Alliance" (*www.positivecoach.org*).

4. While some sports such as football, baseball and basketball allow a coach to offer regular input during a game, other sports such as soccer, tennis and swimming involve little or no coach/player communication during actual competition. *For this reason, practices offer the best opportunities for coaches to influence players.*

5. Do not overcoach in games. John Wooden maintained that a high percentage of his coaching was done in practice, and that his game coaching often involved minor adjustments of strategy. "Prepare your players in practice and let their instincts take over in games," was his advice. This does not mean that you should sit silently on the bench. Game coaching should focus on reinforcing the lessons, skills and other concepts taught in practice.

6. Methods of teaching skills are constantly evolving, and your task is to seek current information, including the most effective instructional techniques for the age group you are coaching.

7. Certain skills, like hitting a baseball, are taught differently by different experts. If you see two contrasting ways of teaching a skill, your job is to evaluate both methods and make a reasoned choice. You may use por-

tions of several techniques and/or tailor instruction to the style, needs and skill levels of individual children.

8. Follow the time-honored tradition of meeting with an expert to learn more. In many cases, this can be done before or after observing the expert's practice session.

9. Invite an expert to do a coach's clinic for your league volunteers, offering information on running practices and teaching fundamental skills.

10. Make the practices stimulating and fun, and be sure you teach fundamental skills.

11. Create an atmosphere of "team." Discuss with your players—*and their parents*—the value of the team experience.

12. Take a personal interest in each player.

13. Do not teach or allow gamesmanship tactics.

Running Good Practices

Young players who enjoy practice will learn more!

Your objectives as a youth league coach should include helping players learn to compete fairly, win with dignity, and deal constructively with losses. Building some competitive aspects into your practices can help you achieve these goals and make practices more fun and stimulating.

Two keys to running a good practice are *preparation and organization.* Here are 15 other important tips:

1. Act confidently, even if you are not!

2. Plan ahead by selecting a few skills and drills to be taught at each practice.

3. It is better for players to have a firm grasp of a few key skills than a hazy recollection of every technique in your sports glossary.

4. Plan the drill sequence and approximate time allotted for each skill.

5. Try to determine an optimum group size for drills. Optimum size may vary with different skills, as well as with the age of the team members.

6. Remember that repetition is the key to mastering a skill.

7. Allow time for scrimmages.

8. Competition in practices should be both realistic and instructive, but don't go overboard. Every drill does not need a winner; employ some competitive drills but make sure competition remains healthy and balanced.

8

9. In sports such as basketball, ice hockey, field hockey, soccer and lacrosse, begin to teach the principles of proper spacing (see page 83).

10. Be a teacher, not a screamer.

11. Incorporate positive reinforcement into the lesson plan.

12. Create an atmosphere of "positive focus," emphasizing that the best reaction to a poor play is not anger, but attention redirected to performing with proper technique.

13. For players at a more advanced level, it is useful to devote some time to "special situations," such as the two-minute drill in football or the hit and run in baseball.

14. Research and bring along a thought for each day that is stimulating, even inspiring.

15. Have one or two practice rituals your players can count on. For example, at the end of each practice, have the players, with raised voices and enthusiasm, slowly jog one lap around the field or court. At the end of the lap, meet in the center of the field/court, clasp hands and deliver a final "coach's message" to conclude the session.

Drills

Every sport has fun drills such as pepper in baseball, "Around the World" in tennis, or full-court dribble drills in basketball. In a basketball drill, a novice player might simply work on his weak hand, while a more advanced player might utilize the spin dribble, between the legs dribble and crossover dribble, all in one trip up the court!

To Demonstrate or Not To Demonstrate?

If you are a skilled player—or were one and retain some of your old skills—by all means demonstrate. Your saying it, and then doing it, will engage the attention of your players. A suggestion for those coaches who decide to demonstrate and have not performed the skills for some time—bone up on them first!

If you are uncomfortable demonstrating techniques you want your players to learn, do not fret. Ninety percent of the college coaches I know cannot or should not try to demonstrate correct techniques. Either they have been away from playing the game too long, or were not highly skilled players to begin with.

Here are some tips:

1. Do not demonstrate if you are likely to embarrass yourself.

2. Choose one or more youngsters on your team to demonstrate skills. Many skilled young athletes enjoy being called upon to demonstrate.

3. Invite a highly skilled high school or college player to spend a practice session with your youth league team. Be sure the player can properly execute the skills selected for demonstration.

4. Pick out one or more effective skills development DVDs to show the entire team. (With young players, limit the showing to 5 to 10 minutes.)

5. Many coaches/lecturers demonstrate the mechanics of a skill without the ball or bat. A basketball coach may demonstrate proper shot technique, i.e., feet shoulder width apart, knees slightly bent, elbows in, fingertip control, eye the basket and follow-through—without even holding the ball. This can be a very effective way to demonstrate without looking foolish!

Your Offensive System

Your offensive system at the youth league level should encompass the following:

1. An introduction to playing in position and the concept of proper spacing.

2. Simplicity, so beginners will not be confused.

3. Reasonable structure to prevent chaos.

4. As the players become more comfortable with the system, add variations to the offense.

5. For higher-level players, make it clear that they need to carry out their assigned role within a system that incorporates some freedom within the structure of the offense.

6. An ultimate goal is an offensive system that incorporates *freedom within structure.* Reaching this goal will take time and patience, and will not happen with beginners.

Your Defensive System

Youth league players may consider defense less fun than offense, but it can become great fun, and a source of pride, especially as players improve at it. Consider the following points:

1. The defense played in team sports should be one that allows players to improve their fundamental defensive skills. This may, for example, mean playing man-to-man defense in basketball as opposed to zone.

2. Defensive execution improves significantly with proper techniques — beginning with proper footwork.

3. Good conditioning significantly improves defensive performance.

4. This is your chance to teach young athletes a strong work ethic, because defense is all about work!

5. Reinforce the concept that defense is also about helping each other — about teamwork.

Research several offensive and defensive systems, and choose one in each category you feel will be most effective.

Coaching the Scrimmage

Scrimmages in many team sports, whether intra-squad or inter-squad, present great teaching opportunities. Here are some tips:

- It is instructive to talk to athletes during scrimmage play, as long as you do not overdo it.
- Don't ruin the scrimmage by stopping the action after every play.
- Film a scrimmage — this can be a great teaching tool.
- Don't confine your scrimmages to full field or full court — use half of the field or half of the court to reinforce offensive and defensive principles.

Correcting Bad Habits

Helping an athlete "unlearn" poor techniques and replacing them with proper techniques is one of the most challenging coaching tasks.
Here are 12 tips:

1. Helping a child unlearn a bad habit and instead learn a good habit requires a certain level of expertise and patience.

2. Before you take on the task of tinkering with a child's shot or batting swing, make sure what you are going to suggest is correct.

3. If you are not sure, see if you can get an expert to spend time with you, the athlete or the entire team.

4. If you decide to do it, tell the child the following: "You have developed a bad habit in your shot (or throw, or whatever) that can be corrected. It's

going to take hard work and patience on the part of both of us, and I'm willing to put the time in if you are."

5. If the child is willing, you need to begin by breaking the skill down into parts.

6. Focus first on proper stance and footwork—then work your way up, e.g., knees, upper body, technique, etc.

7. Put the ball or bat down! It is often best to have a child practice proper skill techniques without the ball, bat or any equipment involved. This allows a child to concentrate on proper mechanics while "learning" or "relearning" the skill.

8. Take away the target. While coaching at the University of North Carolina, Dean Smith had his players—including one Michael Jordan—stand in front of and shoot against a wall in order to check arc, backspin and follow through without worrying about the target.

9. Videotaping can demonstrate what a player is and is not doing correctly. Once a child achieves correct form, make a DVD to reinforce use of proper mechanics.

10. Teach players to use visualization, i.e., mentally rehearsing a desired outcome. Visualization is a process of picturing the perfect performance of an athletic play or skill.

11. Newly learned techniques require *frequent* repetition.

12. Continue to remind yourself that the process of unlearning and relearning takes time and patience.

Other Fun Activities

Very few of your youth league team members are likely to play on a high school varsity team, and even fewer will play at the college level, but *all* are candidates to enjoy the sport. There are some things you can do to nurture that enjoyment.

Trivia Contests

A weekly or bi-weekly ice cream sundae trivia contest on your sport, plus a "Thought for the Practice or Week," can add enjoyment. Keep the trivia contest simple, include some local questions, and perhaps add one fairly tough question that requires some research. You can draw your thought for the week/practice from any number of famous quotation books, some of which are sports specific.

8

Encourage youngsters to work with their parents on the trivia contests.

Sample Basketball Trivia Questions

- How many national championships has the UConn women's basketball team won?
- Lute Olson led the University of _____ to a national men's basketball title.
- Who is the Head Women's Basketball Coach at the University of Tennessee?
- Which retired professional basketball player played in the most career NBA games?
- How many championships did the Houston Rockets win in the 90s?
- Where did Charles Barkley play college basketball?
- How many combined NBA championships do Bill Russell and Michael Jordan have?

A History Lesson or Interesting Story

When coaching a youth league team, consider preparing an occasional history lesson that will help your players appreciate the background and rhythms of the sport. At my basketball camp, I prepare a weekly lesson on New England basketball history. There is always a moral to the story and often an element of humor. There are many books on your sport, and you may be able to unearth some wonderful local sports tales as well. One never knows what bit of lore may spark a youngster's curiosity, nourish that child's love of the sport, or even drive the child's desire to improve.

If you come upon a newspaper or magazine story that you feel will interest your players, clip it and take it to the next practice or game. Ask your players to look for good stories and award a prize to the youngster who brings in "the best story of the week."

If you are working with another coach, this responsibility can be shared.

Take The Team To a Big Game

When coaching a youth league team, try to incorporate a trip to a high school, college or professional game into your season planning. The sights, sounds, smells and excitement of attending that first game have converted many children into lifelong fans. The game can also serve as a teaching trip, illustrating the skills and strategies that your team has been practicing.

Helping with Carpooling. . .Above and Beyond

When you sign on as a volunteer coach, your responsibility does not include carpooling… you are already doing enough. On the other hand, if you choose to get involved, you may be helping in an area that many sports parents — especially single parents — told us is the most challenging they face.

Here is how to help: As soon as you have a team roster, send an email to parents stating that, because transportation can be an issue, attached are the names, home and email addresses, and phone numbers of all team parents. Your email should make clear that, because you are coaching, you will not be part of a carpooling group (if this is your choice), but you hope the roster information will make carpooling easier.

The Car

Our surveys and focus groups have confirmed my parental experience that pre- and post-game car rides have the potential for producing both valuable dialogue and Chernobyl-like fallout.

The Pre-Game Ride

The mood of your child while riding to a game may be as variable as the New England weather and as unpredictable as the outcome of the pending contest. To reduce tension it may be helpful for a player to have a pre-game routine. For example, a house rule requiring a fully dressed and equipped player 15 minutes prior to departure time gives everyone breathing room, not to mention reducing the number of last-minute searches for clean uniforms and equipment and dressing in the car!

One of our focus group moms told me that she allows her young baseball player to select whatever "ride music" he feels will best prepare him for the game. His choices range from visualizing with classical music to mental pumping and energizing with Queen's *We Will Rock You.* (I personally recommend the heavyweight champion of pre-game arias: *Be True To Your School* by the Beach Boys.) If the music that best prepares your child becomes unbearable, earphones are always an option!

Most importantly, take your cue from your child, and do not try to force last-minute advice upon anxious or excited ears.

The Post-Game Ride

Whether your athlete wins or loses, emotions peak immediately following a game. In the close quarters of a car you are the captive audience upon which your child's feelings may be fully unleashed. At this point, your child may direct anger or distress at you, as a *parent*. The proximity and highly charged atmosphere make it all too easy for you to overreact. I propose a strategy of allowing your child "car time" to reasonably vent joy or despair. During this period, avoid engaging in post-game analysis, criticism or blame games.

As the parent/coach, it is important to offer initial empathy and understanding, but save in-depth discussions for later, when your athlete is less volatile. If your son is angry about not playing first base, later is when you remind him about the commitment to the team.

Coaching your child does not have to put a strain on your relationship and can, if you handle it carefully, even strengthen it. If you consistently reinforce the anchor/aspiration philosophy and employ *balance* and *perspective*, the experience can be a positive one—and then some.

Review in Chapter 5 what youth league parents should expect and hope for from a coach, and this will get you off to a good start!

Spacing in Team Sports

"You look like five guys in a telephone booth!"
— Old coaching mantra to untangle bunched up players

Understanding and practicing proper spacing is a vital step toward becoming a team player. In baseball, where positions are relatively fixed, proper spacing and positioning is less challenging for a beginner than in sports such as soccer, ice hockey, lacrosse, field hockey or basketball, where the whole team is in motion. *A good way for a youth leaguer to learn about the importance of positioning as it relates to team play is to learn the concepts of proper spacing.* Here are seven spacing points to keep in mind:

1. Youth teams often resemble herds of children chasing a ball up and down a playing field or court.
2. Watching the herd can be frustrating, but screaming from the sidelines won't help your child. Let the coach teach the "herd" how to untangle!
3. Maintaining appropriate spacing and positioning while in motion requires conceptual thinking which may not begin to develop until the 3rd or 4th grade, or later. Even when conceptual understanding kicks in, proper spacing can remain challenging.
4. An important first step is to tell players that good spacing means moving away from the ball more often than moving toward the ball. With younger players at my basketball camp, we employ drills that mandate moving away from the ball, e.g., "When overplayed, go backdoor."
5. A diagram can help older players understand spacing concepts, but the best way for a young child to begin to understand spacing is for the coach to stop practice, re-position players and explain what each player is supposed to do and why.
6. As your young player begins to understand spacing, point out that in many sports, players who are bunched together are easier to defend than those who are properly spaced. Therefore, the objective of a pass or player movement away from the ball is often to make the court or field bigger — and thus harder to defend.
7. Parents can reinforce a coach's lesson by repeating appropriate practice drills at home. It is easier to do this when other players/siblings join in.

Finally, consider my cautionary verse:

8

Frank Galasso

The Closed Door

In freshman year, he saw his dream
Pass by when coach called out the team.

One score hence, a father now,
He'd lace them up, and show them how.

Each child would shine on court and field
He'd teach them not to ever yield.

"Push hard, don't quit, jump high, run fast."
By proxy, they'd rewrite his past.

Two more score, a grandsire now
He'd sadly face his children's vow:

"We knew whene'er we failed to win,
You would treat the loss as sin.

The door to honor you said was true,
We'll never let our kids pass through."

Chapter 9

PARENT ATTENDANCE AND BEHAVIOR AT GAMES

Attending Your Child's Game

"I like to have my mom and dad watch me play, as long as they behave."
—Comment taken from our surveys

Whether or not you are a serious sports fan, you should make the effort to attend at least some of your child's games. In addition to the pleasure of watching a son or daughter play, parents can observe how their athlete reacts in various sports situations, and help guide their child. If you really can miss that early evening or Saturday morning meeting, remember, your child's sports career is a *finite* experience. One parent wrote, "It felt like it had just begun when it was almost over."

Our surveys show that 87% of young athletes enjoy having parents watch their games. Since it is unlikely you will be able to attend all games, take time to explain to your child any reasons preventing your attendance, including:

- Parent work schedules.
- Other family obligations.
- Babysitting, transportation issues, or schedules of other siblings.
- Distances that prevent attendance at away games.
- Time to attend to emergencies, or important jobs at home that can't wait, such as letting in the plumber.

Sibling Schedules

Parents of two or more of children will encounter inevitable schedule conflicts. When games and/or activities of siblings overlap, *discuss with your children how you will divide attendance at their activities.* Your attendance plan could include the following:

- In the normal course, you will rotate attendance at games/activities for each child.
- When one child has a "big game/performance," you will attend.
- When there are two conflicting "big games/performances," rotate attendance but allow for the rare "*really* big game/performance" to take precedence.
- If one of your children is in the last year of competition, e.g., a senior in high school with no college sports participation planned, you can certainly adjust your schedule to attend a few more of this child's games (though you should never adjust it to the point of skipping all of a younger child's games). In making such adjustments, also consider whether it may be the last Little League or recreational soccer season for a sibling who may not seem intent on continuing in sports.

Parent Behavior at Games

"Behavior is a mirror in which everyone displays his own image."
— German author, Johann von Goethe

Some sports fans have the misguided notion that the purchase of a ticket buys the right to practice rowdy, rude, repugnant, and sometimes dangerous behavior in the stands. Too many sports parents fall short of good game conduct. In many cases, their actions negatively impact others, including their own children. You must follow this guiding principle: *Nothing around the game—from rowdy fans, to demonstrative players, to overbearing parents—should ever become more important than the game itself.*

A Big Challenge

When you attend a game in which your child is competing, your self-restraint is likely to be challenged, sometimes severely. Many parents identify so closely with their child's performance that they take it very personally when a "bad call," mistake, or rough play occurs. At some point during your child's sports career, you can be certain that several of the following situations will occur:

- The coach employs a strategy with which you disagree.
- A fan says something that annoys you.
- An observer makes negative comments about your child.
- The officials make one or more bad calls.
- Your child makes one or more mistakes.
- The coach isn't playing your child.
- The coach does not play your child in the "right" position.
- Teammates do not pass the ball to your child.
- The coach yells at your child.
- Fans or opponents try to rattle your child.
- Your child makes a critical mistake which directly affects the outcome of the game.

Any one of these situations can test your emotional, verbal or physical self-control. Remember, in your own small way, you contribute to the success of each game by behaving properly. Your sports parenting goal is to be a positive role model displaying self-restraint and good sportsmanship.

Act accordingly!

Eleven Behaviors to Avoid

Fan behavior can easily succumb to a "domino effect" when one or more negative, loud, or unruly fans trigger similar behavior among other observers. To help prevent such chain reactions among your fellow fans, at the beginning of the season, ask the coach to present good sportsmanship guidelines which specifically list unacceptable behaviors for parents, coaches and players. Offer to assist the coach by helping to write the first draft.

Feel free to use, or share with the coach, the following points. Some may appear obvious, but because they continue to occur, they're worth mentioning:

1. Do not mutter nasty criticisms about other players. *This incites more parent conflict than any other fan behavior.*

2. Do not needle the officials or opposing players in order to distract them and interfere with the game. Some parents have developed low-volume harassment into an art form.

3. Do not goad other parents into acting inappropriately, and do not join those who do.

4. Do not argue with or respond to the negative comments of poorly behaving fans, especially opposing fans.

9

5. Do not make angry, loud or profane comments about coaches, players, officials or other fans.

6. Do not throw objects of any sort. Believe it or not, this happens!

7. Do not scold or yell at your child—or any child—about poor play, during or after a game.

8. Do not try to communicate with the coach during a game. Let the coach concentrate.

9. Do not yell instructions or try to communicate with your child during a game. Your instructions may embarrass and/or confuse your child and undermine the coach's authority.

10. There is a difference between a positive cheer and an ear-piercing screech. Be supportive of your team, but do not allow your cheering to become so loud or relentless that those around you wish they had earplugs!

11. *Do not become a boorish "rules expert."* Whether or not you have some knowledge of the rules, refrain from loudly correcting questionable calls by officials.

Where to Sit

For a number of reasons, where one sits at a game can become an issue. Sit wherever you are most comfortable. You may want to take a folding chair in case you choose to sit away from a group of fans, because:

- Sitting near opposing fans subjects you to a barrage of hostile comments.
- Some parents use game time to loudly socialize and gossip.
- You find it stressful to watch your child perform, and sitting alone helps you maintain your equilibrium.
- Your team's verbal assault squad makes it unpleasant to sit with the group.
- You fear you may respond with unpleasant comments when you hear criticisms of your child.
- You prefer to focus quietly on the game without feeling obligated to engage in polite chitchat. If people want to talk, tell them you will touch base after the game.

Whether it is enjoying the camaraderie of the crowd or sitting alone at the far end of the field, it is your *right* to enjoy watching your child's competition from whatever vantage point you choose. I often find solitude an agreeable game companion!

If your child expresses a preference regarding where you sit, I would be inclined to honor such a request, because it might help your child maintain focus on playing, without mental distractions associated with looking at or hearing mom or dad.

Your Child is Wronged

There are few things in competitive athletics that are more gut-wrenching than watching an unprovoked punch or kick inflicted on your child. However difficult, you must remain in your seat and stay out of any conflict, unless your child is seriously hurt, or in danger due to a lack of adult supervision on the field or court. If you must help your child, do not display anger or engage in verbal or physical encounters with anyone!

The bad spill, while occasionally due to an intentional act, is most often misinterpreted. Fans, parents and coaches tend to overreact when they observe hard contact, especially if contact is to sensitive areas of the body.

Remind yourself:

- At the youth league level, the overwhelming majority of hard contact is accidental. When a youth league player takes a hard fall it is usually caused by an opponent who accidentally gets tangled up with your player.
- Not to display a frequent and foolish fan reaction to hard contact, such as yelling at the opponent involved, or the opposing coach.
- If hard contact is intentional, it is the referee's job to sort it out.
- There are times when a referee won't see such plays, and other times when the referee's judgment will differ from yours. Whether or not you agree with the call, make a commitment to the following principle: *the rules and referee calls are incontestable!*
- Parental overreaction to hard contact may negate your athlete's learning the valuable lessons of competitive self-restraint and self-control, which are necessary to athletic success.

Mature sports parents must maintain self-control even when their child has been intentionally wronged.

The Personal Time Out

Just as players may need a time out to deal with physical or emotional fatigue, sports parents may need to take a break from viewing. If your reservoir of emotional control is depleted, and you can no longer bear to watch,

9

feel free to move your seat, get refreshments, take a walk, watch a game on another field, or go away and read. Far better to take a break than to turn into a rude or belligerent fan who makes a regrettable mistake!

According to sports psychologist Dr. John Sullivan, "Children have an opportunity to learn physical, mental and emotional self-discipline from sports, and part of the learning process is watching how their parents act at games."

The Parent's Need to Express Frustration

If your need to release frustration is best accomplished verbally, rather than through exercise or some other activity, you should first recognize the distinction between public venting at a game, which you should not do, and private venting to a spouse or friend, which can be very therapeutic.

Four tips on parental venting:

1. It is important to choose carefully the person to whom you vent. Try to pick someone you can trust to keep your feelings confidential. A spouse or someone not involved with the team might be a wise choice.

2. Use caution in discussing your frustrations with other team parents, because:

   • Your complaining may result in unintentional but implicit criticism of their child or other teammates.

   • Venting may well appear to diminish your "team first" commitment, and contribute to a corrosive cycle of parental complaints.

3. Do not vent in front of your athlete. You risk undermining your child's respect for the coach and team while detracting from the "team first" commitment that adds great value to the sports experience.

4. Again, maintain your self-control in public—and do your venting in private!

What About Reading a Book or Newspaper During the Game?

In most cases, your child knows when you are present and rightfully expects your undivided attention.

As a rule of thumb:

1. When the game is being played, even if your child is not in the game, you must watch, not read.

2. During pregame or halftime, there is nothing wrong with reading. In fact, it might even help you relax.

What If You Do Something Stupid

*"If you own up to your mistakes, you don't suffer as much.
But that's a tough lesson to learn."*
—Philanthropist and former Chrysler CEO, Lee Iacocca

Anyone involved with sports for any length of time has probably done something stupid.

You know the symptoms: you succumb to a rush of anger or adrenaline, and lash out verbally or physically. After your anger drains away, you feel an overwhelming sense of embarrassment and contrition.

Highly respected former Cincinnati Reds third baseman and manager Ray Knight experienced such an episode at a youth league softball game. While coaching his 12-year-old daughter, Knight was unfairly badgered by the father of an opposing player, and made the mistake of retaliating in a physical way. In recounting his mistake to *Sports Illustrated*, Knight said, "I'll tell you how much it hurt me. My girls didn't even get to play in that league this year. My remorse is immense."

If you make a mistake, here are four tips:

1. *Quickly* apologize to those you offended, even if it means mending a fence with someone who had a hand in breaking it.

2. Do not qualify your apology with excuses. Admit you were wrong, *and refrain from words of equivocation.*

3. Use the experience to learn, change, and show others that mistakes need not last forever. You begin this process by quietly but firmly reasserting your personal commitment to model behavior. Your reputation may be temporarily bruised, but most people will be forgiving, *especially when they observe your good behavior.*

4. Move on, but promise yourself that you will never repeat your mistake.

Intense circumstances, especially those involving children, can provoke good people to act out in ways they never imagined possible. If you feel you are about to lose control, take a deep breath, count to 30, and consider the unfortunate consequences that could result from irate behavior, including the fact that parent outbursts at games are now a media lightening rod. You may even find it helpful to promise yourself a reward for maintaining your self-control.

Pearl Buck once wrote, "Every great mistake has a halfway moment, a split second when it can be recalled and perhaps remedied." *Never have I seen the decision by a parent to enter a conflict at a sporting event prove to be a better choice than to retreat from a conflict.*

Your Player Asks You To Stay Home!

"If you are guilty of pressuring behavior, your child may be too frightened to be honest in response to your questions. Thus, a careful, and often difficult self-exploration is necessary."
—Sports Psychologist, Dr. Bridget Murphy

Thirteen percent of the young athletes we surveyed did not want parents at their games. Not surprisingly, two of the three most common reasons cited were bad parent behavior and excessive pressure to perform. The third reason was simply player nervousness when a parent watches.

If your child is reluctant to have you attend games, you need to take an honest look at your behavior, and try to determine why the reluctance exists. In seeking the answer, first consider whether you are guilty of any of the following:

1. You are too intrusive. You yell instructions to your player, undermining the coach and causing embarrassment, confusion and distraction.

2. You criticize the officials.

3. You criticize the other team's players or coaches.

4. You criticize players on your child's team.

5. You argue or become rowdy and demonstrative.

6. Your cheering is too loud and non-stop.

7. You cause embarrassment by hanging around the bench checking up on your player, or showing too much affection in public.

8. You try to give advice to the coach.

9. You become angry if your child makes mistakes or the team loses.

All of these behaviors are embarrassing to your child and other players. Every team member can identify the overbearing team parents.

After your self-analysis, have an honest conversation with your child regarding your behavior. Do not try to argue or debate your behavior with your child. You are trying to elicit their honest feelings and feedback without the child being afraid of your anger or reprisal.

Too Much Pressure?

If your young athlete asks you not to attend games, it might be because your child feels you are constantly pressuring her to perform. Begin by asking yourself whether you expect your child to meet unfulfilled athletic needs of your own.

Then ask yourself and your child whether:

1. Your child feels you are too critical. Do you dissect every performance and burden the child with harsh instructions as to what should and should not have been done?

2. Your child fears disappointing you or letting you down. *If so, you need to repeatedly convey the message that your love and approval are not based on sports performance.* (This is also an appropriate message for the child who simply feels nervous when you are watching.)

3. You are sending the message that you are too personally invested in the details of your child's sports career. *Remember, this is your child's sports career, not yours! Sports are intended to be an enjoyable extracurricular activity from which your child is supposed to benefit, not suffer — or watch you suffer!*

After listening to your athlete, carefully analyze your behavior. This may include soliciting honest input and opinions from people who are familiar with you and your child's sports situation. Then carefully consider how to modify your behavior and your expectations, and be sure to let your child know you are planning to do so. *Remember, it is not your right to take the joy of sports away from your child.*

In contrast, if your child states that your presence is nerve-wracking, and you have determined through discussions with your child, and others, that you are not exerting too much pressure or misbehaving, simply tell the child that all athletes must learn to perform in front of fans, including mom and dad.

Too Nervous?

There are a few parents who find it excruciating to watch their child's games. They either stay away, or their anxiety and distraught state during games convey the wrong message to their child. Parents in this category need to evaluate their over-involvement, and consider how such imbalance affects their child's experience.

The 11 Danger Signs of Parental Over-Involvement

Occasional annoyance or discontent over some aspect of your child's sports activities is typical, and not a reason for serious concern. However, regular practice of a number of the following behaviors indicates you have a problem.

1. You obsess over the statistics of your young athlete.

2. You feel the need to videotape every game, and you scrutinize the tapes for your child's performance errors.

3. You become angry if your child has a bad game, or makes what you believe are foolish mistakes.

4. You easily become angry with your child's teammates, because you feel their lack of skill or performance is holding back your child's "stardom." (This is different from occasional irritation at a "ball hog.")

5. Your anger at your child's teammates includes regular and unfiltered venting of your disgust.

6. You conduct regular "performance evaluations" with your child.

7. You become depressed when your child performs poorly. Your "overriding need" is for your child to succeed, rather than concern for your child's needs.

8. You are too nervous to watch your child play.

9. You are continuously angry with the coach over your child's playing position, lack of playing time, or the coach's strategy.

10. You continuously push for external rewards for your child, such as awards or media recognition, and give little consideration to such internal rewards as fitness and camaraderie.

11. You devote a disproportionate amount of time to a child's sport, neglecting other responsibilities.

If you find yourself guilty of many of these behaviors, you have become too personally invested in your child's "games." You should take immediate steps back from your child's activities and try to adjust your mindset, emotions and behavior. In some cases, such adjustments may require professional help.

Your role at games is to be a supportive, well-behaved parent, while watching your athlete pursue enjoyment and proficiency at the child's own pace.

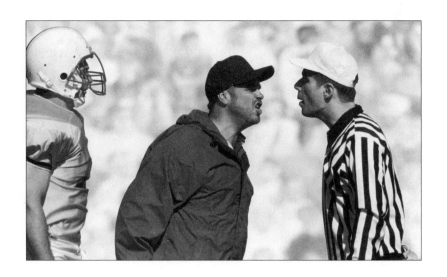

Chapter 10

TREATMENT OF OFFICIALS

"Without them there is no game." —Anonymous

"Every coach, player and fan who screams at a referee should try officiating a game—just once." The late Paul "Frosty" Francis made this statement when he hired me for my first head coaching job at Kingswood-Oxford School in West Hartford, Connecticut. At the time, Frosty was a senior administrator at K-O and a nationally respected college basketball referee who later became Executive Director of the International Association of Approved Basketball Officials. Following Frosty's advice, I refereed a summer camp championship game. From that experience, I gained a greater understanding of and respect for the difficult role of officiating.

We have all experienced the urge to scream at an official over a questionable call. Before you succumb to this temptation, consider one conclusion we have drawn from administering National Sportsmanship Day:

The single worst influence on a young athlete's conduct is the misbehaving parent in the stands, not, as some parents would like to believe, the athlete on television who is a poor role model.

Eight Points to Consider

"Imagine the job description: You're to run around in the mud on a Saturday afternoon and accept the malicious abuse of up to 40,000 people for 90 minutes plus injury time. Pay negligible."
—English novelist, Nicholas Royle

Here are eight points you may want to think about before discussing treatment of game officials with your player:

1. If you are prone to barking at officials, you must curb that behavior. If you don't, whatever advice you offer your youngster about respecting officials will be rendered meaningless.

2. One of your most important goals should be to help your young athlete develop respect for officials, including an understanding that officiating is a very difficult job. Making the correct call often involves the critical act of positioning—being at the correct angle to see and make an accurate call. Even for experienced officials, it is sometimes impossible to get positioned quickly enough to make the right call.

3. Some fans believe it is acceptable to incite bad behavior in other fans. Unfortunately, some assume this to be a right (and rite) of fandom, a mindset that creates problems, even at the youth league level. Do not allow yourself to be pressured into poor behavior by another fan or group of fans.

4. At the youth league level, be particularly sensitive to youngsters who are officiating. Anyone running a youth league knows how difficult it is to enlist volunteer (or underpaid) officials, and leagues must often recruit their referees from the ranks of high school or college students. Among the most offensive displays of poor sportsmanship is a coach or parent trying to influence a young referee through intimidation. If you find yourself acting this way, you really need to take a step back and consider whether you should be at the game.

5. Generally, the least experienced officials will be those who work youth league games. The better umpires and referees often move up the officiating ladder, leaving those learning to make calls on the same field with those learning to make plays. Many parents assume favoritism is the reason behind poor or inconsistent calls, when it is often a lack of experience, skill or knowledge.

6. Officials may be intimidated or make mistakes, but very few officials act with intentional bias. Two good reasons are:

- Most officials are fair-minded people who have a love of a particular sport and a desire to help. This is especially true of underpaid or volunteer officials at the youth league level.
- By the high school level, the pay increases and the evaluation process becomes quite demanding. In most regions, game officials are graded

10

by the head coaches and, at times, a supervisor of officials. Low grades mean fewer games or demotion to a lower competitive level.

7. In some sports, officials may have to make literally hundreds of split-second calls.

8. Participants and fans are *highly* subjective. This statement requires no research!

Eight Things to Tell Your Child

1. Begin by saying, "Throughout life we all deal with people who are charged with enforcing rules. Being rude, argumentative or hostile to officials does not improve the game for anyone. I'm not going to act this way in the stands, and neither are you on the field."

2. The vast majority of great athletes "zone out" the official and focus on playing the game. This is a very valuable objective for a young athlete. Tell your child, "If a bad call or series of bad calls occurs, don't let this distract you. Discipline yourself not to worry about what just happened. Stay in the present and focus *only* on the next play."

3. An athlete who loses self-control after an upsetting call can hurt personal performance and that of the team. Tell your child that the best way to help the team is to avoid becoming overly emotional and, instead, aim for a "focused zone" within which the best players operate.

4. Strongly emphasize that officials take a dim view of being questioned, let alone scolded by an 11-, 13-, or even 21-year-old. And, take my word, certain officials make the offender pay. Referees are human and, with a few, there exists a subtle, perhaps unconscious, element of "payback"; poor behavior may well be remembered by the official on the next close call.

5. Teach your child that officials respect athletes who display a good attitude, give 100% to their task and let the referees do their job without interference. Many people we encounter in the athletic arena show up again at other stages of our lives—including officials!

6. It is realistic to tell your child that some coaches make a practice of trying to intimidate officials, and that their blustering tactics may sway a few officials. Over the long haul, however, it seldom works to a coach's advantage and can result in "referee payback."

7. Help your child understand that it is no more likely that an official will make all calls correctly, than it is likely a player will make all shots.

8. Tell your child that complaining to referees allows the child to get into the very bad habit of favoring excuses over execution—a habit that, unfortunately, often crosses over to other areas of life.

Are Games Really Lost Due to a Bad Call?

Years ago, I attended a basketball coaches' meeting the week after "March Madness" had run its course. Whining about tournament officiating led the league's supervisor of officials to address the group.

"How many of you watched at least 10 games during March Madness that did not involve your own team?"

Every hand went up.

"How many of you can stand up and name one game you watched, not involving your own team, where an official dramatically influenced the outcome of that game?"

Not one hand went up, and the supervisor had made his point. When thinking about all of the games you watch, you probably remember bad calls, especially those in the closing minutes or late innings of a game. But even in sports with minimal scoring, I doubt you will pick out more than a few contests where you can honestly say the official cost the team a game.

"It All Evens Out in the End"

This common phrase associated with officiating is usually, but not always, true. The fact is, officiating does not always even out at the end of each game, or even over the course of a season—especially at the youth league and middle school levels where officials may be the least experienced and knowledgeable. This is the reality of referees taking on extremely difficult jobs.

What if the Umpire Blows the Championship Game?

Those who have competed in a big game know that the outcome lingers, sometimes for years. For some players, the importance of a big game is almost surreal.

Learning how to behave in a situation that may be both unfair and heartbreaking is a worthy discussion topic well *before* the big game approaches. When and if such a circumstance arises, the goal for you and your child is to rise to the highest level of honorable competition. Maintaining good decorum in a high-pressure game is difficult, particularly if there are questionable calls down the stretch. But if you are looking for carry-over value from the sports experience, handling a crushing and perhaps unfair defeat with dignity and honor is as valuable a lesson as sports can provide. Your ongoing efforts to teach your child to keep sports in balance may not lessen the immediate pain of a loss, but it will help a player accept and recover from a defeat without feeling the whole world is in ruins.

What If It's the Last High School Game?

It may be your youngster's last high school game, but it is just the beginning of that youngster's journey in life. I do not deny the hurt, but I am positive of two things:

- One of sports' most valuable contributions is to help us prepare for and deal with disappointment.
- You can assure your child that, over time, while the joy of victory or the hurt of defeat will still be felt, it will lessen. What will not lessen will be the satisfaction of having behaved properly, whatever the outcome.

Judgment Call Versus Misinterpretation of the Rules

A coach has every right to question an official over misapplication of the rules, and this must often be done within seconds. Such justifiable protest is different from screaming over a judgment call. When a referee makes an error on a rule, protesting must be left in the hands of the coach. If you are knowledgeable about the rules and you see an important rule misapplied, without drawing attention to yourself, try to make the assistant coach aware of the misapplication.

If a player sees a misapplication of the rules, it is that player's responsibility to inform the coach, who then handles it.

Referee Dishonesty?

"The actions of one should not indict the masses." — Anonymous

A key subplot in my 1990 novel, *Are You Watching, Adolph Rupp?* involves a basketball referee falling into gambling debt and fixing several games. When one such real life incident occurred in the NBA 17 years after the publication of my book, many people asked for my reaction. My response in 2007 was the same as in 1990: Umpires and referees are an overwhelmingly honest group. At the professional level, they are subject to intense security checks that extend both on and off the field/court.

The last Major League Baseball umpire accused of gambling was one Richard Higham, who was fired and banned from the game way back in 1882. No referee gambling scandals have ever been reported in the NHL or NFL. My advice to you and your young athlete: Do not be jaundiced in your view of sport by any one isolated incident.

Three Final Points

1. Try refereeing! I don't mean to be glib. If you find that you lack appreciation for the job of the official, try refereeing. There are dozens of summer leagues and youth leagues looking for volunteers. At high school age, encourage your child to officiate one or more youth league games. Both of you will gain appreciation for a job as essential as it is under-appreciated.

2. Never argue with officials. Teach your child that when playing in a game, the referee's interpretation and enforcement of the rules are incontestable. I am certainly in favor of making a child aware that some inequities in life demand protest. But do not allow your child to think that either of you have a "civil right" to behave boorishly over a referee's call.

3. Officials are probably the most selfless group involved in sports!

SECTION III

PROBLEMS AND CHALLENGES

Chapter 11

THE UNPARALLELED VALUE OF TEAM

"THE TEAM, THE TEAM, THE TEAM"
—Coach Norman Dale's mantra in the movie *Hoosiers*

If you want your child to learn some good lessons about the value of team, schedule a family viewing of *Hoosiers*! Gene Hackman's portrayal of Coach Norman Dale is brilliant, but what I like best about *Hoosiers* is the way the movie poignantly reinforces what sacrifice and commitment to "team" can do for a group of young athletes.

A Vital Goal

Helping a young athlete develop a "team first" mindset is an important task that far too many parents are failing to undertake. Why? Because they themselves don't possess a genuine commitment to the team. Parental attitude and commitment to a team can strongly influence a child's development as a team player. A "team first" attitude offers learning opportunities and rewards that extend well beyond yesterday's victory. On the other hand, a selfish perspective can make a team experience less productive, even painful.

Three Important Steps

"It's amazing how much can be accomplished if no one cares who gets the credit."
—UCLA Basketball coaching legend, John Wooden

There are three team steps that parents must accept and promote if they want their child to embrace a lasting commitment to a team.

Step I: Be an Advocate for the Team

Consistently advocate for a genuine commitment to the team, not just when team goals conveniently coincide with your player's individual goals, and especially when team goals may be in conflict with what you or your player want. Such an attitude will help you and your athlete derive greater satisfaction from the team experience.

Team advocacy means setting aside the most common form of improper sports parent advocacy, that of lobbying for special treatment of a player, whether for a starting position, a different playing position, or more playing time. Such misguided advocacy intrudes upon a coach's prerogatives; if granted, such requests are often at the expense of a teammate just as worthy or more worthy of the playing time or position.

Parental lobbying and a "my child first" attitude detract from team goals. These attitudes prevent your child from developing the lifelong advantages which accrue to team players. *Learning to be a team player is often cited in our surveys as the most valuable benefit of team sports participation.*

Step II: Avoid the Victim Syndrome

Steer away from, and steer your athlete away from, the victim mindset that is corrosive and all too prevalent in team sports. You have undoubtedly heard some or all of the following refrains:

- My child has a poor coach.
- My child's coach plays favorites.
- My child is unfairly penalized by bad officiating.
- My child is playing the wrong position.
- My child doesn't get enough playing time.
- My child's teammates never pass the ball.
- My child's teammates are poor players.

Believing your child is a victim is a mindset that is easy to succumb to and hard to shake off. Whether this negative attitude originates with a parent or with a complaining player who feels mistreated, it is unproductive for everyone involved. Do not convey this attitude to your player, and discourage it if your athlete begins to demonstrate such a mindset. Refusing to accept an attitude of victimization is different from allowing a child to express frustration over a difficult situation, and then helping the child deal with the frustration in a constructive manner.

Whatever the assigned team role, teach your athlete that productive results are best achieved by a "can do" attitude, rather than by an "it's not fair" mindset.

Step III: Distinguish Between Internal and External Goals

Internal goals: Incorporate into the sports experience objectives such as effort, teamwork, fitness and camaraderie.

External goals: The pursuit of recognition such as awards, statistics and press clippings.

A weakness of the sports culture is that it too often exalts external rewards, and gives short shrift to internal rewards. One strength of the positive team experience is that it fosters balance between internal and external goals. Teach your young athlete the value of noble internal goals, including:

1. Internal goals are more about judging yourself by your own measuring rod rather than by what others might accomplish, what others think of you, or what others expect you to accomplish.

2. People often feel good about themselves when they achieve their objectives through internal goals such as effort, teamwork and unselfishness.

3. Too much focus on external goals is selfish and defeats the valuable process of team building.

4. External goals can be a positive source of motivation as long as these goals are balanced with internal goals. External goals are often achieved as a byproduct of effort and attention to one's internal goals; they often go hand in hand!

5. A joyous activity is often characterized by being so absorbed in the activity that you forget yourself and lose track of time. Internal goals often result in this wonderful state of mind.

6. An obsession with external goals can cause selfishness and, over time, unhappiness and regret.

At the beginning of, and at strategic points throughout your child's sports career, reinforce the value of those selfless internal goals that do not show up in the newspaper but bring great meaning to the sports experience—and to one's life.

Youth League Concepts For Building A Commitment To Team

"(Winning), after all, is the ultimate test not of the quality of single men

but of their capacity to work together and accept common sacrifices."

—Author Luigi Barzini

Developing a commitment to team is an incremental process that should begin when your child is a youth leaguer and be reinforced throughout your child's sports career. Teach the following five concepts to help your youth leaguer understand what it means to be on a team:

1. When you sign up for the team, you may not get to play your favorite position. Since a team cannot have five goalies or three first basemen, you must do whatever job the coach assigns.

2. Your good attitude is very important and can affect other members of the team. A good attitude includes:

   • Enthusiastically doing what the coach says.
   • Not complaining if you do not like the assignment.
   • Not saying bad things about your teammates.
   • Being supportive of and helping your teammates.
   • Being proud of doing your job, however big or small it may be.

3. Even if other players do not do what the coach says, such as sharing the ball or staying in position, *you should.*

4. The most enjoyable team experiences are those when the team works together, not when you are trying to be the star.

5. Individual accomplishments of unselfish athletes are always admired, particularly when a team is successful. Many of the best players in team sports history, including Larry Bird, Sheryl Swoopes, Tim Duncan, Peyton Manning, Mia Hamm, Sue Bird, Bill Russell, Steve Young, Wayne Gretzky and Derek Jeter have shared a team-oriented, unselfish approach.

Regularly remind your youth leaguer that both good and bad attitudes are contagious, and that being an enthusiastic, unselfish player benefits everyone on the team. Point out that the highest praise an athlete can receive is to be told by the coach, "You are a real team player, and your unselfish approach makes everyone around you better!"

Six Team Goals For Your Youth Leaguer

Parents should encourage a youth leaguer to set the following team building goals:

1. Put team goals ahead of your personal goals.
2. Try to be the hardest worker on the team.
3. Try to be the most enthusiastic player on the team.
4. Try to be the most coachable player on the team.
5. Try to maintain a positive attitude which will help energize both you and your teammates.

6. Most importantly, care about your teammates, including those with whom you have little in common. Parents can draw a "circle of caring" and explain that on a new team a player may already know and care about a few teammates, but should work to widen that circle of caring to include every team member.

Nine Advanced Team Concepts
For High School and College Athletes

"I play not my eleven best, but my best eleven."
—Legendary Notre Dame Football Coach, Knute Rockne

It is frequently parents who have difficulty accepting a youngster's role, especially if their child is not starting or starring. Rather than complain, parents should try to understand and accept the value of team play. You can reinforce the concept by making the following points to your young athlete:

1. **Making a varsity team is an achievement and offers a chance for team members to be part of something bigger than themselves.** Tell your child, "Now that you are on the team, your goal should be to help improve the team in every way possible."

2. **For the greater good of the team, individual players must make personal goals secondary to team goals.** By the time a player reaches high school, this non-negotiable team demand should be an integral part of the athlete's mindset.

3. **Accepting one's role.** Often a player's greatest challenge is accepting his role on the team and performing that role with *diligence and enthusiasm.* Diligence and enthusiasm are central to a team's success, regardless of the player's role. If a player is unwilling to accept his role, the whole team will likely suffer.

   Even if your child is on the bench, encourage and reinforce a "team first" commitment by asking the following questions:

   • Are you doing everything possible to improve your skills and those of your teammates, especially in practices?
   • Are you ready to play your best if you are needed?
   • Are you displaying a positive attitude?
   • Are you encouraging a positive attitude in your teammates?
   • Are there any unattended jobs which you can do to help the team?

   Suggest to your player that he try to excel at a "no glory" job that will help

107

the team, such as cheering from the bench or working extra hard in practice. Make sure your player reads the 16 leadership goals for all team members in Chapter 21.

4. **Value your teammates.** The best players must value and acknowledge the contributions of all team members. As basketball legend Red Auerbach preached, "Once a player becomes bigger than the team, you no longer have a team."

5. **More enjoyment.** Reinforce the notion that a "team first" athlete usually enjoys the experience more than a "me first" athlete. Selfish players often miss out on the fun, shared experiences, and deeper satisfaction that come from a genuine commitment to the team.

6. **No strutting.** Tell your player not to harm the team concept by calling attention to himself after making a good play.

7. **Enjoy the team's success.** Tell your athlete that, however big or small a role, every player should have the goal of experiencing joy from the team's success. And you should support this goal!

8. **No selfish risks.** Remind your athlete that players who take selfish, unnecessary risks and repeatedly step outside their role invite the displeasure of the coach and may be justifiably benched. An example would be the basketball player who has an unreliable dunk shot but who, on a breakaway, still decides to opt for the high-risk dunk rather than the sure layup.

9. **Statistics.** Tell your youngster that effective team players never worry about personal statistics during a game. They "lose themselves" as they focus on executing their assigned team role.

Team Views of Two Legends

- **Russell on ego.** In the rush toward individual stardom, emphasis upon "team" is often forgotten. Celtics Hall of Famer Bill Russell wrote, "Everything you do begins with yourself, but for you to use ego to win, you have to make it all about your team. Winning is a team sport and can only be accomplished through team ego." The Boston Celtics have won a record 16 NBA championships, yet have never had a player lead the league in scoring.

- **Lombardi on love.** In the book, *When Pride Still Mattered,* former Green Bay Packers lineman Bob Skoronski shared Vince Lombardi's view of love and team. "You might have a guy playing next to you who isn't perfect, but you've got to love him, and maybe that love would enable you to help him. And maybe you will do something more to overcome a difficult situation in football because of that love. Coach Lombardi didn't want us to be picking on each other, but thinking, 'what can I do to make it easier for my teammate?'"

Both men knew that caring about one's teammates makes the sports experience more meaningful and more enjoyable.

Individual Freedom versus The Good of the Team

Staying Within The Assigned Role

"My son would gain 100 yards a game if they'd run the ball."
"My daughter could score at least 20 points a game if the coach would tell the other players to give her the ball."

Unfortunately, comments of this sort are not unusual. They illustrate a mindset among certain athletes and parents, who believe the coach's strategy limits individual achievements and athletic glory. Parents and players who think this way ignore the core objectives of team play, especially the unselfish performance of assigned tasks which leads to team success.

Both parents and athletes must accept the fact that, regardless of an athlete's skill, very few athletes who play a team sport are given the green light to try anything they choose. This reality can be frustrating, especially for those with a "me first" and not a "team first" attitude. Many players are encouraged by the coach to freely execute two, three, four or perhaps even more skills, *but* they are also told by the coach not to attempt other tasks. A coach may say, "You are a fine shooter from 12 feet out, but I don't want you shooting from beyond 15 feet, because your percentage drops significantly from that range." Good coaches teach a "freedom within structure" approach; they want their players to execute assigned tasks freely within an offensive and defensive structure in which a player distinguishes between a worthwhile risk and an ill-advised gamble. Your goal as a parent is to accept the coach's expertise in these matters, and tell your child to do the same.

The Ultimate Team Test

One of the biggest challenges facing any serious player is how to handle playing behind someone. Help your young athlete by offering the following points:

- In practice and during your off-season training regimen, you should work as hard as you can to beat out fellow teammates for a starting position. Striving to win a starting job is at the very core of individual and team improvement.

- If you don't get the starting job once the season has begun, here are two "team" goals:
  - In practice, you should continue to do your best to win the starting job. Your effort not only will help you, but will also help those playing ahead of you. Such effort is a hallmark of the true team player, and of successful teams.
  - Once the game starts, you must discipline yourself to root for any teammate on the field or court, including any teammate who is playing ahead of you at your position. If you find yourself rooting against anyone playing ahead of you, you must realize that this is the act of an immature, selfish player. Discipline yourself to be ready, and when your chance comes, go into the game and do your best.
- Being able to selflessly root for a player ahead of you during the game is perhaps the ultimate test of being a true team member. If you can get to this stage of selfless ambition, you have really accomplished something!

The Big Picture

The quality of selflessness can be enhanced by helping a young athlete understand a vital element of life's big picture. Here is your message: "At certain stages, things might not go as perfectly as you want. But during these stages of imperfection or disappointment, there are almost always opportunities to grow and to become stronger and wiser.

"Make it your objective to learn from your disappointment so you will become more successful at the next stage!"

The Courage of the Benchwarmer

"It is courage, courage, courage, that raises the blood of life to crimson splendor."
— Playwright George Bernard Shaw

It is interesting how many of our surveyed "successful people" were not stars, or even starters, yet still placed *great* value on their sports experience. Sports helped these people develop an unselfish, determined work ethic that has served them well.

When I speak to student-athletes on college campuses, I often make the following point:

"Courage comes in different forms. Some of the best kids in America are non-scholarship college athletes who sit on the bench, yet give everything for the team. Those of you who are in this category have a special brand of courage, and I like your chances in life!"

Building Trust Through the Team Experience

In team sports, trust can be defined as a shared belief that team members can depend upon each other to achieve common goals. The team sports experience often encompasses a number of factors inherent in trust building, including:

1. Coaches who behave consistently and who keep their word, provide an atmosphere in which trust can develop.

2. Building rapport through experiencing and sharing the emotional and physical challenges of a season.

3. Bonding. Teenagers need to develop trust in someone other than Mom or Dad. This process is especially valuable for youngsters who may not have close family relationships.

4. The neglected or abused child. Many young people who have been subject to physical or emotional abuse find within their team a group of people who genuinely care about them and in whom they can place their trust.

5. Revealing one's feelings. This staple of trust building is common in sports due to the intense emotional investment of players in the well-being of the team and in each other. Over the course of a season, team members will share many inner thoughts, knowing that fellow team members will treat their feelings—and failings—as if they were their own. Such open and honest communication is at the core of the team sports experience.

6. The importance of respecting differences and working together. When a team is working toward a common goal, one tends to forget about a person's color or religion. Team members must know they can depend upon each other, despite any differences.

7. Widespread dependence on one another. Such interdependence often transfers from the field or court into other aspects of the lives of team members. "I know I can always depend on my former teammates," was a common view expressed in our surveys.

8. It is important to show empathy and support when a teammate is vulnerable. When weaknesses are exposed, other team members should try to be sympathetic, supportive and helpful, not critical.

A Famous Example of Vulnerability

Bill Russell is perhaps the greatest team player in sports history, yet even Russell expressed vulnerability. In a fabled playoff game against the Wilt Chamberlain-led Philadelphia Warriors, with only seconds remaining, Russell made an errant inbounds pass. A basket by the Warriors would eliminate the Celtics from the playoffs. During the timeout that followed the turnover, Russell pleaded with his teammates, "Guys, get me off the hook!" Moments later, John Havlicek stole the inbounds pass, sealing the victory for the Celtics, setting the stage for another world championship, and giving rise to play-by-play commentator Johnny Most's legendary bellow in fourth octave, "And Havlicek stole the ball!"

Russell said that such expressions of vulnerability were common among his teammates, and that the positive response of the other Celtics built an extraordinary trust within the team.

The Limits of Loyalty

By the time a young athlete reaches the high school varsity level, the bonding opportunities through sports are powerful. The "all for one and one for all" motto pervades many locker rooms. Yet, there can be a downside to this mentality; closing ranks to protect bad behavior such as hazing, bullying or sexual harassment is all too common in team sports.

The unbridled loyalty to fellow teammates should never go beyond what is right or include looking the other way when a teammate behaves badly. Nor should such a commitment to team cross the line into an "us against them" mentality characterized by arrogance or disinterest in other schoolmates.

The Six Qualities of the Ideal Team Member

1. Effort in and out of season which results in improvement in the sport.
2. Friendship with some team members and a genuine interest in all team members.
3. Selfless ambition directed toward the well-being of the team. This includes:
   - Rooting for all teammates during the game, including those playing ahead of you.
   - Being far more concerned with the good of the team than personal statistics or honors.
4. Observance of team rules in and out of season.
5. Adhering to high standards of behavior in and away from the sport.
6. Being coachable.

The Carry-over Value of "Team"

"Cooperation is one of the three basic principles of evolution—the other two are mutation and selection. Cooperation is essential for life to evolve to a new level of organization."— Director of the Program for Evolution Dynamics at Harvard University, Dr. Martin Nowak

Many parents are not pleased with their child's team experience if the child is not starting or starring. When a player senses this message—and you can be sure a child will—it is likely that her pleasure and enthusiastic contribution to the team will be diminished. You must display and promote the attitude that there is honor in being a hard-working member of any team, no matter what position or playing time is involved. You must also remember that a major strength of team sports is that it helps counter those selfish actions by children of all ages.

America's First Head Coach

In 1776, George Washington faced what appeared to be an impossible task. With vastly more troops, experience and weaponry than General Washington's untrained forces, the British were considered to be the greatest military power in the world.

In seeking ways to motivate his men, General Washington recognized that his first task was to let each and every one of them know that, regardless of their rank, they were of great importance to the mission of independence. And so, he sent the following dispatch to be read to his troops, "This is a cause so worthy that all posts are honorable."

Send a similar message to your young team member!

A Simple Question to Ponder

With overwhelming evidence at hand about the long-term value of being a team player, why would you not wholeheartedly support a commitment to "team?"

Finally, consider my two short poems on the profound value of team:

Frank Galasso

The Value of Team

When a child discovers an interest in sport
And fame and glory become the dream,
Point out that a jewel of a grander sort
Is the value and joy of being on a team.

Frank Galasso

True Diversity

When we put our hands together
Before the game, in prayer
Black hands, white hands, Christians, Jews
United by how much we care
Our coach would bellow
"We are one,
And there is room for every fellow."

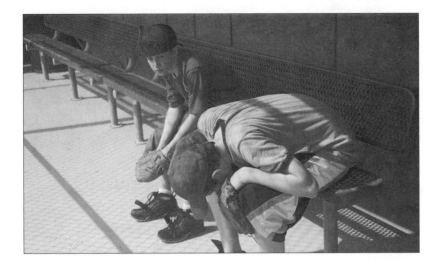

Chapter 12

GETTING CUT

"When one door closes another door opens." —Anonymous

"Getting cut was my first serious encounter with emotional trauma," wrote one surveyed athlete. For those players who have a passionate love of their sport, and who have engaged in consistent, rigorous practice with the goal of moving up the competitive ladder, being cut can be a severe jolt. For many other youngsters, however, being cut is more a short-term disappointment than an enduring psychic wound. And for a great many, the cut opens up new and better opportunities in another sport or activity.

The Fallibility of Coaches

In sports like swimming, it is the stopwatch, not the coach, that makes most selection decisions. In sports where the coach must use his best judgment to choose team members, he utilizes criteria he deems important to overall team success. The use of some subjective, non-quantifiable factors in making cuts can leave any coach open to error, but does not lessen the legitimacy of the process. All team cut decisions involve some subjective "team chemistry" factors such as attitude, work ethic and being a team player, and there may be some *very* close calls when eight players are competing for two places on a team.

The Responsibility of Coaches

Prior to selection of the team, the coach should:

- Establish clear selection guidelines including physical skills, level of conditioning and the importance of team play and attitude.
- Have the guidelines approved by the school or league administration.
- Hold a pre-season meeting well in advance of tryouts. At the meeting, athletes should be given the selection guidelines so they know how to prepare.
- Make known any absolute team roster limitations.
- Remind players that many factors involved in selection are judgment calls, and may be influenced by a player's attitude, character and work ethic, and team chemistry.

Final Cut Factors

Even if there is some flexibility in team roster size, many coaches base decisions on three realities:

1. In some sports, too many players make it difficult to run a good practice.

2. Keeping everyone happy, especially those who get little playing time, can be very challenging. This is especially true with skilled athletes who have worked hard to reach higher levels of competition, and who look upon playing time as the reward for their efforts.

3. A youngster who wants to remain on a team even when told she will be "the last person to play" may, as the season progresses, develop a far different attitude after working hard and not being rewarded with much playing time. Although there are some athletes who can deal with little or no playing time and still be a positive influence, many athletes are too immature, selfish or disappointed to handle such a role.

A coach's final cut decision may also involve any number of the following elements:

- As noted, a large number of athletes trying out can involve close calls and difficult choices for a coach.
- A school or league policy on roster size.
- Physical facilities may limit practice time and space and, thus, the number of team members.
- Budgetary issues like the number of uniforms or at the college level, the amount of travel money available.

- At the high school or college level, some coaches choose a junior or senior and provide the opportunity for the underclassman to play JV or freshman—and then move up the following year. Michael Jordan's high school coach made this decision in MJ's sophomore year, not because he didn't realize Jordan's potential, but because he knew that what the sophomore needed most was game experience.
- The senior who has come up through the system, worked hard, and displayed a good attitude is often given roster preference over an underclassman, unless there is significant disparity in ability.
- Some coaches cut the senior and select the younger player with better skills or more potential to improve. This comes under the "choose the best athlete" and/or "grooming a younger player for next season" approach, whatever the age or grade of the youngster.
- Sometimes a coach must choose by position, needing a player to fill an empty spot. "I needed a catcher, not three first basemen," said one surveyed baseball coach on this matter.
- A coach sometimes cuts a skilled but less flexible player whose skills cannot transfer to a needed position.
- Some positions, such as pitching, require many players to do the job.
- A coach may justifiably cut a more skilled player whose attitude will detract from the team's chemistry. One surveyed basketball coach said, "When it comes to my 10th, 11th and 12th men, attitude and work ethic are the primary considerations."

Some Improper Reasons for Being Cut

- Some coaches are influenced by politics. Being the child of a school administrator, friend of the coach, large donor or board member may exert subtle (or not so subtle) influence on a coach's decision, whether or not the coach even acknowledges such influence.
- Favoritism, different from politics, may play a role in decision-making, though coaches may not even be aware of their bias. This occurs at all levels, and favoritism sometimes becomes even more of a factor in try-outs when a parent/coach is evaluating his own child or a friend of his child.
- Some coaches are influenced by parental pressure. To avoid conflict, the coach yields to badgering by an aggressive parent.

What If Your Child Is Cut?

Your first job is to offer comfort and empathy and make yourself available for listening and discussion. *If appropriate, this is also a good time to remind your youngster how proud you are of his effort. It is also a time to remind yourself that some children reach the limits of their athletic ability and are simply not quite good enough to make a middle school or high school team.* After the initial shock subsides, explain that:

- Acceptable expressions of anger, sadness or disappointment should be made at home.
- You don't expect the child to play the role of victim or engage in public whining; these are not good ways to handle the disappointment of being cut (or any other team conflicts).
- Negative comments or displays of disrespect toward the chosen players are unacceptable. The coach, not the players, made the selections.

Do You Meet with the Coach?

"Torture the statistics enough and you can get them to say anything."

—Anonymous

No.

Many angry parents want an answer to their question "why was my child cut?" Coaches cannot always answer this question in terms that are acceptable or understandable to a parent, and should not have to justify all of their decisions. When parents try to lead the coach into a statistical/skill discussion, e.g., How many points did my child score in tryouts? How many assists did my child have? Did Jane score more points than my child in tryouts? — and so on, they are ignoring many factors that enter into putting a team together. In most cases, the coach has made final decisions based on what is best for the team as a whole, including many non-quantifiable qualities such as teamwork, attitude and work ethic. By the high school and college levels, favoritism is not as much a factor as some distressed parents seem to feel. Under pressure to succeed, the vast majority of coaches at these levels choose those they believe will win games and contribute to team chemistry.

The Next Step

By contrast, it is *most* appropriate for your player to meet with the coach. Tell your wounded warrior the following:

- "Like it or not, everyone must deal with, and make adjustments to, unpleasant decisions made by others. It's up to you to decide what happens next."
- "Even if you don't like the coach, you should say goodbye, and end the relationship in a civil, mature manner." Explain to your player that she may have ongoing or future contact with the coach, or later need a reference/recommendation. Whether or not your child intends to continue in this or any other sport, this is a good opportunity to learn the 'high road' value of leaving on a positive note.
- "If you wish to stay with the sport, and perhaps try out for the team at a later stage, ask the coach to suggest ways you can improve."

The Eight Options

While your player considers future plans, make it clear that you expect the player to engage in some worthwhile activity, and that a hidden value of being cut is often the discovery of a new opportunity. Point out the following options:

I. Stick with the Sport

Many young athletes choose to work at improving their skills in hopes of making a team the next season. If a youngster chooses this route it is worthwhile to say, "Coach, I understand your reasons, but I'm only a sophomore, I love the sport, and hope to play in the future. Do you have any suggestions I can use to get better?" Most coaches will respond favorably to such a mature approach. Plus, working hard on these suggestions may bear fruit.

If a youngster is cut as a 7th grader, or even as a sophomore in high school, there is plenty of time to practice and improve in that sport. Halls of Fame are stocked with athletes who used an early disappointment to train until they were a valuable team contributor.

II. Look for Another Team

Communities and schools often have intramural/recreational leagues or other teams such as AAU, YMCA and YWCA, Legion, and Boys and Girls Clubs on which a youngster can continue to compete and enjoy the sport. Your league/travel player may enjoy sticking with the new option, or later decide to try out for a school or high-level travel team. For the player who already wants to "try out" again for the team from which she was cut, regular game experience can help her improve. (Again, it can be beneficial for an athlete to meet with a coach to obtain improvement tips.)

III. Second Look Policy

Some schools have a "second look policy," where a cut player is given a chance to return for one or more "second look" practices. If a coach employs the second look policy and/or appears open to adding a player or two, any decision will be strongly influenced by what impact the added player will exert on team dynamics. A coach may be persuaded by a player who honestly makes his case by stating:

- I love the sport.
- I will be the hardest worker on the team.
- I will never complain on the bench.
- I will be a role model by displaying a good attitude and unselfishness. (Suggest that your player review the 16 goals for all team leaders in Chapter 21.)

Before your athlete sets off for his "second look" or to make his case with the coach, be sure he understands the hard work involved and intends to keep any commitments he makes to the coach and team!

IV. Becoming a Team Manager

Being a team manager offers as many opportunities for developing successful life skills as playing a sport — perhaps even more! If your child loves the sport and wants to continue involvement by being the team manager, suggest that she consider both the benefits and demands of the position, including:

- The value and importance of a job requiring organizational skills, the ability to work with people, and complete discretion when dealing with confidences of coaches and players.
- It can be a great addition to a résumé. The coach is often the first person turned to for a reference and can be quite helpful with job or college placements. Many coaches develop a long-standing relationship with their team manager.
- Team managers may get to work out with the squad, travel with the team, develop friendships and occasionally earn a future position on the team roster!
- At the college level, some team managers are paid, and a few Division I positions offer scholarship assistance.
- Your youngster may enjoy the opportunity to work with coaches and players who share a common love of the sport.

In reflecting on team managers who took their positions seriously, I am struck by the number who are now leading highly successful lives.

V. Focus on Another Sport

Whether it is learning a new sport or focusing on a sport an athlete has already played, some middle school, high school and even college athletes may be able to switch to a sport which more closely meshes with their physical traits and skills.

Several years ago, a family friend called me in a state of gloom because her son, who had been an all-star youth league basketball player, had been cut from the high school freshman basketball team. The boy was a good athlete but *very* small. My honest opinion was that the coach did him a favor (albeit unwittingly), because the boy's lack of size would have made basketball increasingly difficult.

I told the mom that the young man should begin to look at sports in which his size was not a hindrance.

"But won't he be behind other kids who have already played those sports?" the mom asked.

"Depending upon the sport, that may be true," I responded. "But he's only a freshman and, because of his athleticism and work ethic, he is probably not so far behind that he can't catch up with some athletes in the new sport."

I reminded her that "one of sport's most valuable assets is 'the journey.' The process of reaching the goal is half the fun."

In this particular instance, I was aware of a new wrestling program that was being planned at the boy's high school. I told the mom about the proposed program and that amateur wrestling was a wonderful sport, as long as the athlete refrains from taking on unhealthy solutions to solve weight problems. The boy looked into it, joined the team and ended up being captain in his senior year.

As difficult as it seems at the time, an early cut can be turned into an opportunity for some players. Many fine athletes begin with a sport that is not the best match for their skills or physical characteristics. An early cut may spur a youngster to try a new sport which may be better suited to her physical and/or emotional makeup.

VI. Becoming a Coach

A number of cut players discover an opportunity to continue in their sport as a coach. For the high school senior, it may be helping with the school's freshman team or a local youth league squad. For the college player, it may be serving as a scout for the school's program, or coaching a local youth league or high school freshmen or JV team. There are many fine high school, college and even professional coaches who suffered a cut and decided to stay with the sport through coaching.

VII. Becoming a Referee

Almost every community has a shortage of referees. Referee supervisors welcome the opportunity to train young aspirants, who must often study and pass a certification test. A high school student may be assigned to officiate a youth league game, a college student may be assigned to officiate a high school freshman or JV game. "Plus," as one young referee said to me, "I get something I never got as a player—a paycheck!"

VIII. Focus on a Non-Sport Extra-Curricular Activity

After analysis, some players realistically decide that continuing competitive sports would be an uphill or losing battle, and instead choose to pursue exciting, challenging and fulfilling new extra-curricular activities.

Extreme Steps

When a child is cut, and parents cannot accept the decision, they occasionally take steps such as hiring an attorney, complaining through the media, or making the cut an issue with the coach, AD, league or school board! I am opposed to such actions and the embarrassment they cause a child.

Sports can offer moments of great joy and satisfaction as well as extreme disappointment. Being cut from the team can be upsetting, but with your help, your youngster can turn the experience into a learning process by taking time to consider future plans and trying new things.

When I see parents overreacting to their child's sports disappointments, I am reminded of a good friend who anguished over every bad bounce of his son's basketball career.

"As I look back on it," he said, "it was not as important as it seemed at the time."

If a cut signals the end of a high school or college player's "official" career, help your athlete remember the valuable lessons hopefully learned. Also remind your youngster that some of the most enjoyable benefits of sports can be found in recreational settings. I know quite a few high school and college players who participate in intramurals and love playing without the extreme time demands and stress placed upon a varsity athlete.

Chapter 13

"MY CHILD IS NOT GETTING THE BALL"

"The fault, dear Brutus, is not in our stars, but in ourselves. . . ."
—Shakespeare

Several years ago, I attended the opening game of my town's basketball league for 8- and 9-year-old girls, the majority of whom were unskilled beginners. After the final buzzer, I observed one of the players getting into a car with her mom, who had not attended the game. Within seconds, the mother and daughter got out of the car and approached the coach, who was leaving the gym with his own daughter, also a member of the team.

The mother confronted the coach with the statement, "My daughter was not passed the ball." When finished, she told her daughter to "tell the coach what happened," which the youngster did with obvious reluctance. The mom then asked, "What are you going to do about it?"

The rookie coach seemed stunned and at a loss for words. I had just watched the game and it was easy to recall the girl in action. She was a novice whose lack of skill and experience were apparent. I was disappointed by the mom's handling of the matter for a number of reasons, including:

- The mother automatically believed that her daughter's description of being "frozen out" was accurate, despite the fact that she had not watched the game.
- The mother failed to calm down and reflect on an emotional issue before acting.

- The mother used extremely poor judgment by impulsively confronting the coach and doing so in front of her daughter and the coach's daughter.

- The mother should have observed one or more games and then, if still concerned, advised her daughter on the best ways to approach the coach.

- If nothing positive resulted from the daughter's discussion with the coach, the mother could privately and politely discuss her concerns with the coach by asking how she could help her daughter, not by demanding that her daughter be passed the ball.

The mother turned what might have been a learning opportunity into a confrontational encounter that embarrassed her daughter. *Parents should never raise player/team "problems" with the coach in the presence of any team members or their siblings.* Clearly, the mother should have waited and given more thought to the "problem" before approaching the coach.

When a parent and young athlete are concerned about the athlete not getting the ball, it is important to look at possible reasons why.

Six Reasons Young Players Do Not Get the Ball

1. One or more teammates may be genuinely selfish players.

2. Teammates may appear to be selfish players because they do not understand the importance of passing or do not have the skills to make passing an integral part of their game.

3. Teammates may not know how to look for, or be able to find, an open player.

4. Teammates may not have developed the split-second skills required to make proper passes even when they see an open player. This is *very* common in youth league play.

5. Your child may not be doing what is necessary to get the ball.

6. Your child may not yet be skilled enough to make passing to him an attractive option.

What to Do

When your child complains about not getting the ball, rather than offering sympathy, blaming "ball hogs," or inappropriately complaining to the coach, there are positive options available. Make some or all of the following points to your child:

1. "Not getting the ball now doesn't mean you cannot become a successful player who regularly gets the ball, if you work at it."

2. "Yes, some of your teammates might not pass the ball enough, but just blaming others doesn't help anyone."

3. "It is your responsibility—and opportunity—to work on your skills and improve your game so teammates will want to pass to you! Skilled players usually get the ball more often, whether by being in the correct position to receive a pass, or by simply hustling."

4. "Teamwork is contagious, so make an effort to pass to teammates who are open. This may encourage teammates to return the favor when you are open."

5. "As you work toward improving your offensive skills, you can, right now, try to do other things to help your team, like defense and hustle!"

6. Offer the following tips:

   - Players need to "get open" to receive a pass.
   - Ask the coach to teach you proper footwork to "get open" and then practice the footwork.
   - When you are open, you must communicate this to your teammates either verbally or non-verbally.
   - Do not repeatedly yell, "I'm open" if you are not open.
   - Being open may only last a second or two, *so you must repeat the "free up" process each time you don't receive the ball.* Failing to repeat the free up process is a major weakness of many players.
   - Do not repeatedly run toward the ball. Moving away from the ball often presents better scoring opportunities.

Instructional Leagues versus High-Level Competition

"I'll be 'fair' in everything I do, but the players won't be 'equal' with regard to on-the-court playing time. If I gave everybody equal playing time, it would not be fair to the team as a whole. People who deserve to do more should do more."
—Duke Head Men's Basketball Coach, Mike Krzyzewski, on his "fair but not equal policy."

In instructional leagues, it is reasonable for coaches to emphasize equal playing time, sharing the ball and reinforcing passing skills in practices and games. As players develop, fairness most often equates to what's best for the team, and what's best for the team becomes the most important factor not only in determining playing time, but who gets the ball and when. In more advanced leagues, good passers use discretion. With the game on the line, it is not fair to expect a player to pass to a teammate who is likely to make a poor play. This will not help a team that has worked hard to achieve victory, or boost the confidence of a moderately skilled player who fails to make a key play. In high-level competition, a coach will emphasize wise passing choices.

The Ball Hog

A team might have a true "ball hog," especially at the youth league level. This ball hog is often a skilled player and/or good athlete who thinks nobody else on the team can make the play. Unfortunately, there are some coaches who allow this selfish behavior, and sometimes the ball hog is the coach's child! In such situations, encourage your child to continue to work on self-improvement. Remind your athlete that some of the best lessons in sports come from learning to deal with difficult situations!

If by chance your child is a "ball hog," do not ignore it. Explain that such selfishness will impede development as a player and hurt the team. Make it clear that most good middle school, high school and college coaches look for team players. Also share an interesting fact with your youngster: *no NBA or NCAA national basketball championship team has ever been dominated by a ball hog.*

The Offensive Strategy

In team sports such as soccer, basketball and football, the coach's offense may dictate how often your child gets the ball. A player not getting the ball much at the high school level may have little to do with a selfish teammate, but may relate instead to an offensive system installed by the coach.

What do you do?

Nothing. This is not your job! Let your child handle the situation, understanding that the coach has the right to employ an offense based on what is in the best interests of the team.

A team member who has a problem with an offensive philosophy should take the responsibility to deal with the coach. The player could say, "Coach, I believe I can help the team more if I become a bigger part of the offense." A child who takes this step needs to offer good reasons, including a plan regarding how this will help the team. Remember, it's still the coach's call.

Dealing with ball hogs and imbalance in team play by working hard to improve one's own skills and teamwork can be a valuable learning—and leadership—experience.

Larry Bird — It's All in the Footwork

When basketball great Larry Bird was a young player, he was not getting the ball as much as he wanted. He realized that he would continue to be guarded by quicker players. To combat this, "Larry Legend" practiced his footwork for hours and developed a "free up" move which allowed him to break loose from a quicker defender and receive a pass from a teammate.

Despite being slower than most of his defenders, Larry Bird's ability to consistently "free up" was a key to his phenomenal basketball success.

One can only wonder what might have happened had his parents complained to the coach, "Larry's not getting the ball enough. What are you going to do about it?"

Finally, consider my verse on the value of willpower:

13

Frank Galasso

Willpower's Reward

The first requirement
Simple grit

To amend techniques
For balls not hit.

Then, exulting
When they do land in

Discovering resolve
Can produce a win.

The exhilaration of doing it
The satisfaction of earning it.

Chapter 14

PLAYING FOR A DEMANDING COACH

The Firm and Fair Coach

"A teacher affects eternity; he can never tell where his influence stops."
— American writer, Henry Brooks Adams

Several years ago, Dee Rowe, my great post-graduate year coach at Worcester Academy, taught a course in sports studies at Middlebury College. The students were told, "Be on time, do not slouch, remove all hats, and treat everyone with respect." At Coach Rowe's request, I addressed the class. Just prior to my lecture, several students approached me, and their spokesman stated that, "Coach Rowe's old-fashioned discipline and genuine interest in his students never goes out of style." "It's been wonderful, totally wonderful—my best experience at Middlebury," added another student.

Dee Rowe is one of many sports educators whose high standards and expectations have guided young athletes, and in many cases pushed them to achieve things they never considered possible. Competing under the guidance of such a coach can be a valuable benefit of sports participation.

Why Playing for a Firm and Fair Coach is Valuable

In our surveys, athletes of various ages and backgrounds expressed appreciation for challenging and difficult periods in their lives—such as playing on a high school or college team, a stint in the military, or a three-week Outward-Bound program. A demanding leader pushed them to develop self-reliance, trust in teammates, and showed them that they could sustain the physical and mental effort required to accomplish their goals.

When evaluating their personal development, many people credit experiences that taxed them mentally, emotionally and physically. Once a season ended, or a task was completed, they felt an enormous sense of accomplishment and satisfaction.

Character Lessons from Our Forefathers

It his wonderful book *1776*, for which he won a Pulitzer Prize, historian David McCullough reminds us that the lives of George Washington and his contemporaries were "hard," "inconvenient" and "precarious." McCullough linked these three harsh descriptions to a virtue possessed in considerable measure by General Washington and many of his colleagues—character.

McCullough's astute observations on the character of our forefathers explains why I strongly value the firm and fair coach who, in the overall "education" of athletes, may make things:

- A bit hard—tough drills and rigid behavior codes.
- A bit inconvenient—early morning practices or late-night trips.
- A bit precarious—uncertainty of a starting job or playing time.

Many American youth are in dire need of such challenge and rigor. It is often the firm and fair coach who provides these "character building" experiences.

At What Age Do Athletes Benefit?

Youth Leaguers

I am totally opposed to a drill sergeant approach with youth leaguers, but I have no problem with coaches demanding respect for the rules and age appropriate consequences when rules are violated. It is important for a youth league coach to have the dual objectives of teaching correct fundamental skills, while making the sport enjoyable. For most youngsters, enjoyment is not merely related to their success at learning the skills and winning games, but is also tied to age-appropriate coaching techniques and the playing atmosphere. Insufficient discipline can result in an unpleasant atmosphere in which little learning, team building and enjoyment are possible.

Older Athletes

"The art of raising kids, and then resilient adults, is challenge and master, challenge and master. You do not want to raise your kids stress-free because then they're not prepared, they're not equipped." —Dean of the Mount Sinai School of Medicine, Dr. Dennis Charney

With mature athletes on high school and college teams, and even some middle school travel teams, the role and style of the coach changes. The most respected coaches are those who treat players with firm, consistent discipline, stress responsibility for one's actions, emphasize teamwork, and teach youngsters how to set and work toward goals. Because they care so much about a player's personal development, these coaches brook no excuses when a young athlete is undisciplined or fails to put forth effort.

Adults in the workplace *never* like to be yelled at. Paradoxically, we found that many high school and college athletes do not mind being yelled at on occasion by their coach, and many told us they think it is a necessary part of improving in sports. "As long as it's not the only form of communication, I have no problem with it," said one surveyed athlete. "I get worried when my coach stops yelling at me!" said another.

14

What to Expect and How to Help Your Athlete

If your child is playing for a taskmaster coach, be prepared for some challenges. Expect emotional swings and volatility over the course of the season. As a parent, keep in mind the following points:

I. Listen, But Don't Step In

When your athlete complains, be willing to listen and offer advice when appropriate. Since player complaints about too much work and discipline often come with the territory, do not impulsively intervene in an attempt to make things easier for your athlete. Most serious athletes value improvement and appreciate a coach who can help them improve. Young athletes often find that sticking with a tough sports regimen eventually generates its own rewards. An exception to no parental intervention is when systematic bullying, abusive behavior, injuries, physical threats, or unethical practices are involved.

II. Learning to Handle Criticism

Positive reinforcement is an effective coaching tool, but a coach must also deliver honest critiques in order for a player or team to improve. The tough coach may be the one who helps your child learn to deal with criticism, a quality lacking in many people, including adults, and one that is important for all of us to grasp.

After offering his generous critique of my novel, *Are You Watching, Adolph Rupp?*, the late James Michener told me, "If you continue to write, be prepared for criticism. Every book that I have ever written has been criticized by someone. I often think that my ability to deal with criticism dates back to playing sports for tough coaches in high school and college. They taught me to handle criticism in a careful and constructive manner, and that experience has been extremely valuable to me as I have gone through life."

When dealing with a coach's criticism, tell your child the following:

- "Don't let the coach's loud voice or delivery style prevent you from hearing the message."
- "Stay focused, be respectful, look the coach in the eye when he is speaking, and listen carefully to the words."
- *"Do not take it personally* if instructions are given in an angry, loud or abrupt fashion. Stay calm, and visualize how you will carry out the coach's instructions."

Experiencing variations of intensity in a coach's style, such as quiet praise one minute and harsh criticism the next, help teach an athlete to handle tough challenges, avoid emotional reactions, and stay focused.

III. The Value of Observing Rules

If you want your child to derive long-term benefits from sport, you should be happy when your child's coach takes enough interest in his players to enforce the rules and not look the other way. When I was a senior in high school, my tough yet beloved basketball coach, Joe Lane, left no doubt about personal responsibility and the consistent application of the rules for all players—whether starters or substitutes.

In the locker room before an important road game, I told Mr. Lane, "My mother forgot to pack my red uniform socks."

"It's not your mother's responsibility to pack your socks, it's yours," he replied. "You are out of uniform and you're not starting tonight."

When I reacted with the impertinence of youth, Mr. Lane informed me, "You won't start the next game either."

During that game I was quite upset with his decision, but I later appreciated that team rules are incontestable. And, I never again forgot those long red stretch socks!

IV. The Passionately Raised Voice

Joe Paterno of Penn State and Gail Goestenkors of Texas are wonderful coach educators who are tough, fair, and enthusiastic, and they don't hesitate to yell at a player or team to make a point. A parent, randomly entering the "classrooms" of these coaches, might be stunned by hearing vehement language or a raised voice, but selective use of these tools is not abusive. High school and college coaches use language, volume and tone of voice as tools to motivate, guide and inspire players to achieve excellence.

Gary Williams, Head Men's Basketball Coach at the University of Maryland, once said, "I have a gym language and I have a language away from the gym. I never cross the line with those two things." Coach Williams is known as a tough taskmaster who raises his voice on a fairly regular basis, yet his players admire and respect him. "He is my true friend," said Juan Dixon, former University of Maryland All-American.

V. The Gift of Delayed Gratification

The firm and fair coach is particularly skilled at providing an experience that includes delayed gratification. Many surveyed former athletes pointedly told us that their sports experience taught them to appreciate the importance of delayed gratification.

Respected Programs and Delayed Gratification

Firm and fair coaches at many respected high school programs make it known that, whenever possible, upperclassmen, particularly seniors, are rewarded with playing time and other considerations. The "senior reward" concept is rooted in the diligence and loyalty required for a player to work up through the system. Such a concept is a valuable tradition in many of the best high school programs. Sometimes injuries occur to a senior, or a younger player is clearly superior. But the notion of competing in a highly respected program that expects and rewards the efforts of upperclassmen is an example of delayed gratification that works! Coaches at these programs understand not only the benefits of such an effort-based system, but the pitfalls of freshmen and sophomores being awarded playing time and acclaim before being mature enough to handle it. The old saying, "be careful not to get discovered too early," applies here!

Fewer and fewer colleges employ the senior reward concept for a number of reasons, not the least of which is the constant pressure on college coaches to win—immediately. Yet such high school and college effort-based programs that honor the senior almost always provide a positive experience for those athletes who have the persistence and fortitude to stay the course.

If your child is competing in such a program, you should be happy that delayed gratification is a part of the child's athletic experience.

14

Positive Carryover

I have found that students who are able to handle the challenges of delayed gratification achieve a much higher level of success than those who do not. From the resolve required to achieve a good grade in a class of little interest, to participating in a sports practice regimen that might not bear fruit for months or even years, delayed gratification is borne of the self-discipline and self-control that seem essential to success in life.

Parental Advocacy or Intrusion?

One veteran coach said, "Last year, I was watching the practice of a fellow coach who seldom raises his voice. On this particular day, the team was not responding to some changes he was making to the offense. Two or three times, without using any profanity, he hollered at several players to 'get with it.' The next day, a parent complained to the school principal about the coach's 'verbal abuse' at the prior day's practice. Fortunately, the principal realized that this parent was being far too sensitive, and that the coach was a fine man trying to shake mental cobwebs out of a few players. Unfortunately, not all principals are as discerning or supportive, and more and more parents feel it is their duty to 'protect' their child from the rigor of a challenging undertaking or a coach's discipline."

As a parent, you must carefully look for the difference between a good, firm coach and an out-of-control coach, one who is either mentally or physically abusive and harmful. If you believe the coaching environment is damaging to the players, you have the right to talk to the proper officials. Take care, however, not to make a snap judgment based on one or two impressions. The occasional raised voice is not going to harm the players.

Everyone Makes Mistakes

Coaches are no more perfect than are parents, and, on occasion, coaches may not keep their calm, controlled demeanor. One characteristic most leaders have in common is passion, and sometimes expressing that passion is part of the game! An occasional passionate outburst may be acceptable; consistent abuse or bullying has no place in sports and should not be tolerated by administrators.

The Good of the Whole

The firm and fair coach is committed to doing what is best for the group—yet is also skilled at knowing when to offer positive feedback to individuals. *"He sure didn't coddle me, but boy were his kind words ever meaningful,"* said one surveyed ex-athlete.

The Payoff

"Our chief want is someone who will inspire us to be what we know we could be."
—American Poet, Ralph Waldo Emerson

Many high school and college youngsters may be at a stage in life where they need a non-parental adult who teaches the values of teamwork, discipline and hard work. A coach is in a unique position to help youngsters develop these qualities, because the activity he governs is so important to many athletes.

Rigorous practices help teams get ready for tough games and unfriendly environments. However upset your child may be during the season, the tough coach or teacher is often the educator most appreciated later in life. Before complaining about the coach's firm hand, consider the words of the Persian poet Sá Di, "The severity of the master can be more useful than the indulgence of the father."

Many former athletes consider their demanding coach to be their "guiding conscience" through life—the person they do not want to disappoint.

14

THE LIFELONG MENTOR

"Just one firm, forthright and caring mentor can help a wayward child become a responsible adult. I am the beneficiary of such a mentor—my high school coach."
—Taken from statement of surveyed leader.

When interviewing candidates for positions at the Institute for International Sport, I frequently hear from former athletes that they benefited from the experience of having a "real mentor"—their coach—on whom they can depend throughout life. This view is often reflected by their coach's name almost always appearing atop their reference list!

Conversely, it has been striking to interview candidates who have not played sports, and who indicate that they lack such a mentor. One interviewee said it this way, "I interacted with a number of my professors, and I don't consider any of them to be mentors. Many of my athletic friends consider their coach to be the mentor I wish I had."

Our surveys confirmed that coaches appear to be in a class by themselves as mentors and lifelong friends to those they "taught." Here are six reasons why:

---

1. An athlete spends many hours together with a coach, sharing emotional moments and intense conversations. Our surveys make clear that, within the sphere of education, coaches spend by far the most time with students.

2. Many coaches feel that mentorship is an important part of their job.

3. Many athletic departments include character development/relationship building as part of the coach's job description. No one does this better than Princeton's Athletic Director, Gary Walters, who implemented an acclaimed mentor/character-based coaching program at Princeton.

4. There is a powerful bonding process that often takes place between players and good coaches. Contributing to the bonding process is the shared passion for their sport.

5. Inherent in the sports experience is a robust combination of joy and adversity—success and failure. With good coaching guidance, many athletes learn what the poet Byron wrote: "Adversity is the first path to Truth," and what historian Edith Hamilton wrote: "The fullness of life is in the hazards of life. And, at the worst, there is that in us which can turn defeat into victory." Many credit their coach/mentor with instilling this lesson.

6. Honesty. At the core of the firm and fair coach/player relationship is the coach offering honest feedback. The player must be prepared to receive feedback maturely and constructively—and even consider the criticism as a compliment! An old adage applies here, "When a coach is on you, it means the coach thinks you can get better!"

One of the most valuable benefits of the sports experience may be the acquisition of a trusted lifelong mentor.

Finally, here is the verse that I wrote in honor of my four great coaches, Bob Devlin and Joe Lane at St. John's High School, Dee Rowe at Worcester Academy and George Wigton at Bates College:

Frank Galasso

The Captain of Our Ship

The grandest trip in all my years
Was a lively mix of joy and tears.

Our leader, a man above reproach
Then and now we call him coach.

Parts of the journey were surely not sweet
The harshest of his means are now obsolete.

Emotions of youth would sink and soar
Ruddered by a man tough to the core.

At every practice, the coach would say
"Being on this team is more than play."

Each day a score of lessons learned
The constant message, "achievement is earned."

When I head out to work each day
Those lessons help me find my way.

For at the base of his coaching science
Was teaching his players self-reliance.

14

Chapter 15

THE NEED FOR ATHLETES TO EXPRESS FRUSTRATION

"It is easy to fly into a passion—anybody can do that. To be angry. . .at the right time. . .
and in the right way is not easy, and it is not everyone who can do it. . . ."
—Aristotle

The Importance of a Good Listener

Many predicaments in sports and life are best handled by providing a person with the opportunity to voice her frustrations. Some coaches are receptive to this form of dialogue, others are not. In fact, it is fair to say that a common weakness among many coaches is a reluctance, even unwillingness, to engage in meaningful discussion with frustrated athletes.

When a young college friend of mine was not named men's basketball captain for his senior year, he was so disappointed that he seriously considered not playing. The captaincy issue was especially upsetting, because this young man possessed exceptional athletic and leadership skills. We had a lengthy discussion in which he expressed his frustration and disappointment, and I then advised him to set two goals:

1. Play with the objective of deriving as much joy as possible in your final season.

2. Take advantage of the many leadership opportunities available to non-captains.

The young man accomplished both objectives and, in the process, broke the school scoring record. He later told me that he would have quit the team had he not been able to discuss his anger, sadness and disillusionment.

How to Handle a Range of Emotions

My many conversations with frustrated players and sports parents helped me recognize the following points related to sports competition and emotional well-being:

1. The intensity of the sports experience makes it important for an athlete to have an outlet for frustration, anger and disappointment which can stem from any number of problems, including poor personal performance, losing, little playing time, a personality clash with a coach, or difficulties with teammates.

2. Many athletes need guidance on when, where and how to vent. This includes:

   - Establishing a rule of "no public venting." While expressing emotions plays an important role in the sports experience, there are far too many athletes and parents whose displays of anger or distress are too public or inappropriate and are later regretted.
   - Explaining to your child the importance of venting only to people who can be trusted not to broadcast the athlete's feelings.
   - Knowing when it is or is not appropriate to go to the coach to discuss frustrating problems.
   - Recognizing that venting may be all the athlete can do in response to a tough situation, and that after the needed period of venting, the athlete, with guidance from you, may have to personally determine the best method for coping with a problem.

Tips When Listening to Frustrated Athletes

While emotions of the moment, especially joy or sorrow, are readily accepted in the sports arena, there is still an "off the field" culture in which many athletes are hesitant to express their feelings. *Wise parents encourage athletes to give healthy expression to their feelings when away from the athletic arena!* Whether or not your child's coach encourages or even allows venting and subsequent discussion, you should encourage your athlete to use you as a trusted sounding board.

Here are some important tips:

1. Athletes who do not feel free to vent are at increased risk of becoming so

frustrated or angry with their sports experience that they stop trying, quit, or, as sports psychiatrist Dr. Ronald Kamm points out, "Even act out violently on the athletic field."

2. Listen carefully to what your athlete is saying. Acknowledge your young- ster's feelings, and try to understand what is being expressed. Offer a safe, non-judgmental environment. Initial discussions are intended to allow a child to unload and feel better for having done so.

3. While listening, keep these points in mind:

   • Your child might be complaining about something that cannot be changed, such as the personality of a teammate or coach.

   • You must understand your role and the inherent limitations in your ability to make changes. A complaining substitute player may not deserve to be a starter, but whether or not you agree, it is the coach's decision.

   • It is not your job (or right) to try to rescue your child from typical sports difficulties. Learning to deal with obstacles and frustration can be an important developmental step in becoming self-reliant.

   • It is your right, and sometimes your responsibility, to intervene if your child complains about unethical or unsafe practices, abusive behavior, and/or rules violations.

4. When your child feels better, discuss positive attitudes and actions the child can work on, even if the source of frustration cannot be eliminated. If you do not feel you have enough sports experience to give helpful advice, seek someone who does.

5. If, after your child has vented, you and your athlete believe there is an issue which needs to be discussed with the coach, it is up to all but the youngest athletes to take appropriate steps to deal with the coach.

6. If your child remains overwhelmed with anger or frustration after you have listened and offered advice and/or enlisted the aid of an experienced sports person, the expertise of a child psychologist or psychiatrist with knowledge of sports may be needed.

Venting and the Coach

Wise coaches are interested listeners. Regrettably, many coaches are reluc- tant or unwilling to listen to an athlete's problems or engage in thoughtful discussions during the season, when an athlete most needs a sympathetic ear.

15

This is unfortunate, since some problems can only be dealt with by a head coach or assistant coach.

One former college football captain quit his team during his senior year when he became extremely frustrated with his coach. He told me that his frustration stemmed from the coach's "closed door" policy which shut off any important communication between the coach and players. The football team was losing, and players desperately needed an ongoing dialogue with some member of the coaching staff. Instead, the captain was overwhelmed by complaints from his teammates and then felt hamstrung when he could not communicate the team's needs to any of the coaches. The head coach's "tough it out" policy resulted in widespread quitting.

During the season, high school and college head coaches must put reasonable limitations on the amount of time they devote to problems of individual players, and therefore should delegate some of this responsibility to assistants. In some high school and college athletic programs, this need for communication is recognized, and an assistant coach may be assigned the job of "designated listener." At many colleges, academic advisors and even sports psychologists are also available for this purpose. Such a support system does not accompany most sports experiences at the elementary, middle, and high school levels, which is why you may be your child's most important and valued listener.

When the Coach is the Problem

In some situations the coach may not be the most desirable recipient of an athlete's venting, just as a boss is not always the best choice for the unleashing of an employee's complaints. This is especially true if the coach is the source of your athlete's frustration.

Tell your player that, in addition to parents, some of the following people may be good listeners and sources of advice, *especially if these people know and understand the coach:*

- Assistant coach
- Captain or other teammates
- Teacher or professor
- School counselor
- Sports psychologist, psychiatrist or athletic counselors

Venting With a Teammate

Much therapeutic venting takes place among teammates. It is important to know the difference between therapeutic venting based on frustration and idle gossip. Emphasize to your player that expressing anger and frustration to a trusted confidant is helpful for letting off steam and then thinking more clearly about what steps, if any, the athlete might take to alleviate the frustration.

Caution your young athlete on two points:

- It is best to confine venting to trusted teammates who will treat concerns as confidential.
- Therapeutic venting can sometimes cross over to corrosive backstabbing. Be careful that venting is not borne merely of jealousy, or done in a way that creates friction on the team.

Buster's Sports Wisdom

During a frustrating high school sophomore season, I considered changing schools. My dad arranged for me to meet with someone I admired and who was well-known for his sagacity, a man named Lester "Buster" Sheary. Many people in New England consider Buster to be the greatest basketball coach in the region's history. He coached several All-Americans at Holy Cross, including Hall of Famer Bob Cousy. Buster's 156-36 record still stands at the top of Division I men's basketball.

Upon retiring, Buster took an interest in helping kids deal with sports issues and personal problems, using a wonderful combination of firmness and understanding. During our meeting, Buster listened to my concerns, made constructive suggestions about my game, and then stated, "Two years ago, you chose this high school program. You made your bed, now lie in it. Stay where you are, stop whining, stay focused, and things will be fine!" He left no doubt that he cared about my well-being.

After listening to him praise and scold me, I began to thank him for his advice.

"Don't thank me now, Danny," he said gruffly. "Thank me by doing the same thing for kids when you're an adult."

I am grateful that I stayed at my high school, thanks to Buster's selfless directive.

Many communities have someone like Buster, someone with a special ability to guide young athletes. If your child is in need of such guidance, look around for a Buster Sheary.

15

Chapter 16

QUITTING

"The first time you quit, it's hard. The second time, it gets easier.
The third time, you don't even have to think."
— University of Alabama Hall of Fame football coach, Paul "Bear" Bryant

When a player says, "I want to quit," parents have a responsibility to look at the whole situation, including their child's relationships with the team and coach, work attitude, and physical and emotional condition. Because there are valuable lessons to be learned from sticking with a difficult task and trying one's best to overcome problems, allowing a young athlete to quit at the first sign of problems is not a good lesson for a child of any age.

Quitting Due to Injury

The world of competitive sports offers little tolerance for quitting, but situations do exist when quitting a team or sport may be the only reasonable choice. A severe injury can instantly dictate a halt to play, whether for six weeks, six months, or forever. More subtle injuries may appear minor to a parent, coach or player, but could result in prolonged, even permanent, damage if play continues. Many limping ex-jocks easily identify with Tom Wolfe's splendid portrayal of the excruciating daily pain of fictional ex-football star Charlie Croker in the novel, *A Man In Full*.

While quitting as a result of a sports injury is a fairly straight-forward decision, there may be less clarity involved in guiding a player who wants to quit for other reasons. Deciding factors vary for youth league, middle school, high school and college athletes, and you may need to help your player determine if, and when, a decision to quit is an appropriate one.

Youth League

Early Steps to Help Prevent Quitting

Few children begin a sport with the intent of quitting. At the youth league level, however, there is a chance a child will want to quit when things do not go well. To help minimize this possibility, there are several steps you should take before your child begins an activity.

I. Beware of "Yuppified Overbooking"

Take a careful look at the whole range of your child's activities, and determine whether sufficient open time exists for adding a new sport or team.

Is it necessary to drop an activity to make space for a new one? I know students so overscheduled with lessons and teams that they go to two or three activities after school. This overbooking often stems from a parental competitive urge to ensure their child does everything better than other children. Be fair to your child by allowing a few select activities for maximum focus and enjoyment.

If your budding athlete has too many commitments, it is up to you to discuss this with your child, and help your child select which activities to keep and which ones to drop before signing up for any new sports.

II. Research the Activity

Does your child really want to play the sport? Try to determine whether a particular sport is one your child wants to learn or continue to play, or if your child is signing up merely to please you or maintain a "family tradition." Be careful not to pressure your child this way. When your child shows an interest in a sport, research the following:

- How long is the season?
- How many practices and games are scheduled each week?
- What are the times and locations of practices and games?
- Can young players sign up with friends on a team? Your child may be intent upon playing with a best friend and may not wish to play if placed on a different team.
- Can a player request a specific coach?

148

- Can team placement be done to aid carpooling? If not, can you get your child to every practice and game?
- What is the coach/league policy regarding missed practices?
- What is the coach/league policy regarding missed games?
- What is the league policy regarding playing time?

Do not assume it is the league's obligation to accommodate all requests, including teaming up with a friend or being assigned to a specific coach. There may be good reasons not to grant such a request, especially if it disrupts competitive balance among teams. Also, such requests can run counter to the self-reliance objective of the sports experience.

III. The Commitment

When the decision has been made to sign your child up for a sport or team, it is time to have a discussion about completing the season. *A youth leaguer who begins a sports season with clear expectations is far less likely to suggest quitting when circumstances become difficult or unpleasant.* You may wish to make the following points:

- "Any sport involves hard work as well as fun, so be prepared to give your best effort."
- "I hope the playing experience will be enjoyable for you, but even if it is unpleasant because the team is losing or you're not playing as well as you would like, I expect you to complete the season."
- "You may be taking a spot on the team that another child dearly wants, so don't take the spot and think you can quit because you don't like something."

Testing Different Sports

A youngster should be able to "test" a number of sports and, after a season or two, feel free to drop those that are not a good fit. However, the same rules regarding seasonal commitment and quitting should apply to any sport your player is "testing."

To Quit or Not to Quit

What if your youth leaguer joins the team, starts the season, and then wants to quit?

Research and preseason guidelines can help establish expectations and head off most problems, but no amount of groundwork can fully prepare you

16

and your player for the wide assortment of troubles that can arise. In some situations, quitting should never be a choice, while in others, it may be the best solution.

Do Not Accept These Eight Reasons For Quitting

Some kids are ingenious at devising excuses. Here is a sample of some common complaints that are inadequate for quitting:

1. "I can't play well enough. I stink." Tell your player, "No one gets better by quitting. Among the reasons you are playing is to learn fundamental skills. The only way to improve is to practice, play more, and make sure you get help from the coach if you're having trouble with some skills."

2. "My teammates are lousy." Point out, "No one guaranteed you a great team. Your job is to work your hardest. If you're so much better than your teammates, see if you can help them. Your good attitude encourages the whole team and makes things better for everyone."

3. "My friends aren't on the team," or "I don't have any friends on the team." Remind your child, "We discussed this possibility and no one promised that your friends would be on your team. Making new friends can be an important part of playing sports."

4. "My coach is mean." This calls for some careful listening to your child's reasons, and unobtrusive observation of the coach. If it turns out the coach is not really mean, and your player is simply unhappy with the coach's style or personality, explain that, "The coach isn't there to make everyone love him. He is coaching to teach you skills and help you learn to be a team player."

5. "It isn't fun." This too requires investigation to get to the root of the problem. All sorts of things can take the "fun" out of an activity. If your player is not getting the expected star billing, playing position, or winning team experience, these are not valid reasons to quit.

6. "I want to do something else." This is not a good enough reason to override the importance of honoring what is probably a short-term commitment.

7. "I'm not getting enough playing time." Gently remind your child, "You are free to work harder to earn more playing time."

8. "I'm not getting the ball." The complexity of this frequent complaint requires that you read Chapter 13 for detailed advice.

In most of these cases, a youngster's desire to quit involves minor adversity, frustration, or disappointment of some sort. I do not believe it is helpful to allow a child to quit under such circumstances, especially when most youth league seasons only last 6-12 weeks.

Parent "Quitting"

"The tree of deepest root is found least willing still to quit the ground."
—Poet Hester Lynch Thrale

Unfortunately, it is not always the youngster who wants to quit a team when things are not perfect. Misguided parents, who want to keep a child from facing any unpleasantness, sometimes pull a child off a team for frivolous reasons. After her nine-year-old daughter attended two basketball practices with a coach known for his expert instruction and kind approach, one mother told the league administrator, "Susie and her coach are not well-matched, so I'm taking Susie off the team." In this case, Susie had taken a spot in a fully enrolled league.

Eight Reasons Why Quitting Might Be a Viable Choice

If your youth leaguer repeatedly states, "I want to quit," and cannot clearly state why, perhaps it is due to one or more of the following situations, and the child's best interests would be served by being removed from the team or sport. There may also be times when a parent realizes a decision must be made, even if the child opposes the idea.

16

1. It becomes apparent that your child has no desire to learn or play the sport, but signed on to appease a parent who expected the child to play for an improper reason such as upholding the "family tradition" of playing that sport. Remember, ask your child first, and listen carefully to the answer before your child signs up for a sport.

2. Some early youth leaguers discover they simply cannot function in a team sport, because they may be too physically or mentally immature to play on a team. Parents will have to determine when the misery of such a mismatch outweighs any value in finishing the season. If this is the case, you might consider individual lessons in a sport such as swimming or tennis while the child matures enough to give team sports another try. Be aware that some children never like team sports.

3. Your child finds out that the physical nature of a sport such as football or ice hockey is much more punishing than expected. There is little point in

forcing play upon an undersized child, or one who is unhappy with the amount of contact. Continuing such endeavors can lead to physical and/or psychological problems.

4. A coach fosters an environment of intimidation, fear or constant pressure. If this is the only style a coach uses, and a child is continually anxious and unhappy, it may be best to withdraw the player. I know a Little Leaguer who, at age nine, played for a coach who acted like a Marine drill sergeant. The two and a half hour practices, three nights a week, quickly came to feel like torture and the boy went home feeling less and less competent after constant scolding. His parents debated whether to allow him to quit, and decided that he should stick it out. The boy never again played baseball, although he enjoyed the sport before he had the misfortune of playing for that coach.

5. A coach is unwilling or unable to discipline players engaging in acts of bullying or harassment. Unfortunately, the coach's child or the child's friends may be the worst offenders, feeling they have special license. This is obviously a difficult subject to discuss with the coach, so I suggest unobtrusive observation of the situation and discussions with your child. Try to determine whether the coach appears aware of the "bullying" and ignores it, or whether it is done out of earshot of the coach. If a coach seems unaware of the problem, have a confidential discussion with the coach, in which you ask the coach to put a halt to such behavior. Point out that your player feels like quitting. If, after the conversation, the coach takes no remedial steps, the resiliency of your child must be your guide. Children who are unable to deal with bullying, and are miserable, may be better off leaving such an atmosphere.

6. An injury or extended illness can dictate withdrawal from a team, especially those injuries requiring complete rest. The macho mantra of "playing through the pain" is ill-advised unless undertaken after medical experts have diagnosed the pain and granted permission to continue playing. *If there is any question regarding an injury, do not let a child or coach persuade you to allow play without the go-ahead from a sports medicine expert.*

7. You and your athlete find that the coach demands an unreasonable time commitment which far exceeds that which you were led to believe from your research. Such a time demand may be unworkable for your youth league player and/or your family's schedule.

8. You find that your athlete cannot keep up with essential schoolwork because of the time and stress demanded to play a particular sport.

Final Steps Before Quitting — Youth League Level

If you and your child believe there is a serious enough problem to consider quitting, but you believe the season may be salvageable, ask your child to stick with it for a little longer. During this time, contact the coach and politely ask that your conversation remain confidential. Point out that:

- You appreciate the coach's volunteer efforts and time commitment.
- Your child is having a difficult time.
- Specify the reasons things are not working for your child.
- Ask the coach for any ideas which could help the team experience work for your child.

A courteous, unemotional call or email may help a volunteer coach recognize that one principal obligation is to respond to the needs of each child. Words of encouragement from the coach can often turn the experience around. If a coach does not respond well and your child is still miserable, quitting may be the best course of action.

An Important Suggestion!

If your child expresses a desire to quit but sticks it out, once the season has ended, make sure to tell your child:

- "Resolve can get you through a lot of problems in life — as you just found out!"
- "I want to commend you for clearing this hurdle. I'm *very* proud of you."

Higher Level Competition and Quitting

The Natural Sports Pyramid

Studies point out that a high percentage of youngsters who engage in youth league sports stop playing by middle school or high school. One "dropout" study reveals that nearly one-third of the 10-year-old athletes playing organized sports have stopped competing by age 13. Other studies cite statistics demonstrating that between 70% and 80% of players in organized sports have dropped sports by the ninth grade.

Some critical interpretations of these studies conclude that the primary culprits causing youth leaguers to quit are overbearing youth league parents and insensitive youth league coaches. In fact, the *major* reason that fewer kids are playing competitive sports by middle school or high school is the competitive narrowing of playing opportunities at each level. Spots on amateur

16

sports teams decrease in pyramid fashion, from a base of youth leaguers, to a very small pointed top composed of the best Division I college players.

In *many* towns in America, you will find a scenario similar to the following: A town's youth league soccer program may have 400 girls and 400 boys participating over four grades, e.g., grades 1 to 4 or grades 5 to 8. In the same town, the one and only public high school offers roster spots for only 40 girls and 40 boys at the four-year high school, with 20 boys and 20 girls on their respective high school varsity soccer teams, and 20 boys and 20 girls on their respective high school JV soccer teams. Opportunities similarly decrease in many other sports. By ninth grade, sign-up recreation leagues are often replaced by AAU/Club teams with competitive tryouts.

In high schools with larger enrollments, competition to play on a varsity team can be even more severe for an aspiring young athlete.

Ten Reasons Athletes Stop Playing Sports

By the time a child is ready to play on a middle school, high school or college sports team, many things in the athlete's life may be changing. Some youngsters play effectively through middle school and drop sports in high school; others play in high school and then drop sports in college. But at each level, fewer players continue in competitive sports, and the reasons may include:

1. The playing opportunities are drastically reduced for large numbers of youngsters when varsity, AAU/Club, and elite travel teams are the primary vehicles for competitive play. The fewer available team slots are awarded to those who possess higher-level skills and are willing to make a serious commitment of time and effort.

2. Many middle school or high school youngsters self-select out of a sport when they assess the playing ability required on a high school or college varsity team. Some players realize they cannot play at the next level and decide not to try out for the team.

3. Some students choose to participate in extracurricular activities which they find more interesting or valuable than sports. Dance, art, drama, band, school newspaper, school yearbook, and language clubs may gradually or suddenly edge out a sport as competition for the student's time. "It took me awhile, but I finally realized that my son was happier—and better off—in the school band than on the school football team," said one parent.

4. Former multi-sport youth league, middle school, or high school players quit some sports in order to focus on one sport in middle school, high school or college.

16

5. Some youngsters who casually played sports do not want to devote the time or effort required to continue playing at the next level.

6. Students who are skilled enough to play in high school or college may quit because the time demanded by their sport prevents their pursuit of a rigorous academic program or limits their academic choices. This is particularly true at the college level. It is interesting that over 50% of recruited Ivy League athletes quit their varsity sport before their senior year. One surveyed Ivy League student who dropped his sport to pursue medical school said, "Ivy League athletes often drop out of their sport because they are not on athletic scholarship, find another extra-curricular activity of greater interest, and/or recognize that the time devoted to sports will detract from their studies. In my case, it was forgoing a varsity sport so I could attend my classes and labs without being worried about practices or games."

7. Some athletes simply lose interest or enjoyment in playing due to constant parental/coach pressures.

8. Some varsity high school and college athletes quit because of a lack of playing time.

9. Some athletes quit because an injury will not allow further play on a sustained basis.

10. Finally, quitting is often fostered by a parent who consistently criticizes the coach or other team members and, as a consequence, sets up an excuse for the young athlete. Remember, your job is to guide your young athlete, not to encourage the habit of blaming others. If you need to vent about your child's sports situation, make sure you do it with someone other than the child!

16

THE COLLEGE ATHLETE AND THE RIGORS OF ACADEMICS

While addressing student-athletes at over 100 colleges and universities, I have encouraged athletes to discuss how college sports affected their grades and their choice of a rigorous academic major. While many student-athletes have told me that the disciplined routine of sports helped them develop a more disciplined approach to their studies, others made clear that the time, focus and stress involved in competitive sports significantly reduced their effectiveness as a student.

If this is true of your college athlete, particularly a student-athlete at the Division III level without an athletic scholarship, removal from the varsity should be given serious consideration. Your job is to remind your student-athlete that academic achievement should come before sports. If the student-athlete decides to quit the team, either during or after a season, then your message should be, "If you make this decision, you must also buckle down and become a serious student!"

Avoid a Hasty Decision

I know many former high school and college athletes who quit a team and who now wish they had given greater thought to their decision. These former athletes did not appreciate that quitting meant the end of their team sport opportunities. If your accomplished athlete becomes so emotionally overwhelmed by a problem, fatigue or a perceived social need that he wants to quit, try to help your child see the big picture, including possible long-term consequences of a hasty departure. You have the experience to know that quitting may temporarily solve one problem, but lead to other undesirable consequences. *Point out that decisions with long-term consequences, such as quitting or transferring, are often best made after the season, when the athlete is less distressed and able to think more clearly.* Your role is to help guide the child away from a hasty decision while considering how to best deal with a problem.

Four Steps Your Athlete Should Take Before Quitting

Step I: Identify the Problem and Talk It Out

If your player is considering quitting a team, your first step is to help your youngster identify the problem. Conversations should be non-judgmental, allowing your athlete to sort out perceptions and feelings about why things are not working. The unburdening process sometimes helps a frustrated athlete organize thoughts and feelings clearly enough to establish a plan of action for dealing with any problem.

You could start your conversation by asking some or all of the following questions—and be prepared to listen:

- Are you unable to adequately complete your schoolwork?
- What isn't working well for you on this team?
- Do you feel you are contributing to the team?

16

- Do you believe your efforts are not appreciated or not being acknowledged?
- Are there specific problems with your coach or teammates, and if so, what are they?
- Do you feel you are putting in too much time and effort for too little payback?
- Are you simply too exhausted to feel like continuing?
- What, if anything, can be changed that would make you want to remain on the team?

Sports psychologist Dr. Bridget Murphy tells us that, "Far too many athletes of all ages suffer from too little physical and mental rest and recovery time." Your job as a parent is to monitor and enforce adequate sleep and nutritional routines, as well as to determine whether a particular sport, team or season is simply too demanding for your child's physical and emotional stages of growth.

Step II: Meet with the Coach

A dedicated athlete should not quit without making an honest effort to work things out through discussions with the coach, since some problems can only be addressed or solved by working with the coach. In most situations, it is an athlete's responsibility to set up any meetings.

- Have your athlete contact the coach and request a meeting during non-practice hours. No coach wants an athlete to quit, and a competent coach should recognize that one of his most important responsibilities is to help an athlete get through a difficult period. Open communication is the best way to achieve this. Prior to the meeting, suggest to your youngster a role-play, perhaps with you acting as the coach. Often, a "heart to heart" with the coach can make what seems like a hopeless situation not so hopeless after all.
- The parent's role should generally be limited to that of home advisor, unless a parent needs to remove a sick or injured child from play, and the player or coach pushes to continue play.
- Youngsters may be so afraid, ashamed or embarrassed that they would prefer to quit without contacting the coach. In this situation, your first step is to remind your young athlete that the mature way to handle the matter is for the young athlete—not you—to schedule a meeting. If the young athlete still resists, I recommend that you call the coach and explain that your child is experiencing a problem, is frustrated or

16

fatigued, and is thinking about quitting. Make it clear that you would appreciate any guidance and support the coach can offer your child. No coach should refuse such a request and should willingly meet with your youngster.

- Sometimes the player/coach relationship is the problem, and a meeting with the coach may not produce any solutions. If this is the case, your athlete must weigh the pros and cons of continuing to play for the coach, and then decide whether to finish the season or quit.

Step III: Consider Taking a Break

If it becomes evident that your player is suffering mental fatigue or burnout due to ongoing problems or an intense, extended playing season, it may be time for a break. There is a clear distinction between a six-week youth league program and the multi-season activities of some highly competitive athletic teams. Suggest that your player ask the coach for permission to take a break before making a final decision about quitting. Depending upon the extent of your child's fatigue and dejection, the coach's opinion, and the team's schedule, a break could last several days, one or two weeks, or more. Such a break may allow an athlete time to regroup and gain a better perspective from which to make important decisions. Many college programs have athletic counselors who can help facilitate a needed break.

When Basketball Hall of Famer Dave Cowens was at his peak with the Boston Celtics, he developed severe mental fatigue. He approached Red Auerbach, the legendary coach, general manager and president of the Celtics. Many in Auerbach's position, with the pressures of winning weighing on every decision, might have tried to convince a player as valuable as Cowens to stay and tough it out. Auerbach recognized that this was a delicate situation and that Cowens would be best served by taking time away – which he did. Following a "sabbatical" of several months, Cowens returned to the Celtics and performed brilliantly.

THE FAKED OR PROLONGED INJURY

An athlete faking, exaggerating or prolonging an injury may be exhibiting symptoms of a problem beyond the physical injury itself. Whether consciously or subconsciously, the player may be reacting to emotional pain every bit as excruciating as pain inflicted by a physical injury. How you handle such "injuries" depends upon the actual scenario, but I suggest a cautious and gentle approach.

A real injury may have been misdiagnosed or not properly treated. If you suspect this may be the case, obtain a medical review with a sports medicine physician. If the review reveals no problem, it may be that the athlete fears re-injury and needs to be gradually reintroduced to play while regaining confidence.

An athlete may suffer such deep mental fatigue or burnout that he translates his "psychic pain" into a "bodily pain" without an awareness of doing so.

A player who intentionally "fakes" or claims a physical injury might believe it is the only acceptable way to attain a desperately needed mental health break without appearing weak or less dedicated. Most athletes who choose this course find it too painful and embarrassing to confide in anyone.

No player wants to admit to faking, exaggerating or prolonging an injury, so when coaching I never questioned a player's "self-diagnosis," but told the player, "You can come back when you're ready." This face-saving method allowed an athlete time and space to work out a problem. In more extreme cases, the athlete may be in need of professional counseling.

Step IV: Other Sources of Help

While parents and coaches are vitally important resources for a youngster to consult regarding quitting, the counsel of outsiders may also be valuable, especially if a parent or coach has become part of the player's problem. Consider seeking help from:

- A former coach for whom your child played the same sport or another sport. The coach may have valuable insights from working with your athlete, and expertise on how to guide the youngster.
- An older and wiser ex-coach or ex-athlete in your community who can approach the situation in a kind but objective manner. Many distressed young athletes have benefited from the caring and expert advice of former sports figures.
- A professional psychologist, psychiatrist or sports psychologist. Such a professional is often best able to help a youngster who is overwhelmed by stress, fatigue or other personal problems. Many colleges have pro-

fessional counselors available to help young athletes deal with such issues.

"Know When to Hold 'Em and Know When to Fold 'Em"

As a parent, try not to be so rigid about "finishing what one starts," that you cannot discern when quitting may be a valid choice. Quitting must be considered on a case-by-case basis, keeping in mind both the short-term and long-term pros and cons. It is vital to allow your child to learn to overcome obstacles, develop resiliency and derive satisfaction from one's efforts. But do not force a child to remain in an unbearable or damaging situation.

Six Final Questions Before Your Child Quits

Whether because of tougher competition, time constraints, or changing interests, if your child plans to quit a sport, there are six questions I would ask the child:

1. Do you understand this could be end of your team sports experience?

2. Do you understand that you might regret the decision at a later stage of your life?

3. Since there are only a few weeks before the season finishes, why not try to get through this season, and then make a decision on your future sports career after you have had a break?

4. Are you thinking about what you want to do with the time you once used for sports?

5. Would you consider trying a new, less stressful sport for reasons of fitness and enjoyment?

6. If you quit, do you have a plan to continue getting exercise? Make sure to tell your child that many competitive athletes who drop their sport lose their motivation to remain physically fit. Sports psychologist Dr. John Sullivan points out that, "Those involved more for physical excellence than physical fitness often face a tough fitness transition when the commitment changes from varsity to recreational. Many athletes in this category feel they have lost their goal." If your child decides to drop out of sports in favor of other worthy extra-curricular activities, it is important to encourage the child to maintain a physical fitness regimen.

16

A Public Withdrawal

In the 1964-65 basketball season, two high school big men were already drawing national attention. One was 7'2" Lew Alcindor of Power Memorial High School in New York; the other was 6'9" Ron Teixeira of Catholic Memorial in West Roxbury, Massachusetts.

In much publicized college decisions, Alcindor chose UCLA and Teixeira chose Holy Cross. Alcindor would soon change his name to Kareem Abdul-Jabbar, lead UCLA to three straight national championships, and then go on to become one of the greatest players in NBA history.

Teixeira played well enough at Holy Cross but was frustrated with the coaching style of Crusader mentor Jack Donahue (who had actually been Alcindor's high school coach). Midway through his junior year, after trying to work things out with the coach, Teixeira sent shockwaves through college basketball by quitting the Holy Cross team. His decision also opened up an avalanche of analysis, including a wonderful classroom discussion led by my teacher at St. John's High School, Jay Foley.

Mr. Foley—himself a Holy Cross graduate—devoted an entire period to discussing the various elements of Teixeira's highly-publicized decision. Mr. Foley urged us to look at the matter with an open mind. He pointed out that Teixeira was a brilliant student who had tried his best to resolve the problems with Coach Donahue, and who, in quitting, was making a decision of principle. *He further suggested that Teixeira quit not just because he was frustrated, but because his frustration was clearly an impediment to his studies.*

Teixeira went on to great success in life. He received an MBA from the Amos Tuck School at Dartmouth, and has enjoyed a distinguished career in business. From an athletic standpoint, he switched from basketball to karate, where he earned a black belt.

As I think back on Ron Teixeira, it strikes me that he traded basketball for what he felt was a higher purpose—the peace of mind that would allow him to train his mind.

I recall Mr. Foley saying that, "sometimes quitting actually takes more courage than staying."

Chapter 17

SHOULD MY CHILD PLAY ON A TRAVEL TEAM?

"To say yes, you have to sweat, and roll up your sleeves,
and plunge both hands into life up to the elbows."
—French playwright, Jean Anouilh

Research Results

In our survey, we found that 66% of Division I college varsity athletes, 63% of Division III college varsity athletes and 58% of high school varsity athletes competed or currently compete on travel teams in the same sport they play at school. On average, the college varsity athletes began playing on travel teams at age 12, the high school varsity athletes at age 11.[6]

Making the Decision

Signing on with a travel team involves a difficult decision that may present sports parents with a "right versus right" dilemma. It is right for a talented youngster to want to play against high-level competition with the best available coaches, as it is right for parents to want to protect young players against too much "sports pressure."

Meeting the wishes and needs of both parties is possible if parents do not allow an activity to be carried to an extreme. Any extracurricular activity in which a child becomes seriously involved, whether music, dance, theater or sports, brings with it increased time demands, expense and commitment. If you have a growing athlete who is not neglecting studies in pursuit of sports, it is perfectly reasonable to investigate whether a travel team would meet the athletic needs of your child, and whether the team activities are structured in a way that can work for your family.

Points to Consider Before Your Child Joins a Travel Team

1. How good is local league and school competition? Does your player need a travel team in order to play competitively, work with good coaches and improve skills? Some geographic areas are "hotbeds" of excellent play in particular sports. Your child may be fortunate to find all these needs locally without joining a travel team.

2. What long-range sports goals does your child have? Is it to enjoy playing against good opponents, to make the high school varsity team, to be awarded a college scholarship, or to play at a professional level? Do you think playing on a travel team will help your child meet these goals?

3. If you are a parent who does not like sports, do not allow your dislike to limit your child's sports participation. Avoid excuses like, "we don't have the time or money," when your real motive is to simply avoid extensive involvement with sports. In his wonderful principle, "The Golden Mean," finding that mean between deficiency and excess, Aristotle cautioned against the perils of not only excess *but* deficiency!

At What Age Should My Child Start to Play on a Travel Team?

The best age to start will be highly individual and varies by sport. Some youngsters have the skills, focus and desire to play on a travel team at age 10 or 11, while many others are better off waiting until age 13 or 14. The sport and types of teams available, as well as the skill level and personality of your child, should be your guides. Consider the following points before making your decision:

1. Success in athletics often results from a love of the sport.

2. Natural athletic ability at a young age does not necessarily translate into successful and enjoyable travel team play. A youngster needs the desire and maturity to fulfill the obligation.

3. After researching a team, try to gauge whether the time commitment and level of work match your child's skills, focus and maturity.

4. At some point, improvement in every sport requires competing against other good players. This may or may not require a travel team, and, as

noted, will depend upon your location, your child's sport, and the assortment of leagues and players in your locale.

5. Exceptionally promising and/or skilled players are most apt to require travel team competition to achieve their athletic goals.

Gauging Your Child's Readiness

If it is clear that working with better coaches and higher-level players requires travel team play, try to objectively analyze whether your child is ready to play on such a team by reviewing the following:

1. Are you, or your athlete, the driving force in wanting your child to play on a travel team? If it is only you, your child should not join the team. The travel team is not a "parent badge of honor."

2. How important to your child is playing on the travel team? Does your child really want to play for a team because of love for the sport, or is your child just trying out because:

   • Friends or former teammates are doing so?
   • You are pushing, and your child does not want to disappoint you?

3. Is your child's grasp of fundamental skills and playing level advanced enough to benefit from higher level coaching and competition?

4. Do you and your child understand the increased time and intensity of the competition involved?

5. Is your child mature enough to understand that tradeoffs exist? Can the child accept less social activity, more structure and, with the exception of the summer season, more pressure to be organized and get homework finished?

If your child is younger than upper middle school, burnout could very well be the result of travel team play before a child has the requisite desire to take advantage of tougher competition, better coaching, and more practices and games. If you are uncertain, it may be better to wait an extra year or two before taking on this commitment. There is no evidence to suggest that waiting a year or two at this young age will be a deterrent to later success in the sport.

Researching Teams

If your child is serious about playing and has the skills and required dedication, start researching team options available for your child's sport.

1. Take time to investigate variations among coaches and teams within a

17

league or organization, as well as those in different organizations, such as different junior/senior legion baseball teams, or Babe Ruth or AAU/Club baseball teams. In some cases, coach/team choices are limited by geography and/or school district.

2. Is the coach someone with whom you and your child want to work?
   - Does the coach genuinely care about kids?
   - Based on feedback from former and current players and their families, do the coach's style, work ethic and disciplinary rules seem reasonable to you and your child?
   - Is the coach firm and fair with high expectations, or so concerned with winning that high-pressure tactics are used?
   - Does the coach have good teaching and communication skills?
   - Does the coach enforce good sportsmanship?

3. Does the coach propose that playing on the travel team means specializing in the sport year-round?
   - Playing on a travel team need not mean specializing in a sport to the exclusion of other sports. Your child should be free to play only part of the year on a travel team.
   - If your child is a multi-sport athlete and only wants to play part of the year, discuss this with the coach.
   - Some extreme coaches expect athletes to sign a year-long commitment not to play other sports. This is unacceptable, unless your child has the very rare passion to want to play only one sport for all seasons that year.

4. Older athletes are often scheduled more heavily than younger players, but I have seen extremely rigorous travel schedules for some young teams. Check the following:
   - The length of the "season"…all year, half year, quarter year.
   - Estimated number of practices per week and length of practices.
   - The number of games and tournaments. These vary according to the regular school season for the sport, the summer season, or the off-school season for the sport, e.g., fall baseball or spring soccer.

5. Check the geographic locations involved in the team/league playing schedule.
   - Where are the home fields and practice sites? They could be in your local city/county or in a neighboring county.
   - Where are the opponents' fields?
   - What is the travel distance to most competitions? Travel distances vary greatly from sport to sport and from one travel team organization and

17

locale to another. A team may have a group of competitors all within a 60-mile radius unless the team attends district or regional playoffs. Check carefully, so you will know what is involved.

- If out-of-town games present a problem, determine ahead of time if your child can carpool with other teammates.

6. Is there a preseason team/parent meeting at which parents and players are allowed input into the schedule? Are schedules preset by the league or coaches?

- Some teams vote on the number of tournaments to be entered and the greatest distance the team is willing to travel for "typical" games or tournaments.
- Certain organizations allow teams to enter as many or few tournaments as they choose. Other organizations, such as Legion baseball, may set the summer schedule in advance of player selection.
- Coaches may or may not be involved in setting schedules for individual tournaments, and some tournament schedules are set just prior to their start date, when final entries are received.
- What is the coach's policy on family vacations or a child attending a sports camp? Your child may have to make a decision about what activity is most important—a week or two of camp or playing on a team.
- For summer teams, find out how many tournaments begin during the work week. Parents who cannot go out-of-town during the work week must make arrangements for their player to travel with another family or the coach.
- Inherent in any team commitment is the possibility of advancing in the playoffs. This extends the season and often adds out-of-state or regional travel. If your child signs up, you are committed until the season ends!
- Try to find out possible dates for the extended season in case the team makes the playoffs.

7. From Boy Scouts to Little League, youth programs are finally recognizing that background checks of adult supervisors and volunteers are a must. *Demand that your program perform this process.*

8. What is the cost? I have seen costs range from no fees to as high as $800 a month. Be sure estimated costs include fees for the league, uniforms, tournaments and coach's pay. Then estimate travel expenses, including food and hotels for you and your child. If your child is asked to play for a team and your family cannot afford the expense, find out whether there are any league sponsors offering financial aid.

17

Transportation Safety

If there are out-of-town games involving travel and overnight stays, and your child will not be riding with you or an approved parent, *you must check out transportation issues.*

1. Who are the van/car drivers?

2. Do any of the drivers have criminal records or serious traffic violations, e.g., DUI, reckless driving or speeding? It can be uncomfortable asking a coach for such information, *but your child's safety should be your first consideration.* Many states now have websites for checking traffic violations and criminal records.

3. Is the van/car well maintained, e.g., decent tires, brakes, etc.?

4. How many people does the van/car safely carry, and are there enough seatbelts?

5. Is there strict enforcement of a policy prohibiting players or coaches under 21 from driving?

6. On long trips, does the coach drive more than 8-10 hours before calling it a day? Does the coach take sufficient breaks while driving?

7. Are there car rules on noise and other distracting behaviors?

Out-of-Town Supervision

For out-of-town, overnight trips, investigate who will supervise/chaperone players.

1. Are there clear, established rules for the team chaperones?

2. Are there enough adults to adequately monitor players?

3. Who supervises in hotels? This is a very important duty, because most road trip problems occur in hotel rooms after curfew. One parent described a tournament for 14-year-old baseball players where young men stayed up until 3:00 A.M. watching adult movies. In addition to having watched unacceptable material, players were too exhausted to play well the next day. In another instance, a basketball coach caught a 15-year-old player drinking and removed him from the team. The player was quite shocked and insisted that former coaches had "winked" at player use of alcohol.

4. What times are curfew and lights out, and are they enforced?

5. Are the players required to stay with the group or sub-group during all non-game activities away from the hotel? Does each group have a supervisor and check-in times?

6. Are there clear check-out rules for parents who wish to take their player away from the team to eat, drive home, etc.?

Playing Up

Mature, highly skilled young athletes are sometimes invited by coaches to "play up" on a team, i.e., play with older athletes against older athletes. If your child is invited to play for such a team, you will have to make a careful judgment based upon your knowledge of your child's skills, maturity, and the sport involved.

An important element of sports success is bringing an athlete along at a pace fast enough to challenge a player and allow improvement, but not so fast that the player loses confidence or interest in the sport. The age at which a young athlete "plays up" depends upon the individual and even the sport.

We asked the following question of high school and college coaches:

If an athlete shows an advanced skill level or potential for improvement, do you think the athlete should "play up," i.e., play on a team with older athletes against older competitors?

Sixty-seven percent of college coaches and 70% of high school coaches told us that *advanced athletes* should play up, and offered the following points:

- College coaches recommended that highly skilled athletes begin to "play up" at age 13.
- High school coaches recommended that highly skilled athletes begin to "play up" at age 12.
- Coaches who did not feel that playing up was appropriate pointed out the possibility of a youngster losing confidence.
- Most coaches agreed that the decision to play up depends on the sport, and *they were much less inclined to recommend playing up in physically punishing sports like football or ice hockey, where there is a greater chance of injury.* [7]

If your player accepts an invitation to "play up" on a travel team, point out that this will be an apprenticeship during which your child should observe and learn from both the good and bad habits of older players. Try to help keep the experience in perspective in case your child receives less playing time, or is less successful than when playing with one's own age group. The player who

17

wants to improve usually understands that this is part of the challenge. On the other hand, a highly skilled young athlete may be resented by older athletes who are not as gifted. Prepare your youngster for this possibility.

The Travel Team Contract

Contract: *An agreement between two or more parties for the doing or not doing of something specified.*

A current trend among travel teams is to require a player and/or parent to sign a travel team contract. Some contracts have reasonable expectations that serve to put the player and family on notice regarding the extent of the commitment and expected standards of behavior. Other contracts may be excessive in their demands.

What is Reasonable?

Reasonable expectations include a player commitment to:

- Attend all practices and games, except for illness, family emergencies or a pre-approved excuse from a practice or game.
- Exhibit good behavior both on and off the field. Good behavior includes following team rules, exhibiting good sportsmanship with an emphasis on respect toward all teammates, opponents and officials, no fighting and no use of drugs or alcohol.
- No other team membership/sports activities during the travel team season of three to five months.

What is Unreasonable?

Unreasonable expectations may include:

- A contract in which the player agrees not to participate on any other teams for an extended period of 8-24 months.
  - Some specialized players are comfortable with this kind of extended commitment.
  - If your player is a multi-sport athlete and a travel team coach wants your player on the team, you have a right to negotiate a "seasonal" team contract with a shortened time commitment.
- A commitment to an excessive number of practices.
- Unreasonably long practices.
- An unreasonable number of games.
- Excessive fees.
- Excessive transportation and overnight travel expenses.

It is up to parents and players to carefully review the commitments demanded in any team contract. Obviously, summer season athletes may be able to tolerate a more demanding schedule than during the school year. Look at whether a contract differentiates between the summer season and school season.

If the contract terms are extreme, you are free to discuss them with the coach and travel league administrators. If you believe the time commitment demanded during the school year is excessive, you and other parents may present what you feel are reasonable practice and game schedules. If the coach and league administrators are not willing to listen to reasonable input, then they are probably too intense and unbalanced regarding the importance of sports as an extracurricular activity.

If your athlete really wants to play for a high-level, demanding team and is willing to make the commitment, you must evaluate whether your child has the skills and maturity to balance schoolwork and a demanding travel team schedule.

Overscheduling Versus Honoring a Commitment

You and your child need to understand that joining a travel team involves a commitment to the team. Many teams set clear rules about not playing on a second team during the specified travel season. *In the absence of a specific rule, do not allow a youngster to join another sports team during the "travel team season."*

Overscheduling is imprudent for many reasons, and parents should be careful not to impose their own desires and Type A behaviors upon their child's schedule or let a child badger them into signing up for two teams. Reasons not to overschedule include:

1. The travel team loses the benefit of a player's full mental and physical commitment to that team. Even if a player manages to attend all games and practices for both teams, a child may be too tired to focus and perform well for both teams.

2. When joining a travel team, you want your child to learn the importance of making a decision and fulfilling the obligation that comes with the decision. Overscheduling allows a child to only partially fulfill multiple commitments instead of making good choices.

3. Sports can be exhausting. Young athletes are growing children who should not be pushed to their limits or allowed to exhaust themselves

17

both physically and emotionally. An excess of sports and any other extracurricular activities can leave a child stressed and weary with no free time. Why would you or your child want this?

4. There is a much higher risk of incurring repetitive motion and overuse sports injuries, especially when fatigued.

5. During the school year, studies will likely suffer.

6. There is a greater likelihood of a child "burning out" or just quitting a sport or activity.

7. Neither adults nor children get to do everything they want at the same time. Why allow a child to juggle too many simultaneous commitments?

Overlapping Seasons

A multi-sport athlete may occasionally find that one sport season extends into playoffs and overlaps the beginning of a new sport season, e.g., basketball overlapping baseball. If you have a multi-sport athlete, you or your athlete will need to clarify beforehand, with both coaches, how possible overlapping seasons will be handled. A child should not be attending two practices a day, and weekend games may be in conflict. If an overlap is for a brief period, both coaches may allow alternating practice days and a missed game or two at the beginning or end of a season. *Any lengthy overlap is unfair to both teams and to the child.*

Will My Elementary or Middle School Child Be Left Behind?

Parents sometimes fear that without travel team play their child's athletic growth and competency will lag behind and lessen their child's chance of making a high school team. Travel team coaches often play upon this fear as a recruiting tool. They may also use this fear as a justification for demanding single sport specialization. More often than not, such coaches selfishly want to keep their best athletes on their team year-round. Our research found that 76% of college athletes were multi-sport varsity athletes while in high school!

While our research shows that a majority of varsity high school athletes (58%), Division I varsity college athletes (66%) and Division III varsity college athletes (63%) play or played on travel teams, it also reveals that a healthy percentage of varsity high school and college athletes did not play on a travel team. Travel team play does not guarantee qualifying for a high school or college team! Worried parents who cannot locate a travel team that works for their child should consider the following points:

17

1. A number of average players may be on travel teams because their parent or a friend's parent coaches the team.

2. Politics may also be involved in team selection when children of recreation league coaches get spots as "parental rewards" for their volunteering. The players in both of these categories will someday run into an objective coach.

3. Some travel team players peak early, due to one or more of the following factors:

   - Large size and/or early growth spurt.
   - Practicing long hours.
   - Playing in a significant number of competitive games.
   - Benefiting from good coaching at a young age.

(Also, the small, highly skilled player who excels in elementary or middle school may find that lack of size becomes a disadvantage in high school.)

4. There are a number of natural athletes who may not need extra play to maintain and improve the skills required to be competitive. Many of these athletes adapt quickly to the requirements of their particular sport.

5. The non-travel team player may experience a growth spurt or further physical development in high school. Some late bloomers are simply awkward and uncomfortable with their bodies until they have more fully matured.

If your elementary or middle school child is not playing travel but continues to play and works to improve, do not be surprised if your player becomes as good as or better than some travel team players!

The "Sensible Travel" Team vs. The "Excess Travel" Team

A major problem for promising elementary and middle school athletes, eager to play against good competition and learn the fundamentals of their sport, is that too many travel team programs go way too far—literally and figuratively—with youngsters of this age. It is not uncommon to see an elementary/middle school "Excess Travel" Team program involve 12-14 weeks in two separate seasons, along with one or more games on each weekend day, three practices per week and other expectations—resulting in an excessive commitment of time and energy.

A travel team program for youngsters in the age range of 8-13 need not include an excess number of games, a lengthy season (or seasons), or numer-

17

ous trips to far away game sites. The "Sensible Travel" Team concept that I recommend encompasses the following points:

- An eight-week schedule played during the traditional season of the sport, e.g., fall soccer, winter basketball, spring or early summer baseball, etc.
- Two practices per week.
- One weekend game for the first seven weeks, and a Saturday-Sunday "Round Robin" in weekend eight to close out the season.
- With the exception of rural and certain other locales, games should be played within 20 miles of the players' homes.
- Excellent coaching.
- A try out and cut policy, for this is still a program offered to young people who are serious in their interest, and anxious to engage in challenging competition.
- A reasonable minutes/innings per game policy that affords all team members some playing time. (This policy may need to change by upper middle school.)

Two Special Additions

- Invite—and compensate—a highly competent area coach to put on two or three special clinics, which are run in conjunction with an actual practice. Adding two or three clinics by a respected coach who is willing to "complement" the efforts of the head and assistant coaches can add great value to the experience. (Conversely, you may invite two or three different experts to conduct the two or three clinics.)
- A team trip to a local "big game," be it a high school, college or professional game.

Such a "pilot concept," geared to the motivated young player but not administered in the "excess zone" so common among young travel teams, works! If you would like your child to be involved in a positive travel team experience at a relatively early age, utilize this concept. With good long-range planning, you will find it fairly easy to gather a group of teams in your region for a season of fun, exciting competition, skill development and camaraderie which will leave one weekend day open in weeks one through seven.

A Bonus for You!

This approach will also land you squarely in the "Golden Mean" zone about which Aristotle wrote—the mean between deficiency and excess!

Impact of the Travel Team on Families

Sports travel teams are frequently criticized for being disruptive to family life. For teams with extremely demanding schedules, there is validity to this criticism. However, your good research should provide you with information needed to make sound decisions. Interestingly, some families told us that the travel team was one of the few "balancing" activities pulling mom or dad out of the office and offering time for unhurried conversation with their player.

Here are two different experiences described by our survey participants:

PRO: A single mom wrote, "I have one child and both of us are happy with the travel team experience. We have gotten closer as a result of traveling together, and I have met many new friends."

CON: From the parents of three children, "It was too disruptive to the family and we had little time for the activities of the other two kids."

Your decision—and it is a parental decision—must be based on the needs and particular circumstances of your family. In families with more than one child, I have seen problems develop when the whole family feels forced to attend games. Conversely, I have observed other families who enjoy attending games together. Some siblings dislike sports; some parents resent a large portion of their free time being consumed by team activities. On the other hand, parents who take turns with team activities often find they enjoy their time alone and the increased communication which can accompany the child's activity.

Suggestions to Reduce Family Stress

1. Do not expect siblings to attend a lot of games, and do not force them to attend if other arrangements can be made.

2. Whether it is sports, music or drama, a parental "divide and conquer" strategy is the only way some families keep up with extracurricular activities of more than one child. While most children appreciate it when their parents attend their games, they also understand that this is not always possible; parents have obligations to other children.

3. Parents should not feel guilty for taking turns attending games and tournaments, because this rotation allows:

   • One parent some needed time off from travel duties.

   • Parents to rotate responsibility for children staying home or engaged in other activities.

   • Flexibility when work schedules do not permit both parents to travel at the same time.

17

- Parents to save some vacation days for non-team activities.
- The bonus of one-on-one time alone with each child.

4. If a big family event is planned, see if your child can be excused from play, and make the request well in advance. If not excused, arrange for your player to travel with another team family.

5. Discuss possible travel and carpooling arrangements with your child before joining a travel team so your player understands what is involved.

6. For single parents, scheduling and logistics can be complicated, but travel teams are still possible.

   - Plan to alternate attendance at activities if you have more than one child and schedules conflict.
   - Carpooling may become necessary due to work schedules or when required by activities of other children. At the beginning of each season, try to determine which team parents are responsible drivers and are willing to share carpooling duties.
   - When a sibling does not want to attend a weekend tournament or away game, try to make arrangements with parents of that child's friends. Offer to return the favor.
   - When you cannot attend out-of-town tournaments, plan ahead so your travel team player will have a family to help with rides and rooms.

Hard-Nosed Realities of Many Travel Teams

On most travel teams, policies and strategies associated with high-level competition are in effect. These strategies, as well as the intensity of workouts and playing schedules, often increase incrementally with the age of the players and include:

- A tryout and cut policy, including the possibility of former players being cut in favor of new and better players.
- Teams employing strategies to win, which means:
  - Coaches play the best members of the team.
  - Teams may impose stringent attendance rules for practices and games, including one such as "three missed practices and you're out."
  - Teams may have members who get little or no playing time except during practices.

Remember, playing time, playing position and strategies are not within your parental domain. These are coaching prerogatives.

On the Bench

If you think there is a chance your child might be a substitute, discuss the challenges involved. Is your player willing to devote a lot of time and energy to attending practices and games with little expectation of playing time? Your athlete may believe that hard work and competitive practices are the best ways to significantly improve and move up in the lineup. It is better to anticipate and discuss the possibility of being a substitute, than to have a disappointed player who may want to quit the team mid-season. On most travel teams, your child is probably taking a spot that another child wants. Remind your child to think carefully before accepting a place on the roster.

Eleven Characteristics of a Good Travel Team Experience

1. An environment which fosters a love of the game.

2. Coaches who emphasize the pursuit of excellence and good sportsman-ship as opposed to merely the pursuit of winning.

3. Coaches who teach age-appropriate skills with a focus on good funda-mentals and who incorporate strategies and teamwork into their instruc-tion. A travel team with skilled players often results in team members learning to depend upon and appreciate each other!

4. For younger players, there should be less pressure and intensity and a less rigorous schedule.

5. Good competition.

6. A seasonal—not year-round—commitment.

7. Summer teams should have more players on the roster to allow for fami-ly vacations, summer camps, etc. Summer teams should allow a few planned, excused absences, especially when the coach is notified well in advance.

8. During the school year, reasonable scheduling of weekend tournaments, including travel distance and number of games.

9. Costs which are not excessive and/or teams which offer some financial aid to those who cannot otherwise afford to pay.

10. Well-planned practice sessions. The length of practices should be age-appropriate and adjusted for the summer or school year.

11. Well-planned first aid and emergency practices.

17

Who Makes the Final Decision?

You do. You must judge both your child's readiness and your ability to handle the logistics. If your child makes the cut, really wants to play for a travel team, and the commitment looks manageable, agree to a "test season" and go from there.

AMATEUR SPORTS AT ITS BEST

Many travel or summer league teams are guided by skilled, unselfish coaches, and funded by generous individuals or organizations. The Durham (NC) Post 7 Senior Legion Baseball Team was coached by Lew Weatherspoon, who doubled as a Red Sox scout. Coach Weatherspoon revelled in the opportunity to help his players learn, compete and improve their game. For student-athletes who wanted to play college baseball, he also helped find an appropriate match.

In the best tradition of a firm and fair coach with high expectations, Coach Weatherspoon enforced three simple rules for all his teams:

- Be on time.
- Hustle.
- Respect the game and its participants.

The American Legion Durham Post 7 raises money through bingo and other activities to cover the costs of coaches, umpires, team uniforms, and tournament fees for junior and senior Legion teams. There is no cost to the players, unless it is shared hotel expenses at tournaments. The legionnaires payback? The good feeling of providing young men with a wonderful summer of baseball, camaraderie, and life lessons learned through sports.

For every unscrupulous coach or athletic footwear company manipulating young amateur players for attention or profit, there are many more travel coaches and sponsors who participate for the right reasons.

17

Chapter 18

PLAYING ON TWO TEAMS IN ONE SEASON

"To go beyond is as wrong as to fall short."
— Confucius

A few young athletes, even some early youth leaguers, have parents who mistakenly allow them to sign up for multiple sports teams in the same season. It is often the "skilled athlete" who is granted this privilege. Parents enjoy the "star" status accorded their player, coaches want winning teams and players relish the action and attention.

Coaches and teams have the right to expect a full in-season commitment from players and their parents! A high school baseball coach wrote, "If a high school pitcher is playing weekend AAU tournaments, he will have to miss a pitching rotation during the week, because we keep a pitch count. This is why I forbid in-season overlap of teams." Forbidding such overlap is well within the authority of a varsity coach, and such a policy should be supported by you.

A different and common scenario involves the multi-sport athlete whose high school, club, or AAU coach in another sport pressures the athlete to participate in regularly scheduled off-season "scrimmages, clinics or skill development programs" while the athlete is playing an in-season sport. These "clinics" do not formally schedule games or competitions in order to get around multi-team prohibitions. Such off-season programs are fine for single-sport athletes—or multi-sport athletes who are truly off-season—but they are inappropriate and unnecessary for in-season athletes.

Coaches may pressure players and their parents by implying or stating that the athlete will be left behind if he doesn't participate in such programs. Your job is to eliminate this pressure by forbidding these "organized overlaps." Your "in-season" multi-sport athlete can sharpen "next season" skills informally and during free time. Remember, our surveys confirm that the majority of college varsity athletes were multi-sport athletes in high school!

Many problems inherent in playing for two teams can be avoided if parents act responsibly and establish clear rules. In most cases, rather than signing up for multiple teams, athletes who feel a particular recreation league, travel or school team is not meeting their needs can seek a team which plays at a level at which the athlete is challenged. If necessary, advanced players can "play up."

Unless you can be shown very compelling reasons to make an exception, your paramount rule should be *one team or program per season!*

Thirteen Problems with a Multi-Team Commitment

"If one factor of production is increased while the others remain constant,
the overall returns will relatively decrease after a certain point."
—The Law of Diminishing Returns

Even if your player's coaches and the State High School Association allow a multi-team commitment, likely problems when playing for two teams include:

1. Failing to teach your athlete that difficult choices are sometimes necessary. Busy student-athletes cannot do everything they want, because time and energy are finite commodities.

2. Parents who allow excessive sports activity send the message that sports are more important than academics and proper rest.

3. You may be teaching your player that one does not have to follow the team rules involving missed games and practices.

4. The morale and attitude of other team members may suffer, because scheduling exceptions for your player display favoritism.

5. Your child cannot give a "best effort" to either team.

18

6. Your child fails to understand the importance of making a full commitment to the team.

7. The overworked youth league, middle school or high school athlete whose body is still growing faces serious risk of overuse and repetitive motion injuries.

8. Players risk spending so much time on sports that schoolwork suffers.

9. An athlete who squeezes in schoolwork may be too rushed or too tired to properly concentrate.

10. Coaches competing for a player's loyalty and best effort place an athlete in a stressful position.

11. Coaches may teach playing skills and/or demand positions be played in contradictory fashions, causing confusion and forcing players to switch back and forth to please different coaches.

12. Your physically stressed and mentally exhausted player is at increased risk of burnout.

13. Finally, playing on a closely-knit team is one of the great joys of sports. Athletes jumping from one team to another over the course of one season often lose this benefit.

Making a Choice

When faced with making a choice between competing teams, ask your athlete to consider personal short-term and long-term sports goals, and make a list of the pluses and minuses of each team, including:

1. Is the level of competition best suited to the player's needs?

2. Which team will offer the best coaching?

3. Which team will offer the best opportunities for improved skill development?

4. Which team will offer satisfactory playing time in the desired position?

5. Which team will most value your contribution, and will this help your playing experience be more meaningful?

6. For high school players wanting to play in college, which team offers the greatest college recruiting exposure?

7. What is the frequency of the practices and games of each team?

8. What is the travel time to the practices and games of each team?

18

9. Which team has players and a coach with whom you would most like to associate?

10. Taking in all factors, which team will offer the most challenging playing experience?

11. Taking in all factors, which team will offer the most enjoyable playing experience?

Ask your youngster to review these lists and discuss the choice with you. Take into account each coach's philosophy on key issues such as sportsmanship. If more information is needed, suggest a discussion with the coaches. Make it clear that once the choice is made, you expect a full season's commitment.

A POSSIBLE SCENARIO

A high school athlete competing on the varsity basketball team receives notice of a Sunday lacrosse "showcase" clinic. The clinic will run over six consecutive Sundays in January and February, and the literature makes clear that college coaches will be present to scout prospects. Your varsity basketball player, who also plays varsity lacrosse, asks to participate in the clinic. What do you do?

You say no, because:

- A varsity athlete has a commitment to the in-season team—and that team only—during the course of the particular season.

- In this case, competing in a Sunday lacrosse clinic could very well result in an injury to the player and/or the player being a "tired athlete," neither of which are fair to the in-season team. Before each varsity season begins, unless rare extenuating circumstances exist such as in swimming, make it clear that your athlete's commitment is to the varsity team and the varsity team only! (Professional teams are well aware of the injury risks associated with playing another sport during a particular season. When Los Angeles Laker Vladimir Radmanovic separated his shoulder while snowboarding during the 2007 NBA All Star break, he was fined $500,000 for his transgression.)

Inquire if your young athlete's school has a policy regarding participation on two teams in one season. If not, suggest to the athletic director that a well-developed policy be implemented.

Exceptions to The One-Team Rule

"There is no useful rule without an exception."
— Physician Thomas Fuller

There may be extenuating circumstances in which playing on two teams serves the needs of your athlete without seriously penalizing either team. Swimming is a sport where overlap of club and high school seasons is common. A serious swimmer may truly want to help the high school team but realizes the high school team suffers from:

- Less skilled coaching.
- Scarce pool time at poor locations.
- Little opportunity for high-level training and competition.

For these types of reasons, swimmers sometimes join two teams. In such cases, parents must place limitations on the overall level of activity, or else the benefits will be outweighed by the disadvantages of multi-team play.

Suggestions for Swimmers

Tom Slear is a frequent contributor to *Splash Magazine,* the official publication of USA Swimming. At my request, Slear made the following suggestions to swimmers faced with the school versus club choice:

"When deciding whether to commit to both a club and a high school team, or to pick one over the other, keep in mind that each has specific missions which don't always overlap. High schools offer sports within an educational context. In a practical sense, this means that not every effort will be made to hire the best available coach, or to ensure that a team gets to participate in the highest level of competition possible.

"The first inclination of high school athletic directors is to hire coaches from within the faculty. The most qualified applicant won't necessarily get the job. The same applies when putting together a schedule. The top priority is not necessarily exposing the athletes to the best competition, but scheduling nearby opponents to hold down expenses and miss as few classes as possible.

"Club teams, on the other hand, take a different approach. They hire the best coaches they can afford. They go to the best competitions for which parents are willing to pay. Most importantly, they allow the best athletes in a particular area to train and compete together, a coveted situation that high schools can't match because of their geographic restrictions on enrollment.

"But clubs are no match for high school teams in two critical areas: notoriety and peer respect. The reality of sports coverage by America's news media

18

is that it doesn't happen athletically unless it happens on a school team. I once had an Olympic swimmer tell me that his high school championship was covered exhaustively by the state's largest newspaper. Yet a few weeks later, when, as a club swimmer, he finished fifth at the United States nationals, there was not a word of it in the newspaper. Club members typically labor anonymously while less talented high school athletes get written about in the newspapers and noticed by their classmates. It's unfair, perhaps, but that's the way it is.

"After weighing the pluses and minuses, make a decision that carries with it a firm commitment. The worst scenario is to tell a high school coach that you want to be a member of the team and then miss many of the practices and competitions to meet obligations with the club. Before the season, be truthful with each coach about what you want to do. After you get their feedback, settle on the best course of action. Then tell the coaches what you plan to do and stick to it. Such forthrightness will minimize, if not eliminate, complications." [8]

Making Two Teams Work for Your Athlete

If extenuating circumstances, such as those which may exist in swimming, cause you and your athlete to seriously consider what should be a *rare* two-team commitment, it is your responsibility to research the schedules, establish clear rules, and convey those rules to your athlete and all coaches *before agreeing to allow your child to participate on two teams.* Your overall objective is to structure your athlete's level of activity so it is the same or only slightly more than that demanded when playing on one competitive team. This may take the form of more formal competitions and fewer practices. Try to meet this objective by taking the following steps:

1. *Keep practice activity to a level commensurate to one team.* Review team practice schedules with both coaches and your player and be sure both coaches agree to a "practice rotation" between teams. *Do not allow dual practices on any day or a practice on a competition/game day.*

2. Both coaches and teams need to know when a player will be in the line-up. Review competition schedules and establish agreement with both coaches about which games/meets a player will attend if there are dates when both teams have competitions. When school and club seasons overlap, schools usually compete during the week and clubs on weekends, but you must be wary of excessive competitions. A game/competition should supercede a practice for either team on any given day.

3. If there are too many games and schedule conflicts, you must tell your player to pick one team unless both coaches are clearly willing to have a "half-time" team member.

4. Players need a day off for physical and mental rest. Do not allow games on both weekend days on a regular basis. If dual schedules demand regular weekday competitions as well as games on both weekend days, you should not allow participation on two teams.

5. If both coaches agree to your rules for sharing your athlete, make it clear that you expect them to support your youngster's efforts for both teams, or you will instruct your player to select only one team!

Without parental limitations on excessive activity and a clear plan for controlling a two-team commitment, your child will be physically and mentally exhausted, which is unfair to all those involved, and especially detrimental to your child's ability to perform as a student and enjoy being a child.

Dueling Coaches

Many middle school and high school athletes find themselves in a tug-of-war between their school and club teams. Whether or not there is seasonal overlap, a player who competes for both a school and club team may find one or both coaches fighting for attention and loyalty. Club and AAU coaches (and personal trainers/coaches) are especially guilty of undermining school coaches by sending negative messages about playing time, the high school coach's teaching skills and even teammates! Such messages are inappropriate and may cause a player to question the other coach and feel torn between competing loyalties.

What to Do

Explain to your player that coaches sometimes behave inappropriately because they want a player's full focus. If one coach criticizes the other coach or team, encourage your youngster to deal with the problem by taking the following steps:

1. Politely tell the offending coach, "Please don't make negative comments about my other team or coach."

2. Tell you about the comments.

3. Tell you if the coach continues to undermine the other coach after being asked to stop.

18

If a coach continues such tactics, it is proper for you to let the coach know that your player does not want to be placed in such an awkward position. Make it clear that if the practice continues, your athlete will not be allowed to play for the offending coach.

Team Overlap with Elite USA Federation Teams

Elite USA Team athletes often wish to compete on their high school or college teams. A serious lacrosse player might find that a USA Team lacrosse tournament is scheduled prior to the end of a high school season. If a USA Team player skips such a tournament, the chances of making the final USA Team are slim or eliminated. In some states, a high school lacrosse player competing on a USA Team may be violating State Association rules which prohibit participation on other teams during the high school season.

If you think your player will be penalized by association rules, be prepared well in advance to provide evidence to the State High School Association that USA Team participation will not be excessive, and request permission for your player to compete. You must be prepared for a "no" answer, and plan accordingly. A choice of teams may become necessary if permission to compete is not granted.

State High School Association administrators are trying to protect children from excessive sports participation, but they may not be up-to-date on the specific requirements of elite USA Team participation in each sport. Share information on your youngster's sport that will be helpful for association decision-making. Encourage the USA Federation to establish a working relationship with your State High School Association in order to develop rules and schedule tryouts and tournaments in a manner which does not unjustly penalize the elite high school player.

And, of course, if your elite player has a potential overlap with a USA Federation team event, you must clear this with the high school coach well in advance.

At the college level, some coaches are reluctant to release their players to compete for USA National teams. I am aware of one such instance which caused great friction between the player and coach. Erica Wheeler, former USA Olympian and member of the Board of Trustees of the US Track and Field Federation, points out, "An athlete who competes at a national federation's championship or on federation sponsored teams does not conflict with NCAA policy. Competition dates and team travel dates for national federations are published well in advance, and the college coach would generally have plenty of time to plan around any conflict with the college sports schedule. Elite level high school players being recruited by college programs should get a clear idea from the head coach at each school regarding the coach's policy on elite USA team participation."

Change of Sport Season and Team Overlap

A basketball player who is also a baseball player may be on a successful basketball team competing in a post-season tournament. When this happens, the baseball coach needs to be informed about the basketball tournament schedule so the dual sport player can be excused from baseball until the basketball season ends. Such overlaps do not usually extend past 7-14 days. Most schools wisely require a player to finish one season, including post-season play, before beginning practices in the next sport.

Summer Teams

There is tremendous variation in the number of days, practices and intensity demanded by summer teams and leagues. It is acceptable for an athlete to play on two summer teams that practice and play once or twice a week with little or no overlap. If a dual commitment involves regular overlap, you probably need to enforce your "one team per season" rule and suggest selecting the team which adequately challenges your youngster. Honoring a commitment to a team still applies in the summer!

18

Chapter 19

LEARNING THE FUNDAMENTALS
OF LIFELONG SPORTS

"Athletes do not win on emotion, they win on proper mechanics."
— UCLA Basketball coaching legend, John Wooden

A Special Gift

Regardless of whether your child wishes to compete in one of the lifelong sports, give the child the "gift" of early lessons to properly learn the fundamentals of one or more of the following sports:

- Swimming
- Tennis
- Golf
- Depending upon your locale, sailing, squash, horseback riding or skiing.

Many people take up these sports later in life because team sport options decline as early as middle school and almost disappear by adulthood. The opportunities to participate in individual sports such as tennis, swimming or golf continue throughout life, and a healthy percentage of older "rookies," perhaps even you, wish they had learned correct fundamentals in their youth.

A Distinction and a Strategy

There is a big difference between aggressively pushing a child into team sports and gently, but firmly, introducing a child to a few lifetime sports.

19

Every child should be taught to swim for obvious safety reasons. With lifelong sports such as tennis and golf, I propose that your child, one sport at a time, take lessons or clinics once or twice a week over a period of several months. If you expect a child to maintain these fundamental skills, it is a good idea to follow up with periodic clinics, lessons or camps every nine months to a year. Remind your child that it will be much easier to return to a sport if basic skills are maintained over a number of years. If you are an adult rookie, you might enjoy taking lessons so you and your child can practice and play together! If you already play, use your skills to enjoy practicing with your youngster.

But I Hate Tennis!

Some worthwhile activities may require an assertive approach with a reluctant child, particularly in the introductory phase. If your child says, "I hate tennis," your response could be, "I am not saying you must regularly play the sport after lessons. However, you may want to swim, play tennis, or golf when you are older, so I want you to properly learn the basic skills. It will then be up to you to decide how much you want to use these skills. If you choose to practice and improve your skills, you will find the sport more enjoyable to play."

Many a child who anticipates hating tennis, golf or swim lessons arrives at quite the opposite view when properly introduced to the sport. Whether it's smooth, efficient swim strokes, tennis strokes, or golf swings, your 10-year-old will probably appreciate them at age 25, 35, or 50, and will surely appreciate your role in fostering a fit-for-life philosophy!

Use a Real Teaching Professional!

If you are going to invest time and money on lessons in these lifetime sports, find a professional instructor who is highly skilled at teaching proper fundamentals, while making the experience enjoyable. Swimming lessons are generally well taught in either town recreational or club settings. I do not believe this is the case in many town recreational tennis or golf programs. Town programs often employ part-time teenagers and adults who may possess good playing skills, but may not possess effective teaching techniques or experience. Many recreational programs (which double as vacation, daycare and after-school services) have youngsters spend a large portion of time playing matches using incorrect fundamentals, which then become bad habits.

Good teaching pros have a way of tailoring instructional methods to best suit each player. They also have an eye for picking up on mistakes and correcting them. Without early lessons from a skilled teacher, your beginner will like-

19

ly develop bad habits and be confronted with a reality of most sports — *unlearning bad habits is a very difficult task, even for a gifted athlete.*

If the cost of private lessons is prohibitive, talk with other parents about sharing the cost. Lessons taken with friends may be more fun and appealing to your child, not to mention less expensive! There are also a number of professionals who will reduce their fee, or even do some *pro bono* work.

Early instruction in the fundamentals of lifetime sports is a good investment that may one day result in your offspring saying, "You know, I never appreciated how valuable those lessons were until I had to play golf with my boss!"

19

Chapter 20

ATTENDING A SPORTS CAMP

"All things seem possible in summer." —Anonymous

Parents may fondly remember their childhood weeks at summer camp which typically included activities such as swimming, canoeing, hiking, archery, arts and crafts and horseback riding. Such camps, in pastoral settings, continue to prosper, but a new generation of specialty sports camps has emerged to meet the needs of young athletes. Some specialty camps have highly skilled instructors, while others, whether or not the directors admit it, are little more than fancy babysitting services. A well-run sports camp should offer excellent instruction of fundamental skills and competitive playing strategies in a fun atmosphere.

Should My Child Attend a "Specialty Camp?"

In our surveys, we asked parents of youth league, high school and college athletes if their children attended (or still attend) a sports "specialty camp" in the summer, e.g., basketball camp, soccer camp, baseball camp, tennis camp, etc. The results were:
- Seventy-two percent of youth sports participants attended or attend a sports specialty camp.
- Eighty-five percent of high school varsity athletes attended or attend a sports specialty camp.

193

- Eighty-seven percent of college varsity athletes attended a sports specialty camp in their youth.[9]

When a child develops an interest in a particular sport, attending a good specialty camp can be highly beneficial for development in that sport. I usually recommend day specialty camps for elementary and middle school athletes, and overnight specialty camps for older, more experienced youngsters (middle school and high school) who ideally have attended day camps, understand the kind of work involved and what can be achieved. An added advantage of attending high-level specialty camps is introducing the athlete to the "sports network" of high school and college coaches and athletes.

Matching Your Child's Goals to the Camp

Successful selection and attendance at a sports camp, whether half day, full day or overnight, requires you and your child to look at your child's immediate goals and research camps to find the best fit. A bad camp experience is often the result of a poor match between the type of camp and a child's interests, skill level and goals. If your youngster wants to attend camp in a sport, but has had little playing experience, you obviously need to select a camp which includes excellent basic instruction for beginner/intermediate level players. Enrolling a novice in a camp geared to advanced players could be extremely discouraging!

Proper research will help you determine whether a camp offers an appropriate level of instruction and playing time to meet your child's needs. If you are introducing a young child to a new sport, consider starting with a half-day camp, usually 9:00 A.M. to noon, or look for a full-day camp, usually 9:00 a.m. to 3:00 or 4:00 P.M., which tailors the activities and pace to different age groups. There can a big difference between a full-day, outdoor soccer camp in a hot climate, and a full-day, indoor basketball camp in an air-conditioned or well-ventilated gym.

Multi-Sport Camps

Multi-sport camps, sometimes called "all sports camps," offer an excellent method of engaging youngsters in a variety of sports without making a session-long commitment to just one sport. Most such camps are designed for youth leaguers, with day camps usually requiring a minimum age of 5 or 6; and overnight camps usually requiring a minimum age of 9 or 10. Many young campers enjoy the variety of activities found in multi-sport camps, and such camps are useful for campers who do not have a favorite sport, who want to explore new sports, or who may be too immature to enjoy the intense focus required in some full-day, single sport camps. These multi-sport camps are intended to provide variety rather than the advanced instruction often found in single-sport camps.

Single-Sport Specialty Camps

Single-sport specialty camps vary widely, with some serving an age range as wide as 6 to 18 years. Whatever the range, it is important to determine whether the ages and skill levels are broken into appropriate divisions, so a novice 8-year-old is not matched against a skilled, stronger 12-year-old. Depending upon your location, you can often find both local day and nearby overnight specialty camps for popular sports, but for less common sports, youngsters may have to travel to overnight camps.

The single-sport specialty camp with excellent instruction is also a good method for introducing the camper to fundamental skills of "life-long" sports such as tennis or golf. Young players who have had some instruction in these sports also find camp a good place for periodic tune-ups and practice of playing skills.

Summer is the best time for an athlete to work on improving skills. One high school ice hockey coach wrote, "During the season, individual practice time is restricted and the focus is more on team concepts than individual skill development. During the summer, players can focus on personal improvement." Picking the right specialty camp can be an important part of an athlete's improvement plan. Specialty camps with good competition allow an athlete to gauge proficiency against other skilled players and determine areas requiring attention.

Some typical "specialty camp" age ranges and areas of focus include:

- Ages 6 to 14, with a focus on teaching basic fundamentals and incrementally competitive games.
- Ages 15 to 18, with a focus on teaching advanced fundamentals, conditioning and competitive games, but still broken into appropriate skill groups if camp enrollment allows.
- High school showcase/invitational camps that cater to established high school players who hope to be recruited by colleges. These "elite" camps are designed to showcase high school players, so college recruiters can observe players competing in multiple games each day. An aspiring athlete or parent should ask for a list of head and assistant college coaches who have visited the camp in the past two years.
- Some high school showcase camps have minimum combined SAT and

grade point average requirements. These assure coaches from academically selective colleges that most attendees present meet their college's academic requirements. More detailed information on showcase camps is found in Chapter 29.

THE VALUE OF TRADITIONAL CAMPS

"No pleasure endures unseasoned by variety."—Roman Statesman, Publius Cyrus

In your desire to provide your athlete with the tools to excel in a sport, do not forget that many of the traditional "in the woods" camps offer children an experience that incorporates outdoor fun, learning and sound values.

Camp Becket in Becket, Massachusetts (*www.bccymca.org/becket*) recently celebrated its 100th anniversary. For a century, the camp has taught youngsters how to swim, sail, build campfires, play capture the flag and revel in the outdoors. Every Sunday there is a non-denominational church service, and every day campers see the following Becket mottos in log cabins and the dining hall:

- Do your best.
- Help the other fellow.
- I can and I will.
- Manners maketh the man.
- Peace through understanding.
- Each for all—all for each.
- Play the game.
- Better faithful than famous.

Offer your young athlete the opportunity to attend such a camp for an interesting and worthwhile change of pace and an experience the child might treasure.

Help in Finding the Best Camps

Parents and athletes looking for a good "specialty/showcase camp" may use college coaches as an excellent source of information. College coaches visit showcase camps to observe players, and they are in a good position to evaluate the various camp programs and levels of competition. Most college sports programs have an assistant or head coach willing to share recommendations for specialty/showcase camps in their sport. Other sources for camp recommendations could be current high school and college athletes and their parents, local high school coaches, travel team coaches, and area teaching professionals. Begin your search in the fall, because camps may be full by January or February.

Specialty Camps Held on College Campuses

Specialty sports camps administered by college coaches are usually well run, because:

- Most college coaches want their camps to reflect well on their school and program. A good college coach does not want to damage a program's reputation by running a poor camp, especially when camp may be a component of recruiting and public relations.
- College coaches are usually highly skilled teachers and are proficient at selecting skilled staff. Many of their staff members are high school coaches with proven teaching skills.
- Junior counselors are often outstanding college players. *Young campers love to watch, listen to, learn from, and be with these excellent athletes.*
- Most colleges have excellent facilities.
- Camps are designed to make a profit, and a camp will not remain profitable unless it is well run!

Researching the Camp

You should obtain references for any camp with which you are unfamiliar. *The best references are from parents of current and former campers.* If you do not know any camp parents, the director should be willing to provide such references. Camp literature may be unclear about important issues such as the camp's level of instruction, the daily schedule, and the professional expertise of the instructors, so take time to investigate:

1. Professional staff.
   - What is the professional expertise of the primary instructors? Good camps have very strong adult senior counselors and a mix of mature high school and college athletes as junior counselors.
   - What is the camper/counselor ratio? A ratio of 6:1 or 7:1 is optimal. If the ratio exceeds this range, there may be little individualized instruction and less chance for improvement. Individual sports may require even lower ratios.
2. Structure of the Day.

- What is the daily schedule of the camp?
- Are there blocks of time devoted to teaching skills?
- Are there blocks of time devoted to "supervised stations" at which the skills are practiced and fine-tuned with the instructors?
- How many games are played? There should be daily competition, but at some sport camps, campers mainly play games and receive little instruction in fundamental skills. This may result in reinforcement of bad habits.
- Are physical activities broken up to allow snacks, water breaks, and cooling off periods?
- Are there lectures? Many camp lectures are too long and unproductive. In my 25 years of running camps, I have found that eight-minute mini-lectures, emphasizing one or two skills and immediately followed by 30-45 minute supervised teaching stations, are most productive. Exceptions are made for well-known highly skilled guest lecturers.

3. Level of competition. If camps accept a range of ages and skill levels, find out whether instruction and competitive play are broken into appropriate groupings. An advanced 13-year-old tennis player would be bored playing against beginners the same age.

4. Facilities. Are there adequate facilities such as courts, fields, etc., to keep all groups properly active? Do players/teams spend a lot of time waiting to play? Find out what happens if there is a week of rainy weather; are indoor facilities available, and can skills be taught and practiced indoors? Ask for the rainy day schedule!

5. How are campers evaluated? Is the camper sent home with a detailed evaluation which can serve as a personal improvement guide?

6. Find out if there are any recommended pre-camp conditioning routines. Some "unseasoned" campers develop such sore, blistered body parts that after the first day or two they have difficulty participating in certain activities. Any high school camper should report to camp in shape and ready for a rigorous week.

7. Are there any special values or themes promoted by the camp? For example, are sportsmanship, fair play and respect included in instruction, or is there tacit endorsement of cutthroat competition and winning at any cost?

8. For overnight camps, obtain information on lodging, food, and nearby medical facilities. Geographically remote sports camps may actually need medical staff onsite. For all camps, expect to provide your "permission

for medical treatment" forms, and confirm that senior counselors have First Aid training.

9. At intense overnight camps, is sufficient time allotted for proper rest? Hard work is fine as long as campers get enough rest. Ask for a daily schedule.

10. For overnight camps, obtain specific information on the presence of adult supervisors in dorms. Unfortunately, some teen/college counselors may not have the maturity to provide safe, disciplined overnight supervision.

11. What is the camp's policy on bullying and hazing? Good camps have firm, clear policies on both issues.

Special Requests

If you have a special request, and if your child may not want to attend if the request is denied, seek an answer before finalizing an application. *Always ask well in advance, and follow up with a written request on the application.* Here are three possible requests — and possible answers:

1. Your child wants to play for a specific coach. The director says no, because that coach is being assigned to a different age group.

2. You request that your large and talented 8th grader be placed on a high school team. The director gives you a *provisional* yes, with the understanding that this decision is subject to change if your player appears to be overmatched.

3. You request that your child be placed on the same team with a friend. The director gives you a *provisional* yes, with the understanding that this decision is subject to change if it upsets the competitive balance of the camp teams.

In individual sports such as tennis and golf, it is easier to make skill level and/or coaching changes than in team sports such as basketball or baseball where teammates are learning to play as a cohesive unit and one change can affect the whole grouping.

Position Requests

When a youngster attends a sports camp with the specific goal of improving in a position such as point guard or quarterback, *it is reasonable to expect a significant amount of the camper's time — in teaching stations and in games — to be devoted to that position.* If you do not receive a clear answer to this type of request, look for a camp that agrees to it!

Two Examples

Basketball

Your child wants to play point guard, either in anticipation of playing this position on the high school team or to practice these skills in the hope of playing "the point" in college. Positions assigned in most basketball camps are relatively fluid, so, if your child wants to play a specific position, make this arrangement well in advance, and get a clear commitment from the director.

Baseball

Many baseball camp applications require a player to specify the one and only position to be played during camp. At youth league and middle school teaching camps, it is reasonable to request that your child play and learn a new or secondary position. By high school, parents and players must investigate whether a camp is structured to allow learning new or secondary positions, or whether the camp is designed for teaching advanced techniques, competitive games, and fine-tuning of positions for established players. At high school baseball showcase camps, many of which are held on college campuses, teams depend upon players having sound skills to support the team. A novice catcher on a team of high school all-stars could compromise the purpose of the camp! Some large camps may provide both instructional and advanced level teams, but you need to ask the right questions before enrolling.

With research, you should be able to find a camp that will agree to your child's position request.

The Position Camp

There are quarterback camps in football, pitcher camps in baseball and softball, big man and point guard camps in basketball, goalie camps in hockey and soccer, and many other position camps in a variety of sports. Most position camps are staffed by counselors who possess an in-depth knowledge of the particular position. A high percentage of these camps are effective at teaching the core skills and nuances of the particular position. Local or regional coaches, especially college coaches, can generally point you in the direction of a good position camp.

The Reluctant Camper

Young campers, even those who have participated in selecting their sports camp, may become apprehensive before, or on, the first day of camp. By using a team approach, parents and camp staff can usually turn an anxious youngster into a happy camper. To make this strategy work:

- Parents should do their homework before choosing a camp, and involve their young athlete in the review and selection of the type of camp.

- Parents should try to anticipate and discuss any foreseeable hurdles with their camper.
- Bring up the idea that new experiences can be scary, and emphasize that it is okay to talk about such feelings. *Parents should remember that one objective of camp is to allow a child to learn that he can master a new experience.*
- If you have specific concerns, do not wait until the last minute to contact the camp director. Most camp directors and staff appreciate communication, and they can employ "preventive steps" to ease adjustment when given advanced warning.
- If your child is very shy, you may want to make arrangements for your camper to attend camp with a friend. Camp directors often accommodate requests to be on the same team if requests do not mismatch skills or create competitive imbalance. Explain to your camper that the friend may not always be in the same activity group, and the friend may also enjoy making new friends.
- Remind your camper to follow the rules. A youngster who is constantly being disciplined is less likely to learn and be a happy camper!
- Emphasize to your child the idea of finishing what one starts. Strongly discourage your child from asking to quit a program in which you have invested time and money, unless there are extreme circumstances the director refuses to address.

Removing an unhappy camper should be a last resort used only in extreme situations such as those involving safety, ethics or bullying. Reasonable exceptions are injuries, other health problems or exhaustion. The latter is fairly common, especially when a camper is not given any "summer break," particularly from one camp to another.

Involving Staff With Camper Complaints

If your camper reports unhappiness about some aspect of camp, before making an excited call to the director, try to determine whether your child's distress is caused by an unacceptable situation which can and should be remedied, or an individual disappointment that the child must try to overcome. Situations in which a director or senior administrator should be contacted include:

- Another camper bullies your child.
- Your child is in the wrong age group. This may or may not be intentional since skill placement may take precedence over age, or there may be

a clerical error. An older child can certainly handle an age error by bringing the error to the attention of a counselor or the director.

- Your child's coach uses profanity or humiliating tactics while coaching.
- The staff does not take proper care of an Epi Pen, an inhaler or some other medical necessity for your child.
- The shy child simply needs some extra attention to get over the initial hump.

In situations such as these, the camp director should be notified immediately by email, a phone call, or at pickup or drop off. Most directors appreciate feedback, because problems cannot be addressed if they are not clearly communicated. Many situations can be corrected with communication initiated by a parent. If you have not notified a camp staff member or the director about a correctable problem, do not complain after camp has ended!

When addressing such issues, remember:

- Children are not always accurate, complete or clear when trying to explain a problem.
- Be considerate when making your contact, e.g., no calls too early in the morning or too late at night except for real emergencies! At pick up or drop off, wait until a senior administrator or staffer is available if you need to privately discuss a problem. Do not interrupt staff during supervised activities.
- Calmly explain the problem, and calmly listen to the answer.
- Again, do not wait until the camp session is over to complain about a situation which could have been handled with early communication.
- Questions dealing with minor details should be directed to camp staffers, not the director.
- Do not pull a child out of camp without giving the camp staff a chance to explain and/or correct a problem, and your child a chance to deal with a "corrected" situation.
- Allowing a camper to quit should be a last resort used only for serious, unresolved problems.

Constructive Suggestions

If you have constructive suggestions for camp improvements, either in scheduling or other details, share them with the director by letter or email. It is unlikely the camp schedules or programs will be changed during a session, but any director should be receptive to suggestions that could improve future sessions.

When Not to Involve the Director/Camp Staff

It is up to you to encourage your camper to deal with some types of problems, either by learning to live with a problem or taking personal initiative to change a situation. Parents are a camper's best resource for listening, brainstorming and suggesting methods for dealing with such problems. Examples of problems for which director contact is inappropriate include:

- Your camper likes the coach on another team better. Any special coach requests must be made in advance, since teams based on age and skill levels are prepared long before camp begins.
- Your camper asks for a new team because the current team is not winning.
- Your camper expected to be the team star and is let down because this is not the case.
- Your child's feelings are hurt because a "best" friend is enjoying the company of other campers.
- The lunch is not as good as mom's!

All of these possibilities should be discussed before camp begins!

"I'm Not Getting the Ball!"

This is a very common occurrence at soccer and basketball camps, especially with beginners/unskilled players. Do not overreact if your young camper comes home with this complaint. A brief conversation with your child's coach may be appropriate if it is to discuss what your child must do to improve. Tell your child, "You are in camp to learn and practice the skills necessary to get the ball in the future!" Chapter 13 provides detailed information on this common issue.

Don't Quit

"Withdrawing a child after one day often says more about the parents than the camp program."
—Camp parent who also served as a camp counselor

I remember a rainy day when two friends arrived at camp to begin their week. Both children showed reluctance to attend the camp. One parent stated, "We have paid for this, you agreed to it, and you are going to stick it out." The other parent gave in to the child's protest and allowed the child to leave camp. At the end of the week, the child who stayed claimed that it was her best experience ever!

Before signing up for camp, listen to your child's opinions and be sure to remind your youngster that he is making a commitment to attend the full session. A high percentage of first-day unhappy campers end up being fifth-day happy campers!

Refund/Dropout Policy

Camps must enforce strict dropout/refund policies that prevent parents from signing up a child and then withdrawing the child for anything less than a medical emergency. Camp directors hire staff, rent facilities, purchase uniforms and insurance, and plan facility and equipment use based on enrollment, and therefore need to employ clear refund/dropout policies. Most camps will publish their refund/dropout policy. If you register your child for camp, you should honor the commitment unless there are extenuating circumstances, such as a medical or family emergency.

What About Financial Aid?

Most camps fall into the category of small businesses, while others are administered by non-profit organizations such as churches or the YMCA/YWCA. Small businesses need to make a profit, but they should also be willing to give back to the community. Many camps do so in the form of a low-key, quietly administered financial aid program.

Financial aid is seldom addressed in camp brochures, because camp owners/directors fear financial aid requests would be overwhelming. The beneficiaries of camp financial aid are often those who ask and make a good case for receiving aid.

If your research leads you to several camps where the tuition exceeds your budget, do not be reluctant to approach the camp director via email, letter or phone call, and state your case. Few will offer full scholarships, so you should expect to pay a portion of your child's tuition. Some local businesses will sponsor deserving athletes at good camps, so do not be afraid to ask!

My Camp Philosophy

For more than a decade, all of my camps (*www.doyleprograms.com*) have been fully enrolled with waiting lists, and our rate of return is very high. Whether it is my multi-activity Camp Renaissance or my Basketball Camp, I have the following objectives:

1. Camp is administered in a safe environment.

2. Campers learn the concepts of fair play and teamwork.

3. Camp is a place for positive socialization, and bullying is not allowed!

4. Campers learn fundamental skills in their sport or sports.

5. Campers learn the benefits of physical fitness.

6. Campers learn that if they work at something, good things can happen.

7. Campers will aspire to one day become camp counselors.

8. Camp is reasonably priced and I quietly provide financial aid for those I feel are in real need.

9. The staff is a mixture of experienced adults and bright, enthusiastic young people, who are positive role models.

10. Staffers are knowledgeable enough, and flexible enough, to work effectively with youngsters who have different aptitudes and levels of interest.

11. Campers and parents know that I am active at camp and not merely lending my name, and will be available to address any problems.

12. The staff works to create an environment where campers look forward to each camp day.

13. Encouragement of parent feedback. Each day I station senior staff members at the entrance from 8:00 to 8:40 A.M. to listen to parental concerns and address the issues.

My objective is for these 13 points to add up to great fun and valuable lessons.

THE SCHOLAR-ATHLETE GAMES

Since 1993, the Institute for International Sport has administered both the World Scholar-Athlete Games and the United States Scholar-Athlete Games at the University of Rhode Island. Other Scholar-Athlete Games have been held in locales such as Northern Ireland, Australia and Israel. Speakers and performers have included the likes of Bill Clinton, Elie Wiesel, Rudy Giuliani, Shimon Peres, Bill O'Reilly, Joan Benoit Samuelson, Bill Bradley, Aretha Franklin, Sir Roger Bannister and George Mitchell. Participants must be nominated by their schools, and must possess honor roll status and proficiency in one of the sports or arts offerings.

The Scholar-Athlete Games are an example of a summer program that requires early contact by the family/school. For more information, visit: (*www.internationalsport.com*).

Final Suggestion

For some lighthearted camp humor and good lessons, listen to Alan Sherman's recording of "Camp Granada."

20

SECTION IV

CULTIVATING LEADERSHIP THROUGH SPORTS

Chapter 21

WILL SPORTS HELP YOUR CHILD DEVELOP LEADERSHIP SKILLS?

"He who has never learned to obey cannot be a good commander."
—Aristotle

Whether sitting on the bench or serving as a veteran team captain, a sports experience can help any youngster develop leadership skills. For all team members, sports can serve as a valuable laboratory for learning to follow directions of a coach or teammate. Team sports may also be a child's first opportunity to observe how different leaders react to stressful or adverse conditions with good, bad or mediocre leadership techniques.

Our Survey of Leaders

"Remember that the best leaders never stop learning."—Abraham Lincoln

We surveyed 500 of the most successful career professionals in America about their experience, if any, in sports—and their views on leadership. Included in this distinguished group were college presidents, CEOs, Governors, Senators, attorneys, doctors, and even a former U.S. Supreme Court Justice! We learned some interesting facts from these leaders, including:

- Eighty-seven percent of the 500 told us they had played competitive sports. (Competitive meant playing through and/or beyond the 10th grade.)

- Ninety-eight percent of those 435 sports participants said their experience was positive and quite helpful later in life.
- Only seven players were college team captains, and only 29 players were high school team captains.
- Many pointed out that because they had not been great athletes, they learned the value of following the commands and directions of the coach and captain.
- Many told us that observing teammates and coaches awakened their interest in various facets of leadership. Observing leadership is an especially valuable benefit of the sports experience, one open to all participants, regardless of athletic ability.
- Many remarked that sports taught them five essential qualities of good leadership:

1. Learning to deal with disappointment. A number of successful leaders told us that their sports experience helped them cultivate the ability to learn from disappointment, deal with it, and move forward without dwelling on it.

2. Competitive self-restraint, a term used throughout this book, is a mindset which involves remaining focused and resolute without overreacting or losing control.

3. Learning the value of teamwork and the importance of fostering a team atmosphere.

4. Self-discipline. Many successful leaders felt that their sports experience acted as a catalyst for their lifelong focus on self-discipline.

5. Sports helped many leaders learn two key facets of responsibility:
   - Taking responsibility for one's own performance and actions.
   - Meeting one's personal responsibility to the team.[10]

The 16 Leadership Goals for All Team Members

Being on a team, including being team manager, presents your child with opportunities to cultivate leadership skills. Encourage your child to set attainable leadership goals which are not dependent upon athletic ability.

The following 16 goals can help every team member, regardless of athletic ability, develop leadership skills:

1. Follow team rules.

2. Try to be the hardest worker on the team.

3. Try to be the most enthusiastic player on the team.

4. Try to be the best-conditioned player on the team.

5. Observe and reflect on the leadership traits of the team captain and coaches.

6. Master the plays.

7. Care about your teammates; this includes being supportive and never back-stabbing.

8. Maintain your sense of "balance" when adversity strikes.

9. Put team goals ahead of personal goals.

10. Inspire confidence by demonstrating self-control.

11. Try to be the most coachable player on the team.

12. Reach out to those team members with whom you have little in common.

13. Try to energize your teammates with your positive attitude.

14. Learn to accept the coach's criticism without taking it personally.

15. Treat disappointment or failure as feedback, followed by a quick return to normal.

16. Consistently adhere to high standards of behavior and be a role model who demonstrates respect toward all members of the team and school community.

Establishing high personal standards raises the bar for other team members. When a coach has a group of players who aspire to these goals, the whole team benefits!

The 21 Non-Negotiable Responsibilities of a Good Captain

"Since the honor of being a captain will stay with you for life, confers responsibility as opposed to privilege, and will always appear on your résumé, treat the honor with respect."
—St. Mary's College of Maryland Head Women's Basketball Coach, Barbara Bausch

If your child is elected team captain, it may be helpful to have a discussion about the team captain's role, beginning with this point: "You may have been elected captain based on your ability as an athlete, not because of your leadership skills. It is your responsibility as captain to try your best to be a good leader, as well as a skilled athlete. Take advantage of this leadership opportunity by cultivating your leadership skills."

Remind your new captain to meet the 16 leadership goals for all team members, plus understand that to be a good captain, an athlete must devote attention to developing essential non-physical leadership skills. One surveyed leader said it this way: "Just as developing sports excellence requires practice, so too does developing good leadership skills."

Discuss with your captain the following 21 non-negotiable captain responsibilities:

1. A good captain encourages teammates to aspire to the 16 leadership goals for all team members.

2. A good captain is approachable.

3. A good captain acts as a team sounding board, listens carefully, and in this role helps direct the thinking of teammates toward positive goals.

4. A good captain takes special care to acknowledge the contributions of those on the bench.

5. A good captain never shows favoritism or promotes cliques.

6. A good captain must be at his or her best in the tough times.

7. A good captain fosters the concept of "sharing the credit."

8. Whether the team is on a winning or losing streak, a good captain must demonstrate optimism and inspire hope.

9. A good captain serves as a link between the coach and team.

10. A good captain understands that a leader is still a team player.

11. A good captain works as hard or harder than anyone on the team.

12. A good captain conveys a belief in oneself and in one's teammates.

13. A good captain makes the effort to bond with every team member, including freshmen and sophomores and those with whom the captain has little in common.

14. A good captain is trustworthy, and by consistently doing the right thing regardless of the circumstances, fosters an atmosphere of trust.

15. A good captain conveys the message that an atmosphere of trust does not mean acceptance of improper actions or behaviors by team members.

16. A good captain observes all team rules, including those on drugs and alcohol.

17. A good captain conveys the message that bullying or humiliating teammates damages team building and trust.

18. The best captains are able to achieve an exalted form of leadership called "selfless ambition." Great captains are able to direct their ambition and

passion toward the success of the team, more than toward personal success.

19. A good captain sets aside personal problems to show genuine concern for teammates in need of support.

20. A good captain adheres to the highest standards of behavior, recognizing that misbehavior by an athlete can have a ripple effect and damage the athlete, sports program, school and family.

21. Finally, a good captain sets the goal of doing such an excellent job that his or her captaincy serves as a model for future captains to follow.

The Challenge of Peer Leadership

A captain's job can be especially challenging, because a captain has no inherent power or enforcement authority over peers, such as that available to a coach. The captain must lead by example, developing trust and demonstrating genuine respect for the value of all team members. Learning this form of peer leadership is very valuable.

The peer leader must also refrain from a negative action employed by some young people in leadership positions—bullying.

My Captaincy Plan

As a young basketball coach, it became clear to me that electing the next year's captain(s) at the end of the season was fraught with problems. As a result, my captaincy plan involved an election during the following Christmas season. I chose this course because I realized that a basketball captain elected in March might not be the same captain elected the following December, when leadership was really needed. I also wanted to see which of my returning players:

- Showed the most leadership and diligence in the spring and summer.
- Reported back to school in shape.
- Worked the hardest—and demonstrated the most effective leadership—during preseason.
- Played well in early games.
- Demonstrated leadership in the early season—on and off the court.

By the time of the captain's vote, the players had been able to carefully analyze each candidate, and there was little doubt in anyone's mind who the best captain(s) would be. While I always reserved the right to overrule a vote if I felt the choice was not in the best interests of the team, I never took this action. I always found the Christmas vote to be well thought out and fair.

Our surveys confirm that many present and former athletes would have voted for a different person for captain had the vote been taken at a later stage, e.g., once the following season had begun.

Some coaches oppose late elections, because they want a captain available to oversee off-season activities. I believe off-season activities can be a time to motivate team members who want to develop and demonstrate leadership skills. My observation is that off-season leadership will be apparent—with or without the formal title of captain.

Most importantly, by the time the vote is taken, there will be no doubt who deserves the honor.

MY RECOMMENDED CAPTAIN — ELECTION CALENDAR

FALL SPORTS: Captains should be elected in August (during preseason) or after one or more regular season games.

WINTER SPORTS: Captains should be elected in November (during preseason) or after one or more regular season games.

SPRING SPORTS: Captains should be elected in February/March (during preseason) or after one or more regular season games.

I realize that this plan will prevent high school spring sport athletes from listing a captaincy on their college applications and resumes. Yet this is a case of "the good of the whole" trumping the good of the individual. Another advantage that I have found with this plan, particularly when captains are elected once the season has begun, is that such a plan often gives the team a "boost."

Voting for a Captain

"He that judges without informing himself to the utmost that he is capable, cannot acquit himself of judging amiss."

— British philosopher, John Locke

For many young people, a captaincy vote will be among their first truly important ballots. Tell your child that a thoughtful, objective vote for the most qualified candidate, not just the most popular or best athlete, reflects maturity.

Six Preliminary Analysis Steps

Voting for a captain should involve the following steps:

1. All team members should read and carefully reflect upon the previously listed 21 "non-negotiable" responsibilities of a good captain.

2. Skill level should be a factor, though not the only factor. To be successful, teams will generally need to call on the talent of a highly skilled player. Thus, the voter should consider "in-game leadership," which often requires a high level of skill.

3. Some highly skilled players are excessively selfish and arrogant, and thus unworthy of the captaincy. Other highly skilled players are shy and reserved, and have no interest in team leadership outside of their personal performance. The voter should consider what impact not electing the best player will have on the chemistry of the team. A strong leader can maximize the athletic skills and performance of other players.

4. Even before the season ends, players should observe and think about candidates for the next season's captaincy. Players should ask the coach when the vote will take place, since many votes occur without advance notice and leave little time for thoughtful consideration of candidates.

5. If co-captains are a possibility, players should consider candidates whose skills and personalities complement each other.

6. Finally, in the preliminary analysis, the young athlete should winnow the list of potential captains to two or three.

Do You Vote for Yourself?

Tell your child, "Only if you believe you are one of the most qualified to be captain." Captaincy is very alluring for some, but an honorable competitor will vote based on what is best for the team. A good captain plays an important role in the success of the team; a bad captain can seriously hurt the team's chances for success. A captain vote should reflect fair and objective analysis of a candidate's effectiveness; it should not be an example of selfish decision-making!

Everyone Cannot Be Captain

Our surveys made clear that many "adult leaders" were not elected team captains in their youth. Some of these adult leaders pointed out that, due to their lack of playing skill and/or experience, their teammates made the right choice in not electing them captain. "In my adult world, I do have the kind of confident leadership skills required in my present position. Yet I did not possess enough sports skills to be a 'confident leader' on my high school team, and thus did not deserve to be captain. However, team play did allow me to observe the leadership skills of others, which proved to be invaluable," was the way one surveyed leader responded to this issue.

CAPTAIN CANDIDATE EVALUATION CHART

Four Core Categories Rate Low to High: 1-10	Name:	RATE
1. Level of effective leadership during the game.		
2. Level of effective leadership during practice.		
3. Level of effective leadership in the off-season, including off-season training regimens and other team-related activities.		
4. Level of effective leadership in terms of "selfless ambition", i.e., able to best direct ambition and passion toward the success of the team, more than toward personal success.		
	Subtotal	

Seven More Important Categories Rate Low to High: 1-5		RATE
1. Level of effective leadership as a team sounding board, committed to listening carefully, and in this role, helping to direct the thinking of teammates toward positive goals.		
2. Level of effective leadership in terms of being at his or her best during the tough times.		
3. Level of effective leadership in terms of fostering the concept of "sharing the credit."		
4. Level of effective leadership in terms of working as hard or harder as anyone on the team.		
5. Level of effective leadership in terms of connecting with every team member, including all substitutes and those teammates with whom the candidate has little in common.		
6. Level of effective leadership by adhering to the highest standards of behavior, recognizing that misbehavior of an athlete can have a ripple effect and damage the athlete, sports program, school and family.		
7. Level of effective leadership in terms of serving as a link between the coach and team.		
	Subtotal	
	TOTAL SCORE:	

What If Your Child is Not Elected Captain?

There are many instances in sports when a deserving youngster is not elected captain, and it can hurt. A captain is sometimes elected based on athletic ability and/or popularity, with little consideration given to other aspects of leadership. If your child feels deserving of the captaincy, but is not elected or appointed, use this as a "teachable moment." Encourage your child to handle the situation with dignity, and remind your youngster of two points:

- Just as the vast majority of surveyed leaders did, you can develop and practice leadership skills without being captain.
- Many athletes who are not elected captain become great leaders, and many within this group used the non-election as a source of motivation.

Parents must understand that they have no role in the election or appointment of a team captain, only a supporting role in guiding their player's personal development.

The Five Leadership Areas for Non-Captains

Explain to your player that sports activities break down into five broad categories, with each category offering some of the leadership development opportunities listed in the 16 leadership goals for all team members. All non-captains are free to practice leadership in any category, but it may be helpful for athletes to begin in the categories in which they feel most comfortable.

I — In-Game Leadership

In-game leadership opportunities are often based on a player's position, skill or both. Honestly advise your non-captain that in-game leadership often results from natural talent coupled with a practice regimen that develops superior skills, and almost always falls to a highly proficient player. Many in-game leaders work hard to achieve excellence, and they use their excellence to help their teammates perform at an optimal level.

Athletes will follow the lead of a reliable, skilled player they believe can get the job done. These in-game leaders often have the experience and mental toughness to perform in the most adverse of circumstances, and the confidence and skill to take competitive risks — and deliver in clutch situations!

II — In practice

Leadership during practice may rely less on pure talent and more on:

- Focus
- Hard work
- Hustle
- Mastery of the plays
- Unselfishness
- Enthusiasm
- Optimism
- Respectful treatment of teammates.
- Punctuality
  In the minds of many coaches, punctuality equates to "Lombardi time," as espoused by the great football coach Vince Lombardi, i.e., arrive early and stay late!

III — In the locker room

Locker room leadership demands:

- Putting team goals first.
- Not bragging about oneself.
- Encouraging and supporting those players who are struggling.
- Never backstabbing or belittling another player or the coach.
- Being optimistic.

IV — In-season but away from games or practices

All players may lead by example when they:

- Follow the rules, including curfews and no drugs or no alcohol.
- Stay positive even when losing.
- Support younger players in need of good role models.
- Eat a balanced diet and get proper rest.
- Do other things to stay healthy such as wearing a hat in cold weather, dressing properly based on climate, showering after practice and, in general, approaching good health as an "obligation" to the team.

V — Off-season

Non-captains become positive role models, and thus leaders, when they:
- Work the hardest to improve skills and conditioning.
- Encourage other players to do the same.
- Are available to work out with teammates in a joint effort to help every team member improve. (This is part of the year-round "you can depend on me" culture of successful teams.)
- Follow out-of-season rules, especially those on alcohol and drugs, and continue to be a role model for teammates.

Throughout the year, a real leader will behave with dignity, exhibit the traits of diligence, honorable competition and competitive self-restraint, and will refuse to bully or allow bullying of any team member or other student.

Senior Leadership

This term is commonly heard on high school and college teams throughout America. Coaches often provide seniors with special opportunities to lead in each of the five categories. In a sport such as football, with many players, there are plenty of opportunities for non-captains to exhibit leadership.

Selfless Ambition

"Selfless Ambition" is a vital quality of great leadership. While many leaders are extremely ambitious and passionate, the very best are also selfless enough, and mature enough, to direct their ambition and passion toward the well-being of their team or company, not themselves.[11] Selfless ambition is an essential leadership concept to follow in sports for all team members — coaches, captains and players alike. Indeed, the concept is at the very core of effective teamwork. Not all successful coaches or team captains practice this inspired form of leadership, but some of the most successful and admired do — University of North Carolina men's basketball coach Roy Williams, former UConn women's All-American basketball player Rebecca Lobo, and former NFL star Steve Young are some examples.

The earnest pursuit of "selfless ambition" is a worthy goal for captains — and all other young athletes — who aspire to be effective leaders. Those who are able to achieve this goal in sports will likely find positive carryover value to other forms of leadership — and personal relationships. In fact, it is often this very type of "selflessly ambitious" leader who ends up being considered a great leader!

CLASSIC IN-GAME SELFLESS AMBITION

One of the greatest sports rivalries of all time was Bill Russell versus Wilt Chamberlain, and as a teenager I attended at least six of these classic duels in the old Boston Garden. From watching Russell compete against Chamberlain (and recognizing my bias as a Celtics fan), I developed a clear respect for Russell's unselfish court leadership.

When Russell walked onto the court, it appeared to me that his principal objective was to make all of his teammates "leading men." Wilt, in contrast, seemed to want his teammates to be his "supporting cast." There were some years when Wilt decided that he would lead the league in scoring, and he expected his teammates to react accordingly. Another year, he actually chose to lead the league in assists, and his teammates were expected to play in harmony with that goal. Russell, on the other hand, always seemed dedicated to helping the other four men on the court be the best they could possibly be, an essential quality of the unselfish leader.

In his 13 years in the NBA, Russell's teams won 11 world championships. In head-to-head competition, Wilt's teams beat Russell's only once for a world championship.

Three Sports-Related Leadership Opportunities

Sports provide high school and college age students with three valuable leadership opportunities:

I—Officiating

Many youth leagues will call on high school or college students to serve as umpires or referees. The students are generally paid a modest or even attractive fee and given the opportunity to practice nine "good judgment" leadership skills:

1. Fairness

2. Common sense

3. Conflict resolution

4. Professionalism

5. Focusing amidst distractions

6. Quick, firm decision-making

7. Perspective—young officials quickly understand what it is like to be the person making tough decisions.

8. Observing leadership and benefiting from mentorship. Many young officials are assigned to work with a more senior official whose role is to teach and mentor the newcomer.

9. Responsibility—the official bears responsibility for the well-being of the game.

All nine characteristics are essential elements of good officiating.

Inform your child that a requisite quality of a good official is to block out all criticism from the sidelines. Officiating also requires a commitment to self-control, even when others lose theirs.

Officiating can be a valuable leadership and personal growth experience, but will not always be a pleasant one. Be careful not to put your beginner into a league that is characterized by highly competitive play and emotional fans and coaches. Warn your child to be prepared for disappointing, irrational reactions from players, coaches and fans including, unfortunately, parents.

Finally, have your young official learn the rules and attend any league training sessions for officials/umpires before taking to the court or field.

II — Volunteer Coaching

Youth leagues often provide opportunities for high school and college students to serve as assistant coaches. (Some college students serve as head youth league or high school freshmen/JV coaches.) Such an experience provides a high school or college student with a number of valuable leadership opportunities, including:

- The opportunity to observe the leadership style of the head coach, other league coaches and league administrators.
- The opportunity to practice some of the leadership principles your child admires.
- The opportunity to deal with unpleasant problems and to observe how the head coach deals with different issues.

If your high school or college student decides to coach, encourage a focus on teaching skills and motivating the players—and to refrain from yelling or criticizing, for such actions have no place in the role of a young coach working with younger children. An excellent resource for a volunteer coach, be it a high school or college student or parent, is the Positive Coaching Alliance (*www.positivecoach.org*).

III — Camp Counselor

Sport camps present many fine opportunities for volunteer or paid employment. Few summer jobs offer as many leadership opportunities as camp counseling.

When applying for a counselor position, share the following points with your young athlete:

- Apply very early. It is often a good idea to make initial contact with the camp director as early as the autumn prior to the summer program.
- Make it easy on the employer to communicate with you. If you call the potential employer, and the employer is out or busy, leave the message, "I will be happy to get back to Mr. Jones at a more convenient time," rather than, "Could you have Mr. Jones call me back?"
- Be respectfully persistent.
- When the position is attained, and before the first day of camp, tell your child to follow the credo that I always share with my children when they head off for a job, "Do such great work that your employers will wonder how they ever got along without you!"

Leadership and Respect for Non-Athletes

"At Andover Academy, I learned to appreciate students who were
engaged in non-sports activities like the theatre, debating and so on."
— Head Coach of the New England Patriots, Bill Belichick

At his International Scholar-Athlete Hall of Fame induction ceremony, Roger Bannister told his audience, "When I was a boy growing up, I never looked reproachfully at others not involved in sport. Indeed, I always tried to take an interest in the activities of others, especially when I knew little about the activity. It is a shame when a top athlete basically shuns other schoolmates, for, in truth, it is the top athlete who really loses out."

Help your athlete understand that the overall success of a school or community is dependent upon the interaction and involvement of all its members. Try to counter the culture of "jock arrogance" that precludes young athletes from becoming true school citizens. Make it clear that you expect your player to display respect for all students and take an interest in the activities of all members of the athletic program, school and community. Encourage your athlete to be open-minded and to try to appreciate activities beyond sports. Such a mindset offers lasting benefits.

Real Sports Leaders are "School Citizens"

When Mike Krzyzewski was considering leaving Duke to become the head coach of the Los Angeles Lakers, a Duke dean made this comment. "I hope he does not leave for he is a true university citizen."

Being a true citizen of a school—from attending a school theatre presentation to standing for student government office—is a frequently missed opportunity of the "hubristic jock." Some coaches are to blame for this missed opportunity because they discourage participation in any campus activity other than sports.

Wrapping oneself in a garment of athletic conceit is not only ignorant, it also holds a child back from appreciating, and perhaps even taking an interest in, other worthy school activities.

Leadership and Humility

"Nobility is rooted in humility." —Anonymous

Many people I interviewed about leadership told me that a quality they look for in leaders, but often fail to find, is humility. When asked to identify a leader who demonstrated humility, many interviewees struggled to name even one! By contrast, when asked to name individuals with leadership qualities such as optimism, passion or vision, they had no trouble reeling off a string of examples.

When leaders with humility were named—Jesus Christ, Gandhi, Ronald Reagan, Bono, Jimmy Carter, Colin Powell, Mother Teresa, Nelson Mandela, Elie Wiesel, George Mitchell, and Pope John Paul II—they were all individuals whose leadership is universally admired.

While humility is clearly not a quality shared by all leaders, it is one that many of history's greatest and most respected leaders share. Sports figures such as Tony Dungy and Joe Torre, who display a genuine and self-effacing humility in their leadership, are greatly admired, and they should feel good knowing they set a positive example for others.

One interviewee stated, "I admit I don't see humility in every leader, but when I do, I really respect that person!"

Not a bad legacy!

Competitive Self-Restraint and
the Changing Face of Sports Leadership

"A coach should be a teacher, not a dictator."
—UCLA Basketball Coaching Legend, John Wooden

Some years back, I had a conversation with Calvin Hill, a former All-American at Yale, All-Pro with the Dallas Cowboys, and an International Scholar-Athlete Hall of Fame inductee. I asked Calvin what he felt was the most important lesson his son, Grant, had learned at Duke playing basketball for Coach Mike Krzyzewski.

Calvin said, "There were many, but one that stands out was Coach K's composure under pressure. This quality was reassuring to all the Duke players, particularly in tight situations. Grant knew that in a tied Duke-Carolina game with 30 seconds to go, he could look at his fiercely competitive coach and see a leader in full control of his emotions."

I was so intrigued by Calvin's story that I attended a Duke game, and focused on Coach K's leadership style. At a number of junctures, including the final exciting minutes, I saw exactly what Calvin meant. Many of the Duke players on the court looked at their coach and saw a model of competitive self-restraint. It was clear to me that Coach K's demeanor fueled confidence in his players, and that they learned from his example.

For those of you who grew up playing for or observing coaches whose leadership was based on fear and intimidation, things have changed! A firm, controlled and reasoned approach is more effective over the long-term. Gail Goestenkors, Kay Yow and Phil Jackson are but a few of the contemporary coaches who follow John Wooden's principle of "teaching not dictating."

Transitioning from Athletic Leadership
to Non-Sport Leadership Roles

"If you command wisely, you'll be obeyed cheerfully."
—English clergyman, Thomas Fuller

There is an important distinction between the sports leadership of a coach or captain and the leadership required in the adult workplace. A vital element of a coach or captain's leadership involves preparing and motivating a group of athletes to compete at peak physical performance and, during competition, to draw upon the physical courage essential for sports success. This often involves the sports leader employing a raised voice to passionately stir the emotions of the team.

Some young athletes who respond well to, and learn from, the competitive physical/emotional style of leadership often required in sports, have difficulty transitioning to competitive but restrained civil leadership in the workplace. This may be particularly true for athletes who play under an admired, hard-line coach whose "tough love/raised voice" leadership is highly effective with athletes, but which usually has no place in the adult workforce and may even be counter-productive.

A young person learning sports leadership must be reminded that when transitioning to the adult workplace the hard-line, raised voice, emotional leadership style employed by coaches and team leaders must give way to the pinnacle of great adult leadership, i.e., "inspired standards," as described by leadership expert Jim Collins and often used by coaches like Dave Hixon of Amherst College.[12]

The Hassenfeld-Hogg Center For Sports Leadership

The Institute for International Sport Hassenfeld-Hogg Center for Sports Leadership (*www.internationalsport.com*) opened in 2008 on the URI campus. The Center provides leadership training to coaches, captains and student-athletes throughout the world. The coaches' leadership seminar program aims at helping coaches greatly enhance their skills as sports educators, and offers sports education leadership certification. The captain and student-athlete program offers the participants clearly stated, valuable leadership concepts that can be utilized not only in their sports careers, but throughout life.

My Eighth Grade Sports Leadership Experience

By the time I reached the eighth grade at St. Peter's Grammar School in Worcester, Massachusetts, I already had plenty of experience putting together informal games of pick-up basketball or baseball with my friends. Yet because I felt we had an especially strong eighth grade class of athletes, I wanted my class to do more than play pick-up with each other. The school was administered by the Sisters of St. Joseph and there was no male physical education teacher or coach on the staff. As a result, I took it upon myself to take two steps to address our lack of organized school sports competition.

The first step took place during October, when I contacted St. Bernard's Parish, administrators of a Worcester grammar school basketball league. Over the course of a month, I made several bus trips to the St. Bernard's Parish Rectory to meet with the priest in charge of the league, who finally agreed to admit our team. I then filled out forms, recruited a coach, coordinated transportation to the games, and convinced a neighborhood merchant to donate uniforms. In that '62-'63 basketball season, our team won the St. Bernard's league championship, and then went on to win both the regional and New England championships.

The second step took place at the end of the basketball season. There was no baseball league for Worcester Catholic grammar schools, and so I founded one, naming my friend, Billy Costello—two years my elder—as league president. I employed some of the contacts made in the winter basketball league, and put together a six-team grammar school baseball league. I recruited umpires and made arrangements through the City of Worcester to use the local parks for games. The Worcester Catholic Grammar School Baseball League was active for over a decade, until a number of Catholic grammar schools were forced to close due to declining enrollment.

Many years later, when I was coaching at Trinity College, the *Hartford Courant* ran a story on my eighth grade sports leadership experience. I received considerable feedback on the article, including a call from a local teacher who made two points:

- It was sports that provided you with the venue for such young leadership.
- In today's world, such an endeavor would be nearly impossible, given the tourniquet-like grip of adults on youth league sports.

The primary reason that I developed the Center for Sports Leadership is my belief that sports can play a valuable role in helping young athletes—and coaches—develop leadership qualities. The simple reason is that sports is one of the best "early laboratories" for the practice of leadership. I was fortunate to have had such an experience as a young boy in an activity that I dearly loved.

Finally, my brief verse on one core leadership quality:

Frank Galasso

Leadership

Every athlete should well take heed
The varying ways adults may lead.

Of certain coaches, a player may say
"That self-centered style is not the way."

The most astute, first sight observe
The leader's role, foremost to serve.

SECTION V

MEDICAL ISSUES

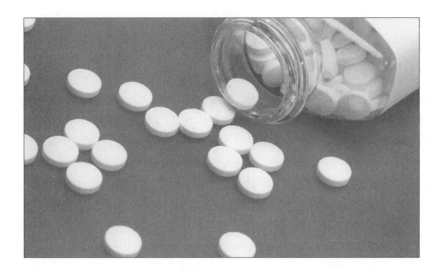

Chapter 22

MEDICATION AND THE YOUNG ATHLETE

"I've been afraid to provide information on my son's medical treatment because some adults,
on learning of his diagnosis, either 'label' him or expect him to be difficult."
—Mother of one of my sports campers

P arents of children diagnosed with Attention Deficit Disorder (ADD) or Attention Deficit/Hyperactivity Disorder (ADHD) debate whether disclosure of their child's diagnosis and treatment will put their child at a disadvantage. Some children have already experienced a coach or teacher who, upon learning of the diagnosis, expected the child to cause behavior and discipline problems in the group. Such parental concerns led me to seek the opinion of a highly respected sport psychiatrist regarding medications and young athletes.

Dr. Ronald Kamm

Dr. Kamm is an adolescent and adult psychiatrist specializing in sport psychiatry. His many activities include consulting with high school, college and professional teams, treating elite athletes in all sports, and serving as past president of the International Society for Sport Psychiatry. Dr. Kamm notes that a sport psychiatrist is a physician who treats athletes young and old, sometimes with medication, to "help athletes reach their full potential."

Dr. Kamm's Seven Points about
ADD/ADHD, Medication and Young Athletes

1. Parents and coaches need to understand that inattentive, impulsive, aggressive or "wired" behaviors are not willful, but a manifestation of a brain malfunction in ADD/ADHD children.

2. ADD/ADHD is not a "fad" diagnosis, as suggested by some critics. The ADD/ADHD brain is structurally different from "normal" children, and abnormalities have been consistently noted on the MRIs and Spect Scans of these children. Along with structural abnormalities, chemical deficiencies in neuro-transmitters are responsible for a child's inability to control impulsiveness, inattentiveness and hyperactivity. Medication re-establishes a necessary chemical balance.

3. ADD/ADHD prevalence ranges from 4% to 12% in the United States with boys three times more likely to have it than girls.[13] While many parents hope their child will outgrow an ADD/ADHD condition, as many as 65% of those diagnosed as children continue to have the disorder as adolescents and adults.[14]

4. Diagnosing and treating children with ADD/ADHD may minimize danger in sports. Inattentive and impulsive behaviors increase physical risk such as getting hit with a baseball or lacrosse stick or using poor judgment on gymnastics equipment.

5. Prescribing medication for an ADD/ADHD child is no different from prescribing insulin for a diabetic. Dr. Kamm states, "In both cases, the patient is merely being helped to be normal. In the case of the athlete, prescribed medication is not a performance enhancer; rather, it is a performance enabler allowing an athlete to perform with fewer handicaps imposed by the ADD/ADHD condition."

6. An untreated ADD/ADHD child will often have difficulty spending the time needed to perfect sports skills.

7. In general, ADD/ADHD children do best in sports where there are few breaks in the action. Continuous action sports like soccer, ice hockey, wrestling, and martial arts are best. Sports like baseball, football, softball, and golf, with their long, frequent breaks, can be more problematic.

How Sports Participation Can Benefit a Child Taking Medication

Dr. Kamm feels that the benefits of sports participation can be especially important for a child athlete taking medication, for a number of reasons:

- If the ADD/ADHD is under control, sports settings help promote socialization and cooperation skills within an environment where rules can be learned and successfully followed.
- ADD/ADHD children respond well to structured workouts and routines, and sports programs can reinforce the self-discipline skills practiced in these routines.
- Proficiency in a sport helps a child develop a well-earned sense of accomplishment and self-esteem, a nice counterbalance to the frustration often experienced by ADD/ADHD children in the academic setting.
- Sports participation provides a youngster with opportunities to practice and develop impulse control, a valuable skill for children with ADD/ADHD.

Can Discipline, Not Medication, Be the Answer?

A number of child-rearing experts believe that ADD/ADHD children do not need medication, only more discipline. Dr. Kamm points out that while a few children are so undisciplined they may display behaviors similar to ADD/ADHD children, those accurately diagnosed with ADD or ADHD may well need medication in order to function normally. Some children, including child athletes, benefit from carefully prescribed medication that addresses behavioral issues that discipline alone cannot. Dr. Kamm points to a recent study in which a group of children given appropriate medication did significantly better than a group of children given no medication and whose parents and teachers underwent extensive behavior modification training.[15]

Discipline is no substitute for medication; medication is no substitute for discipline. All children need reasonable, consistent discipline, and some children need medication as well. When rules are broken, effective discipline includes consequences, not just words or equivocation. ADD/ADHD athletes can also benefit from an athletic environment in which behavior modification techniques are tailored to the particular sport—and young athlete. Dr. Kamm's website, (*www.mindbodyandsports.com*), contains practical advice on this matter.

The key to any decision regarding use of medication is to enlist the services of a reputable medical professional with whom you are comfortable. Do not hesitate to get more than one opinion on such an important matter. Parents of children using medication should be careful to keep the medicine regulated for effectiveness during sports activities so children may function safely. Recent advances in some medications make treatment easier; some prescriptions require only one dose daily.

Additional Questions for Dr. Kamm

1. Should a parent of a child diagnosed with ADD/ADHD discuss the child's diagnosis and treatment with the coach?

   Dr. Kamm: "A parent should tell the coach about the athlete's diagnosis, particularly when a child is young. A child's first experience in youth sports is often crucial in deciding whether the child will stay involved over the years. Ideally, parents should call the coach before the first practice to let him know of their child's diagnosis, and try to enlist that coach's help in their child's treatment. Explaining to the coach that Johnny, due to his diagnosis, can be talkative, inattentive and disruptive in group activities, can help the coach see Johnny as having an illness, rather than an attitude, when the behavior arises.

   "The parent can also share with the coach those strategies that have been most effective with Johnny. The coach would ideally pass these strategies on to his or her assistant. For instance, how does Johnny respond to criticism? To instruction? Parents should ask for and expect complete confidentiality from all coaches.

   "Generally, if a child is being adequately treated with medication and family therapy, disruptive behaviors can be satisfactorily managed before the child begins his sporting career. In any case, the coach should be informed, and enlisted as a member of the treatment team. Like teachers, coaches can provide clinicians with important feedback about how well treatment is working. This includes college coaches who are, after all, teachers who should be made aware of symptoms that may interfere with an athlete's optimal performance. The coach can help, e.g., maintaining eye contact, and asking if the athlete understands after instructions are given."

2. Should a youngster being treated with medication for ADD/ADHD or depression continue or alter the medication during sport practices and competition?

22

Dr. Kamm: "ADHD medications need to be tailored to the needs of each individual child. In school, some need their maximal dose during their second period math class, some during after-school homework, and some during family dinner.

"Athletes have varying needs for these medications depending on their sport. A hockey goalie with ADHD may need his medication to be at classroom levels, lest he be distracted by crowd noises and events, and lose sight of the puck. Some child-athletes find that ADHD medication 'mellows them out.' This can be a positive effect for an overly aggressive tennis player who throws his racquet and loses focus after missing a point, but negative for a defensive lineman in football, who depends on his aggression to bull past the opposing lineman and make a play. In such a case, on practice or game days, the medication can be withheld, or a short acting preparation can be given in the morning, so that it is out of the athlete's system by game time.

"The newer ADHD (long acting) agents now last 8-12 hours. If they start to wear off during after-school activity, a short-acting medication can be given on top of the long-acting dose to cover the athlete during competition."

3. At what stage in an athlete's career — youth league, high school, college or elite national or international competition — will an athlete face the possibility of a prescribed medicine being banned? Does this vary by sport?

Dr. Kamm: "In general, at the youth sport, club or high-school levels, an athlete need not worry about a physician-prescribed medication being banned. For the most part, it is only when an athlete enters international competition, or competes in college, that the bans go into effect. However, even then, a Therapeutic Use Exemption may be applied for, and granted, if the athlete is examined by several physicians, if alternative medications have been tried, and if it is felt that withholding the banned medication would cause a significant impairment to the athlete's health.

"Some high schools randomly 'drug test' athletes, but most medications prescribed by a physician either don't show up on the test or can be readily explained by a doctor's note."

4. Are any or all prescription medications for ADD/ADHD, or other mood and anxiety disorders, considered banned substances by any of the national or international sports governing bodies?

Dr. Kamm: "In recent years sports governing bodies have taken a more enlightened view toward the prescription of some medications. Others however, continue to be banned, and some banned only in competition. Parents should check the NCAA website at *(www.drugfreesport.com)* or USADA *(www.usantidoping.org)* for drugs banned by the US Olympic Committee and for information on the Therapeutic Use Exemption."

Stimulants—The most frequently prescribed medications for ADHD (Adderal, Ritalin), are banned by the USOC and NCAA. They are thought to energize the athlete and give an unfair advantage. Strattera, however, is currently permitted.

Antidepressants—These medications (e.g., Prozac, Zoloft, Wellbutrin) are now permitted.

Sedatives/Most Tranquilizers—Prescribed for anxiety, these are now permitted.

Beta-Blockers—Inderal is sometimes prescribed for performance anxiety. It is banned (in competition only) for riflery in the NCAA. Banned (in competition only) for riflery, gymnastics, diving, wrestling and some other sports by the USOC.

Alcohol—banned (in competition only) by archery, karate and skiing.
Anabolic Steroids—Prohibited at all times, both in and out of competition. (Note: Information provided by Dr. Kamm on banned and non-banned substances is based on the agency rules as of the publication date of this book.)

Supplements—the USADA Dietary Supplement warning is instructive and should be heeded:
USADA DIETARY SUPPLEMENT WARNING
Many dietary supplements (vitamins, minerals, amino acids, homeopathies, herbs, energy drinks), which are sold over the counter or through the Internet contain substances that are prohibited by the World Anti-Doping Code or the NCAA.

Since anti-doping rules make the presence of a prohibited substance in an athlete's urine a doping offense regardless of how the substance got there, any athlete who takes a dietary supplement does so at his or her own risk of a positive test and a doping violation.
(2005 United States Anti-Doping Agency)

5. Should parents worry about prejudice against their children because their

prescription medication is on a banned substance list?

Dr. Kamm: "No. Particularly if the child is seeing a psychiatrist or a sport psychiatrist well versed in psychopharmacology. Medication that is on the banned substance list can be tapered far enough in advance of testing that it will be metabolized out of the body and not show up 'positive' on a test. Even stimulants are permitted in most sports as long as they are not used 'in competition.'

"The fact that a child at a lower level of competition is taking pre-scribed medication banned at a higher level should not concern a coach or league as long as the child's behavior or performance is not adversely affected by the medication."

Dr. Kamm and other physicians in sports psychiatry continue to work earnestly to convince sports governing bodies to re-examine their bans on substances that treat medical disorders. As mentioned above, antidepres-sants and tranquilizers can now be prescribed without penalty for athletes with depression and anxiety. Youngsters and adults who need treatment to function normally should not be penalized by having to forego neces-sary medical treatment just because they achieve a high level of athletic success. In the case of youth leaguers, middle school and high school ath-letes, the best advice is not to worry about future problems with a sports governing body. Do what is best for your child now.

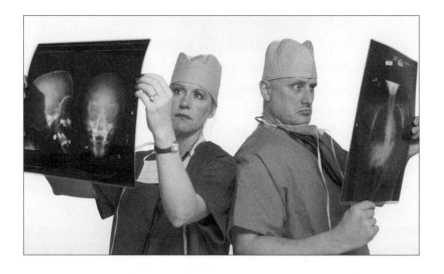

Chapter 23

TREATMENT OF SPORTS INJURIES

"There be some sports are painful."
— Shakespeare

While there is no evidence to suggest that those who coined the phrase "no pain, no gain," were Shakespearean scholars, pain and sport have a close relationship that extends back for centuries.

Dr. Kevin Speer — Sports Medicine Expert

Dr. Kevin Speer takes exception to the notion of always playing through pain. *"Continuous pain is not part of youth athletics,"* states Dr. Speer, an orthopedic surgeon specializing in sports medicine. "The protective and reparative properties of youth are so profound that continuing pain is a clear indication that something is wrong."

A former scholarship football player at Indiana University, Dr. Speer spent nine years as the Director of Duke University's prestigious Sports Medicine Program. Now in private practice in Raleigh, North Carolina, he is one of the most respected professionals in his field.

Twenty Vital Points from Dr. Speer

During a lengthy discussion, Dr. Speer made numerous points that merit your attention. I will relate 20 of them, beginning with one as fundamental as it is important.

I. Tell Me if it Hurts!

Young players often do not tell a parent about an ache or pain for fear of being kept out of a game. They sometimes tolerate considerable discomfort in order to participate, and might unknowingly aggravate a mild injury which, with a short rest, would completely heal. Without rest or treatment, the injury might turn into a condition requiring more extensive treatment, rehabilitation or even removal from the sport.

"You want to create a home environment where the young athlete is not reluctant to talk about aches and pains, one in which the athlete recognizes that some aches and pains are symptomatic of a condition that must be looked at," said Dr. Speer.

II. Don't Be Macho — The One Week Rule and Early Assessment

In the interest of your child, be wary of the macho sports ethic of playing with pain. For the older college player and adults there are aches and pains which are often part of the game. With younger athletes though, particularly those who do not have regular exposure to a sports medicine expert, Dr. Speer recommends, "always err on the side of caution, and if any painful condition continues for more than one week, it needs to be assessed. *I cannot stress enough the importance of early assessment!*"

Dr. Speer related the story of a 14-year-old baseball player whose shoulder pain, for one year, required 2-3 Aleve prior to pitching or throwing. The boy's unstable shoulder progressed from being a playing problem to an everyday problem. When the boy could no longer raise his arm in class, his parents finally admitted that it was time to seek professional help. With early treatment, this would have been a preventable condition. Instead, the boy will never again play a sport involving an overhead throwing, swimming or swinging motion.

Dr. Speer emphasizes, "Do not wait to have any continuing pain assessed by a sports medicine professional." Continuing pain does not necessarily mean constant pain, although it may, but a pain which continues to be present during play or during a particular motion or action while playing, even after a week of rest.

III. "Safe Pain" or "Unsafe Pain?"

In evaluating an athlete's condition, Dr. Speer first tries to determine whether the pain is what he labels "safe pain" or "unsafe pain."

"Safe pain" — "safe pain" means an athlete's condition has been assessed and all considerations requiring treatment have been excluded. "In other words, it's a benign ache or pain accompanying sports participation, and enduring it will not produce any long-term problems," said Dr. Speer.

"Safe pain" categories might include:

- Recovering sprain—still tender but okay to play.
- Bruises or cuts that are not severe.
- Inflammation diagnosed as "safe pain."
- Achy sore muscles after not having played, or from extensive playing in a short period of time. (Achy pain is common during the first week of any sport pre-season practice.)
- "Safe growing pain," such as in the heels of some children, but only after the painful area has been diagnosed.

"Safe pain" in these situations means it is okay to play if the child can and wants to play with it.

"Unsafe pain" — "Unsafe pain" involves some condition which, if ignored and untreated, will get worse with time and may require greater treatment and expense, a longer time away from play, and possible permanent damage. *"It is best to assume any continuing pain is unsafe until medical diagnosis has determined otherwise,"* said Dr. Speer.

"Unsafe pain" categories may include:

- Emerging repetitive motion injuries, often called overuse injuries, to bones or soft tissues such as ligaments or tendons.
- Any pain or continuing discomfort involving growth plate areas (around joints) especially in children experiencing a growth spurt.
- Stress fractures—soccer and other running sport athletes often play with minor foot pain until stress fractures become debilitating and break even further.
- Severe sprain/strain of ligaments, tendons or muscles which could further tear and require surgery.
- Unstable joint— e.g., shoulder or knee.
- Concussion—any head bumps/concussions must be reported to parents and coaches, and *never* play following loss of consciousness or trauma to the head without permission from a physician.

"For parents and players who avoid medical attention out of fear of missing games, the strategy may backfire, and result in more missed games than if early proper treatment had been undertaken," said Dr. Speer.

23

IV. Growth Plates — A Developmental Process You Should Understand

In simple terms, the growth plate is the portion of the bone where growth occurs, near the ends of the long bones and close to the joints.

"There is an age at which a child's rapid adolescent growth leaves the growth plate wide open, vulnerable to injury, almost like marshmallow," said Dr. Speer.

This stage of rapid growth usually takes place in girls ages 10-14, and boys ages 12-16, though of course each child's growth pattern varies.

When a child experiences pain around a joint during these growth stages, Dr. Speer explains, "I look first at the bone because it is the weak link. The older they get, the more growth slows and the weak link transfers from the bones to soft tissues, usually the ligaments. Pain in an elbow or knee may feel the same at 12 years and 16 years of age, but the tissues damaged are probably different and treatment is different."

According to Dr. Speer, the only treatment for bone is rest. For soft tissue, there may be rehabilitative treatments available. Preventive exercises are sometimes prescribed to strengthen muscles and help avoid sports-related injuries to bones, ligaments and tendons.

V. Repetitive Motion or Overuse Injuries

There are many sports in which a specific motion or series of motions is performed over and over, resulting in injuries such as those frequently seen in the arms and shoulders of swimmers, tennis players and baseball players, or the knees and feet of soccer, lacrosse and field hockey players. There is no single point at which a player suddenly suffers a repetitive motion or overuse injury, but rather, according to Dr. Speer, "the athlete's repeated motion wears down the bone or soft tissue fiber by fiber until it fractures or tears, preventing further play, sometimes permanently." Dr. Speer further adds, "The athlete's level of discomfort or pain may seem acceptable and then the weak link simply breaks down with little warning. This is another example of the importance of early assessment and employment of early treatment and preventive techniques. Such treatment may preclude more severe damage and a lengthy loss of playing time."

VI. Sudden Impact or Single Event Injuries

As indicated by the name, these injuries are the sudden and accidental occurrences to be found in any sport, and include broken bones, lacerations, severe sprains, strains, bruises and concussions. A twisting turn or fall may be the source of injury, but sudden injuries often occur as a result of hard contact with other athletes. The football player who gets tackled and tears the cartilage in his knee has suffered a single event injury. As Dr. Speer points out, "Most injuries in this category are part of the sport and, in many cases, you can't prevent them." *If protective gear is available, be sure your athlete properly uses such equipment.*

VII. Chronic Pain and Burnout

Sports medicine experts tell us that *youngsters who play with chronic pain are far more likely to experience burnout than those who do not.* Parents and coaches who push a child to play while in pain, or even allow it to continue, are increasing the likelihood of two things:

1. A child losing the joy of playing and then quitting.

2. A child becoming injured and being unable to play for a longer period or perhaps permanently.

VIII. The Importance of Expert Evaluation and Treatment of Your Child's Sports Injury

If you think "sports medicine experts" aren't for youth leaguers, think again! Non-specialized medical treatment may be adequate to excellent for simple lacerations, sprains, bruises or fractures. There is, however, a big difference between the treatment and rehabilitation of an injury for a return to activities involved in daily living (which would be regular orthopedics) as opposed to getting back to playing a sport which may push a specific body part to its physical limits. Typing on a computer does not strain an elbow or shoulder injury the way playing baseball, tennis or swimming does. Treatment and rehabilitation by sports medicine experts may make the difference in a child's post-injury success or failure at their chosen sport. The added vulnerabilities of a growing body may make specialized, expert treatment even more necessary.

IX. Even the Experts Have Sub-Specialty Areas of Expertise

Within the field of sports medicine, there are sport-specific experts with extensive training and experience related to particular sports and injuries which accompany those sports. These injury specific experts practice the latest surgical techniques and rehabilitation protocols. For example:

- Orthopedic physicians for "overhead athletes" typically treat arm and shoulder injuries common to swimmers, volleyball, baseball/softball, lacrosse, and tennis players. Even within this specialty there may be only a few surgeons with the technical expertise and experience to perform, for example, the "Tommy John surgery." Named after the great ex-Yankee hurler, "Tommy John surgery" is, in medical terms, ulnar col-

23

lateral ligament reconstruction with an autologous graft. In laymen's terms, this is when a hairline tear to the inside elbow ligament occurs in a baseball pitcher. Even a minute tear cannot heal 100% without reconstructive surgery, and can ruin a pitcher's career. If your child suffers such an uncommon injury, find the most qualified surgeon. You want the specialist who regularly performs this type of treatment, not the general orthopedic surgeon. Following surgery, the surgeon will want your child to see the sports medicine rehabilitation therapist who specializes in arm and shoulder rehabilitation and long-term preventive programs for such injuries.

• Sports with extensive stresses to the lower extremities, e.g., soccer, lacrosse, basketball, football, and cross-country may produce foot, knee, and leg injuries, both from repetitive motion/overuse and sudden impact events. The highly technical and ever changing field of sports medicine sees dramatic improvements in surgical and rehabilitation techniques each decade, and even from year to year. "We are light years ahead of even five years ago," is the way David Roskin, sports medicine rehabilitation specialist at Duke University Sports Medicine program, describes the progress. Surgeons and rehabilitation therapists who specialize in treatment of these injuries are best able to diagnose, treat, prevent further damage, and enable a safer, faster return to play.

The Little League Pitcher—A Case Study for Proper Treatment

Dr. Speer describes a "Little League star" as an example of what he calls a "textbook" injury.

A 12-year-old pitcher complained of mild shoulder and elbow pain late in the Little League season. A respected general orthopedic surgeon told the boy that it was probably a pulled muscle or tendon, and that if it felt better after two weeks, the youngster could resume playing on the post-season all-star team, with no further need for visits. (Dr. Speer notes that at this point a more thorough evaluation, X-rays or an MRI could have shown emerging stress fractures to the "soft" growth plates.)

The boy rested, felt no pain and returned to action in two weeks. When on the mound, he was closely monitored by a "pitch count," a practice commonly used at all levels of baseball to make sure that pitchers do not over use their arms. Despite this safeguard, an end of the summer evaluation by Dr. Speer, due to the boy's occasional mild shoulder discomfort after pitching, indicated the child had developed stress fractures in the growth plates in his shoulder and elbow, although he complained little about the elbow.

Treatment, rest, and rehabilitation required 14 weeks, and thereafter a continuing regimen of arm exercises. The exercises were designed to reduce stress to the growing joints and growth plates through the strengthening of surrounding muscles.

This boy was lucky. The stress fractures were mild and diagnosed early enough so there was no permanent damage. According to Dr. Speer, "had he continued to ignore the mild discomfort and played AAU baseball through the fall, he may well have ended his pitching career at that point."

David Roskin of Duke points out that, "College teams are littered with former pitchers who are playing the outfield or infield because they did not properly care for their pitching arm at age 12, 13 or 14."

X. After an Injury—The Rehabilitation Process

The sports medicine physician will diagnose and establish a treatment plan for your injured child, but most effective treatment plans require a rehabilitation program designed by the sports medicine therapist. Rapid changes in sports medicine make it well worth your effort to find the most "sport appropriate" therapist for your child's type of injury. Protocols of only 10-15 years ago may now appear to have been designed during the "dark ages."

The Therapist—A Key Player

The therapist is a key player in safely returning your child to sports activities, and the therapist who has played sports and is familiar with your child's sport will be able to relate to your child, gain his confidence and offer a supportive relationship. As Roskin explains, "There are 10 different therapists in our Duke clinic and one is a woman who is a dancer. If a dancer comes in, I may know how an ankle works, but I don't know anything about the motions of a pirouette. It makes no sense for me to plan a course of therapy when the dancer/therapist can offer in-depth knowledge of dance requirements combined with therapeutic techniques. On the other hand, I do have an in-depth knowledge of baseball and its requirements, and I do rehabilitation and prevention programs for baseball players and 'overhead athletes' of all ages."

The bodily motions involved in daily living and those of sports are vastly different. Since sports participation imposes so much more stress, *the best chance for a long-term safe return to play is through a program of exercises designed to adjust the body, step-by-step, to the stresses experienced in sporting activities. Once injured, treated and returned to play, athletes who want to stay in the sport should continue a home program designed to prevent re-injury.*

The Fearful, Injured Player

After an injury and/or surgery, many youngsters are fearful of returning to

23

full play. These players can be helped by a knowledgeable rehabilitation specialist's support. The supervised, step-by-step increases in sports activities help an athlete gain confidence and safely return to play. A good sports therapist will advise when, and at what level, play should commence.

Injured players who suffer unresolved psychological trauma may require referral to a sports psychologist or child psychologist.

Stick with the Plan

Do not be tempted to skip the rehabilitation process to avoid the "extra" expense. Roskin tells us that good sports therapists have learned that keeping kids in the program is the only way to safely return them to play. "This means paring down the rehabilitation steps to include only those necessary exercises, and teaching kids how to do the exercises at home with periodic check-ins." He warns against trying to finish a program too early to "fit insurance." Many therapists will tailor the therapy sessions to fit insurance needs if you check requirements in advance and work out a plan. A premature return to play increases the probability of re-injury, thus starting the healing and rehabilitation process anew.

XI. The Injured Child — A Surprise Benefit

For many injured youngsters, the slow return to competition may feel like an eternity. Dr. Speer usually tells the athlete, "this is going to be a very maturing experience for you. To come through this successfully you are going to learn discipline and patience. It's slow, boring and methodical. First, you must follow the rehabilitation and exercise programs. Second, you must have a sense of duty to yourself not to do the things you shouldn't do when away from supervision."

The end product, a healthy return to action, often means the athlete has mastered two very important life skills — self-discipline and patience.

Cousy's Lucky "Break"

Basketball legend Bob Cousy once broke his right arm in high school. During the extended healing period, "the Cooze" did everything with his left hand — eating food, opening doors, writing school reports, *and* dribbling a basketball for hours on end! Years later, he credited this injury with making him a better player. "It was during this time that I really learned how to go to my left, a key factor in whatever success I enjoyed as an athlete," said Cousy.

XII. Four-Party Decision Making

An athlete may fear letting down the team or not appearing stoic or tough enough more than he fears further injury. For these and other reasons, you not only have the right, but the obligation, to be a fully informed decision-maker when determining whether, or when, your child plays, or plays hurt.

The four parties involved in decisions regarding athletic injuries to children may end up aligned as follows: coach and player versus parent and physician/therapist.

23

The first two parties are often the least cautious about the consequences of injuries; the latter two parties are often the most reasoned. (Although some parents are as stubborn as players or coaches in failing to seek treatment, or trying to return a child to play too early.)

Dealing With the Coach When a Player is Injured

When your player is injured you may find it a difficult task to deal with the coach. Coaches may have sports expertise, but few possess in-depth knowledge about injuries or the physiology of the joints. "There is often a bit of a blind spot here," says Dr. Speer. "Some coaches are simply not receptive to information from parents or physicians."

Compounding the problem is that many kids, perhaps even yours, have little sense of their boundaries or of possible long-term harm. If a coach is pushing your child to play when it is possibly unsafe or too early following an injury, follow these guidelines:

- Don't let the coach and child decide when it "feels okay to play." You and your child's medical expert should be the primary decision-makers.
- A child may "feel okay" long before a safe return is possible, especially in repetitive motion injuries.
- The parent *must* be the child's front line advocate for a safe return to play.
- If necessary, have the doctor talk to the coach and explain the medical basis for the decision. Most physicians are willing to do this.

XIII. What About Playing in the Big Game or the Last Game of the Season?

Depending upon the type of injury, sport, position played, time of the season, and the age of the child competing, a physician may, with specific guidelines for the game, appropriately allow a child to play the big (or last) game. Remember, though, these "big game decisions" should be made by the sports medicine expert, not just by the coach and the athlete.

XIV. Are There Other Techniques to Help Prevent Sport Injuries?
The All Important Warm-Up

Warming up is the one mechanism in injury prevention which Dr. Speer considers indispensable. Youngsters should not walk out onto the field and just start playing. They should first engage in light jogging or some other gentle aerobic activity to get the muscles lightly warmed up before starting more intense play or practice. *The light warm-up should always precede any stretching.*

XV. To Stretch or Not to Stretch?
Age is a Key

Most children and adults have gone through the pre-game ritual of stretching. When asked whether this actually helps young children prevent sports injuries, Dr. Speer explained, "I never tell them not to stretch, but I insist on a light warm-up prior to any stretching. The importance of stretching is pretty much related to a youngster's age." Youth league players from the ages of 5-12 generally do not require significant stretching. Stretching, however, becomes more important as athletes climb the age ladder. By 15, Dr. Speer recommends that athletes be stretching and by 20 "it is mandatory."

"If a 20-year-old fails to stretch he or she probably won't be playing long," says Dr. Speer.

After an athlete has been injured, stretching is vital. In most cases, post-injury rehabilitation includes very specific warm-ups and stretches.

XVI. Do Young Athletes Need Weight Training?

Physicians and athletic leagues usually categorize young players by four major age groups:

- Early youth ages 5-10
- Upper youth ages 11-14
- High school
- Collegiate

Is weight training recommended for players at any of these four age levels?

Early Youth Ages 5-10: Children in this age range are simply too physically and mentally immature, and lack the knowledge and self-discipline to have even possible minor benefits outweigh the risks of weight training. In this age range, children lack the necessary hormones for weigh training to make any difference. Dr. Speer states, "Without testosterone and a more mature metabolic profile it's a pointless exercise." Any strengthening format for a particular sport would simply involve practicing and playing the sport without over-doing it. Regular play activities such as running, swimming, biking, skating and outside games offer adequate fitness and strengthening for youngsters in this category!

Upper Youth Ages 11-14: Even at this age range weight training will not be all that helpful, but it can be a time for learning and understanding proper techniques. Dr. Speer tells us, "The child this age will not see big gains in strength because it is not physiologically possible. If you see a very muscled 14-year-old, he is probably more physically advanced age-wise, or he could be using androgenic aids."

In this age range, an athlete who either wants a program to prevent injury, or has already been injured and is in rehabilitation would use resistance bands, with heavier bands as the child grows. Older athletes in this age group may be allowed very light weights. Resistance band protocols may be especially helpful in strengthening and balancing muscle groups in arms, shoulders, backs and chests of "overhead athletes."

High School and College Athletes: Large variations in growth patterns may still influence the point at which weight training has the most useful benefits for young athletes in high school and college. Athletes this age are clearly developing the metabolic profile necessary to obtain benefits from weight training. The sport chosen may also dictate whether a weight regimen is of serious benefit. For example, athletes in injury-prone positions/sports may find preventive programs especially beneficial. Also, a wrestler might gain more sports-specific benefits than a cross-country runner.

Is Supervision Required in Weight Training? From the start, a child must be under the direction of somebody other than his peers. When beginning a program, seek out a sport therapist, physician, or personal trainer for advice on how to properly lift and train. Periodically thereafter, as the child grows and lifting abilities change, get an updated training program and re-check techniques being used.

Dr. Speer feels it is *never* a good idea to allow dead lifts and heavy squats for any age high school athlete. "They may try to mimic what they see a 20-year-old doing at the local gym, but it is not a good idea," said Dr. Speer.

Frequency Guidelines? The general adage of training every other day with 48 hours rest in between sessions is still reasonable. If a child wants to do some training every day, have him alternate upper body and lower body exercises. Mr. Roskin and Dr. Speer tell us that resting three to four days in between sessions is also fine. Just do not lift intensely more than every 48 hours for any particular body part!

XVII. Preventive Therapy Programs

Sports rehabilitation specialists can be very valuable allies in helping youngsters prevent sports injuries. Many of today's athletes play longer seasons or even year-round. This extended activity places more stress on youngsters growing bodies than the "seasonal play" of past decades. If your child plays a sport position with a high possibility of repetitive motion injuries (e.g., baseball pitcher's shoulder or elbow, soccer player's knees or ankles, swimmer's or tennis player's shoulder), it may be well worth taking the preventive step of having your athlete see a sport therapist for a program designed to minimize the risk of certain injuries, and to help keep your child playing safely.

A rehabilitation specialist such as Roskin will examine and evaluate an athlete's physical development, observe the child's mechanics and investigate the athlete's level of play. Roskin will then design an age-appropriate program for incrementally strengthening and balancing the different muscle groups used in the sport. The program may include proper warm-ups, resistance stretch bands, free-weights, and appropriate sport protocols for throwing, pitching, swinging a tennis racquet, etc.

Athletes who wish to stay in their sport may be advised to perform their exercises/protocols three days a week for maintenance of their muscle groups. Roskin points out that as the athlete grows, her program may require 6-12 month checkups for re-evaluation and updating.

XVIII. Educate Your Child About the Basics of Injuries and the Value of Expert Treatment

You do not want your child to be afraid to tell you, the coach, the trainer, or the doctor the truth about an injury. According to Dr. Speer, one important way to achieve this objective is to educate your child about the fundamental points of injuries, e.g., the single event injury versus the repetitive motion/overuse injury.

As part of your task, tell your young athlete that a respected professional has, as a principal objective, the goal of keeping the athlete in competition, not preventing the athlete from competing. In other words, you want your youngster to develop a trust in the expertise of the sports medicine specialist.

It is your job to teach your child the importance of honest communication regarding ongoing discomfort and pain incurred during sports activities! Discussions with many former college and professional athletes reveal that a *very* high percentage of these adults wish they had been more careful when dealing with their sports injuries. A number of former athletes also indicate that their current choices of fitness activities and recreational sports are seriously restricted by prior sports injuries.

XIX. A Great Idea! Organize a Sports-Medicine Forum for Your League or Area Leagues

Among the many fine suggestions offered by Dr. Speer, one especially good one is for sports parents and league administrators to arrange an annual community symposium on the issue of sports injuries. The idea is to contact local sports medicine experts and enlist their participation in a "live forum." The experts should include a sport's medicine orthopedic specialist, a sports rehabilitation specialist, and a certified trainer, who discuss the importance of the one-week pain rule, proper early diagnosis, treatment and rehabilitation. Depending upon the sports involved, it may be useful to have a coach or trainer demonstrate proper mechanics for particular sporting motions. In addition, a handout list of area sports medicine specialists and recommended trainers would be helpful to parents and coaches.

If you undertake such a project, try to organize the forum for multiple leagues/sports in your area, in order to assure good attendance.

Dr. Speer likes a live interaction approach as opposed to a videotaped presentation, "because it allows those present to have their specific questions properly addressed."

Who Should Attend?

Coaches, parents *and* players. One effective format is to organize the program at a local school in two parts:

- **Part A**—This part of the overall session is devoted to the youngsters (but attended by parents and coaches, all of whom will surely get important information).
- **Part B**—This second part of the session is more adult-oriented. "The youngsters may continue to sit in as long as they are quiet!" suggests Dr. Speer. Otherwise, you might have a team of volunteers supervise the children in the gymnasium or outdoor field during Part B.

Should You Compensate the Professionals?

If you can get a sponsor for uniforms, I'll bet that you can get a sponsor for such a forum. There is, however, nothing wrong with asking the professionals to appear on a pro bono basis (as long as you make good use of the professional's time).

What About Resistance?

Dr. Speer makes a very interesting point about coaches. "Some coaches, certainly not all, are resistant to much discussion about sports injuries. The reason is that they think people like me will keep their players out of action.

"In truth, my role is to keep the athlete playing, not prevent the athlete from being in the sport. I want them to play, *but* I want to find out what it is that needs to be done to *keep them playing.*"

XX. Ten Final Reminders on Intervention and Treatment of Injuries

Dr. Speer estimates that as many as 80%-90% of his surgical interventions on children under age 18 would not have been necessary if early evaluation and treatment had taken place. "If I were allowed to see most children within three weeks after the initial onset of the symptoms, I probably could have invoked a strategy of treatment that would have avoided surgery."

Keep these 10 points in mind:

1. Early diagnosis and treatment generally lessen loss of time from games or competition, and early treatment is most likely to reduce long-term medical costs.

2. Teach your child to always tell you if he suffers *any* head injury or if he has any pain or even "feels" discomort. Some players may not identify discomfort as pain.

3. Keep track of the pain or discomfort and follow the one-week rule.

4. Acuteness/severity of pain is not the only guideline for determining the need for evaluation or treatment.

5. The fact that a child is able to play with the pain does not determine whether it is safe or unsafe pain. Obtain early expert diagnosis to determine whether pain is "safe" or "unsafe."

6. If pain is unsafe, get early treatment and follow the plan of rest, rehabilitation or even surgery to prevent further injury.

7. If given a rehabilitation/preventive therapy program, be sure your athlete follows the plan.

8. "Safe pain" that goes away and later seems to return at the same location may be an entirely different condition. A growing child should be re-evaluated for any "new" or "returning pain" lasting more than one week.

9. A diagnosed "safe pain" which changes in nature, for example the pattern or severity of pain, may require re-evaluation.

10. Diagnosis and treatment from sports medicine experts with expertise in a specific sport is best, because they are most current on the types of injuries, treatments and rehabilitation protocols for athletes in those sports.

SECTION VI

DIVERTISSEMENT!

SPORTS POEMS WITH A MESSAGE

Chapter 24

"DIVERTISSEMENT"

Divertissement — a diversion or entertainment.

I offer such an interlude in the form of seven sport-themed poems that I have written, many of which contain a message or lesson. The accompanying illustrations have been drawn by Frank Galasso. Twelve more of my poems have been incorporated into various chapters.

The Center for Sports Poetry

Poetry has many fine earmarks; it slows us down, helps us to question, contemplate, discover and prioritize. We developed the Center for Sports Poetry *(www.internationalsport.com /cspoetry)* at the Institute for International Sport to encourage young people to write sport-themed poetry as a means of creative expression. Pass the word to your young athlete!

24

Frank Galasso

Distant Memory

That bygone time
When you stole the ball
And made the shot
To win the game
And felt a joy
Unlike any since
Is long forgotten
By all but a few
But never by you!

First Love

He once read
that love
required
an object

aside from family
the first object
of his devotion
was not a schoolgirl

but a round, rubber sphere
taut with air
and tiny, protruding dimples
to aid his grip.

He dribbled it
when dry,
palmed it
when wet.

It accompanied him
on the journey
from push shot
to jumper

served as catalyst
for choosing sides
and seizing lessons
from laurel and loss.

At evening's close
torpid from
the day's pounding
on hot or frigid asphalt

24

the rotund bunkmate
rested
still and sure
atop his bed.

When a shard
of glass
punctured its
rubber skin

Al Banks
the gas station owner
helped him apply
a four-tailed bandage

to halt
its oxygen
from seeping out
and deflating his joy.

He watched it age
the protruding dimples
transforming first
to a smooth, seamless surface

soon deformed
by boil-like air bubbles
that subverted
its stable bounce.

As the fullness of life
unstrapped its
full court press
of joy and woe

he would remain
forever faithful
to that first object
of his love

a starbright, Spalding basketball
which he first saw
resting under
the Douglas Fir

on Christmas morning
1956.

Frank Galasso

Frank Galasso

Real Esteem

It is earned
Not bestowed

By undue praise
Or privileged ways.

It is values implanted
Not favors granted

An ongoing quest
Of principled best.

Frank Galasso

24

The Tightrope of Early Promise

A seven-year-old shows up one day
Dazzles them all with his dashing play.

His speed and agility make them swoon
"This boy will be a great one soon."

And so begins a journey fast
Of favors first, and scruples last.

"You are so special," he hears them coo
"No need to do what others do."

Decades later, faded fame
No one cares about his game.

The wistful theme of his memoir
The soured hopes of the former star.

Perspective

In exhorting the team
To glory and fame
The coach will roar
In tonight's game,
You will all taste more
Than most do
In a lifetime.
Yet tasting real living
Goes past the acclaim
A teenager reaps
From a two-hour game
Scaling sports hills
All well and good
As long as life skills
Are learned and understood.

Frank Galasso

Remembering Priorities

Crossing the finish line
Of a week on the run
He finds quiet comfort
In a bedroom chair
Gazes proudly
At his sleeping son
Protected well
By a teddy bear.

On this week's trip
A gift he bought
A coalescence
Of hope and love
First step en route
To the town's sandlot
He rests on the bed
A baseball glove.

"In coming days
I'll show him how
My tips will help
My boy to shine."

Stops short to muse
On a prior vow.

He'll chase his own dream, not echo mine.

A Shallow Premise

Ramrod straight
Clarion and sure
The doctrinaire coach
Wags his finger and chides

"Sports doesn't
Build character
But it does
Reveal character."

I peel off
The first layer
Of the coach's dogma
By reflecting back

To an athlete
I exalted
In my
Early youth

An older boy
Whose physical skill and steady hand
Had sold the town
On his moral command

But then, with sweep of time
And speed of light
His silky moves
Took unwelcome flight

Unprepared for
The epilogue of sport
And with no market skills
Of any real sort

He plummeted hard
In sad free fall
Seeking condolence
From alcohol

He fathered a son
Yet did not marry
The weight of paternity
Too heavy to carry

When challenges called
Such as raising his son
His common refrain
Was to pivot and run.

A word of advice
To that well-meaning coach
Base your lessons
On a more studied approach

When dispensing guidance
To impressionable youth
Make certain the message
Is rooted in truth

Character is not fixed
In one's adolescence
Nor merely revealed
By physical evidence

Character development
Is a lifelong ascent
With daily chances
For self-improvement

The critical thinker
With judgment astute
Divides undeveloped notion
From moral absolute.

Frank Galasso

SECTION VII

DEVELOPING GOOD SPORTSMANSHIP

Chapter 25

SPORTSMANSHIP—IS IT BETTER OR WORSE?

"Ethics is an obedience to the unenforceable."
— English judge and mathematician, Lord Moulton

Some of the most poignant conversations I have had involved successful coaches and athletes who expressed lingering regret over their "tainted victories." A common theme was: *In looking back on my career, I realize that employing unsportsmanlike tactics to win was not worth it.*

The Roots of National Sportsmanship Day

In 1989, I went to a high school basketball game that significantly changed my perspective on sports. Both teams had losing records and were eliminated from state tournament consideration. Because it was not a high stakes game, I didn't expect either coach to employ tactics of gamesmanship, defined in Webster's Dictionary as "the method or art of winning a game or contest by means of unsportsmanlike behavior or other conduct which does not actually break the rules." And I certainly didn't expect outright cheating.

With a minute left in the game, a player from the visiting team dribbled toward the hoop, charged into an opponent, and was called for an offensive foul. As the two teams headed to the other basket for the foul shots, I noticed that the home team coach made a hand signal to his team. I suspected the coach was employing the old trick of switching foul shooters.

Here is how it works: If a referee calls a foul and there is an appearance of uncertainty regarding who was fouled, some coaches take unfair advantage of the confusion by sending their team's best foul shooter to the line, as if that player had been the one fouled. *Let the referee or opponents figure out that the wrong player is on the line*, is the common directive.

At this particular high school game, neither the visiting team nor the referees noticed the switch. The home team's best foul shooter, not the boy who had been fouled, proceeded to make both ends of a one-and-one. Those two foul shots ended up being the margin of victory.

After the game, I met the winning coach for what I anticipated would be a handshake and a few words of conversation. Drained of color, his face reflected none of the usual satisfaction from victory, and I knew him well enough to raise the issue that was on my mind.

"Look," I said. "I did a lot of dumb things in the name of competition, but I need to ask you something; are you under so much pressure that you felt you had to switch foul shooters?"

"Yes," he replied, and then asked, "Could we go somewhere and talk?"

For the next two hours, we engaged in a thought provoking conversation that was both emotional and cathartic. We talked about why we went into coaching, and we agreed that ambition and the pressure to win often conspired against honor and idealism.

We also talked about the role of sportsmanship in athletics. Both of us acknowledged that this was the first time that either of us had engaged in a substantive dialogue on the issue, and that in our 25 combined years of coaching, neither of us had attended a coach's meeting or clinic at which the topic was addressed. By the end of the conversation, it was clear that such dialogue would benefit anyone associated with sports.

On the drive home, I began to formulate ideas for the creation of a National Sportsmanship Day (NSD). The next morning, I presented the notion to a trusted advisor, my college basketball coach, George Wigton, who was spending a sabbatical semester at our Institute for International Sport. George liked the concept. Six months later, with the help of our two Rhode Island Senators, John Chafee and Claiborne Pell, the United States Congress officially recognized National Sportsmanship Day *(www.international sport.com/nsd)*. On the first Tuesday of each March, NSD is celebrated by thousands of schools throughout the United States and abroad.

Is Sportsmanship Worse Now Than in the Past?

National Sportsmanship Day feedback tells us that the majority of people consider a lack of sportsmanship to be far more prevalent now than even a decade ago.

To that I say: "Beware of the fallacy of the innocent past!"

An Historical Perspective

"Serious sport has nothing to do with fair play... it is war minus the shooting."
— English author and journalist, George Orwell. (Written in 1948!)

I have competed as an athlete and coach since I was a young boy, and I have studied the evolution of American sport from the mid-19th century to the present. On the matter of sportsmanship, the good ol' days weren't always that good.

Charles Alexander's wonderful biography of Ty Cobb provides important insights into Major League Baseball in the early 20th century. One of the greatest all-around players in baseball history, Cobb was also one of the most Machiavellian athletes ever to compete. His many ploys included sharpening his spikes so his intentionally high slides into opponents would produce not only dropped balls but gory wounds and broken bones.

"Always aim for the wrists," was one war whoop from Cobb, a man well-versed in trash talking long before the term became common in sports vernacular.

Alexander's book on Cobb, and Robert Creamer's excellent biography of Babe Ruth, portray baseball in the early 20th century as a colorful and intensely competitive sport, but also one devoid of any widespread commitment to sportsmanship. In the infamous Black Sox scandal of 1919, the Chicago White Sox actually threw the World Series and "Say it ain't so, Joe," was the oft-quoted remark of a forlorn young fan allegedly directed at the accused Joe Jackson, a Cobb-like superstar. Banned for life for his complicity in the Series scandal, Jackson inspired the book *Shoeless Joe*, by W. P. Kinsella, that later became the inspiration for the movie *Field of Dreams*.

Other sports were rocked by wrongdoing as well. College basketball was badly shaken by a series of point-shaving scandals, the first of which took place in 1949 and involved three All-American players from the University of Kentucky, a program that was thought to be "untouchable" to gamblers. Professional football had its share of embarrassments, including a betting scandal in 1963 involving Green Bay Packers star Paul Hornung, who was suspended for a year for wagering on games.

From my days as a young player I remember the hard-nosed competition, the rewards for winning, and the disappointment, even shame, of losing. However, I recall little, if any, attention being paid to sportsmanship. When we started National Sportsmanship Day in 1991, we enlisted the aid of Senators Pell and Chafee to conduct a national survey of sportsmanship programs. The survey found that virtually no sportsmanship programs were in existence in schools or youth/recreation leagues at that time!

25

Reflecting on their observations of and experiences in sports, many people are prone to wistful thinking, and they ignore the cloudy side of the "good ol' days."

The Effect of Television

A fair assessment of the present state of sportsmanship should begin with the effect of television on people's thinking and actions. Driven by ratings, producers often highlight the sensational.

National Sportsmanship Day participants have provided us with numerous examples of television's aggressive and, at times, unbalanced reporting of bad or violent behavior in sport. In one case, a coach pointed to a typical February night when he estimated that 175 college men's basketball games were played. "To my knowledge, there was only one fight in the 175 games, and that fight was featured on the national news."

The media should continue to report on bad acts, yet all of us must assess where those bad acts fall within the context of the overall picture. Remember, when Ty Cobb lacerated an opponent's arm with his knife-edged spikes, the only people who saw it were those in attendance.

25

What is Better Today?

- *There is much more being done on behalf of sportsmanship today than even a decade ago.* In reviewing this premise with college, high school and youth league representatives, every person with whom I spoke confirmed that many sportsmanship programs are now in place. Sportsmanship has become a hot topic!
- *Less fighting because of greater penalties.* The only sport that seems oblivious to the highly effective deterrent of "taking the game away" is professional hockey, which continues to nod and wink at fights, a practice that could be changed with a stroke of the Commissioner's pen.
- *Many parents and coaches are genuinely interested in sportsmanship.* I make this statement based on the widespread commitment of many adults to National Sportsmanship Day programs through their active participation.

What is Worse Today?

- *Increased pressure to win and the availability of drugs have made use of performance enhancing substances, a practice that has made its way down to the high school level.*
- *There is greater disregard for sportsmanship ideals by a harmful subgroup*

of parents. This is not an indictment of the parental majority who support proper conduct and whose exuberance is confined to cheering for the team. There are, however, a growing number of parents who are overly involved, intense, and ambitious when it comes to their child's sports career. They focus only on winning and highlighting their child's play, leaving aside good sportsmanship and ethical behavior. While the majority of parents (and athletes) behave honorably, the small percentage of parents who act out seem to be getting worse in their misbehavior.

- *There are far more displays of player arrogance now than even a decade ago, as exhibited by regular trash talking and excessive celebration.* Muhammad Ali is one of my favorite athletes, but he is also the primary taproot of hubris in contemporary sports. Because he was such an original, and his behavior often contained an element of humor, he seemed more endearing than offensive to his fans. Not so with current trash talkers!

Yet trash talking does not pervade all professional sports.

25

There's No Trash Talking in Baseball!

"Once players reach the pinnacle of their profession, the focus is on behaving properly. Outwardly criticizing another Major League baseball player is considered unprofessional."
—Pitcher Tom Glavine

While at bat in a 1932 game, Babe Ruth was being heckled by the opponents, the Chicago Cubs. The Babe allegedly pointed to center field and hit the ball out of the park. "That kind of burned me and I said 'alright, you bums, I'm gonna knock this one a mile.'" The Babe went on to say, "I guess I pointed, too!"

Such "trash talking" was a staple of the early days of baseball. Yet such "bench jockeying" rarely exists anymore. There are three primary reasons:

1. The Major League Baseball Players Union has created a "brotherhood-like" atmosphere among the players.

2. Free agency has allowed players to leap from club to club, transforming teammates who are friends into former teammates who remain friends.

3. As Tom Glavine points out, the majority of contemporary baseball players are committed to intense competition combined with mutual respect.

Since these are admirable qualities you should reinforce in your young athlete, remember to tell your young star about this fine aspect of America's pastime. [16]

273

Impact of National Sportsmanship Day

"I predict that one of the many benefits of National Sportsmanship Day will be to raise the awareness of sportsmanship and ethical practices among millions of young people, coaches and parents. I am very excited about what this program will do, both on its own, and as a vehicle to encourage schools to create their own sportsmanship programs."

—Senator John Chafee at a 1990 Washington, DC press conference
to announce the creation of National Sportsmanship Day.

I am encouraged by the increased focus on sportsmanship. Our analysis of National Sportsmanship Day demonstrates its impact upon millions of young athletes, coaches, and parents, by favorably influencing their views on sportsmanship and encouraging responsible, sportsmanlike behavior.

Feedback from athletes, coaches, and parents tells us that well-planned discussions on the topic of sportsmanship are quite thought provoking. "The discussions made our athletes—and me—step back and consider what is really important in competition," wrote one college athletic director.

How to Enroll in National Sportsmanship Day

It's easy! Participating schools are provided with a free sportsmanship poster and instructional packet containing suggested activities, role-playing scenarios, right versus right conundrums, essay contests and discussion questions. The packet also provides details on how high school and college teams may enroll in "Team Sportsmanship," a program which involves high school and college teams visiting elementary and middle schools on National Sportsmanship Day. Each school is encouraged to adapt NSD to its own needs. You can receive our free informational packet by downloading it off the NSD website *(www.internationalsport.com/nsd)*.

ALL-AMERICAN SPORTSMANSHIP SCHOOLS

Each year, the Institute for International Sport selects All American Sportsmanship Schools. If your child's school is committed to sportsmanship, encourage a school administrator to nominate the school by visiting: (*www.internationalsport.com/nsd*).

Chapter 26

THE PRACTICAL VALUE OF GOOD SPORTSMANSHIP

Honorable Competition and *Arête*

The Greek word "*arête*" means "goodness/honorable." In ancient Greek athletics, *arête* encompassed the ideals of valor, skill and honor. At its core was the athlete's commitment to compete energetically but within the rules. In the coming years, the Institute for International Sport will aggressively promote our 21st Century version of *arête*—Honorable Competition— to coaches, athletes, and parents throughout the world. Honorable competition is a concept which parents must demand of their child and their child's sports programs.

Does Good Sportsmanship Mean Less Competitive Play?

Many people wonder if a commitment to sportsmanship results in a lesser degree of competitive resolve or intensity. Not at all. Good sportsmanship does not lessen the intense hard work, strenuous practice or competitive play of athletes. It encourages athletes to play seriously but fairly, and while winning is valued, it does not override the rules of fair play and honorable conduct. At its best, sportsmanship helps coaches, athletes, and parents focus their competitive urges within the rules of the game being played.

Extraordinary Courage Where I Least Expected It!

The most notable example of honorable competition I have ever observed took place in 1975, when I took my Kingswood-Oxford basketball team to Prague, Czechoslovakia. We were the first U.S. basketball team to play in a sanctioned tournament in Czechoslovakia, and a common theme among the other seven teams, five Czech and two Soviet, was "Beat the Americans."

Four days after our arrival, we advanced to the championship game, meeting the top-seeded team, Club Sparta of Prague. With less than a minute remaining in the game, and the score tied, one of our players stole the ball from the Club Sparta point guard and raced toward the basket. The Club Sparta guard quickly regained his control, caught up to our player and knocked the ball out of bounds. The referee's vision was blocked, and rather than guessing on the call, he asked the Club Sparta guard, "Who touched the ball last?" Before I could register my displeasure with the referee for placing this decision in the hands of the opponent, the Czech athlete indicated that the ball belonged to the U.S. team. The boy did this in front of a sellout crowd with live television coverage. We scored on the next possession, and went on to win the championship by two points.

When considering the courage and integrity exhibited by that young man, our triumph seemed almost inconsequential. He displayed the real meaning of honorable competition better than any athlete I have ever observed. When discussing our trip, my former K-O players often mention his noble deed.

As the photographer Ansel Adams stated, *"Sometimes it takes an act that touches the conscience to clear the vision."*

Poor Sportsmanship — Why It Happens

While we all hope that our children will not be involved in a display of poor sportsmanship, or a flagrant violation of the rules, it happens! Reasons include:

- Some athletes, including beginners, have never been taught the principles of good sportsmanship.
- Some beginners may appear to intentionally violate game rules, when they really don't have a full understanding of the rules.
- Some athletes are trying to please a parent and/or coach who, knowingly or not, sends the message that winning is everything.
- Some athletes are copying what they have watched on television.

26

- Some athletes have not learned that self-control, self-restraint and integrity are vital components of honorable competition.
- Some athletes know they will suffer no consequences for improper behavior, and may even be rewarded for inappropriate acts resulting in competitive advantage.
- Some athletes are actually taught that an act of gamesmanship or other inappropriate acts can give them the upper hand, and are encouraged to employ such tactics.

Making Good Choices

"But No One Ever Told Me"

Every parent has heard this refrain, and you can expect to hear it again and again, unless you preempt it by teaching positive guidelines for good sportsmanship and pointing out clear examples of unacceptable behavior. From youth league through college sports, your athlete will be presented with numerous opportunities to make choices involving good or bad sportsmanship, and honorable or dishonorable competition. Volunteer coaches, with limited time to work with a team, may not emphasize or even discuss issues of good sportsmanship. It is your parental responsibility to establish clear rules, discuss the rules, and explain what kinds of consequences will result if your player violates your rules for athletic competition.

Point out that rules apply both on and off the playing field, and that regardless of whether a referee or coach sees and calls a transgression, you will impose consequences if you see or hear about incidents of poor sportsmanship.

Guidelines For Athletes

The Five Principles of Honorable Competition

Tell your child that the following principles are at the heart of learning to compete honorably:

1. *Respect the game.* This includes showing respect for opponents, referees, coaches and fans.

2. *Play by the rules, and within the spirit of the rules.* Do not try to get away with cheating or taking shortcuts just because you think no one will notice or catch you. The only real victories are honest victories, untainted by cheating or gamesmanship.

3. *Play your best.* Understand that doing your best does not mean embarrassing or humiliating your opponent.

26

4. *Don't punch back, play harder.* When provoked, an athlete should ascend to the highest level of honorable competition by increasing focus and intensity, not by reacting in an undisciplined, unproductive way.

5. *Employ competitive self-restraint.* Play hard but with self-control.

Since a wonderful benefit of sports lies in the practice of honorable competition, feel free to approach your school or recreation league administrators to request that the five principles of honorable competition be included in program objectives.

Unacceptable Behaviors

In addition to teaching and reinforcing the five principles of honorable competition, it is helpful to give young athletes a specific list of unacceptable sports behaviors. Clear examples make it easier for children to understand, remember, and make correct choices when they are suddenly confronted with difficult situations.

Remember, some of the behaviors on the unacceptable list may not specifically violate game rules, but they do violate the spirit of the rules.

The Dirty Dozen

1. *Fighting,* even if another player starts or attempts to start a fight.

2. Any form of cheating, such as dishonest line calls or fouls.

3. Gamesmanship tactics, including harassment, heckling, trash talking, or other questionable methods to gain competitive advantage.

4. Scolding, bullying, teasing or humiliating one's teammate. At times, high school and college players, especially team captains, appropriately exhort or chastise other teammates, but this is different from simply scolding a youngster who is less skilled or makes a mistake.

5. Arguing with referees, coaches, teammates or fans.

6. Blaming others for your personal errors.

7. Tantrums or displays of anger after a mistake, loss or poor performance.

8. Selfish behavior, including ball hogging, bragging and failing to respect team rules.

9. Intentionally aggressive physical acts which are not part of a competitive, fairly played game. This includes contact intended to hurt someone, to illegally stop or impede a player, or to retaliate and get revenge.

10. Confrontational stances or faces conveying an "I dare you" or an "I can intimidate you" attitude.

11. Extreme self-congratulatory posturing after a touchdown, home run, or basket. This is different from hugging or congratulating a teammate.

12. Profanity or vulgar language.

When you observe any of the above behaviors, use them as a starting point for discussion with your child. Emphasize that many bad decisions and impulsive behavior result from losing one's temper or self-control. *Explain that self-control and self-discipline are essential elements in becoming an athlete who is admired as an honorable competitor.*

The Parents' Role

Youth League

Parents must help youth leaguers formulate and practice ideals of fair play, emphasizing the five principles of honorable competition. During youth league games and while watching sports on TV, watch for examples of good and bad behavior which can be used for casual discussion.

Imposing Discipline

If your child exhibits bad on- or off-field behavior or breaks team rules, who disciplines the child? Your response to poor behavior depends upon the level at which your child is competing, because this influences the balance of responsibility between you and the coach, and your child's responsibility to the team. At the youth league level:

1. During the game, it is just the coach.

2. After the game, if you feel a coach's discipline is adequate, a discussion in support of the coach may follow at home.

3. If the coach fails to discipline, or you believe the coach's discipline is too cursory:

   • Let the coach know that you have no problem if the coach imposes necessary consequences for poor sportsmanship or rule violations.

   • If infractions are minor, give your athlete a warning, and make it clear that next time you will impose home consequences.

   • If more than a warning is needed, choose a home consequence such as grounding, no TV, no video games, or no computer use except for homework.

   • If serious or repeated violations occur, inform your child *and* the coach that your child will sit out the next game.

26

Remember, at the youth league level, a volunteer coach may not have the inclination to emphasize sportsmanship or impose appropriate discipline.

The Most Dreaded Punishment — Missing the Game

One extreme form of punishment, effective with most athletes, is missing a game. In the late '70s, many college basketball conferences changed the penalty for fighting from expulsion from that game, to:

- First infraction — expulsion from that game and the next.
- Second infraction — expulsion for the entire season.

As a result of this effective rule change, fights in college basketball are now about as common as the hook shot!

If you see the need to rid your child of poor sportsmanship and home discipline has failed, taking away one or more games may be the most effective and appropriate decision.

McEnroe's Lesson

At age 30, after more than a decade of frequent outbursts during competition, John McEnroe was finally thrown out of a tennis match during the Australian Open. A series of profanities directed at a chair umpire and his supervisor resulted in the long overdue default.

Many years after the event, McEnroe, a bright and introspective person, commented on the incident. "If someone had done that to me when I was 18, I honestly think that a lot of things would have been different. The message I got early on was that I could get away with just about anything on the court. No one wanted me defaulted. The tournament director didn't want me defaulted; neither did the TV people. But if someone had nailed me, cost me a big tournament, the chances are I would have learned my lesson and not done it again. I mean, I'm not stupid. Tell me where the line is and I won't cross it. The message I got until Australia was that there was no line."

High School Level

Do parents still have a role in discussion of sportsmanship issues? *Yes!*

- At this age, a child will have learned key rules of sportsmanship, and your job is to reinforce these lessons through discussion and consequences.
- It is possible your high school athlete will come under pressure to violate rules. Subtle or unsubtle messages could come from a variety of

sources including teammates, coaches, or other parents who stress a "winning at any cost" or a "pushing the limits" philosophy. As a parent, it is your job to be aware of the sports environment, and intervene when appropriate.

- Should you discipline your high school athlete? In the following three scenarios, it is appropriate to impose home-based consequences that do not intrude upon team activities.

1. You see a pattern of rule or ethical violations unseen by a coach or referee.

2. The coach and referee see, but do not respond, to what you feel are serious or repeated violations of good sportsmanship.

3. The coach and referee notice violations and their response is inadequate.

- Should you take a game away from your high school athlete? Almost never, and only as a *very* last resort. If the coach fails to enforce proper codes of conduct, or encourages misconduct, take these steps:
  - Have a conversation with the coach, making it clear that you find certain behaviors unacceptable.
  - Tell the coach you would appreciate him taking disciplinary action when there is unacceptable behavior from your child.
  - Tell both your athlete and the coach that if it happens again, and goes unpunished, you will have no choice but to remove the athlete from one or more games.

College Level

Whether you are paying for a college education, or your young adult is receiving an athletic scholarship, you must maintain high expectations of your college student. *Your young adult is still under your watch.*
- Do you continue discussions with your young athlete? Most definitely!
- Do you still discipline your young adult or take a game away? No. It is the coach's and school's job to discipline athletes at this level.

There are two larger issues involved here:
1. If you believe your athlete's college team engages in unethical practices, perhaps you should ask your athlete if it is possible to maintain high personal standards while participating on such a team. Such dilemmas reinforce the importance of your child being prepared to make good choices.

2. Does your youngster deserve to be on a team after making unacceptable behavioral or ethical decisions.

26

Your Obligation!

"People do not become happy merely by satisfying their desires. They become happy by living within a belief system that restrains and gives coherence to their desires."
—*New York Times* journalist, David Brooks

The powerful allure of sports success can compromise values that athletes were taught by their parents. Whenever you see your child—including your college athlete—stray from the belief system taught at home, you not only have the right but the obligation to intervene. Your message: "I am not going to allow the bad side of sports to compromise your value system!"

Responsibility!

The "Standards of Behavior" Discussion You Must Have with Your Athlete

Following a speech at the United States Coast Guard Academy, I had a fascinating conversation with several cadets about societal expectations of certain groups, including varsity athletes. The discussion centered around two schools—one a U.S. military academy; the other a non-military private college. A strikingly similar "scandal" occurred on both campuses. The scandal at the military academy received front page coverage in every major American newspaper; the scandal at the private college received only minor local coverage. Virtually the same scandals—vastly different media reaction.

I later conducted an informal poll with several members of the media, presenting to each journalist the following scenario:

- A varsity high school or college athlete commits a bad act, ranging from a violation that requires school discipline (perhaps suspension) to something illegal.
- The same act is committed by a non-athlete (who is not involved in any other high-profile extracurricular activity at the school).

I then asked the journalists if and how media coverage would differ for the two examples.

- Each journalist told me that the varsity athlete's indiscretion would get far more coverage.
- Each journalist told me that even if a varsity athlete committed a lesser offense than a fellow student who was not engaged in a high-profile extracurricular activity, the athlete would still be accorded much greater coverage. "We're talking about 20 to 1 in coverage here...minimum," was the way one journalist explained it.

26

The Ten Reasons Your Athlete Must Adhere to High Standards of Behavior

An important point for your young player to understand is that being an athlete places the youngster in the "much greater public scrutiny" category. Here are the ten reasons why:

1. The behavior of athletes is more closely observed than that of other students—both in school and by the general public.

2. As much as any group, athletes are judged by the company they keep. This fact may require an athlete to disassociate from those who are not adhering to high standards of behavior.

3. The misbehavior of athletes is a media lightening rod—far more so than the misbehavior of most other students.

4. The misbehavior of an athlete can have highly public and embarrassing, if not devastating, consequences to the athlete's personal reputation.

5. The misbehavior of an athlete can be a source of great public embarrassment to the athlete's family.

6. The misbehavior of an athlete can have highly public and embarrassing, if not devastating, consequences to the reputation of the team, coaching staff and school.

7. The misbehavior of athletes can get coaches fired—whether or not the coach had anything to do with the misbehavior.

8. The academic status of athletes, including SAT scores and failing grades, is considered fair game by the media.

9. Rules violations and penalties imposed by a coach on the athlete are considered fair game by the media.

10. Considerate behavior by an athlete produces a generous amount of goodwill; inconsiderate behavior by an athlete produces a disproportionate amount of ill will.

26

Your final message on this issue: "Being an athlete is a privilege which carries certain responsibilities, as well as severe consequences for bad behavior." (Also, share this list with your athlete's coach.)

SELF-MONITORING IN INDIVIDUAL SPORTS & PICK-UP GAMES

In individual sports such as tennis or golf, and in pick-up games, situations arise where there are no coaches or referees to impose discipline or enforce rules. Well before any competition, make sure your child knows exactly what you expect, and understands that you will impose consequences for misbehavior. If, during a tennis or golf match, your child is guilty of serious rule violations, makes dishonest calls or displays unacceptable verbal or physical tantrums, it is your job to impose consequences. At the first sign of misbehavior, depending upon the severity of the transgression, either quietly warn or remove the child from competition.

Jim McDonald, Director of Tennis at Hollow Rock Racquet Club in Durham, North Carolina, states, "If you want to end such behavior it is best to take immediate, firm action. If one of my own children or a member of our tennis team displays such behavior, I end the match. Very seldom does the behavior repeat itself."

A great feature of tennis and golf is reliance on the personal integrity of the players, who are expected to call the lines fairly and penalize themselves according to the rules. The honor code of high-level golf makes cheating unforgivable.

The same need for self-regulation exists in playground and pick-up games, and parents should remind youngsters to make a habit of practicing honorable competition in all settings.

26

Why Be a Good Sport?

There may be times when your child expects practical justification of good behavior. Here are four examples of the practical value of good sportsmanship that you may wish to impart to your children, and to consider yourself!

I. Competitive Self-Restraint

One of the most intriguing exercises we undertook for this book was a survey of 500 highly successful individuals, from U.S. Senators to CEOs. Eighty-six percent told us that they had played sports in their youth. Many indicated that learning to compete while maintaining self-control was a benefit they had carried forward in life. Throughout this book, you will see the phrase "competitive self-restraint" employed to describe this invaluable quality.

People who are able to employ this mindset—whether on the field or in a job—almost always have a clear advantage over those who are unable to control their emotions.

Lesson

Parents should foster the notion of competitive self-restraint in their young athletes, and make it clear that a loss of self-control will result in clearly stated consequences, such as being pulled out of the next game or practice. Taking away a practice or game will almost surely cool the fiery temper of a young player in need of such a life lesson.

II. Parental Behavior at Games

When you attend a game in which your child is competing, your self-restraint is likely to be challenged, sometimes severely. Many parents take it very personally when a "bad call" or rough play occurs.

Whenever you feel that you are about to lose control, you should consider the unfortunate consequences that result from irate behavior.

Lesson

Never have I seen the decision by a parent to enter into a conflict at a sporting event prove to be a better idea than to retreat from a conflict!

III. Integrity Conflicts with Gamesmanship

Integrity is, according to Webster's Dictionary, "a steadfast adherence to a strict moral or ethical code." Gamesmanship is the "art or practice of winning games by use of questionable expedients."

Two clear points have emerged from my lectures at dozens of colleges and universities on behalf of the NCAA Foundation:

1. While most college students can offer a clear definition of sportsmanship, few even know the meaning of gamesmanship, and still fewer have considered how gamesmanship clashes with integrity.

2. Our surveys and interviews show that there is a definite correlation between gamesmanship practices in sports and "shortcuts" in other phases of life.

Lesson

Parents must help young athletes understand the meaning of gamesmanship, and that maintaining one's integrity begins with adhering not only to the rules, but to the spirit of the rules. Parents (and coaches) should share with young athletes a point from ethicist Michael Josephson: "Victory without honor is profoundly unsatisfying." This is particularly true in adulthood.

26

IV. Empathy and the Sports Experience

Some athletes and coaches believe that empathy toward opponents gets in the way of winning. Yet many of the greatest coaches and players are empathetic people who are discerning enough to respect the boundaries of fierce competition.

Young athletes should be presented with these simple guidelines:
- During the game, compete hard but within the rules.
- Know when victory is secured, and do not embarrass an opponent who is already beaten.
- After the game, always treat your opponent with civility and respect.

Lesson

Every parent and coach should make clear to a young athlete that empathy is not only at the core of a moral society, but an essential ingredient to fixing and maintaining relationships. A child who learns empathy will have a richer life than one who fails to cultivate this vital character trait.

Share with your young athlete my short verse on this matter, found on page 287.

Self-Respect

It is impractical to suggest to your young athlete that the "good guy" always wins the game, any more than the "good guy" always closes the business deal or wins the election. It is reasonable to tell your child that the "good guy" maintains his self-respect, and, in the end, may win the respect of others, even of some who do not employ the principles of honorable competition.

The brilliant careers of John Havlicek, Tiger Woods, Chris Evert, Annika Sorenstam, Gail Goestenkors, Joan Benoit Samuelson, Sue Bird, Jack Nicklaus, Jody Conradt, Lute Olson, Mia Hamm, Phil Mickelson, Grant Hill, David Robinson, Roger Federer, and John Wooden provide ample proof that good sportsmanship does not preclude being a great athlete or coach. Some of our most idealized sports heroes are cherished, in part, because of their good behavior on and off the field.

Frank Galasso

The Honorable Competitor

The honorable competitor
Is quick to discern
A valuable lesson
All players need learn:
The noble effort
Required to win
Stops at the point
Of rubbing it in.

Chapter 27

ENGAGING YOUR CHILD
IN SPORTSMANSHIP DISCUSSIONS

"Good communication is as stimulating as black coffee."
—American aviatrix and author, Anne Morrow Lindbergh

Mark Twain once observed that travel is fatal to prejudice. My experience with National Sportsmanship Day has convinced me that good discussion is fatal to bad sportsmanship. A key objective of National Sportsmanship Day is to encourage student-athletes, coaches, parents and administrators to discuss key sportsmanship issues. This is why I recommend that your first step toward engaging your child in sportsmanship discussions is to visit our website at *(www.internationalsport.com/nsd)*.

What You Will Find

The National Sportsmanship Day website will present you with a number of age-based discussion topics and scenarios, including:

- Fifteen discussion questions for elementary and middle school students.
- A series of age-based discussion scenarios, including Right versus Right conundrums for elementary, middle, high school and college students.
- A special discussion topic for high school and college students on the Fourth Amendment and performance enhancing drugs.
- A a series of parent sportsmanship discussion questions.

Right versus Right

The Institute for Global Ethics *(www.globalethics.org)* recommends strategies for teaching ethics and making ethical choices, which I have applied to sportsmanship. Their "Right versus Right" method utilizes situations in which two points of view, neither of which is clearly wrong, and both of which have elements of right, may be in conflict with each other. Such a method helps a young person develop the all-important skill of critical thinking—*the ability to look at things from many sides and to analyze competing ideas.*

Sportsmanship Discussions

Discern: "To perceive the distinctions of; discriminate."
—The American Heritage Dictionary

Parents and coaches may present Right versus Wrong and Right versus Right problems to any age group in order to provoke meaningful discussion about sportsmanship issues. You should select discussion topics which are appropriate to the child's/team's age and sport, and highlight the issues upon which you want to focus. *Young athletes show great interest in sports-related dilemmas, and the good and bad behaviors of well-known athletes, coaches and teams provide interesting topics for youngsters.*

First, try a Right versus Wrong issue and then move to Right versus Right dilemmas. Such discussions offer your child opportunities to consider both sides of an issue, improve problem-solving skills, and develop important values based on honorable competition and good sportsmanship.

I. Topics to Discuss
Right versus Wrong

Topics incorporating a clear Right versus Wrong example are easier to grasp and allow participants to feel confident about their conclusion.

Let's look at some simple Right versus Wrong issues:

1. It is right for coaches to teach aggressive play within the rules, but it is wrong for coaches to encourage dirty play to gain an advantage.

2. It is right for an athlete to work hard to improve, but it is wrong for an athlete to use banned substances to enhance performance, possibly damage one's health, and to pressure fellow competitors to use such substances to "stay even."

3. It is right for alumni to financially support their college athletic programs, but it is wrong for an alumnus to attempt to "bribe" a high school athlete in order to influence the athlete's decision to attend a school.

Right versus Wrong Discussion Example

The star player is caught drinking the night before the championship game, in violation of school and team rules. First, make these points:

- It is right for the coach to penalize the player for serious rule violations by keeping him out of the next game.
- It is right for parents, players and fans to want their full team to participate in the championship game.
- It is wrong for a player who commits a serious rule violation to be allowed to play the next game, whether it is a regular season or championship game.

Discussion Questions

- If the player is penalized, is the coach also penalizing the team, students, parents, faculty, staff, and fans who have worked for and supported the team?
- If the player is not penalized, what message is the coach sending to the rest of the team and to the community as a whole?
- Is the desire to win adequate reason not to "play by the rules?"
- Does the desire to win the championship game ever excuse the failure to enforce the rules?
- Should the level of punishment have anything to do with the importance of the next game?
- Should the punishment be based on the seriousness of the violation?
- Should a leader make decisions based on principle, if that principle collides with public sentiment?

Right versus Right

Right versus Right dilemmas are far more difficult to judge than Right versus Wrong dilemmas. Yet Right versus Right dilemmas provide opportunities for participants to analyze an issue by looking at the merits of both sides. Ask athletes to consider where they stand on the following Right versus Right issues:

1. It is right to expect good decorum on the field of play, as it is right for an athlete to celebrate the joy of a touchdown.

2. It is right for the 6'5" high school basketball player to want to learn the perimeter game to better his chances for a college scholarship, as it is right for his high school coach to want this youngster to play close to the basket and help the team by rebounding.

27

3. It is right for college professors to expect athletes to be serious students, as it is right for college coaches and administrators to want to recruit players they hope will field a winning team and unite the campus.

4. It is right for athletes to do their best during a game, as it is right for the coach not to run up the score against a struggling opponent.

5. And here is one that you may face, if you haven't already: It is right for a youngster with good skills and potential to want to play better travel team competition. It is also right for family members to question this choice because of the cost, the time commitment and travel involved.

Right versus Right Discussion Example I

In basketball and football, each team is given the same number of time-outs. Many coaches save their timeouts for strategic use in late-game situations. Such strategic use often includes what is called "icing the shooter or kicker." "Icing" means that with only seconds left in a game, an athlete who is ready to attempt a field goal or foul shot is subjected to a timeout by the opposing coach. The coach obviously hopes to upset the athlete's equilibrium so he will miss the winning kick or foul shot.

- It is right for a coach who prudently saves some timeouts to be able to strategically use them late in the game.
- It may also be right to suggest that "icing the player" is an unacceptable example of gamesmanship when used against young athletes.

Discussion Questions

Discussions involving "icing the shooter" should include these questions: At what level, if any, is icing unacceptable?

Youth League?
Middle School?
High School?
College?
Professional sports?

Right versus Right Discussion Example II

A high school tennis program has only six team members, the minimum necessary to compete in the conference. The number two player develops a sore elbow, and her parents are torn between allowing her to continue playing or removing her from at least a week of matches.
What should the coach do?

- It is right to rest the player's arm for one week to see if the pain goes

27

away, and if the pain continues, to schedule a diagnostic evaluation.

- It is also right for the team to want the player to compete so the other five players may also compete and avoid forfeiting the matches.

Discussion Question

- Even if the injury seems minor, should the player risk suffering a more serious injury by playing and helping out the team?

This is an example of a tough issue that requires careful thought and analysis. Such an issue pits what is best for the individual against what is best for the team.

II. Tips For Moderating

1. Initiate discussions by asking your child/team to consider whether the problem is a Right versus Wrong or Right versus Right dilemma.
2. When moderating a discussion, do not force your opinion on the child or the team. Remember, this is a problem solving exercise in which opinions may emerge late in the discussions or even afterwards.
3. Pick discussion topics relevant to the team's age and sport, and which provide opportunities to think about the many sides of an issue.
4. Remind the participants that the ramifications of a tough decision are not always pleasant.
5. If appropriate, ask players how they would like to be treated in a particular situation. "Do unto others as you would have them do unto you," is always thought provoking. A child may have a very different reaction if asked to place oneself in a particular situation.
6. Finally, as you engage your child and team in discussion, ask:
   - Based on the circumstances, does one choice seem more principled?
   - Based on the circumstances, does one choice seem better for more people?
   - Even if it is better for more people, does that make it the right thing to do?
   - Based on the circumstances, which side is the most honorable and/or has the strongest argument?
7. Finally, when considering any issue, ask players to look carefully at whether the problem falls into one of four broad categories proposed by the Institute for Global Ethics:
   - **Honesty versus loyalty**, e.g., does the team captain report teammates who drink and violate curfew the night before a game?
   - **Individual versus community**, e.g., do the needs of an injured player override the needs of the team?

27

- **Short-term versus long-term results or consequences**, e.g., steroid use intended to improve strength, but which permanently damages one's health.
- **Justice versus mercy**, e.g., it may be appropriate to dismiss a player for serious rule violations, as it may be appropriate to allow a first offender a second chance.

III. Restating the Issue

At the end of any discussion, it is helpful to restate the issue for your child/team. As an example, let's take "on-the-field celebration"—a common point of disagreement between adults and youngsters.

"Okay, I take the side that it's a team game and players who are too self-congratulatory take away from the value of team play, and lack modesty and good sportsmanship.

"You take the side that sports are supposed to be fun, and players should be allowed to express their joy."

IV. The Resolution of a Tough Issue

As the Institute for Global Ethics suggests, resolution of complex Right versus Right issues can develop through compromise between the two sides.

In the case of on-the-field celebration, the middle ground may lie in a rule that allows the expression of joy as long as, in the judgment of the coaches and officials, the expression is moderate and does not turn into disrespect toward opponents.

V. The Aftermath of a Tough Right versus Right Decision

Because there is merit in each side, Right versus Right issues may take a while for a child to develop a point of view. That viewpoint may change with increasing knowledge and experience. Think about how your own views have changed on issues!

The process of analysis and problem solving may be as important as the resolution. Carefully weighing the merits of both sides of a sports issue, while trying to reach common ground, is a valuable learning process. As noted, a vital step in developing good sportsmanship is thoughtful discussion about issues of sportsmanship. At the end of the discussion, challenge the participants to come up with their own Right versus Wrong or Right versus Right problem for the next team discussion.

The Benefits of Ethical Discussions

"Every scientific advance carries its own ethical challenges."

— Anonymous

Issues of honorable competition and sports-related ethical dilemmas help engage youngsters in serious and stimulating discussion. These conversations offer opportunities for reinforcing the positive values which sports can help teach children. Consideration of the many facets of an issue and thoughtful analysis of problems are learning skills which are valuable for children of any age. Through the use of discussion examples, your athlete may begin to understand that decisions based on principle may not always be popular, but are always worthy of respect — especially self-respect! Such analysis and discussion can help prepare your child for more complex ethical dilemmas that lie ahead — such as the one addressed in the anonymous quotation above.

Be sure to visit the website for Global Ethics *(www.globalethics.org)* to learn more about this organization's fine suggestions for applying ethical discussions to life issues.

Decisions of Principle

Decisions of principle are at the root of an ethical society. Help your child understand this through sports-related discussion and examples.

A True Story

In the championship game of the 2006 Colonial Conference Men's Basketball Tournament, a key George Mason player punched an unsuspecting opponent in the groin. The moment that Jim Larranaga, head men's coach at George Mason, saw the act, he benched the player for the rest of the game, even though the league championship, and a possible NCAA bid, were on the line.

George Mason lost the game. The following day, still uncertain of an NCAA bid, Coach Larranaga suspended the offender for the next game — be it in the NCAA or NIT.

Coach Larranaga was not ordered by any administrator to take either action, but he did so to teach the young man a life lesson, and to remind every player in his program that his rules of conduct were incontestable. Some questioned his decision, feeling the team needed this top player to advance in the tournament. Duke men's basketball coach Mike Krzyzewski took a different view: "I got goose bumps thinking about his integrity."

As history shows, the results of Coach Larranaga's decisions of principle

27

did not prevent — and may have helped — his 11th-seeded George Mason team advance to the 2006 Final Four, one of the most extraordinary accomplishments in NCAA men's basketball tournament history.

Reactions to Decisions of Principle

After relating this true story, remind your athlete that following a decision of principle, the following reactions may occur:

- In the immediate aftermath, the decision of principle is frequently met with anger or disappointment, especially by those directly affected by the decision.
- As time goes on, some people retreat from their prior negative reaction and begin to contemplate the moral courage it took to make the decision.
- The principled decision maker often gains the respect and admiration of others.
- Such decisions often turn out quite well, particularly over time!

A Right versus Right History Lesson!

When the International Olympic Committee awarded the 1980 Olympic games to Moscow, a common fear among non-communist countries was that the Russians would turn the event into a "propaganda show," similar to what Hitler attempted to do with the '36 Olympics (until Jesse Owens ruined his plans!).

Ten months before the 1980 Games were to begin, the Soviet Union invaded Afghanistan, and Jimmy Carter made a decision that is still hotly debated within international sports circles. President Carter pressured the United States Olympic Committee to boycott the Games, which it did. Sixty other countries joined in the boycott, but not U.S. allies such as Great Britain, France and Italy. President Carter's decision was met by praise in some quarters and scorn in others, notably by many athletes who were not allowed to compete.

The Carter boycott decision provides all of the elements of a stimulating Right versus Right decision. Encourage your child's coach (or teacher) to set up a Right versus Right discussion on this issue. Participants should research the main facets of the 1980 boycott, and then address these two "rights:"

- It is right to do whatever one can to protest the violation of human rights.
- It is also right to keep politics out of sports, and allow those who have trained hard to have the once-in-a-lifetime opportunity to compete in the Olympics.

27

The Value of Critical Thinking

When college faculty throughout the United States were asked: *What is the most important objective of a college education?*, the respondents rated critical thinking—the ability to look at both sides and to analyze competing ideas—as the number one priority.

Aristotle wrote, "The mark of an educated mind is to be able to entertain an idea without necessarily accepting it." One's critical thinking skills are enhanced by reading and discussion, including discussion of sportsmanship and other ethical conundrums in sports. Such discussions are not only stimulating, but can also play a valuable role in enhancing your child's critical thinking skills.

27

SECTION VIII

THE COLLEGE RECRUITING SERIES

Chapter 28

THE COLLEGE RECRUITING PROCESS

T he college recruiting process involves a wide variety of issues that are addressed in the following eight chapters. If your child aspires to play college sports, I *strongly* advise you to read all eight chapters. While some may be more relevant to your child's particular needs than others, these chapters will provide you with information that helps clarify what can be a confusing, if not overwhelming, experience.

Your Role in the Recruiting Process

"There are some tasks that require shared responsibility.
The college recruiting process is one of these tasks."
—Former St. George's School (RI) headmaster, Chuck Hamblet

Throughout this book, I strongly advocate for a sports parenting approach that fosters self-reliance in your child. In the case of the college recruiting process, some of the tasks involved should be undertaken by the recruit. However, since this is a *very* time consuming and complex undertaking, not all tasks should be handled by the recruit. Rather, I recommend a "team approach" which involves a sharing of responsibilities among the parents, player, coach, guidance counselor and others.

28

Why the Team Approach?

Handling such a complicated project, without the guidance of adults, is simply too much for a 17-year-old.

Recruiting at all three college levels, Divisions I, II and III, is *highly* sophisticated. Some coaches are ethical recruiters, while others are expedient if not dishonest; *all* know that recruiting is the lifeblood of a successful college athletic program.

Three Reasons for an Adult "Guidance Team"

1. College recruiters are experienced in cultivating relationships, and skilled in employing a range of tactics to sway a recruit—including the "guilt card" if the recruit appears to be heading in another direction."Our coaching staff recruited you first"; "We want you more than the other school"; "We've spent more time recruiting you than anyone else" are three common refrains heard by fickle recruits.

2. The verbal scholarship offer is often a fragile proposition that carries no binding obligation on either side, and is, according to Tim O'Shea, head men's basketball coach at Ohio University, "frequently used by college recruiters as 'recruiting rhetoric only.'"

3. Most high school recruits are uncomfortable saying "No" to an adult, particularly one in a position of perceived power. The objective of the "guidance team" is to buffer the overly aggressive recruiting tactics of some coaches, and to provide wisdom and balance.

Sports Excellence Does Help with College Admission

"Most of the best colleges do not want the well-rounded student
as much as they want the well-rounded class."
—Princeton University Athletic Director, Gary Walters

Translation—a highly skilled athlete or musician often has a major advantage in gaining college admission.

The majority of college presidents, including those at prestigious schools, agree that fielding competitive sports teams is desirable because:

- A successful sports team, even at the Division III level, is often the most direct link between the alumni and the school.

- A successful team creates an atmosphere of optimism and excitement on and off campus, and improves school name recognition. Many schools report that successful teams enhance the number of admission candidates and fundraising, although this point is debated among educators.

28

Schools Which *Do Not* Award Athletic Scholarships

In most non-scholarship athletic programs, each head coach gets to submit a "priority recruiting list" to the admissions office. At virtually every school, this priority recruiting list can help a youngster's chances for admission. "I generally submit 10 men's tennis players each year," stated one Division III tennis coach. "In all cases, they have to fall within the general admission standards set by our school. There is no question, however, that my top four or five tennis prospects will probably be admitted if I recommend them, even if their grades, class rank or SATs are below our average admittee."

Wylie Mitchell, Director of Admissions at Bates College, said, "As long as a prospective student-athlete fits within the range of academic requirements for admissibility, we will consider that student-athlete." Most schools employ a similar policy.

Mitchell further explains, "If Beverly has a 2025 SAT, and is in the top 5% of her class but has no extracurricular activities, and Debbie has a 1875 SAT, and is in the top 10% of her class but has a strong soccer or theatre background, we may well take Debbie over Beverly simply because we think Debbie may contribute more to our campus life. Like most schools similar to Bates, we will not take anyone who falls outside of our academic range. We value excellence in any extra-curricular activity since it demonstrates a work ethic, ability to focus, a commitment to learning and improvement, and sometimes to teamwork. Admissions committees appreciate the expenditure of time and energy necessary to attain excellence in art, sports, music or other extra-curricular activities."

Schools Which Award Athletic Scholarships

There is no question that many schools which award athletic scholarships will accept blue-chip athletes in the *very* lowest range of the school's acceptable standards for admission. This is true at many of the finest Division I academic institutions in America, especially in the high-profile, revenue-producing sports.

When an athletic scholarship offer is tendered, a coach should always inform the student-athlete and parents that the scholarship is dependent upon the applicant meeting the school's admission requirements. No offer is final until a letter of acceptance is received. Problems arise when athletic scholarships are offered before transcripts are reviewed by the admissions office.

28

303

The Academic Index

The "academic index" uses a formula combining SAT, class rank, and SAT IIs to compute a student's index score. Schools establish a range of acceptable index scores which fit the school's admissions parameters. Many schools employ an academic index, but the majority do not "advertise it." If your athlete is considering a school which uses the academic index, ask whether the student's index score falls within the school's range for admission.

When the College Search Should Begin

"It is vital that the high school student be very organized in the college application process. This should begin with the student clearly laying out a written application plan in the summer prior to senior year. The plan should encompass deadlines and goals."
—Assistant Head for Institutional Advancement
Providence Country Day School (RI), Jim Skiff

A youngster should begin to consider college options early in the high school career and absolutely no later than midway through the junior year. Emphasize the importance of looking at all aspects of a school. Far too many athletes wrongly allow sports to dominate their choice.

Your student needs an early start in order to:

1. Perhaps be motivated to work harder in high school in order to meet tough admissions requirements at some schools.

2. Research different schools to determine how they conform to a youngster's academic and athletic interests.

3. Develop a college list which includes schools with a range of admissions requirements—some that will be a reach, some in the middle, and some at which your student is certain of acceptance.

4. Make sure that the student likes all the schools on this list, not just the "reach" schools. This will be difficult to accomplish without an early start.

5. Prepare for the possibility of an Early Decision application.

6. Avoid extra senior year stress brought on by a late start.

Remember, college sports are very demanding and the search should be aimed at finding schools where your athlete can balance academic and athletic goals. *Also, ask your athlete to consider whether each school would be satisfactory if he was unable to play a sport.* Many non-scholarship college athletes quit playing their sport after one or two years of college. (Very few college athletes on athletic scholarship quit.) The Harvard athletic department

28

employs the "broken leg question," i.e., if a student-athlete broke a leg, would the student-athlete still fit in at Harvard without the sport?

Preliminary Steps

At the beginning of the search process, your child should look into a wide variety of schools. With the help of the school guidance counselor or college admissions advisor, a student should first evaluate basic information relating to individual interests and needs, including:

- Location
- Distance from home
- Number of students
- Size of campus
- Campus setting—rural, urban or suburban
- Academic demands and strengths and weaknesses, including departments of possible majors. How does the school match with your student's aptitude and skills?
- Admission standards—see *The College Board's Guidebook, Peterson's College Guide, the College Prowler Series,* and other college guides for detailed information.
- Cost (this may be more important to you than your child!)
- Financial aid opportunities (Ditto!)
- Quality of the athletic program, which includes:
  - The reputation of the coach
  - The tradition and success of the program
  - Skill level required of players, and opportunity to play
  - Athletic facilities
  - Support staff, including academic advisors, strength coaches, and sports medicine personnel
  - Time demanded by the athletic program

To determine which schools might best fit a student's profile:

1. Study the website of each school of interest.

2. If possible, make some informal campus visits as early as the summer prior to the high school junior year or during spring vacation of the junior year. These may be the only times your child will have the opportunity to make college visits until the summer prior to the senior year. Keep in mind that visits during the academic year offer a clearer picture of campus life.

28

3. Contact every school of possible interest and ask to be placed on the admission mailing list, as well as the mailing list of the particular sport of interest. This is most easily done via the school's website.

4. Begin to follow some of the teams under consideration, and if possible, attend some of their games.

5. If possible, ask students—including student-athletes—who attend target list schools for their honest view of their school. *In the case of student-athletes, also ask for honest feedback regarding the particular athletic program of interest.*

Judging Your Child's Athletic Potential For College Play

"The last two people a coach wants to hear from regarding a player's ability are Dad and Mom!"
—University of Louisville Head Men's Basketball Coach, Rick Pitino

The High School Coach and Other Experts

There are many fine high school athletes who misjudge their ability to compete in an intercollegiate sport, and apply to schools which do not match their skill level. At the beginning of the college search, try to obtain the opinion of several experts who are skilled at projecting the most appropriate level of intercollegiate competition for a high school athlete. Start with the high school coach, or club coach, and then approach other experts in your community such as current or former college coaches or players.

The Role of The High School Coach

I believe high school coaches should help with college admissions. Ask your child's high school coach for an honest answer to the question, "At what college level, if any, do you think my child can compete?" Whether or not you like the response, it is important for you and your athlete to know where the high school coach stands on this issue, since college coaches often consult a recruit's high school coach regarding playing ability and character. This answer, and other opinions, may narrow the group of colleges to which your child applies.

While it is reasonable to rely on the advice of certain high school coaches, my recommendation is to get more than one opinion, especially if your child's high school coach has not sent many players to compete at different levels of college play. Some high school coaches are not skilled at projecting the college level at which a high school athlete can compete. If this appears to be the case in your situation, there may be a local high school, AAU/Club or other

28

league coach who has sent athletes to different levels of college play, and is willing to advise you and your young athlete.

It is important to understand that some coaches may push a student to play at the highest level program at which the player can "make the team", rather than trying to serve a player's best interest. Some high school, AAU and Club coaches are "connected" to certain college coaches based on friendships and/or past favors. These relationships can produce subjective rather than objective advice from the high school/AAU/Club coach to the high school prospect. Some high school, AAU and Club coaches also like to boast about the number of players they have sent to Division I programs. "A real problem in the college search is when a young athlete listens to a high school, AAU or Club coach whose interest in and knowledge of college sports is limited to Division I, or is blinded due to a relationship with a particular college coach," said Rick Boyages, former Head Men's Basketball Coach at the College of William and Mary.

Changing Roles

Rick Boyages points out that AAU and Club coaches, who are often with their teams for six or more months a year, have taken on a more prominent "college guidance" role. "It's not that the high school coach has been eliminated as a guidance option and reference. Yet college coaches realize that it can be far more advantageous to cultivate a relationship with a high powered AAU or Club coach who works with a large number of good players every year, than with a high school coach who may only have an occasional prospect."

What if My Child's High School Coach Does Not Want to Help?

Unfortunately, some high school coaches have no interest in helping their athletes with college matriculation. If this is the case with your child's high school coach, try to get assistance from another "mentor" in your community. Make sure that the "mentor" is not a booster of a particular college, for this could result in a possible NCAA violation. Also, make sure that you and your young athlete are pro-active in contacting colleges of interest.

28

College Coaches — A Good Resource

Current and former college coaches are often the most accurate at predicting the level of intercollegiate competition a high school athlete should pursue. Ask a nearby current or former college coach to take a look at your aspiring college athlete. While some college coaches will be governed by self-interest, many will be fair and objective in their analysis. (At certain times, a current college coach would be precluded from observing your player due to NCAA rules.)

If your son wants to play college baseball, and every expert with whom you consult states that the youngster is best suited to Division III, your young man should probably go to a Division III school, if he expects to play.

The Role of the Guidance Counselor

The majority of guidance counselors admit that their expertise does not encompass advising a serious high school athlete about the appropriate level of college sports competition. Said one, "This is why I always employ a 'team approach' which involves the player, parents, coach and, if necessary, other experts."

Guidance counselors are often assigned far too many students to play an active role in the athletic recruiting process of one student. In some schools, the ratio of students to guidance counselors is as high as 480:1! Check the ratio at your child's school.

A Tip

A good way for your child to assess athletic skills is to play against college athletes in summer or off-season scrimmages. In sports such as basketball, soccer, tennis, lacrosse, baseball and softball, this can often be done through summer leagues or in informal settings. The key is for the player to be realistic about such an assessment.

Showcasing Your Talents

"You must stir it and stump it, and blow your own trumpet, or trust me, you haven't a chance."
— English dramatist, W. S. Gilbert of Gilbert and Sullivan fame

Unless an athlete is a highly sought "Blue Chip" prospect, it is important and appropriate for student-athletes to contact coaches at all college sports programs in which the student is interested. This means the student, not a parent, initiates emails, letters and phone calls. Joe Reilly, Head Men's Basketball Coach at Bates College, stated, "Since it is the young man, not the parent, who will be playing for me, it is primarily the young man I want to hear from and get to know."

Coaches in programs with limited recruiting budgets, which include most non-revenue Division I sports and virtually all Division II and III sports, like to hear from potential recruits, *and look for the recruit to show initiative.* "Our coaches always appreciate it when a prospect contacts them, and then continues to show initiative," said Tim Downes, athletic director at Emory University. Bob Schneck, Head Women's Volleyball Coach at the University of Rhode Island, adds, "In sports such as women's volleyball with limited recruiting budgets, if the recruit really wants an athletic scholarship, she must go get it, not wait for the coach to come get her."

The objective of any contact is to generate interest in your student-athlete, and it should be done early in your child's college search, i.e., fall or winter of junior year. *All schools of interest to your child should be contacted since it is not known which programs will be interested in your child.*

Is Senior Year Too Late?

There is no question that coaches conduct many player evaluations during a prospect's sophomore and junior years, and at summer camps prior to senior year. It is also true that the vast majority of college athletic scholarships are verbally offered prior to September of a young athlete's senior year. However, it is inaccurate when a recruiting service or other "expert" tells an athlete that senior year is too late to seek a good sport/school match, particularly at the Division III level. Dave Hixon, Head Men's Basketball Coach at Amherst College, stated, "Coaches, especially at the Division III level, are still receptive to hearing from new prospects during their senior year, particularly fall of senior year. The key is to make it as easy as possible for the coach to evaluate the prospect."

If your player has made no contacts during junior year, here is some advice:

- *Never wait until just before the school's application deadline to contact a coach.*
- Contact all coaches as early in senior year as possible, through emails, phone calls and visits.
- Send the coach a transcript, résumé, game and workout tape and any fall, winter or spring sports schedules.
- It is vital for senior prospects to be *very* proactive in enlisting the help of respected current and former coaches for recommendations and phone calls to prospective college coaches. This is especially true for spring sport athletes, because the college coach will be unable to observe this senior athlete in actual competition.
- If your young athlete happens to know a player at the school of interest, and has competed with or against that player, your young athlete can ask the player to give the coach a recommendation. Many coaches have recruited high school prospects based on the recommendation of an athlete at the college.

28

- As Coach Hixon points out, "Even though, in many cases, evaluations begin much earlier than senior year, a fall or winter sport athlete not applying for early decision at a Division III school still has a good chance to impress a coach and get on the recruiting list. This is so because, at many schools, recruiting lists for regular admission are generally not sent to the admissions office until January or early February."

Coach Hixon also notes that, "If little or no research has been done by the recruit prior to fall of senior year, early decision is probably not a good idea."

Alumni Recommendations

A recommendation by a graduate of the school will generally cause the coach to look at—but not necessarily recruit—the prospect. "I appreciate alumni contact as an introduction to a prospect," said one Division III coach. "But I would never recruit a player without going well beyond the alumni introduction and conducting my own careful evaluation."

The point: an alumni recommendation is a good door opener, but not a deal closer.

What to Send

Try to make it as easy as possible for the college coach by sending the following:

1. A résumé which includes academic information such as class rank and SAT/ACT scores (if available) and athletic information, including height, weight, position and accomplishments/honors. If the college of interest does not require SATs, a candidate must make a judgment as to listing them or not. (For sport résumé details, see pages 333-334.)

2. Schedules of all high school, Club or AAU games.

3. Letters of recommendation from the recruit's coach and, if possible, other experts who have seen the recruit play.

4. A game/workout DVD.

5. The list of any showcase camps the recruit plans to attend and the dates of the sessions.

After initial contact has been made, the prospect should ask the high school coach, as well as the camp, Club and/or AAU coach (if these individuals have enough knowledge of the prospect) to contact the college coach to discuss the youngster's statistics, work ethic, character, ability, potential and any other qualities about which the college coach may want to know.

28

No wise college coach will listen to a parent's evaluation of an offspring's athletic ability. A college coach wants to hear from an expert, and most importantly, wants to evaluate every prospect — first by DVD and, when possible, in person.

Sending the DVD

Some hilarious stories always surface about parents of prospective student-athletes sending "highlight tapes" to college coaches. Pete Carill, the former Princeton Men's Basketball Coach, and a brilliant judge of talent, once called a friend of mine about one of his high school players.

"Coach, Pete Carill from Princeton callin.' Just got a tape on your kid Johnny. Does he ever miss a shot?"

As it turned out, Johnny was a substitute on the high school team whose dad had felt that splicing tapes and producing an eight-minute Larry Bird-like highlight film might actually beguile the sage Princeton coach...which obviously did not happen.

Do Not Deceive!

In recent years, certain high school athletes, in some cases with the help of adults, have employed high-tech methods that go well beyond mere splicing to create DVDs that make them appear much better than they really are. Most coaches are onto this ill-advised ploy. Coach Hixon said, "Even if a coach falls for a doctored DVD, which is highly unlikely, that coach will see the truth on the first day of practice."

My *strong* recommendation: *Do not even consider allowing your child to employ such dishonest techniques.*

What Kind of DVDs Should Be Sent?

Send a workout DVD of drills conducted by an expert. A DVD should also include reasonable portions of games against good competition, and, if possible, against other recruited players. If the sport includes a variety of offenses or defenses, be sure clips show your player performing in a variety of offenses/defenses, i.e., a basketball player in both man-to-man and zone situations. Make sure that the DVD is well produced and "viewer friendly." *If necessary, get help on this important project.*

Eight "Phone/Personal Meeting" Tips for Recruits

While a great deal of coach/recruit communication is done via email, most coaches like to converse with recruits by phone and in person, especial-

28

ly those recruits who appear to be good prospects.

"Phone contact and/or a personal meeting allows me to get a much better handle on the recruit's character, maturity and personality," said Coach Hixon.

Here are eight important "phone/personal meeting" communication tips for the recruit:

1. Be polite.

2. Be enthusiastic.

3. Before you make personal contact with the coach, become knowledgeable about the program. Spend time on the web looking for information about the current status and history of the program.

4. Be honest without being arrogant.

5. Do not *ever* "big time" the coach, e.g., "even though I'm interested in your Division III program, I really feel that I'm a Division I player."

6. If you *really* want to attend the school, let the coach know.

7. Be a "cooperative conversationalist," which means responding with more than yes/no answers. Remember, this is an opportunity for both the recruit and the coach to gather information.

8. Keep a pad of paper next to the phone so that parents and siblings can take accurate messages from coaches, if you are not available.

Do Not Underestimate the Skill Level at Division III

Many parents and high school athletes underestimate the skill level required to compete effectively in Division III. At the more competitive Division III programs, many successful athletes were bona fide high school stars—team captains or all-conference, perhaps even all-state selections. They are often a few inches shorter and/or a few pounds lighter than their Division I counterparts, but as a group they are highly skilled. Related to this topic, here are five suggestions regarding the college search:

- Do not be condescending in your view of what it takes to succeed as a Division III athlete.

- Do not allow your child to overestimate personal ability in comparison to good Division III athletes.

- If Division III is under consideration, do not imply to a Division III coach that your child is really a Division I or II player.

- Be sure to remind your athlete that expressing such opinions to a Division III coach is a turnoff.

- Be aware that certain coaches and guidance counselors know little

28

about Division III college sports. If you find this to be true with your child's coach/guidance counselor, seek other help.

Competitive Imbalance Within the Divisions

Even within Divisions I, II and III, there are many different levels of competition. The very best Division I-A football teams will overwhelm the majority of other Division I-A teams. The same type of competitive imbalance exists in all three Divisions.

In my view, there are really eight levels of NCAA college sports. (This, of course, does not include NAIA or junior college.)

Level I — Division I upper major
Level II — Division I mid-major
Level III — Division I low major
Level IV — Division II highly competitive
Level V — Division II moderately competitive
Level VI — Division III highly competitive
Level VII — Division III moderately competitive
Level VIII — Division III less competitive

If you need to assess the particular level of a college program, review the available information, such as:

- In some Division I sports like basketball and football, there are actually computerized team power ratings. These power ratings are generally published on a weekly basis, and are easily accessed. While by no means perfect, the power ratings will provide you with a good idea of the level of each team in comparison to other teams.

- A number of Division I leagues are subject to power ratings. As an example, the ACC, Big 10, Big 12, Pac 10, SEC and Big East are often at the top of league power ratings in men's basketball, whereas the Patriot League or Ivy League might be at the lower end.

- In Divisions I, II and III, it is common for teams to be ranked not only nationally but regionally. In New England Division III competition, most men's and women's sports have a New England top 10 or 15 poll that is published weekly during the sports season.

- In almost any intercollegiate sport, a Division II or III school will seldom defeat a Division I school. A rare exception is tennis, where some of the very top Division III programs are quite competitive with low-to-mid major Division I programs.

28

313

Playing Down One Level

Based on the eight-level model, knowledgeable coaches often advise eager high school seniors to consider playing down one level from where they aspire to play.

Here are some reasons why:

1. As noted, players and their parents often underestimate the skill required in some college sports.

2. Many high school players overestimate their own ability and seek to play at a higher college level than is realistic.

3. Coaches often push high school players to accept an athletic scholarship or to play in the highest level athletic program with little regard for where an athlete would find the best academic and/or playing fit.

4. More playing time generally offers greater chance for improvement, as long as the competition is still good (which it is at most levels of college competition).

5. If professional sports is a goal, playing infrequently at the highest possible level is not likely to increase chances for a professional opportunity. Some sports professionals, especially "later bloomers" in the NFL, played in mid- or lower-level college programs, (though few NBA players played below mid-major Division I).

Choosing to play down one level will often require your young athlete to stand firm against those, notably certain coaches, who state or imply that playing at the highest possible sports level is the most important aspect of college life. As Coach Hixon points out, "Going for 'balance,' in this case, often takes some real courage — and perspective — on the part of the recruit."

Many ex-college athletes told us they resented the extent of the commitment demanded in return for little playing time. Some, including a number who played on nationally ranked teams, believe they would have been happier playing on a slightly lower level team!

Think of this situation as a "sliding scale" with "competition level" at one end and "playing time" on the other end. The challenge is to find the right point on the scale.

Playing Down Two Levels

Based on the eight-level model, it is *very* rare for a recruit, particularly a Division I recruit, to choose a program two levels down. An exception to this rule would be the student-athlete with top grades who chooses a level VI

28

(highly competitive) Division III school with a top academic ranking over a Division II school, or even a Division I low major. "I knew I had no future as a professional athlete, so I decided to choose Amherst over several low-major Division I programs," said one surveyed student-athlete.

By contrast, virtually all of those athletes recruited by Division I upper-major (Level I) or mid-major (Level II) schools in sports such as basketball, baseball and football feel that they have a chance to play professionally, if not in the United States, then abroad. This is why you seldom see these recruits choosing to "play down" more than one level.

What About the Prestige of Playing at the Highest Level?

In any Division, there are many fine athletes who get little playing time in their program, and who would be starters or stars if they played in less competitive programs within the same level, or at a lower level. Athletes must realistically weigh their desire to play in the "high-level" program, where they might remain a substitute, against the enjoyment of a richer playing experience at a slightly less athletically competitive school.

Too Much Sports Time, Too Little Study Time

"They're adulated when they're playing. But when they get out,
the people who adulated them won't hire them."
—Stanford University football coach, Jim Harbaugh,
on the football program of his Alma Mater, the University of Michigan

College athletes today have far greater demands upon their time than athletes of past decades, so investigate the time demands on any team under consideration, and *ask about the types of careers entered by players who have graduated in the last decade.* Research shows that in certain Division I sports, particularly the "revenue producing sports," virtually no players over the last 10-15 years have gone on to serious graduate study, e.g., medical school, law school or PhD programs.

While this fact causes great consternation among certain college coaches, it is a real issue with factual answers. If your high school recruit is serious about a rigorous major with a view toward graduate school, find out exactly what the players who have competed in the program over the last 10-15 years have done after graduation—since the time commitment of college sports has increased so much.

28

Specific questions to raise might include:

- My daughter's goal is medical school. How many players currently in your program are majoring in pre-med?
- How many former players from your program are currently in medical school?
- Over the last 10 years, how many players from your program have gone on to medical school?
- Over the last 10 years, how many of your players have attended other types of graduate schools?
- What types of graduate schools have they attended?

If it becomes clear to the serious student that varsity competition and a rigorous major at a certain school are mutually exclusive, the student should find another school that will meet educational objectives, knowing that this may mean playing at a lower level of competition, playing intramurals or not playing. Some Division I programs successfully integrate sports and serious academics, but the success of the integration will be dependent upon the program's commitment, as well as the personality, diligence and aptitude of your child.

A Distinct Difference — Having to Win Versus Being Competitive

Whether they admit it or not, many schools foster a culture in which the coach *must* produce a winning team or be fired. Scott Thompson, former Head Men's Basketball Coach at Wichita State, says, "In big time college sports, you are more likely to get fired for losing than for cheating." By contrast, there are many highly respected Division III coaches with .500 or below career records, particularly at schools with stringent admission requirements.

At the Division I level, there is often a *big* difference between the culture that surrounds those sports that are expected to produce revenue for the school and those that are not expected to produce revenue. Other programs, particularly at the Division III level, want to field competitive teams but do not fire coaches based solely on wins and losses.

Why I Like Division III Sports

"Winning the NBA championship was a big thrill; winning the Division III National Championship when I was coaching at Pomona was an even bigger thrill. There is something special about a group of non-scholarship Division III athletes coming together and becoming a real team."

— San Antonio Spurs Head Coach, Gregg Popovich, in a speech at Williams College

In many cases, a Division III sports commitment fits within the educational mission of the college, and most Division III coaches appear to be genuinely committed to an "education first" approach. There are exceptions, and parents and athletes must do their homework! Try to determine where a particular sport and coach fit within the wide range of athletic competition, attitudes and demands upon a student-athlete's time.

Junior Year Abroad

"The ability to play on a varsity team and study abroad in the 'off-season' is, according to students and coaches, a frequent factor in selecting Bates rather than another institution which requires off-season practices."
— Bates College Associate Dean of Students, Steven Sawyer

Another good example of Division III "balance" is the number of Division III athletes who are able to take advantage of junior year abroad (JYA) study. JYA is one of the most enriching educational experiences offered by colleges and universities, and we found that many Division III athletes spend a semester abroad without relinquishing varsity status. Over the past decade, half the students on varsity teams at Bates College studied abroad for at least one semester. By contrast, we could find virtually no Division I scholarship athletes who were able to spend junior year abroad. "The opportunity is non-existent," admitted one head coach of a Division I school.

A Problem in Division III

A number of Division III athletic directors acknowledge that, since there is little NCAA oversight of Division III sports, some Division III coaches make extreme "unofficial" and "off-season" time demands on their athletes, with little fear of consequences. This "pushing the limits" philosophy employed in certain Division III programs makes it likely that the NCAA will soon engage in more oversight of Division III athletics as a whole.

Investigate the "unofficial time demands" for each Division III program of interest.

28

LACK OF MINORITY ATHLETES IN DIVISION III

An unfortunate reality of Division III athletics is that many of its member institutions have few minorities competing on varsity athletic teams. Some blame this situation on a lack of effort on the part of the institutions to recruit minority candidates. I looked into this matter, and found that the majority of Division III schools have active, well-funded minority recruitment initiatives—as well as significant financial aid for minority candidates.

I found the chief "problems" to be the following:

- The vast majority of high school and AAU coaches know very little about Division III sports. Many have done little or no research on Division III sports options, and thus have not given these options a "fair chance."

- Many high school and AAU coaches foster a "Division I only climate" which suggests to a student-athlete that the only valuable college athletic experience is found at Division I.

- Many high school and AAU coaches have little understanding of the considerable financial aid opportunities available at Division III, including for minority candidates.

- Many guidance counselors admit that while they have great expertise in finding the right academic and social match for a prospective college student, they lack expertise in advising on the proper athletic fit. "I have strong knowledge as it relates to good academic or social matches for my advisees," admitted one guidance counselor to me. "But when it comes to advising a young person who also wants to play a college sport, I need to rely on the expertise of coaches and others."

- Division III schools situated in suburban or rural locations often pose initial concerns for minority candidates reared in urban environments.

- There are not enough minority head coaches in Division III, particularly in non-urban schools.

On the plus side, many Division III schools are very anxious to address this issue, including forging partnerships with high school and AAU/Club coaches to better inform them of the many opportunities for their players. A key objective of the Institute for International Sport's work with

28

318

coaches of at-risk male youth—ages 12-18—is to better educate these coaches on the advantages of Division III, including the significant amount of financial aid available at many of these schools.

Another Institute objective is to better inform all parents and student-athletes of the advantages of Division III, and implore them to do their research.

Admissions Lists at Schools Without Athletic Scholarships

If your athlete is applying to a non-athletic scholarship school, the college coach's recommendation to the admissions office may play an important role in the athlete's chances for acceptance. Just as you should be honest with coaches at colleges under consideration, you have the right to ask politely the coach for honest answers to the following questions:

- For what position are you recruiting my student-athlete?
- Who else are you recruiting for this position?
- Has the head or assistant coach seen my student-athlete play?
- Where is my child on the recruiting list you will send to the admissions office?
- What do you feel this means in terms of chances for acceptance?

All final admissions decisions rest with the admissions office. Some overly optimistic coaches paint an unrealistic admissions picture to their recruits, with assistant coaches being especially culpable. Coaches can offer an educated guess as to what their recommendation will mean, but not a guarantee.

Always stay in touch with your student's high school guidance counselor because the counselor can often obtain feedback from an admissions officer.

Controlling Team Numbers

One of the disadvantages of a non-athletic scholarship school is that a coach cannot control the number of recruits in the program, whereas coaches who award athletic scholarships have almost total control in this area. In my first year as Head Men's Basketball Coach at Trinity College (CT), a non-athletic scholarship school, I submitted 13 names to the admissions office, all strong academic candidates. I guessed that eight would be admitted and hoped that three or four would choose Trinity. Twelve were admitted, and 11 enrolled—far more than I wanted.

28

Intentional "Stockpiling"

"Many coaches at non-scholarship schools recruit for attrition. They intentionally stockpile, knowing that a high percentage of their athletes will quit."
—Surveyed Division III coach

Unintentional over-recruitment is a real possibility at all non-scholarship schools, because no one can accurately predict how many athletes will enroll. On the other hand, some zealous coaches at non-scholarship schools deliberately over-recruit so they have many players at each position, and avoid depth problems due to player dropout. I have found stockpiling to be somewhat common at Division III schools, as well as non-scholarship Division I schools, including Ivy League schools.

If your young athlete is being recruited at a non-scholarship school, here are two additional questions to pose:
- How many players do you bring into the program each year?
- Over the last four years, how many players have quit?

Recruiting Large Numbers of High School Athletes to Fill College Beds — A Questionable Practice

College presidents at some Division II and Division III schools, under pressure to fill each class, authorize a practice I find objectionable. At these schools (not the top small academic colleges which generate far more applicants than they can admit), each head coach is required by the administration to generate a certain number of applications from students who play in that coach's sport. The theory is that a men's basketball coach generating 50 applications will see at least 25 admitted. Of that group, 8 to 12 are likely to enroll.

A coach with whom I spoke at one such school objected to the policy for a number of reasons. "First of all, to fulfill my quota, I find myself encouraging kids to apply that I know cannot be admitted, or if admitted, will struggle academically. Secondly, I have had several seasons where I had too many players in the program, which caused me problems and left some kids greatly disappointed."

If your child is being recruited by a Division II or III school, ask the coach if the school employs this dubious "quota policy."

Interpreting Recruiting Letters

Amidst the many types of correspondence from admissions offices, *there are four types of letters a recruit could receive from a coach.* Tom Konchalski, a highly respected basketball recruiting analyst, tells prospective athletes, "The

28

fact that you received an initial letter means a school has 41 cents worth of interest in you!"

The significance of each type of letter varies dramatically.

1. **The typed "personalized" letter that is computer generated.** This type of letter only means that the high school athlete has been identified as a possible prospect by the particular program. High school recruits should know that the program probably sends a similar "personalized" letter to hundreds of other prospects. *View these letters only as an initial demonstration of interest, and absolutely nothing else.*

2. **The hand-written letter or card.** This type of letter may mean there is more than just a preliminary interest in the prospect. Such a letter does not, however, mean that a scholarship or admission to the school is being offered.

3. **The scholarship offer.** A letter from the athletic program offering an athletic scholarship is extremely rare! It is common practice to make the scholarship offer verbally and such offers are non-binding. After a verbal offer is accepted, the school, at the appropriate time, sends the National Letter of Intent accompanied by financial aid documents.

4. **The National Letter of Intent.** This letter, when signed by both parties, binds them to the scholarship offer. The National Letter of Intent is sent out from an institution along with a financial aid document which clearly states the value of the scholarship for one year. These documents are binding on the institution when sent, and are binding on the recruit once the aid document and the National Letter of Intent are signed by the recruit. (Refer to *(www.national-letter.org)* and *(www.ncaa.org)* for further information and frequently asked questions on the National Letter of Intent).

The College Recruiting Calendar
When Schools Can and Cannot Contact Your Child

28

There are *very* few restrictions on prospective student-athletes initiating contact with college coaches. On the other hand, there is a surplus of restrictions on college coaches contacting prospective student-athletes. Each intercollegiate sport in each Division (I, II and III) has a set of recruiting guidelines which you can access by visiting the NCAA website (www.NCAA.org) or writing to the NCAA at: The National Collegiate Athletic Association, 700 W. Washington Street, P.O. Box 6222, Indianapolis, IN, 46206-6222.

The NCAA Recruiting Chart

The following will provide you with a good overview of what is and is not permissible in recruiting, as of this publication date of this book.

	DIVISION I MEN'S BASKETBALL	DIVISION I WOMEN'S BASKETBALL	DIVISION I FOOTBALL
SOPHMORE	**Recruiting materials —** • June 15 following sophomore year **Telephone calls —** • One per month beginning June 15 following sophomore		
JUNIOR	**Telephone calls —** • One per month through July 31	**Recruiting materials —** • September 1 **Telephone calls —** • April call permissible on or after Thursday following Women's Final Four • One during each of the months of May & June. • One on or after June 21 following junior year • Three during month of July following junior year	**Recruiting materials —** • September 1 **Telephone calls —** • One between April 15 and May 31
SENIOR	**Telephone calls —** • Twice per week **Off-campus contact —** • September 9 **Official Visit —** • Opening day of classes	**Telephone calls —** • One per week **Off-campus contact —** • September 16 **Official Visit —** • Opening day of classes	**Telephone calls —** • September 1 — One per week* **Off-campus contact —** • Last Sunday following the last Saturday in November **Official Visit —** • Opening day of classes * Unlimited during contact period
Evaluations and Contacts	130 recruiting-person days during academic year ——Not more than seven recruiting opportunities (contacts and evaluations combined) during the academic year per prospect contacts during prospect's senior year ——No off-campus contacts during junior year ——Not more than three off-campus	85 recruiting-person days during academic year ——Not more than five recruiting opportunities (contacts and evaluations combined) during the academic year per prospect and not more than three of the five opportunities may be contacts ——Practice/competition site restrictions	Six selected evaluation days during September, October and through the last Saturday in November (1-A) 42 evaluation days during fall evaluation period (1-AA) ——Limit of three evaluations during academic year • One evaluation during fall • Two evaluations - April 15 through May 31 (one evaluation to assess athletic ability and one evaluation to assess academic qualifications) ——Not more than six off-campus contacts per prospect at any site ——Practice/competition site restrictions

28

322

	DIVISION I OTHER SPORTS	DIVISION II	DIVISION III
SOPHMORE			**Recruiting materials –** • Permissible
	Telephone Calls – • Ice Hockey – one call to international prospect during month of July following soph. year		**Telephone Calls –** • No limitations * Permissible freshman and sophomore years
JUNIOR	**Recruiting materials –** • September 1	**Recruiting materials –** • September 1	**Recruiting materials –** • Permissible
	Telephone Calls – • One per week July 1 following junior year		Telephone Calls • No limitations
	Off-campus contact – • July 1 following junior year • Gymnastics – off-campus contact - July 15 following junior year	**Off-campus contact –** • June 15 – No more than three off-campus contacts	**Off-campus contact –** • Conclusion of junior year
SENIOR			**Recruiting materials –** • Permissible
	Telephone Calls – • One per week	**Telephone Calls –** • June 15 – One per	**Telephone Calls –** • No limitations
	Off-campus contact – • No more than three off-campus		**Off-campus contact** • Permissible
	Official Visit – • Opening day of classes	**Official Visit –** • Opening day of classes	**Official Visit –** • Opening day of classes
Evaluations and Contacts	50 evaluation days – Softball between August 1 – July 31 80 evaluation days – Women's Volleyball between August 1 – July 31 –Seven recruiting opportunities (contacts and evaluations combined) per prospect and not more than three of the seven opportunities may be contacts. Practice/competition site restrictions	–No restriction on the number of evaluations –Contacts restricted at the site prospect's practice/competition site until such time as the competition has concluded and the prospect has been released by the appropriate authority	–No restriction on the number of contacts and evaluations –Contacts restricted at prospect's practice/competition site until such time as the competition has concluded and the prospect has been released by the appropriate authority

28

323

When you write to the NCAA, make sure to request a copy of the pamphlet entitled "The NCAA Guide for the College-Bound Student Athlete."

The following recruiting issues are covered by the NCAA in depth (believe me when I say in depth!). Some of these policies change from year to year, even month to month, so be sure to obtain updated information. In general, Division I regulations are the most restrictive, and Division III regulations the least restrictive.

- **Telephone calls:** On a Division-by-Division and a sport-by-sport basis, there are specific guidelines regarding frequency and timing of contact with student-athletes by coaches. Extended telephone calls to parents are considered a contact. Division I and II telephone contacts are restricted to one a week for high school juniors and seniors. Division III telephone contacts are unrestricted.

- **Electronically Transmitted Correspondence:** According to the NCAA manual, "electronically transmitted correspondence in the form of email, fax or pager shall not be considered telephone calls." As of the publication date of this book, coaches are precluded from contacting recruits through instant messenger and text messaging. There is an ongoing debate among coaches, athletic administrators and NCAA officials regarding instant messenger and text messaging. Make sure to check the NCAA website for the most updated rules on electronically transmitted correspondence. For now, coaches are allowed telephone, fax and email communication, but cannot use instant messenger and text messaging.

- **Personal Contacts:** There are specific guidelines for when a coach may contact a student-athlete in person, on and off the college campus. Contact rules regulating frequency and timing vary by sport and Division, with the most restrictions on Division I coaches, and few restrictions on Division III coaches. During the contact period, it is permissible for coaches to make in-person, off-campus recruiting contacts and evaluations.

- **Boosters:** Boosters and famous alumni are only allowed to phone or personally contact recruited athletes in Division III programs.

- **Evaluation:** The NCAA defines evaluation as "any off-campus activity used to assess your child's academic qualifications or athletic ability, including a visit to your child's high school or watching your child practice or compete at any site." Each sport has a permissible number

28

of recruiting contacts and evaluations. During the evaluation period, *no* in-person, off-campus contacts can be made with a prospect. The evaluation period is strictly as the term implies—for evaluation only.

- **Dead Period:** During a Dead Period, it is *not* permissible for coaches to make any in-person recruiting contacts or evaluations on or off campus.

- **Quiet Period:** During a Quiet Period, it *is* permissible for coaches to make in-person contacts, but only on the college campus. No off-campus recruiting contacts or evaluations can be made.

- **Official visits:** Official visits, meaning expense-paid visits, are allowed to begin on the opening day of classes of the high school athlete's senior year. A student-athlete may have one expense paid official visit to a particular school and may make official visits to no more than five schools.

- **Printed materials:** The dates when college athletic programs can send

---

TEXT MESSAGING

Make Your Policy Known!

"I'm excited you're looking at Florida State. FSU President T.K. Wetherell and I are friends. When you come to Tallahassee again, let's hook up with each other."
—Florida Governor Jeb Bush, in a text message to a high school recruit!

When text messaging to recruits reached the point of being employed intemperately, if not obsessively, by certain college coaches, the NCAA wisely stepped in. Confronted with anecdotal horror stories such as recruits waking up to 50 or more text messages, the NCAA has, for the time being, banned all coach-to-recruit text messaging.

The NCAA will revisit this legislation in 2008. If the NCAA allows text messaging to return in a more moderate form, you and your young athlete should still exert control over this intrusive practice. Inform all college recruiters that your high school athlete wishes to have reasonable junior and senior years, and should not be distracted by constant text messages.

Also, take the opportunity to use the text messaging issue as a good life lesson for your child about relationships. Meaningful relationships are developed by people who genuinely care about each other; these meaningful relationships do not encompass a coach sending five or six text messages a day stating, "thinking about you," or "we really want you."

28

printed materials to prospective student-athletes vary based upon the type of the material (whether generic or individualized), and whether the school is Division I, II or III. If you have any concern about the fiscal welfare of the U.S. Post Office, take comfort that many NCAA athletic programs are doing their part to keep our postal service healthy! The NCAA is prohibiting "Fed-Ex" packages to prevent schools with large budgets from having an unfair advantage.

- **Written correspondence:** The NCAA has limited "written correspondence" to one written letter/email per day.

(**See Appendix for Division I-A football recruiting calendar**).

The aforementioned points are based on research as of the publication date of this book. Make sure to check the NCAA website if you have specific questions, as these rules can change.

The Official Campus Visit

If your child is being seriously recruited, the coach may offer the youngster an official, expense-paid visit. Division I schools may pay for transportation as well as food and lodging for the recruit. Division I schools cannot pay for parent transportation unless parents drive the recruit to the school, in which case driving expenses can be reimbursed to the prospect. Division I schools can pay for the food and lodging of parents. Division II and Division III schools are allowed to pay for on-campus food and lodging for recruits, and a few have funds for transportation. Most Division III recruits stay in a dormitory. *Make sure to check the NCAA website at www.ncaa.org since the regulations of the "official visit" are frequently being reviewed and altered.*

Whether or not expenses are paid, here are some points for an athlete's consideration during the campus visit:

1. Try to have the visit be overnight and in a dorm.

2. My *strong* recommendation is to try to arrive on Thursday evening, for this will allow a "real collegiate day" on Friday, i.e., attending classes and seeing the school in operation during the week (which is quite different from how the school operates on weekends). At the Division I level, the official visit is limited to 48 hours from the time the recruit steps on campus. If a coach picks up a recruit at the recruit's home, the clock starts at the time of home pick up. If the prospect is picked up at the airport, the clock does not start until the prospect arrives on campus. Thus, if the school hosts the player in a hotel (away from campus) on Thursday night, the official visit does not technically start until Friday morning, and can

28

thus extend through Sunday morning. There are no time restrictions on Division III visits.

3. While on campus, carefully examine the following:

- Dorm life
- Social atmosphere
- Academic atmosphere—attend some classes in areas of interest.
- Athletic culture—for the dedicated high school athlete, the latter is an important consideration because each college will have its own unique athletic culture—some steeped in excess, others more balanced.

4. Try to make sure your youngster stays with a college student-athlete in the sport of interest. The college coach usually makes sure this happens. Understandably, coaches choose host players they hope will make a good impression and say good things about the program. *Make sure to ask a host player and other team members direct questions about the program and coaching staff.*

5. Try to attend a practice and/or game to observe the coaches and players.

6. Try to ascertain the skill level of the returning players in your position. Depending on the time of the campus visit, the sport, and the Division, it may be possible to actually scrimmage with the players, although at the Division I level, no prospect may "try out" in front of a coach.

7. Investigate key areas of interest—like the quality of food!

Sports vary as to the time best suited for a campus visit. Many college programs are amenable to an autumn official visit in senior year. This may be an especially good time for the youngster who is considering early decision or early action.

Early Decision versus Regular Decision

The Advantages and Disadvantages of Early Decision or Early Action

Two important college admissions terms need defining. Most colleges will employ one option or the other, not both.

28

Early Action (EA) means a student applies early to a school, and will be given a decision, but is *not* obligated to attend that school if accepted.

Early Decision (ED) I or II means a student applies early to a school and agrees, if accepted, to matriculate at that school, if financial need is met. The student also agrees to withdraw applications from all other schools.

Burke Rogers, Director of College Counseling at St. George's School, Newport, Rhode Island, cautions that, "Students should only consider applying early decision after careful research and evaluation of all the schools on a student's list. An early decision application should come at the end of a search process, not at the beginning." If a recruit waits until fall of senior year to begin the college search process, there is little chance to even consider an early decision application—another good reason to start the process in junior year!

Rogers also cites the possible advantages of early decision application:

- It takes just one acceptance to produce one enrollment, whereas, in the regular round, it may take three or four acceptances to produce one enrollment. A lot of early decision acceptances can make the lives of admissions officers much easier.

- Early decision will possibly give a candidate a break in both admissions opportunities and financial aid opportunities. In return for the commitment to enroll if accepted, an applicant might receive a slight break in admission standards – the schools might "dip" just a bit to accept a candidate who promises to enroll. (Although this is not the case at highly competitive schools).

- The same is often true with financial aid. An accepted ED candidate may get more financial aid, because more is available at this stage at certain schools.

- In Division III programs, early decision is a very common route for student-athletes to pursue. Coaches like the certainty that comes with early decision applications, just as admissions officers do.

- *By contrast, early action does not provide the college with any greater certainty that the student will enroll.* Thus, the early action candidate is not likely to get as much of a break, either in admission or financial aid in many schools.

Rogers offers two cautionary points about Early Decision:

- You probably should not apply early decision unless you are a viable candidate. If you are depending on a big academic turnaround in your senior year, it is generally best not to apply so early in the fall, before you show your improvement.

- A disadvantage of early decision is that there is no opportunity to compare financial aid offers from different schools.

Rogers makes the following points regarding Early Decision II:

- Many colleges now offer a second round of early decision, wherein a student applies in January and learns the decision in February. A number of colleges realized that many great applicants did not get into their 'top' choice in the ED I round in December, and therefore were still looking for good homes in January.

- Generally, a student who comes up short with one college in the ED round I should consider a slightly less selective college in the ED II round.

Beware of high-pressure scenarios in which a coach pushes a student to submit an early decision application, *sometimes as early as September of senior year,* before a player has had time for careful investigation of all prospective schools. As noted, college coaches love early decision commitments since such commitments reduce recruiting pressure and allow coaches to focus on their team. Many schools also push their coaches to convince recruits to apply for Early Decision.

For those young athletes interested in schools which do not award athletic scholarships, applying as an early decision or early action candidate may provide a better chance for admission. At some, but not all schools, the percentage of accepted applicants is higher for early decision/early action candidates. Admissions offices make acceptance rates for early and regular decision available, so feel free to check the statistics at each school of interest. One admissions counselor stated, "Applying early shows us that a student is genuinely interested in attending our college. . . a factor that is quite important to us."

If a coach asks your young athlete to apply early decision, the young athlete should pose two questions:

1. How much will applying early decision help my chances for admission?
2. How many others in my sports position are applying early?

Coaching Changes

Another disadvantage of early decision is that coaching changes may occur in sports programs. *A student-athlete ready to sign a National Letter of Intent needs to understand that it is a firm commitment to the school—regardless of who coaches.* Consider the possibility of a coach leaving or being fired. Waiting may provide more knowledge of staff changes and time to react accordingly.

Coaching Carousel

"It is not uncommon for a college athlete to play for two or more coaches in a four year span."
— Rick Boyages

Longevity is more the exception than the rule in college coaching, particularly in "arms race" sports such as Division I Men's College Basketball.

28

329

Consider the following—and alarming—number of coaching changes in Division I Men's Basketball over the past five seasons:

> Changes in 2007-2008 season: 57
> Changes in 2006-2007 season: 61
> Changes in 2005-2006 season: 42
> Changes in 2004-2005 season: 40
> Changes in 2003-2004 season: 46[17]

That's 246 changes over the last five years among 336 D-I programs!

Early Decision Risk Factor?

Some propose that an early decision rejection might turn off other coaches who feel they were "second best." Not so, according to several Division III coaches I consulted. "If the player is a good prospect, an early decision rejection by another school doesn't bother me at all," said one Division III coach.

The Advantages of Following the Regular Application Timeline

"Regular" college application deadlines are typically January 15 - February 15 of senior year; "regular" college acceptance times are typically late winter or early spring of senior year. If your high school student has serious interest in more than one college, it is advantageous to follow the regular application time line, particularly if the student did not begin the college search in earnest until fall of the senior year. Colleges may vary in the amount of scholarship and/or financial aid offered, and parents and students need to be able to compare different aid packages.

Getting Off the Wait List

The key to getting off the wait list is "polite persistency" and flexibility. This means the following:

- A wait-listed student must let the college know, in no uncertain terms, of a willingness to attend the college, if given the opportunity—even at the last minute. A letter is the best way to convey this message.
- Whenever possible, the wait-listed student should make an appointment with an admissions officer at the school to personally convey strong interest.
- The wait-listed student should stay in regular touch with an admissions officer via mail, email and an occasional phone call.

Be persistent without being inconsiderate of the admissions officer's time.

28

Coaches have a smaller role with wait lists, because when schools go to the wait list, they are generally trying to fill in voids—gender, geography, etc.

Also be aware that a student who needs significant financial aid will rarely be admitted off the wait list because all of the money is generally gone by the time the wait list is employed.

The Interview

Some schools do not require nor care about a personal interview. Other schools, particularly smaller schools, place *great* stock in the personal interview.

"We rely heavily on the personal interview to judge many things about the candidate, including the candidate's level of interest in our school," stated Wylie Mitchell, Director of Admissions at Bates College.

Find out how much importance each school of interest attaches to the interview, and react accordingly. At many schools, foregoing the personal interview can lessen the candidate's chances for admission.

*Any NCAA rule addressed in this chapter is subject to change. Consult the NCAA website (*www.ncaa.org*) for current information.

THE "LONG ODDS" POSITIONS
That Require Even More Research

There are certain "long odds" positions in college sports, with the position of quarterback heading the list. Many Division I-A football teams will have 8-10 recruited quarterbacks in the program—with only one ball and one starting opportunity. Even in Divisions II and III, a strong program will have 6-8 recruited quarterbacks. In all three Divisions, virtually all of these quarterbacks had been high school stars. Many recruited quarterbacks end up moving to a new position, sitting on the bench, or transferring to another program. Of the 2004 Division I-A programs that ended the season ranked in the top 25, 16 had quarterbacks transfer after the season![†]

If your young athlete is being recruited for a "long odds" position, i.e., a position where there may be four or more athletes in the program competing for one starting job, it may be best to sit back and wait to carefully gauge the best fit. This may mean foregoing early decision or early signing.

28

The "Long Odds" Programs

In terms of sheer numbers of recruits, "long odds" programs are generally the non-athletic scholarship programs found, for example, in the Ivy League, Patriot League or Division III. Some coaches at non-athletic scholarship programs will "recruit for attrition," knowing that a fairly significant percentage of non-scholarship college athletes do not play the sport all four years. I examined two Division I men's basketball programs in the same state with regard to the number of young men who had actually been recruited. One was a Division I athletic scholarship program, the other a Division I Ivy League non-athletic scholarship program. The Division I athletic scholarship program had the exact number of full athletic scholarship recruits the NCAA allowed, 13, in the program, and no other recruited players on campus. The Ivy League non-athletic scholarship program actually had 32 young men on campus who had been recruited to play basketball, only 13 of whom remained in the program. At the scholarship program, not one of the players had dropped out of the sport; at the non-scholarship program, 19 had dropped out!

I also found a number of Division III programs in various sports with high attrition rates. It is surely worthwhile to investigate the number of recruits the coach brings in on an annual basis. It is also worthwhile to examine the attrition rate of the program, and to remember that many recruited non-scholarship college athletes do not play all four years.

[†]Taken from *New York Times* story, August 30, 2005

28

Chapter 29

RECRUITING SERVICES, SHOWCASE CAMPS AND INVITATIONAL CAMPS

"In giving advice, seek to help, not to please."
—Athenian statesman and poet, Solon

Recruiting Services

Should You Use a Recruiting Service?

There are over 100 college recruiting services, the majority of which are Internet-based. These recruiting services are most helpful for non-revenue producing sports, and football because of the large number of prospects. Such services are of little value for high-profile Division I mens and womens basketball, which rely on their own "network of scouts."

A recruiting service will develop a profile of your high school athlete that will, depending upon the level of services purchased, include some or all of the following information:

- Height
- Weight
- Year in school
- Class rank
- Sports statistics
- Speed and strength data

- Honors/awards
- SATs/ACTs*
- Contact information, including home phone, cell phone, home address and email address
- Best time of the day for phone and email contact
- High school coach's name and contact information
- If applicable, AAU/Club coach's name and contact information
- Proposed college major
- Proposed college sport and projected position(s) in college
- Level of competition to which your young athlete aspires
- Geographic area in which the young athlete hopes to attend school
- Several letters of recommendation from coaches who have personally observed your youngster play
- DVDs of the youngster's performance
- A personalized website that is regularly updated

  *For those colleges that do not require submission of SATs/ACTs, the student-athlete must decide whether or not to list the scores. Seek advice from a guidance counselor.

To help develop the profile, a local "scout" who represents the service may evaluate the skill level of your young athlete. Once the profile has been developed, it is the responsibility of the recruiting service to communicate this information to appropriate college coaches and to keep the client apprised of all contacts.

Do You Need a Recruiting Service?

While I am not opposed to such services, keep in mind the following points:

- A recruiting service is not needed just because your child's teammates use one, and your athlete wants the same ego boost.
- Recruiting service reports are most likely to be used by mid-to-lower level college athletic programs. Most nationally-ranked Division I programs pay little attention to reports from such services.
- The recruiting service will not get your child an athletic scholarship. Its role is to put your child into a position to be evaluated, i.e., to position your young athlete in front of the college coach.
- If you consider a service, you should insist on references, including:

29

- ◦ A list of athletes *in your child's sport* the service has helped. Some services are stronger in certain sports than others.
  - ◦ A list of the schools with which the service feels it can exert the most influence, including the names and phone numbers of college coaches with whom the service has established a relationship. The opinions of some services are far more valued than others.
  - ◦ The names and phone numbers of parents who have used the service.
- The sport is an important consideration. Mike Walsh, former Athletic Director at Washington & Lee, and former Head Baseball Coach at Dartmouth, does not feel that recruiting services are of much benefit in some sports. "However," states Walsh, "in a sport like football that must recruit large numbers of athletes, and thus rely on prospect lists, a recruiting service can be very helpful to a high school athlete. Another good reason for using a recruiting service in football is that coaches evaluate football prospects on DVD as opposed to personal observation. A reputable recruiting service can produce a good DVD."
- You, your young athlete, and the high school or AAU/Club coach should consider the following questions:
  - ◦ How much time are we willing to spend on the recruiting process? If your child is a desirable candidate, and if all of you are willing to put in the time, you can probably accomplish as much as most, if not all, of the recruiting services.
  - ◦ How strong are the college contacts of your child's high school coach, AAU/Club coach, or advisor? Certain coaches and advisors have such good college contacts that a recruiting service is not required. Many others do not have good college contacts.

Dave Hixon, Head Men's Basketball Coach at Amherst College, notes that "aspiring college athletes should take the time to develop a résumé which includes most or all of the points addressed in the profile information listed earlier. In my view, for 41 cents and a few hours of your time, basketball prospects, and prospects in many other sports, do not need to spend $1,000 or more on a recruiting service."

An Advantage of Some Recruiting Services is Financial Aid Counseling

College counselors point out that, in a typical year, for every $1 of athletic scholarship money awarded, $122 is awarded in other forms of aid categories, including need-based, academic, merit, leadership and other designat-

29

ed scholarships. It makes no sense for a high school athlete to feel that an athletic scholarship is the only method of paying for college. A clear advantage of some good recruiting services is that they offer advice on how to seek non-athletic financial aid.

A parent who used a recruiting service for his high school athlete told me, "The most helpful aspect of the service was guiding me through the financial aid maze. The service helped me apply for financial aid which I might not have otherwise discovered."

If you are considering a recruiting service, research the extent of expertise the service has in financial aid counseling. As you will see in chapter 31, applying for need-based financial aid can be a challenging process.

Cost

The cost of recruiting services may range from $100 to as high as $3,000 — a figure which strikes me as an extravagant expenditure. For $3,000, you better hope your child will get more than a small portion of an athletic scholarship or aid package!

How Do You Find a Recruiting Service?

Go on the Internet, or ask the high school/AAU/Club coach, guidance counselor or one or more of the college coaches at the schools of interest to your child. There are plenty of recruiting services available, some of which have regional representatives who are in regular contact with local coaches. With research, recruiting services are easy to find.

Here are three suggestions:

- In the early stages of the college search, ask the head coaches at your child's top five or six colleges what they think about recruiting services and which, if any, they recommend.
- If your goal is an athletic scholarship, and you decide to undertake the project without the aid of a recruiting service, make sure you get started in the fall or winter of your high school athletes junior year. As Bob Schneck, Head Women's Volleyball Coach at the University of Rhode Island, states, "in those college sports programs that award athletic scholarships, including women's volleyball, the majority of verbal offers are made before September of the prospect's senior year."
- If your goal is Division III, make sure you get started in the spring of your young athlete's junior year, or early summer at the latest.

29

The Showcase/Invitational Camp

Most team sports have high school showcase or invitational camps which are typically held in the summer, on weekends, or during other school holidays which fall during the sport's off-season. I strongly advise high school athletes to attend showcase camps, because attendance offers excellent recruiting exposure to a large number of college coaches.

How Showcase Camps Help Athletes and Coaches

College coaches no longer travel the back roads from high school gym to high school gym. They prefer to attend showcase and invitational camps, because a large number of good players, competing with and against each other in one location, simplifies their job of evaluation. As Tim O'Shea, Head Men's Basketball Coach at Ohio University, points out, "Coaches have a limited number of evaluation days, as mandated by the NCAA. Thus, it helps us when a multitude of talented prospects are gathered in one locale."

Showcase/invitational camps often provide the following:
- A guarantee that a fairly significant number of college coaches will be present for evaluation. Many camps employ an aggressive marketing approach aimed at letting college coaches know exactly which high school players will be in attendance.
- A handout sheet or booklet for all visiting college coaches which includes an athlete's personal information, e.g., height, weight, age, position, phone number, home address and email address, SATs/ACTs, class rank, name and phone number of high school or AAU/Club coach, and so on. The extent of information provided varies by camp, with high-profile camps usually offering the most information.
- Post-camp mailing/newsletter to college coaches.
- Some information on athletic scholarships, but little if any financial aid counseling.

Be aware that showcase/invitational camps may cater to a specific clientele, such as those aimed strictly for Division I prospects, or Division II or III prospects, or even for athletes with strong academic records! Some of the highest-level camps are by invitation only. As noted, ask college coaches at favored schools which camps they recommend. Be sure your athlete applies to more than one camp.

29

What About Invitational Camps?

Some are more selective than others; most will accept cash, check or credit cards!

Consider these points:

- Invitations are sent to accomplished high school players, usually rising juniors and seniors, less often to rising sophomores or freshmen.
- If your child's high school or AAU/Club coach believes your athlete is a prospect, ask the coach to make early fall contact with the camp, because many summer invitational camps fill up by January or February. A camp director will usually send an invitation to a player who has been given a strong, early recommendation by an AAU/Club, high school or college coach.
- Not every youngster invited is a blue-chipper, but most are quite skilled, creating good competition in the camp games and workouts.
- Tuition is generally charged, but many invitational camps will reduce or waive tuition for blue chip athletes because their participation elevates the camps competitive level and exposure *and* ensures evaluation visits by college coaches.

A New Trend in Elite Camps?

Elite basketball camps have always been administered by individuals other than college basketball coaches. This practice has changed in the last several years, with Division I power programs such as Kentucky, Mississippi, Arizona, Syracuse and UConn all running their own boys high school basketball elite camps.

A mid-major head men's basketball coach offered the following appraisal: "The host college program gains some definite 'indirect' recruiting advantages. Kids in attendance get to hear the head coach speak, observe his style, listen to graduates of the program who are now in the NBA, meet present players and assistant coaches, and view on-campus facilities. I doubt these coach hosted elite camps will be around very long. There will be too much protest from the Division I schools who are not administering them, notably the mid- and low-majors."

How Do College Coaches Feel About Recruiting
Services and Showcase or Invitational Camps?

Most coaches with whom I spoke prefer the camps to recruiting service information. As Coach Hixon of Amherst College states, "At the showcase camp I make my own evaluations."

29

Young athletes can search the web or consult with high school, AAU/Club or college coaches regarding showcase camps in their sport.

Camps Run by College Coaches

A "sport specific" camp run by a college coach on his school's campus (different from "showcase/elite camps") can be an excellent choice for middle schoolers or rising high school freshmen and sophomores. Most of these camps are well run and young players often enjoy:

- Playing in the gym or on the field where their favorite team actually competes.
- Being surrounded by college players who often serve as assistant camp counselors/referees.
- Being surrounded by high school and college coaches, many of whom serve as camp coaches.

The objective of attending such a camp is not so much to be recruited at a later stage, as it is to enjoy the experience. If your rising junior or senior is interested in a particular program and the coach of that program runs an on-campus clinic, enrolling can be a good idea. The young athlete will have the chance to look at the campus, meet players in the program (who are likely to serve as counselors/referees), scrimmage against these players, and perhaps be evaluated by the coach, and establish a relationship with the coach. This relationship may lead to the coach recruiting your child, or recommending your child to another program.

Remember, establishing relationships is a very important part of the recruiting process!

TENNIS RECRUITMENT

College coaches in team sports such as basketball, soccer, baseball, and lacrosse are not the only ones who rely on "showcase" camps to evaluate and recruit athletes. In tennis, we found College Tennis Exposure Camps (CTEC) (*www.collegetennis.com*) and Tim Donovan's Showcase (*www.donovantennis.com*). Paul Gastonguay, Head Men's and Women's Tennis Coach at Bates College, and a former world-ranked player, breaks down college tennis recruiting in the following way:

- Division I—top tier prospects. Many of these top tier high school tennis players will receive Division I scholarships, and less than

29

half of the top-flight players attend College Tennis Exposure Camps. Players at this level compete in USA Tennis National tournaments such as the National Hard Court Tournament, the National Clay Tournament and the Easter Bowl. Top tier high school players may even compete as amateurs in professional "satellite" tournaments. Coach Gastonguay tells us, "Many Division I coaches have budgets to visit tournaments to scout and recruit top tier players."

- Lower-level Division I, Division II and III. Prospects in this range often look to showcase camps to gain visibility. Coach Gastonguay, who serves as an instructor at CTEC, states, "These camps make it easier for college coaches, with limited recruiting budgets, to personally observe and evaluate numerous prospects."

- College coaches also pay close attention to local, state and regional rankings, as well as State high school tournaments.

Brian Shanley, Head Men's Tennis Coach at Salve Regina College (RI), offers two tips to aspiring Division II and Division III tennis players:

   o Join USTA Tennis and play in USTA Tennis individual tournaments before age 16 so you can be ranked and included in USTA Tennis listings. USTA Tennis rankings are scrutinized by Division II and Division III college coaches.

   o USTA Tennis hosts "College Days" for their regions. At these "Days," juniors and seniors can listen to coaches talk about their collegiate programs. Coaches can then watch the seniors go through a series of drills with USTA Tennis staff, and seniors can meet coaches. Due to NCAA recruiting regulations, juniors who attend these "Days" cannot speak with the coaches until after the completion of junior year. Visit (*www.USTA.com*) for information on these "Days."

Other sports have similar showcase camps. Your young athlete should check with the high school or AAU/Club coach, or with college coaches, to find these camps.

29

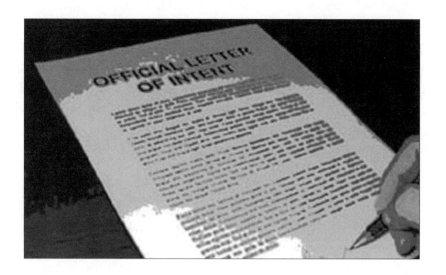

Chapter 30

THE ATHLETIC SCHOLARSHIP

"The soil in return for her service/keeps the tree tied to her."
— Indian poet, Rabindranath Tagore

This chapter will provide details of the "athletic scholarship game," and explore the obligations, expectations and "real value" of the athletic scholarship.

The Fine Points and Murky Nature
of the Verbal Scholarship Offer

"The idea of a verbal offer can be very misleading in that many schools prior to the actual signing period infer to all their recruits that an offer is on the table. This is especially true the further from the signing period you are, and also is endemic among assistant coaches who are not accountable for the final decision. Hence, a great majority of the early 'offers' are in fact more a function of recruiting rhetoric than a genuine offer of a scholarship."
— Ohio University Head Men's Basketball Coach, Tim O'Shea

A letter, phone call or even a personal visit from a college coach does not mean that a scholarship is being offered to your young athlete. When an offer is made, it is likely to be a verbal offer.

There are many areas for confusion when dealing with verbal offers. There are no NCAA rules regarding verbal offers, which means a coach could even make a verbal offer to a 14-year-old. (As Tim Floyd, Head Men's Basketball Coach at USC so imprudently demonstrated when he tendered such an offer to an eighth grade Californian—an act which appropriately outraged the boy's father.) Coaches may fail to point out that the verbal offer is meaningless until an athlete is accepted at the school.

Rick Boyages was the former Associate Head Men's Basketball Coach at Ohio State, and former Head Men's Basketball Coach at The College of William & Mary. Boyages offers excellent insight into the fine points of this process:

"Verbal offers are not binding and are only as good as the 'word' of the head coach with whom you are dealing. Many student-athletes are verbally offered scholarships early in the recruiting process, typically during junior year in high school. By verbally offering a scholarship to a prospect prior to an 'evaluation' period and prior to 'official' visits, coaches still have time to rescind the offer if they feel the player does not perform well enough over the summer. Different sports have different calendars regarding all this.

"Coaches who verbally offer a scholarship 6-12 months early are clearly indicating a *serious* interest in the prospect—as opposed to other coaches, who clearly state that they would like to further evaluate the player before committing themselves to a scholarship offer.

"Sincere, early offers typically come from institutions in the prospect's immediate geographic location. Schools that are close by have probably already evaluated the player on a number of occasions. The recruit may also have been on campus to observe athletic events, attend camps, or compete in local AAU tournaments. Schools can leave a prospect three complimentary tickets to attend home contests. Quite often, the prospect has great familiarity with a university, its coaching staff, and players before a verbal offer is extended; therefore, making an early decision is not as much of a problem.

"*There is no limit to the number of verbal scholarship offers a coach can make.* Coaches can also rescind a verbal offer if another player in the same position, given the same verbal enticement, is first to return with a commitment to the offer. It is conceivable that a coach could stagger a dozen verbal offers for just one scholarship. In most cases, the first player to verbally accept the offer would obtain the scholarship as long as things are honored up until the Letter of Intent signing day (which could be months away). This is quite common.

"Many recruits are informed by a coach that someone else has accepted the verbal offer, thus eliminating them and ending the recruitment process. This is why it is advisable for parents and prospects to 'unofficially' visit the institutions that have expressed an interest in their child early on in the process. In basketball, it is not uncommon for a school with just one schol-arship to schedule 'official' visits with recruits on 3-4 consecutive weekends in September in order to 'squeeze' their top choices into a decision. 'Squeeze' means a college coach giving a recruit a very short time in which to respond to a scholarship offer, sometimes as little as 24 hours. Some coaches disclose all of this and others do not. Deadlines can also be utilized if a coach feels it is 'now or never,' meaning a refusal to immediately accept the offer indicates it is unlikely the player will choose that school, allowing the coach to move on to other prospects…time is money."

A Two-Way Commitment

When both player and coach agree to a verbal deal, the deal should include an *unequivocal commitment on both sides,* including an agreement by the recruit to inform all other institutions of the decision, emphatically putting an end to any further recruitment. The coach should also agree not to recruit any other prospects in the same position, unless clearly stating a reason for needing another player in the same position. The strength of the verbal agree-ment is based on the integrity of the coach and player until the National Letter of Intent signing date. Since a verbal commitment assumes your expec-tation that the opposite party will refrain from pursuing other options, *your word is your bond!*

Remember, nothing is final until financial aid documents and the National Letter of Intent are signed by both parties, and the student receives a formal acceptance from the admissions office.

Pinning Down the Scholarship Offer

"We've done it for many years. That young man from New Jersey (John Bedford—see page 358) *was going through it for the first time. Who has the advantage?"*
— St. Joseph's University Head Men's Basketball Coach, Phil Martelli

You and your child have the right to expect the coach to be honest about his level of interest. However, recruits and their families may have to ask spe-cific questions to clarify any verbal scholarship offers. Coach O'Shea of Ohio University stated, "When it gets to the serious part of the discussion, the recruit and family should not be reluctant to ask direct questions of the coach."

If a scholarship offer has been discussed, but not yet made, ask:
1. Has the head coach seen my child play?
2. For what position is my child being recruited?

3. How many players in this position are in the two classes ahead of my child?

4. Are you offering my child an expense paid visit?

5. Are you offering my child a scholarship?

If a verbal offer has been made, ask questions one through four above, as well as the following questions:

1. At what point will my child hear from the admissions office regarding formal acceptance?

2. How many players in my child's position have you offered, or do you intend to offer, a scholarship in this year's recruiting class?

3. What are their names, and for what schools do they play?

4. Is this an offer for which the first player to accept gets the scholarship?

5. Do you have a ranking preference? Is my child your top recruit at her position or the second or third?

6. Is this offer for a full or partial scholarship?

7. How long does my child have to respond to your offer?

8. If my child says yes to this offer immediately, or in the near future, will you definitely award the scholarship?

9. Do you plan to recruit another player next year who plays the same position as my child?

10. How many players in other positions do you intend to offer a scholarship in this year's recruiting class?

11. What are their names, positions, and for what schools do they play?

The verbal scholarship offer is often a game of "cat and mouse" whereby the coach makes a verbal offer knowing full well that the prospect and family will want to listen to more proposals and/or personally visit a number of schools before rushing into a decision.

Acceptance deadlines can be quite short, sometimes as short as 1-2 days. Coaches cannot afford a long wait for one athlete, and they know that a short deadline may force a player to accept an offer. If your player delays answering, another good prospect may be lost if the wait is too long. Coaches often plan their verbal offers and acceptance deadlines in order to approach the most desirable candidates first, and the others in an approximate order of preference.

A blue-chip athlete may be less pressured with acceptance deadlines, but eventually a coach must insist upon one. Detailed information on the blue-chip athlete is found in Chapter 32.

30

Should Your Player Ask that a Verbal Offer Be Put in Writing?

The NCAA and the Collegiate Commissioner's Association, which administers the National Letter of Intent (NLI), consider the NLI the only binding athletic scholarship offer for a participating school. Due to the aforementioned strategic nature of verbal offers, and the fact that the ultimate decision rests with the admissions office, do not expect the coach to necessarily put all verbal offers in writing. It is, however, reasonable to ask for a written confirmation of an offer if your player accepts a verbal offer and desires written confirmation and details of the verbal agreement. Very few coaches will go back on a written offer since their reputation may be at stake.

Upon acceptance of a verbal offer, a player sometimes issues a press release in order to protect the offer. Athletic departments and/or coaches are not allowed to issue press releases or make public statements about recruits until the formal signing of the National Letter of Intent. Prior to that date, coaches and college officials can only confirm that the athlete is being recruited.

A Question the Coach Has the Right to Ask

A college coach also has the right to ask and expect an honest answer to the question: *How many schools are you considering and where do we stand on your list?* You and your young athlete have the obligation to be honest with the coach, just as your family expects the coach to be honest with you. *It is not just coaches who employ gamesmanship in the recruiting process!*

Rick Boyages points out that there is a recent trend of high school players reneging on their own verbal commitments. Because these arrangements are not binding, high school players are now frequently changing their minds. Common reasons for reneging include a choice made far too early in the process, a pressured decision, or the receipt of a more attractive offer. With verbal agreements, there is always the potential for an honest change of heart or unethical movement on either side of the deal.

As noted, however, a recruit needs to understand that if the coach lives up to his side of the verbal agreement, including not recruiting another player at the same position from the time the verbal agreement was made, the recruit who reneges will likely be putting this coach in a very difficult position. The ethics here apply to both sides!

Promises from Coaches

"Promise: to make a vow to somebody; to assure somebody
that something will certainly happen or be done."
—Encarta World English Dictionary

Things a Coach Should Promise

The only promises a college recruiter should make are:
1. You will be given a fair opportunity to earn a starting position, but I cannot guarantee you will be a starter.
2. I am committed to helping you, and all our players, balance academic and athletic endeavors.
3. In our program, we value and support teamwork, good sportsmanship, integrity, personal responsibility, and hard work on and off the field.
4. We value and maintain long-term relationships with former players.
5. My most important priority is that all of my players graduate.

If a coach makes these kinds of promises, I would give serious consideration to this program and school. A program representing such values can have a wonderful and lasting impact on an athlete.

Things a Coach Should Never Promise

1. I promise you will start.
2. I promise you will get "X" number of minutes, shots, carries, or anything relating to personal statistics.
3. I promise the school will have "easy" courses for athletes which will allow you to focus on your sport.
4. I promise I will not recruit players at your position during your first three years of play. (The coach must obviously recruit an incoming college freshman in your position when you are a rising senior, and, in many cases, even when you are a rising sophomore and junior.)

Under pressure to field competitive teams, many college coaches feel justified in making these sorts of recruiting promises. Stay away from any program or coach who makes such unrealistic and unethical proposals.

Negative Recruiting

Negative recruiting is one of *the* most underhanded practices in college sports. A common ploy is to have someone other than a coach send or email

"negative" articles about other programs to a player. Other examples of negative recruiting by coaches—usually assistant coaches—include:
1. "It's too hard there." Believe it or not, statements of this sort are actually employed by some coaches when a recruit is looking at schools with tougher academic standards.
2. "The coach is on a short-term contract; he won't be there very long."
3. "The players are unhappy—there's a lot of dissension."
4. "The players don't get better under coach so-and-so."
5. "If you go there, you're not going to win, or go to post-season play."
6. "Their style of play will hold you back."

Unfortunately, negative recruiting happens in all three college divisions, and it is far more common than it should be, even in Division III. Be wary about sending your youngster to play for coaches who use such tactics.

The Scholarship Offer Calendar

Many high school seniors are unaware of the "scholarship offer calendar" that exists in college sports. To help clarify this situation, I asked recruiting experts in two Division I sports for their opinions on when—and how many—offers are made at various stages of the recruiting process. I found that in most sports, including Division I women's volleyball and Division I men's basketball, the vast majority of offers are made before September of a high school prospect's senior year.

Division I Women's Volleyball
Likelihood of Verbal Offer Being Made

National Signing Date(s): Early period: November 14-21, 2007; Regular period: April 9-August 2, 2008

Expert: Bob Schneck, Head Women's Volleyball Coach, University of Rhode Island

Comments by Bob Schneck	Uncommon		Common		Very Common	
	Blue Chip High Major	Low to Mid-Major	Blue Chip High Major	Low to Mid-Major	Blue Chip High Major	Low to Mid-Major
Sophomore Year: "We are evaluating sophomores, but are looking for spring commitments from juniors."	X	X				
Autumn of Junior Year: "Blue-Chip athletes will begin to receive offers."		X	X			
Winter of Junior Year: "Blue-Chip and low to mid-major athletes receive significant numbers of offers."					X	X
Spring of Junior Year: "Strongest recruiting of juniors continues into spring with best players committing by end of spring."					X	X
Summer Prior to Senior Year: "The vast majority of programs have made all scholarship offers, though a few may remain in low-to-mid-major programs."	X	X				
Senior Year anytime or Summer prior to College: "Very few scholarships remain. Any offers generally relate to a player quitting or unforeseen circumstances."	X	X				

30

Division I Men's Basketball
Likelihood of Verbal Offer Being Made

National Signing Date(s): Early period: November 14-21, 2007; Regular period: April 16-May 21, 2008

Expert: Tim O'Shea, Head Men's Basketball Coach, Ohio University

Comments by Tim O'Shea	Uncommon		Common		Very Common	
	Blue Chip High Major	Low to Mid-Major	Blue Chip High Major	Low to Mid-Major	Blue Chip High Major	Low to Mid-Major
Sophomore Year: "Early verbal offers made to top prospects, although nothing is binding until college accepts and both parties sign National Letter of Intent."	X	X				
Autumn of Junior Year: "All high-level programs have extended a number of verbal offers to blue-chip recruits."		X			X	
Winter of Junior Year: "Low to mid-major programs are actively making verbal offers."				X	X	
Spring of Junior Year: "If a player has not received a Division I offer by now, it is time to consider Division II and III options."					X	X
Summer Prior to Senior Year: "By this stage, high-major to low-major programs have extended most or all of their verbal offers."			X	X		
Senior Year anytime or Summer prior to College: "This is into the signing period for binding National Letters of Intent. Any offers are probably for back-up players, but chances for any offer are slim."	X	X				

The Rising Popularity of
The Early "Unofficial" Visit

Bob Schneck, Head Women's Volleyball Coach at the University of Rhode Island, cites a growing trend in college programs that offer athletic scholarships, particularly programs with limited recruiting budgets.

"More and more, recruits are out after the scholarship on their own dollar. They are pursuing the coach and the school. This is particularly true of sports like women's volleyball with limited recruiting budgets. If the high school recruit really wants a scholarship, she must go get it, and she must not wait until senior year. Because we cannot call juniors until after July 1, we email recruits who are juniors to encourage them to call us. We also encourage their coaches to tell the recruit of the importance of coming to our campus in the spring of junior year for an unofficial visit—one for which they pay. In our case, we try to bring recruits in to watch our home spring tournament held in early April. We are actually looking for their commitment—and they are looking for ours—at that early date. Our recruiting strategy involves lining up commitments by the end of a recruit's junior year—15 months before she matriculates. Accomplishing this objective allows us to spend time over the summer focusing on rising sophomores and juniors instead of rising seniors, with a major objective of convincing the new junior class to visit our campus in the spring of their junior year. The 'new school of recruiting' is now definitely sophomore- and junior-based, not senior-based, as it once was."

The National Letter of Intent

When a high school student decides to accept a scholarship offer, and has officially been admitted to the school, the youngster is asked to sign a National Letter of Intent (NLI). The National Letter of Intent is sent out from the institution along with a financial aid document which clearly states the specific value of the scholarship for one year. The National Letter of Intent completely binds that athlete to play a specific sport as a freshman at the school providing the scholarship. It also means other schools must stop recruiting the athlete.

The National Letter of Intent is used only by Division I and II schools, because it must be accompanied by the offer of an athletic (not need-based or merit) scholarship. (Division III provides only need or merit aid). The majority of Division I athletic scholarship schools use the National Letter of Intent, and more than half of the Division II schools use it. Most schools that use the National Letter of Intent use it for all of their sports teams, although some Division I schools only use the NLI for revenue-producing teams.

The athletic scholarship is not a four-year award, but a series of one-year renewable financial aid awards. Each school will inform the recipient of this and state the rationale for non-renewal. Typically, only serious academic, disciplinary, personal or criminal problems are grounds for non-renewal and student-athletes always have the right to a formal hearing when this occurs.

"Poor athletic performance is not grounds for withdrawing the scholarship during the period of the one-year award. However, at the completion of the one-year award there is nothing legislatively keeping a coach from non-renewal of a scholarship based on poor performance," states Paul Kassabian of URI. Kassabian futher points out, "If not renewed, the player can go through the appeal process that is offered to all scholarship athletes." See www.ncaa.org for rules governing this issue.

There have been many problems with the National Letter of Intent. For example, the Collegiate Commissioner's Association, which administers the NLI, has been widely criticized for the following scenario: a coach recruits a student-athlete and the student-athlete signs a National Letter of Intent. The coach then decides to take a job at another institution, leaving the athlete, whose decision was based in no small measure on good feelings for the coach, no option but to attend the school. Much controversy and several court cases have resulted from these types of situations.

Rick Boyages points out that some recruits have discovered a safe alternative: "A growing trend is for the heavily recruited athlete to sign non-binding financial aid and admissions documents with the school, which are different than signing the National Letter of Intent. The athlete holds off on signing the National Letter of Intent to make sure there are no major changes in the program. By doing this, the athlete locks in the financial aid and admission commitment from the school, without being locked in by the National Letter of Intent. When an athlete uses this option, one problem is that other schools continue to recruit the athlete until a National Letter of Intent is signed."

A fair question to ask of the coach is, "If my child signs a National Letter of Intent, are you committed to being there for at least next year?"

While a college may release an athlete from a National Letter of Intent when a coach leaves, it is not obliged to, and such a release should never be taken for granted. Before signing the NLI, some athletes wisely make a verbal agreement with the school's athletic director that the athlete will be allowed out of the NLI if the coach leaves before the player enrolls. Recent NLI legislation allows the athletic director to issue a complete release, however, the athletic director still has the option of no release.

Make sure to visit the website for the National Letter of Intent— *www.nationalletter.org.*

COACH "RUN OFF"

The term coach "run off" means that a coach wants to get rid of an athletic scholarship player, and re-invest the scholarship in a more desirable player. Boyages points out, "If the athlete resists being 'run off,' the coach can make things quite miserable for the player. The review hearing, which is presided over by faculty, not coaches, is always available to athletes in this situation."

National Signing Date

Here is a sampling of National Signing dates in the 2007-08 academic year:

- Basketball: early period November 14-21, 2007; regular period April 16-May 21, 2008
- Football: February 6-April 1, 2008
- Women's Volleyball: early period November 14-21, 2007; regular period April 9-August 2, 2008

These times vary slightly from year-to-year.

NCAA Initial-Eligibility Clearinghouse

Whether a scholarship player or a walk-on, all students who plan to enroll as college freshmen and wish to participate in NCAA Division I or II must be certified by the NCAA Initial-Eligibility Clearinghouse.

Prospective athletes must pay a fee and sign a "Student Release Form," which allows the Clearinghouse to provide information to any member institution. The Clearinghouse tells students, "It takes several months for a student's information to be processed, so any college athlete wishing to play a fall sport as a freshman, should take care of registering with the Clearinghouse *immediately* upon completion of the high school student-athlete's junior year." Paul Kassabian of URI cautions that, "Since problems can surface during and after a high school prospect's senior year, taking care of this at the end of junior year can provide the time to deal with such problems."

30

Contact the Clearinghouse at:
The NCAA Eligibility Center
P.O. Box 7110
Indianapolis, IN 46207
Phone: 877-622-2321

"Prisoner of the Scholarship"

"Wherever any one is against his will, that is to him a prison."
—Greek philosopher, Epictetus

The immediate reaction of some who hear this "prisoner" term is to animatedly point out the financial benefits of the athletic scholarship. "I would not have been able to attend college if not for the athletic scholarship," is a common refrain.

While such a position may have rung true in past decades, there is little validity to it now. Financial aid is much more available than athletic scholarships, at a 122-1 rate, and this aid does not include Pell grants or other loans. *Virtually every diligent and resourceful American high school student who really wants to go to college will be able to do so!* While it is true that foregoing an athletic scholarship will likely cause the student to graduate with loans, that student will join the millions of other students who face this financial reality at commencement—and deal with it! The athlete must also consider what it will cost to miss out on a rigorous education.

How Common are "Prisoners of the Scholarship?"

Not very common, but the "prisoner" term was employed by enough surveyed scholarship athletes to convince me that it is worthy of your consideration. The classic "prisoner of the scholarship" is the young athlete who is characterized by some or all of the following:

- The athlete is not reaching sports performance expectations and, as a result, is experiencing great frustration and none of the joy that defined earlier sports experiences.
- The athlete always feels stressed and overwhelmed, and thus unable to meet all of the non-sports commitments of school. Detailed in Chapter 36, the time commitment in many Division I programs is considerable, and often goes well beyond the "legally allowed and countable" hours established by the NCAA.
- Due to a complete lack of free time, the athlete is unable to enjoy a normal college social life.

30

- The athlete does not like the players on the team.
- The athlete does not like the coach. This can be for many reasons, including the fact that some college coaches have little regard for academic excellence. Their unfortunate attitude is reflected by their stated or implied messages about what major to choose, what to do about missing class in favor of practice—all under the mantra "you have an obligation to your teammates and to this program." Some coaches also display a "Jekyll and Hyde" personality transformation from recruiting to actually coaching the athlete.
- Due to the heavy sports time commitment, the athlete does not have time to undertake the major most desired, and gives up the chance for serious post-graduate study in certain fields.
- The athlete has little interaction with the rest of the student body and feels "athletically segregated."

Some scholarship athletes feel no such pressure, and thoroughly enjoy their college athletic experience. Many others, who initially experience the "prisoner" feeling, overcome it through effort, better time management, and the maturing process that often comes with a regimented schedule. But it is clear that not all are able to do so. Stated one scholarship athlete, "When you give up your life for sports, and it's all stress and drudgery, and you see so many other missed opportunities, it's very difficult, and sometimes tempting to get rid of the scholarship in favor of a real college life."

What Does Your College Athlete Do in this "Prisoner" Predicament?

The first step is for the disillusioned athlete to ask: "What can I be doing better?"

The next step is that the athlete may consider quitting or transferring. At this stage, the athlete should consider the ethical issues of trying to keep the scholarship while putting forth less effort in the sport.

Finally, whenever a young athlete feels that the "prisoner" label fits, it is time to consider two facts:

- An important element of college is to experience social growth and enjoyment.
- A lack of academic rigor may well cost more money in the long run than giving up the athletic scholarship!

"If a college athlete decides to give up the athletic scholarship, the athlete must be fully committed to do it for the right reasons—including becoming a more serious student — and staying physically fit," states clinical psychologist Dr. Darrell Burnett.

Obligations of the Athletic Scholarship

"The benefits we receive must be rendered again line for line, deed for deed."
— American Poet, Ralph Waldo Emerson

If your young athlete has done the homework regarding the time commitment, sacrifice and possible tradeoffs that may exist when accepting an athletic scholarship, the athlete must then be aware that accepting this scholarship comes with obligations. I have encountered some Division I athletes who feel that once they accept the scholarship, they do not owe anything other than their modest effort to the program. This is wrong! There is an ethical principle at work here, which relates to the expectations inherent in an athletic scholarship. Expectations include fulfilling an obligation to give one's best effort, and understanding that one's effort not only affects oneself, but the entire team and program.

If your young athlete is ready to accept a college scholarship, make sure the young athlete understands:

- The coaches will be depending on his full effort.
- The team will be depending on his full effort.

Tell your young athlete that, "If you accept the scholarship, your teammates and your coaches have the right to expect you to pursue excellence in the sport."

THE FOREIGN INFLUENCE

In many Division I college sports programs, scholarships are being awarded to a significant number of foreign players. Of the approximate 4,800 men's basketball players competing in Division I schools in 2006, over 400 hailed from foreign countries. Fourteen of the top twenty 2006 Division I men's soccer programs had between 1 and 8 foreign players on athletic scholarship.[18]

How Much Will a Division I Coach Expect?

A great deal! Consider the following statements by surveyed Division I coaches:

- "If I am going to invest $150,000 in a kid, I expect his full commitment to our program."

- "Make no mistake. There is a direct correlation between the arms race at our level, and what we expect of the Division I scholarship athlete."

What are the Obligations of the Division I Scholarship Athlete?

Rick Boyages breaks the obligations down into the following categories:
- Meeting every academic obligation, e.g., GPA, tutorials, class attendance.
- Meeting all individual and team obligations, both in and out of season, e.g., workouts, rehabilitation, strength training and meetings. This means meeting the significant time obligations expected both in and out of season.
- Adhering to both the school and sports program policies that govern conduct.

Boyages was a Division III basketball player (Bowdoin) and Head Men's Basketball Coach (Bates) before serving as Associate Head Coach at Ohio State and Head Coach at The College of William & Mary. Asked to compare the obligations between Division I and Division III, Boyages states, "The overall financial and scholarship commitment of the D-I institution will cause sports obligations to be much more businesslike and intense. Compared to their Division III counterparts, D-I programs possess larger budgets, higher salaried sports coaches, personalized strength and conditioning experts, state-of-the-art training methods, new equipment, and modern facilities. Simply stated, there is a direct correlation between the financial undertaking of a D-I institution's athletics program and the demands on its athletes. The pressure to win in high-profile Division I sports has created a system by which the athletes are consistently pushed to the limit."

The "Walk-On"

The term "walk-on" refers to a non-recruited athlete who tries out for a college team. A number of walk-ons have made important contributions to their college teams, but the odds can be long.

At an athletic scholarship school, a coach invests considerable scholarship funds on recruited athletes. At a non-scholarship school, even at Division III, the coach often uses influence to help a recruited player gain admission. When a walk-on beats out a recruited athlete, it may compromise commitments made to the recruited athlete and call into question the coach's ability to evaluate players. For these reasons, the walk-on faces some serious challenges in beating out a recruited player.

Is it impossible? No. Even Duke men's basketball has had walk-ons on its championship teams, although they have seldom been on the court. While many college coaches have little or no interest in a non-recruited athlete, some will give the walk-on a fair chance at making the team.

WHAT IS THE OBLIGATION OF THE NON-SCHOLARSHIP DIVISION III ATHLETE WHO WAS HELPED BY THE COACH IN THE ADMISSION PROCESS?

If the coach helps an athlete gain admission to a Division III school, it is my opinion that this non-scholarship athlete owes the coach at least one full year of serious effort, the nature of which should have been outlined by the coach during the recruitment process. It is wrong to accept the coach's assistance with the admissions office, and then not even try out for the team, or give less than full effort.

Dave Hixon, head men's basketball coach at Amherst College, makes the following point: "When I sit with a recruit and his parents I explain to them my commitment to their son. A recruited player who chooses Amherst is automatically on the team as a freshman. I think this is important to allow the student-athlete to properly enjoy his first months as a college student and not feel the pressure of having to make the team and thereby passing up many varied opportunities and experiences in order to excessively practice his sport. I also speak to the recruit's commitment. The recruited student-athlete, who has taken a spot in a situation of limited spots, needs to commit to a full year his freshman year. After the freshman year, neither the student-athlete nor coach is obligated, although hopefully both parties work toward the ideal — four years of the college sports experience satisfying to the recruit and the coach."

Whether a Division I scholarship athlete or a Division III non-scholarship athlete, the "obligation factor" relates to doing one's preliminary homework about expectations.

What a "Walk-On" Should Do

If your child is a good athlete who is not recruited, and hopes to play at any college level, including D-III, here are some tips that may make it easier:
- Contact the coach to find out how tryouts are handled.
- There are NCAA forms and medical requirements for all prospective players, and it is up to the walk-on to research and complete these

requirements.

- If your child's high school or AAU/Club coach feels the youngster can help a college program, ask the coach to speak to the college coach. This is *very* important, since it alerts the college coach to be on the lookout for the walk-on during tryouts.
- Follow some of the same procedures previously mentioned, such as sending a game/workout DVD to the college coach.
- Before matriculation, have your aspiring college athlete request an appointment with the head coach, preferably during the coach's "down time." While it is best to meet with the head coach, this may not be possible, especially in football. In this case, arrange a meeting with an assistant coach.
- Consider a school which offers a JV program. A year of JV competition may provide a walk-on athlete a chance to impress the varsity coach and move up.
- Most importantly, make the following point to your walk-on candidate: "On the first day of tryouts, be in top physical condition, be the first athlete to show up, the last one to leave, *and* have the best attitude and work ethic!"

THE JOURNEY OF JOHN BEDFORD

*"College recruiting is so cutthroat and so sophisticated that
kids have to be aware of what's going on."*
—Head Boys Basketball Coach Teaneck High School (NJ), Curtis March

In August 2001, two weeks before he would begin his senior year at Lawrenceville School (NJ), John Bedford and his family received a handwritten note that would place him among the high school basketball elite. He was offered one of approximately 1,000 Division I men's basketball scholarships awarded to rising college freshmen.

The letter from the head coach at the school stated, "I've told John that he has a full scholarship to our college, and now I have put it in writing. This scholarship has the value of approximately $125,000 over the four-year college experience and covers all cost of enrollment at our school. I also want you to know that I will embrace John fully with both arms, treating him as if he was my own son. These are not merely words or an empty promise. My house will be his house. My family will be his family."

John was euphoric about the offer. "It was one of the greatest feelings I ever had," he said. "I felt like I accomplished something great." He was being given the chance to attend, at no cost, one of the rare jewels of college sports —an elite academic institution with a first-rate basketball program.

Or so he thought.

Two months later, the head coach called to rescind the offer, stating that the basketball office was not sure John was an "admissible candidate."

When it became apparent that a Division I scholarship school was no longer an option, John pursued other elite academic institutions with strong basketball programs—all at the Division III level. With honor roll status at a competitive prep school, and 1250 on his SATs, John was placed at the top of the basketball recruiting lists at Williams and Amherst, two premier academic institutions. John was accepted at both schools, and chose to attend Amherst, where he had a brilliant basketball career, leading the Lord Jeffs to the Division III Final Four in 2004 and 2006.

Amidst the whirlwind of losing the scholarship and being forced to pursue other schools, John had forgotten to withdraw his application from the Division I school. To his surprise, he received a letter placing him on the school's waiting list. The waiting list meant that John was an "admissible" applicant if a spot opened up. This contradicted the coach's message that John "might not be admissible, and thus we can't give you a scholarship."

Rather than honoring what was surely a moral commitment to John, the Division I school took the unfortunate position that the coach's hand-written letter was really not an offer, because it was not sent in the form of a National Letter of Intent! At 18, John Bedford was rudely introduced to the world of college recruiting and its technicalities and fine print.

Epilogue: In 2005, a legal settlement between John and the Division I school provided John with funds to help pay for his Amherst education.

Division I Dads

"Fantasy is no good unless the seed it springs from is a truth."
—Author Eurdora Welty

There is an unfortunate type of dad I label a "Division I Dad." While there are a few "Division I Moms," men dominate this category!

The "Division I Dad" is blinded by the prestige of Division I competition. I know one such dad whose son was scouted, but not offered a Division I scholarship. As late as the spring of the young man's senior year, with no offers on the horizon, this "Division I Dad" still clung to his fantasy of a full scholarship for his son. He enrolled his son at several spring "evaluation clinics" where only a few scholarships were available for the 50 or 60 senior players, and those players were targeted as backup or practice players.

Even without a Division I scholarship offer, the dad refused to allow his son to enroll in several attractive Division II or Division III programs. Instead, the son enrolled at a Division I school and pursued his father's dream as a walk-on. The freshman was cut and never played!

The young man later stated that he should have pursued one of the Division II or Division III opportunities in spite of his father's obsession with Division I.

Chapter 31

FINANCIAL AID: A MORE COMMON OPTION THAN THE ATHLETIC SCHOLARSHIP

"To give away money is an easy matter. . .and in any man's power. But to decide to whom to give it, and how large and when, for what purpose and how, is neither in every man's power nor an easy matter."
—Aristotle

A Financial Aid Surprise

Many parents of youth league and high school athletes are surprised to discover a fact related to financial aid and college sports: there are fewer college athletes on athletic scholarship than there are college athletes who are not on athletic scholarship!

Consider the following points:

- There are approximately 150,000 college athletes competing in Division III, none of whom are on athletic scholarship.

- While a number of Division II athletes are on full athletic scholarship, many Division II athletes are not on athletic scholarship, and many others are receiving only a partial athletic scholarship.

- While the overwhelming majority of athletes in Division I revenue producing sports such as football and men's basketball, as well as other Division I sports such as women's basketball, are on full athletic scholarship, a number of Division I athletes in non-revenue sports are not on actual athletic scholarship.

- No athletes in the Division I Ivy League are on athletic scholarship, as the Ivy League follows the "need-based" financial aid philosophy.

What Does this Mean?

It simply means that the majority of college athletes must seek financial aid in the same manner as non-athletes. Here are some tips:

How to Pursue Financial Aid

According to Dr. Matthew Greene, Educational Director of Howard Greene & Associates, a college counseling service, "Even when hoping for an athletic scholarship, an athlete and parent should apply for need-based and merit-based financial aid if they think they need it. In early January of the year a student will start college, submit the FAFSA Form *(www.fafsa.ed.gov)*, the College Board Profile *(www.collegeboard.com)* and Institutional Aid Forms, if required. This is the only way to qualify for need-based financial aid, which constitutes the bulk of aid available from the federal government, the states, colleges, and private organizations."

Burke Rogers, Director of College Counseling at St. George's School (RI) adds, "Many of the most expensive schools also offer the most financial aid. Due to the strong financial aid packages at many of these schools, they can end up being less expensive than lesser-endowed schools for certain students."

Two Financial Aid Realities

- If your child is truly a top-level student who has the qualifications to be admitted to an elite school that offers need-blind financial aid, you can take heart in the fact that the school will provide your child with all of the aid required. Remember that it will be *imperative* for your top student to maintain a high grade point average through senior year. Also, be aware of the ferocious competition for positions at the top-level schools.
- If your child is not in the top student category, early planning will put you in a much better position to explore both academic and financial options.

A Major Challenge

"I finally know what distinguishes man from other beasts: financial worries."
— French novelist, Jules Renard

One of *the* biggest problems that I have observed in the college search process is the following: Many parents who are in great need of financial aid for their child wait until the last minute to begin to prepare what even some savvy financial experts consider to be the daunting financial aid forms required by colleges.

My Essential Financial Aid Planning Model

Begin in your child's sophomore year and *absolutely* no later than your child's junior year. Parents often hear that the college search process should begin with school visits and Internet searches as early as junior year. Wise counsel, yet it makes no sense to begin a search process without including critical financial planning which will allow your student more college options.

Key Steps in the "Essential" Process

I. Academic Analysis

Before you can realistically judge what type of financial aid opportunities will be available to your child, you must work toward developing an objective analysis of your child's college potential as a student. Begin this process in your child's sophomore year by meeting with your child's guidance counselor, or another college counseling expert, to assess the child's current academic status, and how that status might match up with college choices. (Do not listen to any "expert" who says that sophomore year is too early to begin this analysis).

The next step in this analysis occurs in your child's junior year when more information becomes available, including class rank, PSAT and SAT scores. By January of your child's junior year, you and your child should develop a list of colleges that would be of possible interest to your child, and would be realistic in terms of admission. When developing the list, make sure to get the advice of a skilled college counselor. You should also purchase one or more college guide books, and visit one or more of the websites listed at the end of the chapter.

II. Athletic Analysis

Just as you need realistic academic analysis in order to begin to explore college options, you also need a realistic analysis of your child's college athletic potential. Sophomore year is the time to begin to formulate this analysis. Consult with experts, including your child's high school coach and others (see

Chapter 28—for detailed information). For most high school athletes, their potential becomes apparent by sophomore or junior year. Exceptions are those athletes who are truly late-bloomers in terms of growth or skill development. Bear in mind that most prospect evaluation by college coaches is done in the student-athlete's sophomore and junior years.

III. The All Important Financial Analysis

"Families should do these calculations early in the process so that they get at least a ballpark figure about their 'demonstrated need' and 'expected family contribution.' The sooner they have this information, the better!"

— St. George's School (RI) Director of College Counseling, Burke Rogers

As noted, the financial aid forms required by colleges are very complex. Here is an all too common scenario: A parent in clear need of financial aid begins the process of filling out these forms in late-autumn or early-winter of their child's senior year. The parent often finds the forms to be so challenging that either they do not fill them out correctly or they "give up."

If you know that you need significant financial aid, you should complete a "trial" of the required forms in the summer before your child's senior year. You will then learn what information you need to update in January of your child's senior year.

Developing Your Financial Profile

You should begin to develop your personal financial aid profile in your child's sophomore year. This profile will be based on your present income and other financial holdings.

1. Your first step during the child's sophomore year is to gather all of the necessary forms and carefully review them. This will allow you to judge how much expert help you need!

2. Next, develop relationships with experts. There are many experts who are willing to help a diligent family in need of savvy college advice, including financial aid guidance. Look for experts such as:

   - Guidance counselors. The problem with guidance counselors is that many have an excessive number of students assigned to them. That said, a number of guidance counselors have excellent knowledge regarding financial aid forms.

   - An accountant. Any accountant who is familiar with financial aid forms will be able to quickly decipher them. There are many books and websites that an accountant (or you) can review regarding financial aid forms, including those listed at the end of the chapter.

- A successful local person who is active in his or her college. People in this category can be great resources because they may be able to introduce you to admissions and/or financial aid officers at their college, who may take an interest in your case and guide you along.

- A financial aid officer at a local college. Many in this category are quite willing to help guide a parent who shows an earnest desire to help their child obtain financial aid. Burke Rogers states, "I urge families to call the financial aid office at a local college or university, the parent's alma mater or a college where the student is very likely to apply. If approached sincerely and respectfully, financial aid officers are definitely the best source of information for filling out the various forms and are great repositories of advice."

- A college counselor at a parochial or prep school. These professionals are often skilled in financial aid matters simply because the tuition paying parents at these schools expect excellence in this area. Some will be willing to donate a block of time to help a student not affiliated with the school in this process.

- Clergy. Members of the clergy can be wonderful door openers at colleges, or with local graduates of colleges who would be willing to "mentor" you and your child on the financial aid journey.

- You can also seek an arrangement with a financial aid consultant to do pro bono work for you or allow you to pay over time. Doing this over a two or three-year period beginning in sophomore year can be far less taxing financially than beginning early in your child's senior year.

Make an appointment with a financial aid officer or other expert and state your case. Many financial aid officers and other experts are empathetic professionals who will help steer you through the "maze."

Financial Aid Consultants

Contracting with a reputable financial aid consultant can be helpful, especially for parents who only desire financial aid assistance, not the recruiting services addressed in Chapter 29. An example of a well-regarded financial aid counseling service is the aforementioned Howard Greene and Associates *(www.greenesguides.com)*. Financial aid officials at colleges are also highly knowledgeable and should be willing to help with questions, as should certain accountants.

The complications of working with different federal and college financial aid formulas can make working with a financial aid consultant beneficial. Jim Skiff, Assistant Head for Institutional Advancement at Providence Country Day (RI), cautions, "There are a number of fine consultants, and, unfortunately, a number of charlatans. Make sure to check references on any consultant, and make certain to get a clear commitment regarding the consultant's fee structure."

Some consultants will do some pro bono work; most consultants will accept installments from a family in need of assistance.

YOUR CALENDAR

You should develop a calendar with a checklist, which includes the following:

- Sophomore year:
  - Academic analysis profile.
  - Athletic analysis profile.
  - Financial aid analysis profile, which begins by reviewing the forms and the financial aid calculators available on certain websites.
  - Begin to develop relationships with people who might be in a position to help guide you and your child.
- Junior year: Continue the process and complete sample forms.
- Summer prior to senior year: At this stage, you should begin to prepare the financial aid forms. *Do not wait until fall or winter of your child's senior year. An early start might afford you an early review from financial aid officers of schools of interest* thus providing more opportunity to explore various options.

Use the Web!

Burke Rogers encourages parents to use the financial aid calculators available on reputable websites such as *(www.collegeboard.com)* or *(www. finaid.org)*. States Rogers, "These are better than sending away for paper forms, and they are far less expensive than financial aid consultants. Ultimately, most colleges will want electronic submission of this information anyway—it is faster and more reliable for all involved."

When searching for outside scholarship sources, the websites, *(www.finaid.org)* and *(www.fastweb.org),* include a powerful search engine for scholarships based on a wide array of criteria.

In seeking financial aid, the Web can be a great ally!

Financial Aid Realities

"I worked two jobs and my wife worked a part-time job outside of the home and as a full-time homemaker. We sent our four kids to top colleges and received little financial aid. The financial aid system employed at these schools—which was purely 'need based'—seems to almost punish extra effort by certain parents in the workforce."

—Surveyed parent

Many schools in the so-called "elite" category, such as those that make up the Ivy League and NESCAC, are "need based" in terms of financial aid. This means that these schools are committed to meeting the student's financial need based on the Financial Aid Form (FAF).

The good news is that these heavily endowed schools have the financial strength to meet the projected need, as recommended by the FAF. The bad news is that the FAF's view of your family's need might differ greatly from your view! Many hard working American middle class families are not well served by this egalitarian system, and many parents in this group end up suffering from an affliction called "Maltuition." By the time they are finished educating their children, they are in significant debt.

Need-Blind Admissions versus Need-Aware Admissions

According to Burke Rogers of St. George's, need-blind admissions allows admissions officers to make decisions without worrying whether the student has applied for financial aid or not—the college has the resources to provide aid to those students who need it. This is usually accompanied by a guarantee to meet "demonstrated need." Only the wealthiest institutions have the money to institute this policy. Be aware that some "need-blind" offers are heavily laden with loans as opposed to actual grants.

Far more colleges are in the need-aware admissions category. Admissions officers at schools in this category can choose to accept the strongest and most desirable applicants without concern for their financial need; they know the college has the resources to fund the most appealing candidates.

But as Rogers points out, "At some point in the process at most need-aware institutions, there comes a time when the dollars run short, and admissions officers have to pay attention to financial need—and they are most likely to accept students who can pay the full freight. Often this happens for only the last 5-10% of the class. But that figure varies widely with the financial resources of the institution. If an applicant is a marginal candidate and needs financial aid the chances of gaining admission diminish."

Gapping

Gapping involves a college accepting a student but leaving a "gap" between the demonstrated need and the financial aid offer—the student is welcome to attend, but only if able to foot the bill. Rogers points out, "this is a controversial practice, in that it can breed disappointment. An acceptance letter unaccompanied by the necessary funding can be a hollow victory. But at least accepted students have the opportunity to look for outside funding—the door is open to them if they can pay the fees."

Can Sports Proficiency Help?

Yes, if the coach advocates for the athlete with the admissions office. Being a recruited athlete can put your child on a coach's list that will be given special consideration in the admissions office. Being on such a list does not guarantee admission, but it will help, both with admission and, in some cases, with financial aid—particularly at schools that "gap" students based on their desirability.

Beware of Private Loans

"Student private loans is the wild west of lending."
— New York Attorney General, Andrew Cuomo

Due to the limits on federal loan aid, private loans have become a common and often problematic component of college financing. While federal student loan rates are capped by law (6.8% as of the publication of this book), the majority of private loan programs carry variable rates which can soar to credit-card like interest of 20%, or more! The U.S. Congress and a group of Attorneys General are investigating this matter. Rhode Island Attorney General Patrick Lynch points out, "This situation has the potential to force students into heavy debt—even bankruptcy after college graduation."

Here are three *important* tips:

1. *Find out the exact terms of any private loan*, not just the interest rate upon signing but of the variable interest rate that could exist until the loan is paid off. Many students are not aware of the interest implications. Tim Cadigan, Vice President of Washington Trust (RI) points out, "Many of these young people are simply not loan savvy, and are looking for a quick

fix to pay for college. In all cases regarding a private student loan, a parent and child need to have expert and honest advice—and not be duped into a marketing ploy that could have severe ramifications."

2. Be cautious about college officials steering you to private loans. Regrettably, some in this position of trust have steered anxious students to high-interest private loan companies. As one frustrated financial aid officer confided, "I regret to say that some in my profession have been governed more by self-interest than by the interest of the student. In some cases, there have been kickbacks, in other cases it involves simply getting the student into the position of paying for college, no matter what the later cost."

3. Many students sign on these loans, because they have been late in filling out financial aid forms or done a poor job of researching loans. This is another reason to employ the "essential" financial aid strategy.

Tips for Low-Income Families

One of my duties as a Bates College Trustee is to serve on the Bates Trustee Admissions and Financial Aid Committee. In doing so, I discovered the alarming fact that only one in seven low-income youths entering high school will obtain a college degree. By contrast, I learned about the *very* strong commitment of many colleges to students from low-income families. This commitment includes helping low-income parents become more savvy in pursuing financial aid options.

Six Important Points

1. Most American colleges and universities, not just those considered in the "elite" category, are anxious to provide admission and financial aid opportunities to qualified students from low-income families.

2. Many schools have taken important steps to reduce or eliminate loans as part of the financial aid package, thus affording students the chance to graduate without significant debt.

3. Most schools now realize that their commitment to low-income families must include additional grant money for transportation and spending money.

4. If you are a low-income family with a student who desires a college education, schools will be responsive to contact from you—as early as your child's sophomore or junior year—to seek admissions and financial aid advice. Many college admissions and financial aid officers are extremely

busy, but they should never be too busy to offer you advice. The advice will often include directing you to other experts and resources, including suggestions on the best books to purchase and the best websites to visit.

5. Over the last decade, many associated with higher education realized that a high percentage of minority students in colleges were hailing from middle-or upper-income families. While enrolling a higher percentage of minority students was noble, college administrators and trustees realized the importance of significantly expanding the outreach to include students from low-income families and have budgeted accordingly. This outreach is now much more proactive than even a decade ago.

6. As for Grade Point Average and SATs, most admissions offices take into account that children from higher-income families have often been afforded educationally enriching opportunities not available to students from low-income families, ranging from expensive enrollment in the Princeton Review, to a family environment laden with books, theatre, travel, dinner conversation and many cultural benefits that can enhance a child's college application credentials.

Key Advice to Low-Income Parents

"Reading is a kind of sanctuary where human beings have access to thousands of different realities they might otherwise never encounter or understand. Each of these new realities can transform your life."

—French novelist, Marcel Proust

I have observed that many successful college students from low-income backgrounds had a mentor in their formative years—a parent, clergyman, family friend or business person who acted as the child's "opportunity search engine." If you wish to undertake this role for your child, or another child, here are four suggestions:

1. Do your best to motivate the student to begin to read extensively. Point out that reading books will "train the mind" and make life much more interesting.

2. Be proactive—this involves being polite but persistent in seeking the assistance of professionals, many of whom will only be too pleased to help you.

3. Take the same journey that many middle-and upper-class families take—become savvy. You do this by asking questions, meeting with experts, reading books—turning over rocks!

4. If you feel the entire task is too overwhelming, recruit a teammate or two to help you.

Interpretation of "Need" and "Merit" Aid

"In an important sense, all athletic scholarships fall under the heading of 'merit money.' The college determines that the student-athlete will have a positive impact on campus and is thus worth the investment of scholarship money. More broadly, though, 'merit scholarships' go to students who are especially attractive to the college or university for reasons other than sports."

—St. George's School (RI) Director of College Counseling, Burke Rogers

"Merit aid" is typically designated for students with top-level academic and SAT performance, but a few schools use more liberal interpretations of "financial need" and "merit" for outstanding athletes. In one case, an athlete only qualified for partial, need-based financial aid at a Division III school, but was offered a full athletic scholarship by a Division II school. To entice the athlete to attend the Division III school, the aid package was enhanced with a "merit scholarship," although the athlete was only an average student. The best schools offering merit aid have merit scholarship committees which strictly screen candidates, with no unfair advantage given to athletes.

As noted, schools in the Ivy League, and most schools in the NESCAC, offer only need-based aid and do not offer merit scholarships. Many other fine schools, such as Washington & Lee, Hobart and William Smith, Davidson, Claremont McKenna and the University of Rochester, offer both merit aid and need-based aid.

A Huge Increase in "Need" and "Merit" Aid

There has been a major increase in need-based aid. In 1994, $18.6 billion was awarded in need-based aid; in 2004, $39.1 billion was awarded.

There has also been a *huge* increase in merit aid. In 1994, $1.2 billion was awarded in merit aid; in 2004, $7.3 billion was awarded!

Tuition and room and board have also gone up, but not at the same rate as need-based and merit aid. This is good news for families in all income categories, but you must still be proactive in finding the aid.

Negotiating Aid

Carefully evaluate your financial aid awards. Except for certain merit awards, most aid is guaranteed for one year only. Dr. Greene of Howard Greene & Associates recommends that you compare the breakdown of pure grants, parent loans, student loans and work-study in each aid package. A well-endowed school may award more pure grant money and fewer loans than a school with fewer resources.

If your child applies for financial aid and does not receive a satisfactory financial aid package, you can ask the school to reconsider the aid package. This may involve some negotiation on your part. Your hand may be strengthened if another school has offered a more attractive financial aid package. If this is the case, the school with which you are negotiating may require you to show them aid packages offered by the other schools. Burke Rogers notes, "Colleges will consider new information about a family's finances, but few will enter into a bidding war with other colleges about aid offers."

A Possible Option

There are a large number of very fine schools—both public and private—that do not show up in the *U.S. News and World Report* top 50 college or university list, but are strongly focused on recruiting top level students, including athletes. Many of these schools are not constrained in their financial aid policy by need only, and are often quite aggressive in offering attractive financial aid packages. "If we can't win the reputation battle, we can sometimes win the money battle," was the way one admissions officer expressed his school's financial aid philosophy.

While schools in these categories do not offer as much overall financial aid as their wealthier counterparts, many put together extremely attractive financial aid packages for students they really want. According to Burke Rogers, "preferential packaging" is the term used for the financial aid policies of these schools.

Rogers points out, "Not all colleges promise to meet 100% of demonstrated need. When aid dollars are short, they might 'gap' a student—that is, leave a differential between the official 'Estimated Family Contribution' and the amount the colleges require the family to pay. Sometimes colleges will do this with the less desirable students—but conversely they might go the extra mile with the more desirable students. Like a lot of things, it often boils down to impact."

Advantages of "Lower Rated" Colleges

"The number of students graduating from high school has been increasing, and the preoccupation with the top universities, once primarily a northeastern phenomenon, has become a more national obsession."
— New York Times journalist, Alan Finder

There is no denying that a degree from an elite institution such as Harvard or Pomona can carry a certain cachet and a wealth of contacts that can be helpful in various pursuits. Another *strong* advantage of attending an "upper tier" college is that studying in a setting with other bright and motivated students can raise one's own level of performance and intellectual development.

Yet matriculation at such a school does not guarantee life success, and choosing what might be regarded as a "lower rated" school can have its own advantages, such as:

- Many such schools have developed very attractive financial aid/scholarship incentives to attract top-level students.

- Many of these schools have implemented very challenging "honors" programs, and have recruited top-flight professors to teach the honors courses.

- The students in these honors programs have academic credentials similar to students at upper tier schools. Being surrounded by such excellence produces the same "raising the bar" dynamic so prevalent at elite schools.

- Through successful capital campaigns, many of these schools have been able to better position themselves by constructing new facilities such as state of the art libraries, fitness centers and dormitories, not to mention some very attractive international study abroad programs and interdisciplinary majors. "Many in this category are doing a great job in finding ways to gain the 'competitive edge,'" states Rogers.

- A high level student who eschews an elite school in favor of a lower rated school with better financial aid and/or other perceived advantages — and who earns top grades at the school — will likely have similarly attractive opportunities for graduate school and/or entry level job positions as graduates of elite institutions. Major consulting firms have been critized for only recruiting new employees from a small pool of elite institutions. Yet, there are an infinite number of ways other than consulting to earn a living!

- The list of elite schools is far longer than it once was — and by no means includes just the Ivy League. Do *not* assume that a student at Dartmouth is any brighter than a student at Hamilton or Lehigh. There is little difference between the credentials of most in this widely expanded "elite" group, which now includes the NESCAC, the Patriot League and the University Athletic Association — and those students who enroll in the honors programs at the allegedly "lower rated" schools.

In American society, a trained mind accompanied by diligence and the ability to work with people can take one a long way—regardless of the college name that appears on one's jersey!

Say No To *U.S. News and World Report*!

"Those of us committed to higher education tend to bristle at the methodology used in compiling the U.S. News and World Report *rankings or those published by the highly suspect* Princeton Review."
—University of Rhode Island President, Dr. Robert Carothers

Having spoken at over 100 colleges, I have come to the following conclusion: The college ranking systems, such as those employed by *U.S. News and World Report* and the *Princeton Review,* are *grossly* unfair to many wonderful colleges and universities. The elite schools deserve their elite reputations. Yet I strongly advise you to look beyond the rankings for the right fit—academically and athletically—for your child.

A New Trend?

Davidson College, one of the finest and best-endowed liberal arts schools in America, has recently implemented a no-loan policy. This means that Davidson will meet 100% of any accepted student's demonstrated need, with no loan as part of the financial aid package. According to Burke Rogers, "Expect many other well-endowed schools to follow this practice."

Final Thought

"An investment in knowledge always pays the highest return." —Ben Franklin

I am a proponent of attending a top-flight school for a number of reasons, including the fact that moving amongst excellence often produces excellence. Yet such a decision should not result in crippling debt. The "need blind" financial aid philosophy of certain schools is admirable in many ways, and works well for the majority. The fact is, however, that families in a certain income bracket are not well served by this philosophy. I am not talking about families with net worth in the millions; I am talking about families with several children, modest savings, a mortgage, and other expenses that make taking on an additional $40,000-50,000 per year or more in college tuition, room and board *very* taxing.

Life is often about tradeoffs. You and your young athlete must make a careful college decision weighing all factors—including finance!

Recommended Reading

The following books and periodicals are helpful resources for starting the college search, including the search for financial aid:

Books:

Fiske, Edward B. *The Fiske Guide to Colleges—2008.* Naperville, IL: Sourcebooks. 2007

Fiske, Edward B. and Bruce G. Hammond. *The Fiske Guide to Getting Into the Right College.* Naperville, IL: Sourcebooks. 2007

Gold, Jordan and Colleen Byers. *Student's Guide to College: the Definitive Guide to America's Top 100 Schools: Written by the Real Experts—the Students Who Attend Them.* New York: Penguin.

Greene, Howard and Matthew Greene. *Greenes' Guides to Educational Planning: Inside the Top Colleges: Realities of Life and Learning in America's Elite Colleges.* New York: Harper Collins. 2000

Greene, Howard and Matthew Greene. *Greenes' Guides to Educational Planning: The Hidden Ivies: Thirty Colleges of Excellence.* New York: Harper Collins. 2000

Mathews, Jay. *Harvard Schmarvard: Getting Beyond the Ivy League to the College That is Best for You.* Prima.

Pope, Loren. *Colleges That Change Lives (revised edition).* New York: Penguin. 2006

Steinberg, Jacques. *The Gatekeepers: Inside the Admissions Process of a Premier College. New York:* Viking. 2003 (This offers one of the best explanations of how one highly selective college actually makes decisions.)

Thacker, Lloyd, Editor. *College Unranked: Ending the College Admissions Frenzy.* Cambridge, MA: Harvard University Press. 2005

The Best 361 Colleges—2008. New York: The Princeton Review. Random House. 2007

Zmirak, John, Editor. *Choosing the Right College: The Whole Truth About America's Top Schools.* Wilmington, DE: Intercollegiate Studies Institute. 2007

Websites:

http://connection.naviance.com/stgeorges—a good starting point for all college matters—includes links to college websites.

www.stgeorges.edu/—The college counseling page of the SG website—lots of useful handouts available as downloads.

www.collegeboard.com—The all purpose College Board website—includes a college search site and links to college homepages, plus a good section on financial aid.

www.finaid.com—Contains useful information about scholarships and other financial aid matters, including a financial calculator that estimates how much your family can expect to pay.

www.fastweb.org—excellent financial aid resource—includes information about scholarships and a good financial aid estimator.

Chapter 32

THE BLUE-CHIPPER

"In the beginning it's a lot of fun. I mean, you've never experienced anything like it before. But after awhile I started putting my cell phone on silent, asking my mother to pick up calls I didn't recognize. It does get stressful."
— High school All-American and current member of the
University of Connecticut Women's Basketball team, Lorin Dixon

The top-level recruit for a Division I revenue-producing sport receives a thorough education in "excess" which, if not closely monitored, can produce damaging long-term consequences. Highly sought after recruits often develop an inappropriate sense of entitlement that hinders personal growth and achievement. In sports, there are few things sadder than a 35-year-old ex-star who still acts like he is on an athletic scholarship.

Most Division I schools have substantial recruiting resources and are under pressure to reel in blue-chip athletes. There is little in common between the recruitment process in Division I revenue-producing sports and recruiting in Divisions II and III. The Division I process may include the following:

- A beginning volley of high praise or fawning that intoxicates many youngsters *and* parents.
- A continuing series of emails, letters, phone calls, and birthday cards. (To help regulate this situation, the NCAA now prohibits *any* representative of a college's athletic interests, including prominent alumni or celebrities, from any contact with Division I or Division II recruits.)

- Manipulative recruiting tactics that need to be regulated by the family. Some coaches try to use a "friendly relationship" to subtly pressure a recruit into feeling obligated to the coach and school. *Parents must make it clear to all recruiters that their athlete is happy to establish a relationship, but that decisions will be made based on what is best for the athlete, not who acts most like a friend.*
- The feeling of being under siege during the process, and relief when it is finally over!
- A recognition that the process was more excessive than the recruit and family ever imagined possible.

Parents Need to Establish Guidelines

If your child is a blue-chip college prospect, believe me, you will know it, sometimes as early as the ninth or tenth grade. Your first objective should be to create an environment that will protect your child and family from being consumed by the process. A series of conversations with former blue-chip athletes, and their reflections on their recruiting experiences, are revealing. Some indicated they enjoyed being recruited; others found it distasteful; *all agreed on the need for guidelines.*

One former blue-chip athlete told us, "It is essential for the parents and the recruit's 'advisor' to set up clear contact guidelines between the colleges and the blue-chip athlete. In my home, coach calls could be made on Tuesday and Thursday from 7 to 9 P.M. My dad made every coach abide by this rule or risk being eliminated from recruiting me. Without these rules, the situation would have totally disrupted our family." *Strong parental control over the recruiting process is vital!*

The Critical Role of The Advisor

A highly recruited blue-chip athlete needs a trustworthy person to undertake the role of volunteer advisor. This role encompasses the following time consuming tasks:

- Serving as the liaison between the recruit and college coaches.
- Serving as the liaison between the recruit and the media.
- Helping the family develop clear recruiting guidelines with two overall objectives:
  - Afford the recruit the opportunity to have reasonably normal junior and senior years of high school.
  - Assure that the family will not be completely disrupted by the recruiting process.

Selecting the Advisor

Candidates for this role include:

- Parents of the recruit — remember this is very time consuming.
- Your recruit's school or AAU/Club coach.
- A trusted friend.

In many cases, the role can be shared with specific duties assigned.

When considering who will undertake this volunteer role, "job qualifications" to keep in mind include:

- Knowledge of the sport.
- A genuine interest in the recruit's well-being.
- The ability to say no and stand firm whether or not the recruiter is a famous coach.
- The awareness of the *extreme* time commitment involved, and the willingness to take time to do the job properly.
- The integrity to resist inducements that compromise the objectivity of the advisor.

Should the Advisor Be the Coach?

Possibly, but not necessarily. In many cases, the coach can be an excellent choice, but the family and coach must discuss:

- Clear rules regarding all communications about the athlete, including your expectations of what communication you do and do not want to know about. Some coaches who take on the position of advisor also take it upon themselves to discard letters, not return phone calls, and keep the recruit and family in the dark about many communications.
- Star gazing. Some high school and AAU/Club coaches who take on the role of advisor are guilty of "star gazing." When a famous college coach calls with messages of friendship and flattery, the advisor must not forget that the first responsibility is to the recruit.

Advisor Inducements

The advisor for any top-flight recruit is often placed in compromising situations. A high stakes recruiting war may be accompanied by the dangling of perquisites — some within NCAA rules, others forbidden by the NCAA. These may include job offers at the coach's summer sports camp, free tickets, illegal cash payments, or an unethical offer to work as an assistant coach.

A blue-chip athlete needs a competent and trustworthy advisor, or the process will become unwieldy for the athlete and family. Select the advisor as soon as it becomes apparent that your young athlete will be heavily recruited.

Suggested Guidelines for the Blue-Chip Athlete

When schools start to show an interest, to whatever extent possible, have initial contacts go through the advisor. The advisor should:

1. Carefully study the NCAA recruiting process guidelines. This is a *must* for the advisor (See *NCAA Guide for the College Bound Student-Athlete*).

2. Make sure the parents and athlete understand these guidelines.

3. Help the family establish its own limitations on recruiting. Particularly when many schools are involved, even strict NCAA guidelines cannot prevent intrusion into the family's life.

4. Establish *very* strict limitations on phone calls, letters and email. Many families find that a limitation of one correspondence per week per school prevents an avalanche of letters, cards, and other forms of communication. (If the NCAA allows instant messenger and text messaging in the future, make sure to establish equally strict limitations on this intrusive practice.)

5. Put guidelines in writing and send copies to all interested colleges.

6. Make sure that the recruit and family *carefully* read the NCAA regulations on illegal inducements.

7. Help the recruit winnow the list of schools to a reasonable number (6 - 8 schools is a reasonable number).

8. When the list is reduced, the student or advisor should make a personal phone call, and follow up with a firm but polite letter or email to those schools which have been eliminated, in effect saying, "We appreciate your interest in Jane. Unfortunately, Jane has decided to eliminate your school from consideration. Please respect Jane's wishes for no further contact." This is very important, because some schools refuse to take "no" for an answer until the student-athlete has signed a National Letter of Intent. If coaches do not honor the request of the advisor, you or the advisor may complain to the athletic director of that institution.

9. Remember, it is not unreasonable for coaches who have been eliminated to ask why their program has been taken off the recruit's list. Coaches spend a lot of time and effort recruiting, and it is helpful for them to determine what went wrong, or how another school may have done a better job.

10. Help arrange college coach home visits for the 6-8 final schools. I recom-

mend that the list be narrowed to 6-8 before the home visits, because they are important and time consuming. One recruit with whom I spoke actually had 13 schools visit his home, and then cut his list down. "It took way too much time and I should have reduced the number of schools before the home visits," he said.

In most sports, a college program that has *real* interest in an athlete will send the head coach to the home visit.

11. After the home visits, the list should be reduced to a maximum of five schools, which is the limit on Division I expense-paid college visits allowed by the NCAA. The advisor should arrange the official visits, perhaps starting with those which most interest the athlete. Some athletes decide after two or three visits that they need no more official visits.

12. When a coach believes he has a strong lead with a recruit, a common ploy is to ask the player to visit his school first in hope of a quick signing. "Our number two choice plans to visit Friday, so we need your answer by Thursday," is a typical pressure tactic.

Do not be reluctant to contact the NCAA or a college compliance officer at a local school with questions or concerns. The NCAA is very receptive to answering these questions.

In the absence of very strict guidelines, a blue-chip recruiting experience can result in a complete loss of focus on academics.

The Advantages of an Early Choice for the Blue-Chip Athlete

Early choice for the highly sought after player means a decision by the end of junior year or during the summer prior to the senior year. Blue-chip athletes may not be subject to the same admissions deadlines or acceptance dates as other candidates, and there are several advantages to making an early decision. The seemingly endless intense recruitment period will end. Pressures and distractions during senior year are minimized, allowing a student to focus on schoolwork, athletic improvement and social activities.

One interesting issue that arises with an early signing of a National Letter of Intent is the gap between signing and formal admission to the school. In such cases, the coach, prior to sending an NLI, usually submits an athlete's transcript and test scores to the admissions office for a "read." The coach is unlikely to send an NLI if it appears a student will not academically qualify for admission.

Alas, some high profile revenue producing programs have been known to have an academically questionable recruit sign the NLI in order to pressure the admissions office to accept the player. "They get the letter signed and deal with admissions later," admitted a "Big Time Program" athletic administrator.

But Not Too Early

There is a growing trend among highly recruited athletes to make a verbal commitment as early as their sophomore year. I strongly recommend that this type of decision *not* be made at such an early date. The verbal offer carries no enforceable commitment, and many things can change, including the coach!

Illegal Inducements

"A good name is rather to be chosen than riches."
— Proverbs

Illegal inducements offered to recruits are fairly common in Division I revenue producing sports, and rare in all other intercollegiate sports. The buy-off might come in the form of cash, cars, clothing, airline tickets, a loan, tickets to professional games or concerts, a mortgage pay-off, the purchase of a home, or a job for mom, dad or the high school/AAU/Club coach. The briber may be the head or assistant coach, or a "booster" connected with the program, who might be acting without the knowledge or consent of the coaching staff. The primary targets are the blue-chip athlete, the high school or AAU/Club coach, *and* the parents.

The NCAA has very extensive guidelines on illegal inducements, and the penalties are severe. The rules which govern this kind of impropriety have been carefully thought out, and should be observed.

Take the time to read the rules and be sure your athlete does so as well. It is not worth risking punishment for a rules violation or damaging your child's reputation because of a lack of knowledge of the rules or an inadvertent violation. There will be intense scrutiny of all aspects of a blue-chip recruit's life before, during, and after a college decision is made.

The Heavy Recruitment Process and the College Experience Have Nothing in Common

Many former blue-chippers pointed out that their recruitment had little similarity to their actual college experience. "My college recruiters convinced me that playing football would be a work-filled but idyllic period in my life," stated a former scholarship athlete. "Once I enrolled, it was hard work, but certainly not idyllic, especially when I did not make the starting team."

Said another, "When I was being recruited, I was treated like a star; when

I enrolled and another guy replaced me in the starting lineup, I was treated like a substitute."

Almost all blue-chip recruits think they will become highly paid professionals, but only a rare few of this elite group will ever make "The Show."

The Recruit's Obligation — To Inform Eliminated Coaches

Regardless of whether an athlete is a blue-chipper or a Division III prospect, once an athlete makes a final college decision, the coaches at all finalist schools should be personally informed of the recruit's decision. Your young adult should call and thank each coach for the time, effort and consideration the coach has invested in the recruiting process.

Such a call to a coach can be daunting for a 17- or 18-year-old. Nonetheless, it is a call that must be made by the recruit. To make the call less unnerving, a parent should inform all head coaches of the final schools that, "At the end of this process, you will hear from my son personally. Our expectation is that you will respect his choice, no matter what that choice is."

The recruit should be prepared for the coach to restate his case. Unfortunately, a few coaches display anger and rudeness during such calls, which should reinforce the wisdom of the decision. The recruit should be prepared to politely but resolutely stand firm.

A valuable element of the recruiting process is teaching a young person the importance of personally contacting the coaches and ending the recruiting relationship in an honest and dignified manner. Even a disappointed coach should respect a recruit who has taken the time to call and explain his decision, especially since some athletes later decide to transfer.

Final Point!

"You have a special gift. Use it to help others."
— Nelson Mandela to Tiger Woods

A blue-chip high school athlete is in a wonderful position to begin to achieve this objective by simply being courteous to peers, including those with whom the blue chipper has little in common.

NOTE: Any NCAA rule addressed in the chapter is subject to change. Consult the NCAA website (*www.ncaa.org*) for current information.

Chapter 33

THE DIVISION I PROSPECT
WHO DESIRES ACADEMIC RIGOR

"In Division I, it's no longer the preseason, the season and then relaxation.
It's an ongoing, year-round season."
—Associate Commisioner Mid-American Conference, Rick Boyages

If a young athlete is a Division I prospect, you can be virtually certain that athlete will wish to pursue not only Division I competition but, in all likelihood, the highest level of Division I competition possible. So, what if you have a child who is an excellent student with the academic potential to go on to medical school, law school or other serious graduate study, and is being recruited by Division I?

The first thing you need to realize is that accepting the athletic scholarship may well reduce the chances for such serious intellectual engagement. This is not opinion—it is fact. But can the Division I scholarship athlete carve out the time to pursue pre-med? The answer is yes, but only with some *major* pre-college preparation, and *major* in-college sacrifices.

The "Enemy"—Time

The primary educational "enemy" facing the Division I athlete who wishes to pursue a rigorous undergraduate major, with a goal of graduate school, will be *time*. Mike Walsh, former Athletic Director at Washington & Lee and former Head Baseball Coach at Dartmouth, points out that there will be three major time-eaters for the college athlete who is a serious student, especially at the Division I level:

1. Academic requirements, including class, study and research.

2. Sports requirements, including in and out of season practice, strength training, games, travel, meetings and the "sports focus factor" which can be quite consuming.

3. Social life, including personal relationships, parties and down time.

Walsh, and many other intercollegiate athletic administrators and college professors, with whom I spoke, propose that even a serious Division III athlete who is truly committed to a rigorous academic major must forego a good portion of social life. Walsh adds, "For the Division I athlete who is motivated to pursue a very tough academic major, there will be, in truth, virtually no social life—it will be class, team requirements, and all extra time in the library. To a somewhat lesser extent, this is true for the Division III athlete with the same high academic objectives."

A Key Approach—Internalizing Sports Goals

If your young athlete aspires to play Division I sports and undertake a rigorous major, you should encourage the athlete to pursue "selfless internalized sports goals" such as fitness, fun, teamwork and camaraderie (as opposed to an obsessive focus on external goals such as honors, statistics, press clippings and the like.)

I found this concept to be very much in evidence at Division III Caltech, where the undergraduate students had academic pressures that few other students ever encounter. Each day, the principal sports objective of the Caltech varsity athletes with whom I spoke was to reduce the enormous academic pressure they faced. Many accomplished this by setting a goal of *enjoying* the daily two hours of exercise, team building, competition and friendship they found in varsity sports, and not bringing disappointment from the athletic field or gym into the library or classroom. I also interviewed a group of Division I athletes/pre-med majors. They *all* strongly reinforced the Caltech view. Said one, "As a pre-med major and Division I athlete, I look at my daily sports regimen as a welcome break, not as a pressure builder. If it wasn't a welcome break, I wouldn't do it."

For the serious Division I *student-athlete* engaged in a rigorous undergraduate major with the goal of grad school, the "internalizing of goals" approach is advisable, if not necessary. A student-athlete cannot afford to lose academic concentration due to a bad practice or game. *The serious student who wants to play college sports and pursue a rigorous major simply cannot afford to "bring the game home."*

What to Do

During the recruitment period, meet with the academic advisor in the major in question as well as professors at those schools under consideration. The objective of these meetings is to see what is realistic in terms of a rigorous major. Winkle Kelley, Coordinator, Advising Programs for Student-Athletes at the University of Rhode Island, points out, "The athletic-academic advisors are not the best 'go-to people' for this issue; it is the pre-med or pre-engineering advisor with whom the recruit needs to deal at this stage and once enrolled."

This type of careful planning should be done *before* your young athlete signs a National Letter of Intent. "I want to commit to pre-med and I want to find out how it can be done," is the point your young athlete needs to raise and get answered.

Be aware that such a pursuit may encompass the following:

- It may take five years to graduate, not four.
- It will likely involve very busy summers filled with academic course work (and perhaps little opportunity for a summer job, or summers at home).
- It may involve preparing to start school during the summer prior to freshman autumn matriculation.

In other words, it may involve "stretching out" the undergraduate experience to five or even six years, with little down time.

Here are some more important issues to pursue:

- What scholarship assistance can be made available to study a fifth year and/or during the summer? If none is available, will the school be willing to help with a graduate assistantship or some other job for the fifth year?
- If the academic major involves labs, make an arrangement with the coach regarding practices which conflict with labs before signing the National Letter of Intent. Most coaches will agree to a special plan to accommodate labs, and the majority of coaches have options of when to schedule practices. If a coach wishes to accommodate a player with lab assignments, the coach can schedule early morning, late afternoon or even evening practices that do not conflict with the lab. Many coaches are also receptive to an athlete missing a day or two of practice due

33

to labs or other class assignments, particularly if the athlete is willing to engage in individual workouts to "make up the time." (Although coaches will make it clear that only the best players will see the field or court, and that those who are able to devote more time may have a better chance to accomplish this objective.)

- How does the academic advisor in the major of interest feel about courses in the summer? We found that many pre-med advisors do not want their students taking rigorous science courses in the summer, which is another reason why pre-planning is so important.

Eight Other Suggestions

1. Early in your child's formal education, i.e., elementary school, establish a "climate of learning" in your home that begins with encouraging your young athlete to read—and read—and read. "Reading makes life much more interesting," is a point to make.

2. Well before senior year of high school, help your athlete learn of what the Division I experience may be like. Tell your child a real fact: many Division I athletes who want to take on pre-med or go to law school quickly "slide" into an easier major and give up the academic dream in favor of the all-consuming sports dream. This switch of majors often occurs as early as first semester of freshman year. For the serious student who truly desires to attend graduate school, reinforce the notion that significant planning must come into play well before college matriculation.

3. Tell your child that certain majors, e.g., pre-med or engineering, may simply not be compatible with some Division I programs. Stress the "ongoing season" concept, which Division I college sports has become, and that the young athlete may have to make a choice.

4. Make sure to involve the high school guidance counselor in the planning process, and do this early on, i.e., freshman or sophomore year. As part of this process, *make sure that Advanced Placement courses are taken.*

5. Check on the type of tutoring offered at finalist schools. In many cases, athletic tutoring is designed more for the "at-risk student" than the excellent student. (Indeed, several surveyed college athletes who were top students complained that the athletic tutoring is geared for the at-risk student.) If this is the case, try to "negotiate" a one-on-one tutor. This negotiation should take place during the recruitment process.

6. Check on the level of the "academic enhancement" services offered at the

school in comparison with other finalist schools. The one-on-one tutor and academic enhancement center could be real keys to successfully completing a rigorous undergraduate major.

7. Seek out a coach who is genuinely committed to rigorous academic pursuit. You may be pleased to find that a number of college coaches *like* having great students in their program. "It is good for the reputation of our program, and good students do not present the kind of problems for me that at-risk students can present," said one surveyed coach.

8. Finally, since so few Division I athletes are pursuing rigorous majors such as pre-med, you may find that certain schools will "bend over backwards" to help your young athlete succeed in such a major. This could mean a four-year commitment to extensive one-on-one tutoring and other special services from the academic enhancement center. Said one assistant football coach at an upper major program, "If we see a high-profile football recruit who wants pre-med and can do the work, we will do all we can to help that young man succeed. Plus, our Sports Information Director will also make sure that the young man is our poster boy for the next four years!"

It takes a highly intelligent, highly disciplined student to make it through certain majors like engineering and pre-med. It takes a highly intelligent and *extraordinarily* disciplined Division I student-athlete to make it through such a major.

Getting a Fifth Year Paid For

Let's repeat an important premise: The college athlete who desires a rigorous undergraduate major should seriously consider a five-year academic clock.

Getting five years of athletic aid is a bit tricky, but not impossible. Consider two points:

- Since athletic scholarships are renewable annually, technically, a coach cannot offer a five-year guaranteed scholarship.
- According to several Division I coaches and administrators, such an arrangement can be verbally negotiated with a coach, particularly if the "negotiator" is a blue-chip recruit and as long as the athletic department does not have a policy which precludes five years of athletic scholarship assistance.

Why Such an Arrangement is Possible

Division I athletes are eligible for four years of varsity competition over a five-year cycle, which begins on the date of freshman matriculation. Thus, many coaches can theoretically agree to five-years of college athletic scholarship assistance, *particularly if a redshirt year is negotiated, i.e., sitting out a year of actual competition.* During the redshirt year, a player can still practice with the team so that skills are not seriously eroded. This redshirt strategy is typically utilized as a way to improve physical strength, but it can also be useful in relieving pressure from the combination of academic rigor and big-time athletics.

Other Considerations for the Five-Year Student-Athlete

- Risk factor—At the Division I level, it is common for coaches to leave before the five-year period has expired. This is why it is so important to get the commitment properly documented, even with dated notes from meetings/discussions.
- As noted, such a five-year scholarship option depends upon the policy of the *institution* and, frankly, the negotiating power of the prospect (the blue-chipper will obviously have more negotiating power in this matter). Since some schools will provide such scholarship assistance, by all means bring it up. Be aware that the fifth-year scholarship player who has exhausted eligibility might be required by the coach to do something such as serving as a part-time assistant coach (which can be *very* time consuming). The redshirt option eliminates this possibility.
- "Degree Completion Opportunities." For information on degree completion opportunities, visit the NCAA website at *(www.ncaa.org)*.

Peer Influence

There are innumerable studies of different student groups that point to an irrefutable fact: when students are surrounded by peers who have high academic goals, these students are more likely to raise their own academic goals. The Gautreaux program, in which poor families from Chicago were given the opportunity to relocate to suburban middle class areas, is a shining example of this premise working.

This same "Gautreaux concept" applies to a college athlete. If the athlete desires a rigorous major and graduate school, and is surrounded by teammates with no such ambitions, it will require *tremendous* perseverance on the part of the serious student-athlete. Examining the academic status and interests of potential teammates is an important part of the recruit's overall research.

No "Senior Vacation"

For the college prospect who desires a rigorous major and possible graduate school study, senior year of high school is *very important*. "It is imperative that this type of student-athlete treat the senior high school year as a rigorous year of academic work- not a vacation," states Winkle Kelley of URI.

A strong senior high school academic year can:

- Get the student-athlete into the disciplined approach that will be required to balance a challenging college academic load and a varsity sport.
- Test to see if the student-athlete really has what it takes to achieve college objectives.
- Afford the student-athlete the chance to take a number of demanding courses that can be applied to college. "Entering college with a number of credits can be very helpful to the student who desires a rigorous major and possible graduate study," states Kelley.

Point/Counterpoint

While lecturing at Division I schools, I have frequently heard a number of valid points made by Division I coaches and athletic administrators regarding the worthiness of the Division I experience. The advantages they cite—some of which also exist at Division II and III schools—include:

- A highly regimented schedule—in and out of season—which produces a disciplined approach to all aspects of school.
- Expert tutoring which, in many cases, is not available to the rest of the student body.
- A clear focus on a goal.
- The many benefits of being part of a closely-knit team.
- Great networking opportunities. (Although they admit that these opportunities become worthless without proper effort and performance once in a job.)
- Exposure to exceptional leadership. (Some of the finest leaders I have ever observed are Division I coaches and athletic directors.)
- Exposure to a culture of excellence. Many Division I programs exemplify excellence in areas such as preparation, execution and community outreach.
- Much greater diversity and much greater opportunity to meet people from varying backgrounds.
- Some Division I schools report higher graduation rates for student-ath-

letes than for the general student body.

- First class facilities and equipment.
- Opportunities to pre-register for classes which can be extremely difficult to gain access to, e.g., small, popular classes.
- Full access to top-level professionals in sports medicine, weight training, sports psychology and sports nutrition.

As Division I proponents correctly point out, there are many other students on campus who do little academic work and whose idle time is frittered away in undertakings far less desirable than a varsity sport.

The NCAA is also trying to ensure greater academic development for Division I athletes. To hold colleges and universities more accountable for the academic progress of student-athletes, the NCAA has instituted a well-thought-out academic reform plan which emphasizes "progress toward degree", i.e., keeping student athletes on track to graduate. The plan calls for increasing standards at the high school level in order to become eligible to compete in college, then instituting meaningful measures of academic success and accountability at the college level. Thus far, the plan has met with considerable success.

These are all valid points, yet the objective of this book is to present reasoned opinions backed up by facts — and advise you accordingly. In this case, here are three Division I facts that I feel are irrefutable:

1. The time requirements of Division I sports generally begin as early as first semester of freshman year. When this "reality strike" occurs (virtually no social life, and frequent — if not constant — fatigue from practices, games, meetings, classes and library time), many serious and well-meaning Division I student-athletes opt for an easier course of study than that which they had originally intended.

2. If your child is a Division I scholarship athlete, it will be very difficult to pursue a highly rigorous major in preparation for medical school, law school or PhD study.

3. With careful academic preparation, *generally beginning years before college matriculation,* along with a well-thought-out college course plan and the willingness to make considerable sacrifices, such a lofty academic goal can be achieved.

College Objectives/Job Reality

Virtually all students enter college with non-academic and non-sports objectives, such as meeting new friends and enjoying an active social life. And, of course, virtually all students look upon college as a key to future job opportunities. Tell your young athlete that "training the mind" is the first priority, and that the contacts made as a Division I player will do no good if one is not equipped to perform well in one's job.

If your young athlete is able to balance a Division I sports experience and a rigorous academic major—it will be an extraordinary accomplishment. It can be done, but as this chapter suggests, it will be an extremely difficult road.

33

Chapter 34

THE PLUS SIDE OF DIVISION I

"A man, to be greatly good. . .must put himself in the place of another and of many others."
—English poet, Percy Shelley

"M yriad mindedness" means understanding the importance of respecting the viewpoints and ideals of others. It also means being able to disagree without being disagreeable!

Myriad mindedness is a term that all of us need to bear in mind when we examine different levels of college sports; it is no more appropriate for a Division III advocate to assume that all Division I participation is without merit than it is for a Division I advocate to assume that Division III is devoid of athletic challenges.

While I am opposed to the excessive time commitment demanded by certain college athletic programs, and aware of the educational tradeoffs inherent in competing for a number of Division I programs, I am also aware of three facts:

1. Heavily invested in their sport, a number of Division I athletes may well miss out on the opportunity to be engrossed intellectually over the course of their college lives. Yet the term "late bloomer" is not confined to athletes. Many in our society, including overbooked Division I athletes, find their intellectual curiosity awakened at some point during adulthood.

2. I have observed many below average and average students, who were top

athletic prospects, be very well served by a Division I program. Students in this category are often the recipients of excellent tutoring and attention and, as a consequence, often raise their academic profile. "They come into their own with this type of attention," states Winkle Kelley of the University of Rhode Island.

As one Division I athlete, who had entered college as a below average student, told me, "I'm better off in this Division I program—educationally and athletically—than the other alternatives that I had coming out of high school."

3. Suppressing a dream—whether that of the young cellist who aspires to Carnegie Hall or that of the young basketball player who aspires to Madison Square Garden—is unwise. It is far better to foster the balanced "anchor/aspiration approach" espoused in the book.

An important objective of college is to improve one's lot. Because of the time factor, Division I has definitely prevented many athletes from the rigorous academic pursuit that might well have led to medical school, law school, or some other form of intense graduate study. On the other hand, the Division I experience has helped many below average and average students find themselves, prepare for a good quality life, and do very well in their jobs. Said one academic athletic counselor, "Remember, not every student desires to be a doctor, lawyer or engineer, and our society rests on the efforts of many types of noble professions."

While I fret over the number of Division I college athletes who miss out on the opportunity to train their minds as efficiently as they train their bodies, I find many Division I athletes to be highly disciplined, respectful, and in possession of a number of other worthy values such as diligence and passion. Indeed, many Division I athletes have something that a number of other college students lack—a focus on something vitally important to them—a mission. *"Through sports, I feel I'm on my way toward something good; that my life has meaning,"* was the way one surveyed Division I athlete put it.

Their challenge, of course, will be to find something as stimulating and meaningful in adulthood.

Division I or Division III?

In general, I find the Division III sports experience to have significantly more advantages in terms of balance and the opportunity to truly become intellectually engaged. Yet I also realize that Division III is not for everyone,

34

and that many gifted athletes understandably feel the need to test their skills against high-level competition.

The issue here is one of tradeoffs.

- If you choose a high-profile Division I program, you probably miss the chance to pursue a rigorous academic major.
- If you choose a lower level program, you miss the chance to test your sports skills against the best competition.
- If you play in a high-profile Division I program, you may get positive media exposure.
- If you play in a high-profile Division I program, you are subject to intense media scrutiny.
- If you play in a high-profile Division I program, you are accorded the respect and admiration of many fellow students.
- If you play in a high-profile Division I program, you are subject to intense scrutiny by fellow students, and expectations of good behavior by all observers.

It is not the objective of The College Recruiting section to suggest that all Division I athletics are limiting in some way. The objective is to make the young athlete aware of important facts before the college choice is made. For the Division I athlete, the "tradeoff issue" will likely relate to time expenditure, the expectations of the coach, and the awareness that certain educational and/or social opportunities will probably be lost.

The key is for the aspiring college athlete to research and consider all of the facts *before* making a very important decision.

THE FIVE AREAS THAT ALL DIVISION I ATHLETES NEED TO ADDRESS

"In Division I athletics, perception is reality!"
— Paul Kassabian, Director of Compliance, University of Rhode Island

1. Peer influence. Ask yourself three related questions:
   - Do you have friends at your school other than your teammates?
   - Are you hanging around with anyone who is truly a top student?
   - How is your "education" in comparison to other students on campus who are not playing sports? (If you see that many non-varsity students are getting ahead of you academically, that should tell you something.)

(**FIVE AREAS** *continued*)

2. Getting out of your comfort zone. One of your key objectives should be to become a true "University Citizen," which ranges from attending campus theatre productions and lectures, to taking a genuine interest in the activities of non-athletes. The message—getting out of your comfort zone will equate to personal growth and improvement.

3. Your attitude. Many people, including fellow students, will be put off by a Division I athlete who puts on airs. Be aware of two facts:
   - Some, perhaps even many of your fellow students, may re-enter your life at a later stage.
   - Your reputation is being formed now, and will stay with you, for better or worse. The message—expand your "circle of concern" by treating all people well, not just teammates.

4. Scrutiny. You will be scrutinized by the media, fans and fellow students far more than most others on campus. Two messages:
   - A challenge of sports is that acclaim often precedes maturity.
   - Take care not to prove the axiom that, "it is best not to get discovered too early in life."

5. Faculty. Most faculty will be fair in their judgment of you; some will pre-judge you as a mere jock who does not belong in their classroom. The message—be present, punctual, polite, prepared and alert! (And, if treated unfairly, do not be reluctant to make this known to the professor and department chair.)

Chapter 35

THE FINAL CHOICE

"Decide: to succumb to the preponderance of one set of influences over another set."
—American satirist and journalist, Ambrose Bierce

The key to any college decision is to make informed choices, and the information in Chapters 28 - 36 will help your investigation. Neither parents nor students should make a choice without seriously researching the programs under consideration. It is vital for athletes and parents to understand the short-term and long-term tradeoffs involved in different choices, and then together make a choice which best accommodates a student's athletic and academic skills and goals.

Some students have the ability to play Division I athletics and effectively seek academic classes of value, but in general, a Division III experience offers far more balance. The choice must be made with full knowledge of the expectations, commitments and opportunities involved.

A Key Question

"Should I Play College Sports?"

Ivy League institutions report that more than 50% of recruited Ivy League athletes do not stay with their sport for four years. Many college students, despite being fine athletes, opt not to play. "Time" was the deciding factor for most of these students. "I wanted a serious education and felt that devoting 45-50 hours a week over the course of a 52-game baseball season was not going to afford me this opportunity," stated one young man who, after carefully examining the time commitment of Division I baseball, decided to forego a promising college baseball career and accept an academic scholarship.

The college sports experience can be enjoyable, educational and exciting. Plus, being on a team can help a callow freshman make a smooth transition to campus life. Right away, the freshman has a coach/mentor and teammates upon whom the freshman can depend. Be sure, however, that your prospective player understands that there may be little time for activities other than sports and studies.

If your child is serious about obtaining an education, it may be necessary to consider not only the question: "Which college sports program should I choose?" but "Should I play college sports at all?"

Remind your athlete that very few college players end up making a career of sports. The thrill of playing in college quickly turns to frustration when the athlete graduates and finds that college sports failed to provide the requisite skills to compete in the real world. Said one surveyed ex-athlete, "I was 25 when I finally realized that it was better to be well-educated than a great athlete. It was quite a shock!"

The Diploma versus Critical Thinking

"Our current, test driven education…emphasizes rote learning, which is the death knell to critical thinking."
—Author David Elkind

When asked to list the most important objective of a college education, faculty always cite critical thinking—the ability to analyze competing ideas and arrive at reasoned judgments—at or near the top of their objectives for their students. I have addressed student-athletes at more than 100 colleges and universities in Divisions I, II and III. On the whole, I find the student-athletes to be a wonderfully bright and optimistic lot. For the most part, they are goal setters whose principal academic objective is to pass tests and graduate—a worthy aim to be sure.

Yet my observations and instincts tell me that a significant number of student-athletes are more rote learners than critical thinkers—especially those who are spending excessive hours playing and focusing on their sport and who are highly dependent upon tutors.

Encourage your college student athlete to become a critical thinker and to draw the distinction between a diploma and a trained mind. *Ask your student-athlete to meet the Aristotle Critical Thinking Litmus test, which is, as he wrote, "The mark of an educated mind is to be able to entertain a thought without necessarily accepting it."*

A Motivational Suggestion!

When your child is in the seventh or eighth grade, try the following: on a spring or summer weekend, or a beautiful autumn day, take a drive to a good college, and perhaps even attend an athletic event. Allow your child to "feel" the campus and make sure your only message is, "If you work hard enough in school, you may have a chance at a college like this."

Just as watching a great athlete may motivate your youngster to become more serious about his game, visiting an attractive college may motivate him to become more serious about his studies! There is a difference between constantly pressuring your children to get into a good college, and exposing them to options with the hope that such exposure will motivate them to be more diligent students.

35

SECTION IX

TOO MUCH TIME ON SPORTS?

Chapter 36

THE EXTRAORDINARY TIME COMMITMENT
OF MANY COLLEGE ATHLETES
AND A REVEALING PROFILE

"Dost thou love life, then do not squander time, for that's the stuff life is made of."
—Benjamin Franklin

The Time Commitment of College Athletes

A rigorous academic experience is rarely the sole objective of college students. The majority set other goals such as developing friendships and participating in extracurricular activities. I am a *strong* proponent of college sports participation when it contributes to a balanced education. Unfortunately, the time requirements of college sports often prevent many college athletes from devoting as much time to studies as to sports, let alone positioning sports where it belongs, as a true extracurricular activity.

Mike Walsh, former Athletic Director of Washington & Lee and former Head Baseball Coach at Dartmouth, states that college sports, "are asking more and more of the student's soul than years ago. Too many student athletes, even at the fine Division III schools, enter college wanting to get a good education, but because of the enormous time commitment of college sports—an alarming number of athletes are unable to reach this objective."

This chapter describes those time commitments in detail.

NCAA Time Limits

"When I accepted the scholarship, I didn't understand that the football program would own me."
— Student athlete's survey statement

In 1991, in response to an alarming number of college coaches who were demanding far too much of their athletes' time, the NCAA adopted strict time limits for athletic activities, i.e., a maximum of 20 hours per week for "official activities" during the traditional and non-traditional seasons, and one mandatory day off. While well intentioned, the official time limits do not take into account "uncountable" time factors such as travel time to away games, "unofficial" but recommended practices and workouts, training room and rehabilitation activities, time in the locker room, informal meetings, and the all important "preoccupation" factor that is so common among serious athletes. (See Appendix for NCAA countable and uncountable athletic activities.)

Twelve Questions to Pose to the Aspiring College Athlete

"A degree in hand is not always an indicator of educational achievement."
— Former Division I athlete's survey statement

Well before senior year, any high school athlete interested in playing a college sport should be asked to start considering the following questions:

1. What do you want your life to be like in college?

2. Are you looking at the college experience as the last chance to play competitive sports?

3. Do you mainly see college as a stepping stone to professional sports? Is this realistic?

4. Do you aspire to high academic achievement?

5. Do you want to pursue a major/profession requiring rigorous academic work and/or graduate school?

6. To accommodate the time demanded of your sport, will you choose a different major/course of study than you would pick if you were not playing a college sport?

7. Are you prepared to settle on a major that may have little application in later life?

8. Do you realize that college will present you with the best opportunity to acquire skills that are rewarded in a global economy?

36

9. Are you prepared to face the possibility of being constantly fatigued and/or pressed for time—and wish you had more energy for your studies?

10. If you are on an athletic scholarship and benched, will you feel stuck knowing that, if you quit, you may lose your scholarship?

11. If you are not on an athletic scholarship and are miserable about little playing time, will you want to quit?

12. Do you love your sport enough to make the required sacrifices to play at the college level?

Sports advocates like to tell young athletes that college sports opportunities are unique, even "once in a lifetime." Your job is to make clear that college also presents unique, "once in a lifetime" academic opportunities which, for virtually all college students, play the most important role in determining the long-term value of the college experience.

A KEY CHANGE!

Those college sports "traditionally" played in the fall or spring now have "non-traditional" seasons as well. The non-traditional season involves formal practices, scrimmages and, on occasion, games against opposing colleges. (The non-traditional season games are seldom part of the official record.) Here are two examples:

Soccer
- The traditional season for college soccer is the fall, with National Championships played in late-November/early-December (depending upon the Division).
- The non-traditional season for college soccer is the spring.

Baseball
- The traditional season for college baseball is the spring, with National Championships played in late-May or June (depending upon the Division).
- The non-traditional season for college baseball is the fall.

Winter college sports such as ice hockey and basketball have no non-traditional seasons but very long traditional seasons, with extensive activity in the "out-of-season" period.

36

Why is There Such an Extraordinary Time Commitment?

"Few Division I coaches use fewer weeks. Even during the non-traditional season, which has no bearing on wins and losses, most coaches think they need every minute of every day."
— University of Rhode Island NCAA Compliance Coordinator, Paul Kassabian

Most college sports such as soccer, basketball, and baseball were once played and practiced only during their "traditional" fall, winter or spring season. Very few college sports are now so limited. As college coaches realized the advantages of well-planned, scientifically tested training methods, they pushed for extra weeks of practice and more games. Under pressure to win, schools have expanded the playing times of many sports by adding more regular season games *and,* as noted, a "non-traditional season" in which teams practice and compete.

The total number of days/weeks allowed by the NCAA for each sport has become the primary factor limiting time commitments to sports. As you can see in the Appendix, different divisions, leagues, schools, and sports within each division have developed their own system for making use of their allotted number of days/weeks. A Holy Cross baseball player, for example, plays the full NCAA allotted 22 weeks, split into six fall weeks and 16 spring weeks, whereas a UNC Greensboro baseball player splits the baseball time commitment into four fall weeks and 18 spring weeks. Some leagues and schools may place additional restrictions on athletic programs, producing variations in the extent of play, but virtually all Division I and II schools, and the majority of Division III schools, use all of their allotted time.

SAMPLES OF SEASONAL SCHEDULES IN COLLEGE SPORTS

See the Appendix for revealing samples of the seasonal schedules in college sports. The samples illustrate the vast time commitment difference between certain Division I and Division III programs and in certain cases, even within each Division.

NCAA Division I Time Commitment Regulations

- Division I athletes are allowed 132 practice/competition days for most team sports and 144 practice/competition days for most individual sports. These are days that fall within the NCAA 20 hours per week time restriction for both the traditional and non-traditional seasons.
- All practice and competition days must take place during periods stipulated by the NCAA for the particular sport.

- The allowed days are divided into weeks by using six days as a playing week, i.e., 22 weeks (132 days) for teams, and 24 weeks (144 days) for most individual sports.
- *During the "traditional" and "non-traditional" playing seasons,* all official athletic activities are supposed to be limited to 4 hours per day and 20 hours per week, with one full day off. Exceptions to the day off rule are made during post-season conference, NCAA or bowl game play. These in-season time limitations include game competitions and practices, but, as noted, *do not include "uncountable" time such as travel time to away games, time spent in the training room before or after practices and games, locker room activities, and mental pre-occupation with a sport, which is considerable for most serious athletes.*
- *During the "off-season," i.e., the time during the school year separate from the traditional and non-traditional seasons,* all athletes are supposed to be limited to a maximum of 8 "supervised" hours per week, of which not more than 2 hours per week may be spent on coach supervised individual skill workouts. This "outside of playing season" time limitation involves activities supervised or required by the coaching staff, *but there are no time limitations on unsupervised, "recommended" activities undertaken by the student-athlete.*
- Holidays, vacations and post-season play are not counted in these totals. Teams or individuals are often required to practice and compete on these "uncounted" holiday and vacation days.

36

NCAA Division III Time Commitment Regulations

There are no NCAA regulations regarding daily or weekly hours in Division III. Division III institutions must only adhere to the following restrictions:

- Division III individual and team sports are limited to 126 days of play or 21 weeks, with one day off per week.
- NCAA Division III athletes cannot miss class time for practice. Class time may be missed if traveling to an away game or competing in a home contest when the game time conflicts with class.
- Like Division I, practices and competitions in Division III must take place during the periods stipulated by the NCAA for the particular sport.
- Like Division I, holidays, vacations and post-season play are not counted in these totals. Even in Division III, teams and individuals are often required to practice and compete on these "uncounted" days.

The NCAA Manual states that a Division III student-athlete is no different from any other student participating in an extracurricular activity at the college. Interestingly, the manual makes no such point regarding the Division I athlete! Also, consider a striking contrast:

- College athletes are told how much time to spend in athletic activities, and have little flexibility in meeting the demands of their sport.
- Most non-athlete college students choose how much time they spend in their extracurricular activities.

The aforementioned time limits were based on NCAA rules as of the publication of this book. For more information on current NCAA time limits, which vary by sport and division, and are subject to periodic change, consult the NCAA Division I, II or III manuals, all of which can be accessed by visiting the NCAA website at *(www.ncaa.org)*, or consult a compliance officer at a college or university your young athlete is considering.

Are College Athletes Adhering to NCAA Regulations?

According to our surveys, which include Division I, Division II and Division III athletes, many are not! When reviewing the survey time results, keep in mind that the surveys reflect "countable" time, as defined by the NCAA, *but excludes previously noted "non-countable" time.* Our college survey respondents told us the following:

- Thirteen percent spend 11-13 hours a week on their sport *during the season.*
- Thirty-three percent spend 15-20 hours a week on their sport *during the season.*
- Thirty percent spend 20-26 hours a week on their sport *during the season*—an NCAA violation for Division I and II athletes!
- Fourteen percent spend 26-30 hours a week on their sport *during the season*—an NCAA violation for Division I and II athletes!
- Ten percent spend more than 30 hours a week on their sport *during the season*—an NCAA violation for Division I and II athletes!

In other words, the survey suggests that 54% of the respondents are violating NCAA regulations.

What is the Total Time Commitment for a College Athlete During the Traditional and Non-Traditional Seasons?

"You live it."—College student-athlete's survey statement

Whether looking at a Division I, II, or III college, factor in the time devoted to simply getting to away games! While colleges may enforce study time in transit, it is a challenge for many athletes to focus and study during away game travel, especially when tense before a game and physically or emotionally exhausted after one!

Distances between schools within any league, and the geographic features of the region in which the league is located, are the obvious factors differentiating sport travel times, and the reason travel times cannot be included in NCAA time limitations. In most Division III leagues, the average round-trip travel time, *excluding game time*, might be 4-8 hours, but can be as long as 14-15 hours for schools whose location is far removed from other league members. These average times can significantly increase for Division I sports in leagues covering wide geographic areas, though in revenue-producing sports such as men's basketball and football, some Division I programs charter planes to reduce travel time.

It doesn't make sense for a college student to spend significantly more time in sports than in class and studying. If you add travel time, unsupervised individual workouts, time in the training room, team meetings, practices and competitions, it is not unusual for college athletes to spend between 30 and 45 hours a week on their sport activities in the traditional and some non-traditional seasons. The typical number of classroom hours for college students is 12 per week, plus individual study time. Thus, if a college athlete spends 35 hours a week on a sport in-season, and 12 hours in the classroom, the athlete is at 47 hours *before* study time! Remember, athletes are often fatigued when studying, a condition frequently pointed out by college players.

36

SKIRTING THE RULES

It is common to hear players report on ways coaches get around time limitations. One vignette comes from a female Division I scholarship athlete at a top academic school. The young lady reports her coach telling the team after a non-traditional season practice ended, "Now, I am leaving, I am going to get in my car (parked next to the field where she remained for two more hours) and you are free to leave. But, if you want to voluntarily stay and continue to practice, you are welcome to do so."

The player felt compelled to stay for two more hours of coach observed "unofficial, uncounted practice."

What College Athletes Told Us About
Their Time Commitment *Out-of-Season*

"Your non-supervised out-of-season workouts are optional but strongly recommended."
—Written in a letter from a college coach to his returning players

Many college athletes devote significant time in the off-season—supervised and unsupervised—to weight training, conditioning and skill development. Of our surveyed college athletes, we found that:

- Seven percent spend 5 or less hours a week on their sport out-of-season.
- Thirty percent spend 6 to 10 hours a week on their sport out-of-season.
- Thirty-two percent spend 11 to 15 hours a week on their sport out-of-season.
- Twenty-one percent spend 16 to 20 hours a week on their sport out-of-season.
- Ten percent spend more than 20 hours a week on their sport out-of-season.

Even "out-of-season" which, as noted, is separate from the "non-traditional season," 63% of our surveyed college athletes told us that they spend almost as much or more time on their sport routines as in classrooms.

Missed Class Time

Missing class due to a sports commitment appears to be a problem for approximately 20% of those college athletes we surveyed. Remember, the typical college student enrolls in approximately 12 hours of classes per week. The NCAA leaves the monitoring of missed classes up to the member schools.

What Surveyed College Athletes Told Us

- Thirty-six percent missed no class time during their traditional college sports season.
- Forty-four percent missed between 1 and 2 hours of class time per week due to team commitments during their traditional college sports season, (8% to 17% of classes).
- Twenty percent missed between 3 and 7 hours of class time per week due to team commitments during their traditional college sports season, (25% to 58% of classes).

A Division I athletic director wrote, "Missing class is not nearly the problem it was even a decade ago. Athletic directors are mindful of the likelihood of severe faculty and media criticism if teams miss too much class time. We schedule accordingly, which can range from a focus on weekend games to, in the case of well-funded Division I programs, chartering planes."

And yet, protecting the academic interests of those 20% of surveyed college athletes who, in-season, missed 25% to 58% of their class hours, is a problem.

36

412

TWO HYPOTHESES TO TEST!

Hypothesis I: Division I athletes in revenue producing sports, i.e., men's basketball and football, including those who scored over 1950 on their SATs and ranked in the top 10% of their high school class, cannot major in pre-med, engineering, math or other sciences which require labs. This is due to the extensive time commitments of the sport and the major.

The test: Ask coaches in revenue producing sports the following questions:

- Are any of your current athletes majoring in pre-med, engineering, math or sciences which require labs?
- Have any of your former athletes completed a pre-med, engineering, math or science degree (requiring labs) in the last 10 years?
- How much time do your athletes commit to practice, travel, games and other team commitments on a daily basis?
    a. Out-of-season?
    b. In-season?

Ask the Deans of the schools of medicine, engineering, math and science the following questions:

On average, how much time do pre-med/engineering/math/science students at your school commit to class, labs and studying on a daily basis?

Can a student at this school manage a big time athletic commitment in a revenue producing sport and a rigorous major such as pre-med/engineering/math/science?

The answers to these questions should help you either prove or disprove the hypothesis.

Hypothesis II: Many Division I athletes in revenue producing sports major in a course of study that is not linked to post-college career choice or career success. Their coaches want to keep them out of rigorous courses, and the young athletes are happy to comply.

The test: Ask coaches in revenue producing sports the following questions:

- Would you provide me with a list of graduates from your program over the last 10 years?
- Would you provide me with a list of undergraduate majors for such graduates?
- Would you provide me with information as to the current profession of each graduate?

Again, the answers to these questions should help you either prove or disprove the hypothesis.

36

413

Questions To Raise with the
College or University

If your high school athlete is being recruited to play a varsity college sport, it is reasonable for you to request written answers to the following questions, which all colleges should be able to provide:

For Team Sports

- How many days/weeks of the NCAA allotment are used?
- How many weeks are used for the *traditional season?* How many games/dates are played?
- Is there a *non-traditional season?* If so, how many weeks and days per week are used in the non-traditional season? Are games played and, if so, how many?

For Individual Sports

- How many of the allowed NCAA dates of practice/competition are used?
- How many weeks are used for the traditional season?
- How many dates of competition are used? Some individual sports (and a few team sports) hold two competitions in one day. In such cases, the day is only considered one "date of competition."
- Is there a non-traditional season? If so, how many dates of practice/ competition are used?

For All Sports

- What is the average length of daily practice time in the traditional season and, if applicable, in the non-traditional season?
- In the off-season (which is different from the non-traditional season), how many days/weeks are team and individual sport athletes "expected" to practice on a "voluntary but strongly recommended" basis?
- For how long each day?
- Do you ever allow a student-athlete to miss a traditional season practice to prepare for a major test, paper or lab assignment? A non-traditional season practice?
- During road trips, are athletes given materials to make up any missed class work, and are lectures taped? If taped, is it audio or video? When does the athlete receive the tape? Are they overnighted to the athlete while on the road? Are arrangements made for the athlete to listen to or watch the tape while on the road?
- The type of tutoring program, if any. This includes:
  - A realistic view of whether the tutors actually do the work for the

36

student-athletes or foster an approach that involves rote answers on tests. On this matter, you may wish to read about recent scandals at the University of Tennessee, the University of Minnesota and the University of Georgia.

○ If a player has a tutor, does the tutor accompany the team or is academic help available while on the road?

Understand that an extensive tutorial program is not necessarily a commitment to education. Too many athletes at Division I institutions become dependent upon tutoring and fail to develop good independent study skills. Remember, two key objectives for a college student are:

1. To become a critical thinker, i.e., to be able to analyze competing ideas and develop reasoned positions. Among the skills of a good critical thinker is to do as Aristotle proposed, "Be able to entertain a thought without accepting it."
2. To acquire skills required by a global economy.

- Are there enforced study periods during travel?
- How much class time did the team miss the prior year? For away games/competitions, how many days in advance does the team/player leave?
- How far do your teams travel for games/competitions?
- What is the farthest school, closest school, average trip?
- What are the means of transportation?
- How do you use your school vacation breaks? This is an important question to ask. One of the pitfalls of college sports is that many fall and winter teams place little importance on a youngster being home for the holidays.

Will Sports Help Develop Time Management Skills?

Yes, provided the sport involves a reasonable time commitment. In sports programs with excessive time commitments, the benefits of time management are often overshadowed by the need for a student-athlete to simply find time to complete an acceptable amount of work.

If your young athlete is being recruited to play a college sport, find out all you can about the time commitment required by the coach, for this will help you evaluate the coach's true commitment to the scholar-athlete ideal.

Does the Time Commitment Differ Among College Sports?

Yes. Variations exist in the length of the regular season, and other striking

36

differences show up in whether and how a school/league uses a full, limited or non-traditional season. There may also be significant differences in the amount of time actually spent in practices and competitions if one compares a sport such as Division I-A Big Ten football to Division III NESCAC football (see Appendix). Leagues within the same division and even schools within the same league may impose additional restrictions on athletic activities. The Division I Ivy League and Division III NESCAC are examples of leagues with much tighter time limitations on sports. It is worth noting that the NESCAC has produced a number of Division III national championship teams, as well as national champions in individual sports such as tennis.

Other factors you and your student might need to consider include:

- Geography and climate may limit, to some extent, the actual amount of practice/playing time available in sports such as baseball, softball, crew, soccer, lacrosse and tennis, especially if schools do not have appropriate indoor facilities.
- Some Division III warm climate schools actually play a longer baseball season than some northern Division I schools.
- Some individual sports, such as swimming and tennis, may be practiced most of the academic year with limits only on "dates of competition."
- Holidays and vacations are not necessarily days off for some athletes.
  - Winter ice hockey and basketball teams often schedule tournaments during weeks which are not counted as practice or competition days in NCAA totals.
  - Some Division III swimmers told us they must return from vacation as early as January 1 for practices not included in the "allowed days."
  - Spring sports such as baseball, golf, tennis and lacrosse may have no "spring break."
  - If involved in the College Baseball World Series or the NCAA Golf Championships, players may be competing until late June.
  - Many Division I winter sports participants never see home at Thanksgiving or Christmas during their college careers. "Over the course of my four-year college career I was not home once for Thanksgiving or Christmas," lamented a former Division I men's basketball player.

Mike Walsh of Washington & Lee reminds us, "Coaches are given an almost free hand with regard to scheduling games and practices during vacations. In some sports, they have been able to figure out ways to train most days of the school year."

An Enlightened Approach

The Southern California Intercollegiate Athletic Conference (SCIAC) is a Division III league whose membership includes Caltech, Pomona, Cal Lutheran and Whittier. The longest travel time between two schools in the SCIAC is two hours, and most of the schools are within 45 minutes of each other. The league's "non-traditional season" applies to all weeks within the Division III "21-week playing season" which are not included in the traditional season.

In the SCIAC non-traditional/off-season:

- All instructional sessions are voluntary and no class time is missed.
- Each individual student-athlete is limited to a maximum of six hours per week of individual athletic instruction or supervised team activity. All sessions of instruction and activity are limited to a maximum of two hours in length, three days a week.
- No outside competition is allowed during the "non-traditional season," and thus, there is no travel time!

I asked several Caltech student-athletes how they felt about the SCIAC non-traditional season policy. All of them favored it because it gave them an enjoyable and much needed study break without excessive time demands.

The SCIAC is one of the best examples of intercollegiate sports programs contributing to a positive overall educational experience. There are other leagues which foster a reasonable approach to a student-athlete's time commitment, including the NESCAC, which is made up of schools such as Amherst, Bowdoin and Hamilton.

36

The Extensive Time Commitment

"When I started coaching in the '70s, the 15 to 18 hours per week we spent in-season, which included travel, allowed several of my players to major in pre-med. To keep up with the opposition, we are now up to 35 to 40 hours per week, including travel. My present players cannot take on a heavy academic load such as pre-med."

—Division III men's basketball coach survey statement

Playing a sport and achieving academic success is surely dependent upon the abilities and goals of individual athletes, but the amount of time now demanded by many college sports programs *cannot* be good for a student's academic career. Time is a limited commodity and class preparation and learning are now allotted a smaller share of the athlete's time. Over the past several decades, the majority of colleges and universities have shortened their academic calendars to save money. Yet the sports time commitment has simultaneously lengthened, leaving few of the 26 to 30 academic weeks in the average school year free of athletic demands.

The NCAA points out that many athletes get higher grades and practice better time management during the sports season. During my college lecture tours, I always raise this issue with the student-athletes. I have found that many Division III athletes *do* feel that they get higher grades during the sports season. I have *not* found this to be the case with Division I athletes. One interesting example occurred when I spoke at a school which actually had two Division I sports and a number of Division III sports. (There are a handful of such schools in NCAA competition.) When I posed the question to the large group, nearly all the Division III student-athletes present raised their hands to indicate they did get better grades during the season. By contrast, nearly all of the Division I athletes indicated that their grades suffered during the season. Said one, "The time and the exhaustion factors do not allow me to study as much during the season."

Better grades during the season may result from a variety of factors, including:

- The athlete's day is more structured.
- The coaching staff supervises enforced study times in an athlete's day.
- More academic support is offered and tutoring is required due to sports schedules.
- The athlete has less free time and is less likely to spend time "partying."
- Athletes register for "jock" courses and/or take fewer courses in-season.
- Many college athletes shy away from rigorous majors, allowing more latitude for students to be full-time athletes, and at best, part-time students.

If you believe your athlete cannot handle the time required by sports and simultaneously become well-educated, consider summer classes, an extra year, or schools with lighter sports demands.

The "Time Profile" of the Division I Men's Basketball Player

During my 2004 summer basketball camp, I delivered a lecture on the importance of "practicing with a purpose." After telling the campers about Bill Bradley's summer practice regimen when he was a high schooler in Crystal City, Missouri, I invited a high school camper and one of my college-age counselors—a fine Division I player—to join me on the court. I asked the high school player to estimate the number of AAU and high school varsity games he had played over the last 12 months, and the average number of minutes he had played in each game. The young man estimated that he had played in 52 games over this time span, at an average of 20 minutes a game—a total of 1040 minutes - or 17 hours and 20 minutes of actual game competition.

I then asked the Division I college player to review the amount of time he spent on his summer practice regimen. To bolster my "practice with a purpose" message, I wanted the young campers to begin to understand the disparity between the number of minutes a young athlete might play in game competition, and the number of minutes a serious and successful Division I player devoted to individual practice sessions.

As I walked the Division I player through his summer practice schedule, I noticed the jaws of several of my senior staff members literally drop! As the session ended, Jack Casey, my program director, and former star at Division II Saint Anselm, approached me and said, "I was stunned at the hours the young man spent, and with his systematic approach. Nothing like that existed when I was at Saint Anselm, and I was considered by most to be a very dedicated player!" Jack's view was later echoed by a number of other staff members, several of whom had played college basketball in the '60s and '70s.

With great precision, the Division I player described his summer workout schedule, which included a rigorous weight training program, four individual skills development sessions, two or three summer games a week, and three or four 2-hour "runs" (scrimmages), which took place at my camp late each afternoon, and involved a number of high level players from around Connecticut convening to play with the college players on my staff.

The picture he painted was one of total immersion, and it was clear that the immersion was paying off in a basketball sense. The young man was a very high level player who had clearly improved each year, due in no small measure to his rigorous training regimen.

At the time of this 2004 presentation to the campers, I was well into the writing of *The Encyclopedia of Sports Parenting*. The Division I player's comments caused me to look carefully at the time commitment of serious athletes, with the objective of developing a series of time profiles in Volumes I and II. The Volume I profile which follows will be that of the Division I men's basketball player. Volume II will include profiles of college athletes in various sports and Divisions, high school athletes, and a look at younger athletes in "time intensive" youth sports such as gymnastics and swimming.

36

The Process

Phase I

I developed the Division I men's basketball profile through a series of steps, which began in the summer of '04 and extended through spring '07. The first phase involved a series of "time" discussions with college players at my camp, with other college athletes I met during my college lecture tours, and with college coaches. I was always on the lookout for information on the "time factor", not only in Division I men's basketball but in a variety of college sports. What I found in Division I men's basketball is an extraordinary time commitment which encompasses not only the "countable hours," as addressed in the NCAA Handbook (see Appendix), but the significant "uncountable hours" demanded of the Division I men's basketball player. "Those time factors defined as 'non-countable' really do take up a great deal of time," admitted a Division I coach. The D-I Men's Basketball Profile includes both the countable hours, as well as the non-countable hours. You will note that the profile does not include the all important "preoccupation factor" which is a major time item among dedicated college athletes.

Phase II

Once the Division I men's basketball profile was complete, I had the profile reveiwed by several college basketball coaches. While some expressed angst over unflattering information about the time commitment in their sport, none found fault with the profile. "I hate it because I know it reflects poorly on us, but it is accurate," stated one coach.

Another common reaction among coaches was the "more is better" theme as it relates to a well-planned, intensive year-round practice regimen. "It may be an extraordinary time commitment, but it works. Plus, to keep up with our competition, it's what we must do," confided one coach to me.

Phase III

Finally, I asked one of the most enlightened thinkers in college sports, Rick Boyages, Associate Commissioner and Director of Basketball Operations in the Division I MAC Conference. I was particularly interested in Rick's assessment because his expertise encompasses a distinguished college playing career at Division III Bowdoin, as well as a highly successful coaching career in both Division III and Division I. I knew that Rick had a thorough handle on the time commitment of Division I men's basketball players, as well as an admirable commitment to education. Rick corroborated that the hours addressed in the profile are, in his words, "very real."

The Division I Men's Basketball Player "Time Profile"

(See the Appendix for full details on the Division I Men's Basketball Player profile.)

The following graph illustrates a year-round "time profile" for a Division I men's basketball player.

Three important points:

1. None of the following "seasonal" schedules factor in how much, if any, time is spent in injury rehab.
2. The following profile does not take into account the "preoccupation with performance" factor, which is of major significance for many college athletes.
3. The following profile takes into account many NCAA "non-countable" but required activities demanded of the Division I Men's basketball player.

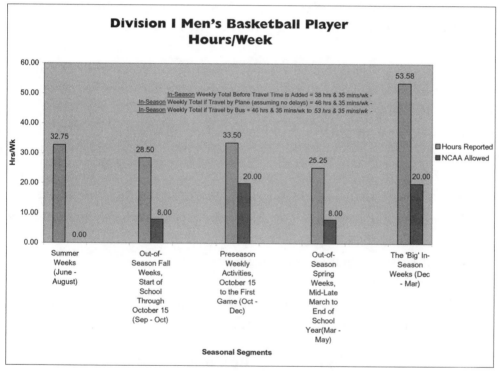

Division I Men's Basketball Player Hours/Week

In-Season Weekly Total Before Travel Time is Added = 38 hrs & 35 mins/wk -
In-Season Weekly Total if Travel by Plane (assuming no delays) = 46 hrs & 35 mins/wk -
In-Season Weekly Total if Travel by Bus = 46 hrs & 35 mins/wk to 53 hrs & 35 mins/wk -

If, for example, 46 hours & 35 minutes minimum per week is devoted to basketball in-season, and a minimum of 10 hours per week is devoted to class time, the Division I men's basketball player is at 56 hours & 35 minutes per week *before* study time. Is there any wonder that very few Division I men's basketball players undertake rigorous undergraduate study or attend graduate school?

Twelve Other Important Points of Interest

1. Athletes who have suffered injuries may perform rehabilitation and

injury prevention exercises which can add an additional 40 to 60 minutes per day, 3-7 days per week.

2. Athletes who need pre-practice/game taping can add 15 minutes per day, i.e., 1.5 hours per week.

3. Away games may involve missing 1-2 days of classes, depending upon whether the team is playing on a weeknight or a weekend.

4. When missing classes, players obtain assignments in advance, and there are monitored study periods on the road.

5. Almost all Division I men's basketball players participate in their league's post-season tournament.

6. Approximately 29% of the men's Division I basketball programs play in post-season NCAA or NIT tournaments, extending the number of weeks and involving as much or more time as the in-season weekly time commitment.

7. Almost all Division I men's basketball programs schedule play during Thanksgiving and Christmas vacations, because vacations are not included in the "official" NCAA weekly time limitations.

8. Fifty-two percent of Division I men's basketball players we surveyed were home at least a portion of Thanksgiving Day, but away the rest of the break.

9. Sixty percent of Division I men's basketball players we surveyed were home at least a portion of Christmas Day, but away most of the break.

10 Some Division I men's basketball players spend considerable interview time with the media.

11. Out-of-season activities can range from hosting recruits to meeting with alumni.

12. Of the Division I sports we researched, Division I men's basketball is clearly among the most time consuming.

What Should the College Do?

When confronted with the time issue, many college coaches and some administrators become defensive. Such a posture often precludes a careful look at the time expectations imposed on student-athletes. A far better approach would be to conduct—every three to five years—a detailed "time commitment study" of all student-athletes at the school.

My hope is that the information offered in this chapter will encourage those involved in college programs to carefully study the time commitment demanded of their own athletes.

WHAT PLATO MIGHT THINK

"Physical training should complement philosophical education for the best of men."
—Plato

One of the earliest "sports programs" in Western civilization was located outside the walls of Athens in a shaded grove known as the Academy. Its founder, Plato, not only lectured on philosophy but insisted that his students undertake a rigorous physical fitness and sports regimen.

The intercollegiate experience should be the most glowing sports example of the mind-body harmony that was practiced at Plato's Academy nearly 2400 years ago. In a number of instances, it is not. Excess time devoted to sports precludes many student-athletes from achieving real intellectual development. Professor John Cole of the Bates College Classics Department stated, "The athletic excesses practiced at too many American colleges and universities would have disheartened Plato."

Many surveyed ex-college athletes now regret their failure to become proficient in anything except their sport. A student's most valuable commodity is time, and your athlete must make educational decisions to prepare for a lifetime, not just the short-term bragging rights from athletic success.

36

	Time Profile of the Division I Men's Basketball Player		Time Spent in Hrs/Wk - Subtotals	NCAA Countable Hours
I	The Summer Weeks (June - August)		32.75	
2	Out-of-Season Fall Weeks, Start of School Through October 15 (Sep - Oct)		28.50	8.00
3	Preseason Weekly Activities, October 15 to the First Game (Oct - Dec)		33.50	20.00
4	Out-of-Season Spring Weeks, Mid-Late March to End of School Year (Mar - May)		25.25	8.00
5	The 'Big' In-Season Weeks (Dec - Mar)		53.58	20.00
5a	In Season Practice Time	25.25		
5b	Games	13.33		
5c*	Travel Time	15.00		
	* 5c varies based on bus or plane travel. See details in appendix			

Time Profile of the Division I Men's Basketball Player				
	Span of Mnths	Time Spent in Hrs/Wk - details	Time Spent in Hrs/Wk - Subtotals	Comments
				According to the NCAA manual, Division I and Division II student-athletes may not, while school is in session, participate in countable athletically related activities for more than: In Season = 20 hours per week and Out of Season = Eight hours per week.
1 The Summer Weeks (June - August)	Jun - Aug			Few Division I players take more than one to two weeks off from their summer basketball training regimen, and the majority follow a summer routine similar to the left chart.
Weight Training		8.25		
Playing in Leagues and Organized Pick-up		14.00		
Individual Workouts/Shooting/Skill Development/Fun Play		9.00		
Jogging/Conditioning		1.50		
Total Hours Per-Week (Jun - Aug)		32.75	32.75	
2 Out of Season Fall Weeks, Start of School Through October 15 (Sep - Oct)	Sep - Oct			During this period, the NCAA allows a player 8 hours of "coach supervised activities" allocated among 5 days per week and divided as:
Weight Training		7.50		· 2 hours on-court instruction. (May be used by coach for scrimmages, small group or individual practices.)
Runs/Full Court Scrimmages		14.00		· 6 hours off-court activities divided among weight training, plyometrics, meetings with coaches and video reviews.
Individual/Small Group Practice Sessions (Including Individual Shooting Practices)		4.50		
Meeting with Coaches		1.50		
Reviewing Video		1.00		
Total Hours Per-Week (Sep - Oct)		28.50	28.50	
3 Preseason Weekly Activities, October 15 to the First Game	Oct - Dec			Division I teams are allowed six days of formal preseason practice per-week. The NCAA allows 20 hours of coach-supervised activities which are included within the time totals to the left.
Daily Practice		25.50		
Weight Training		2.00		
Individual Practice Sessions		3.00		
Team Meetings, Including Individual meetings with Coaches		3.00		
Total Preseason Hours Per Week (Oct - Dec)		33.50	33.50	
4 Out-of-Season Spring Weeks, Mid-Late March to End of School Year	Mar - May			Many Division I players take one to two weeks off after the season ends.

36

424

		Span of Mnths	Time Spent in Hrs/Wk - details	Time Spent in Hrs/Wk - Subtotals	Comments
	Time Profile of the Division I Men's Basketball Player				*
	Spring Activities Include Weight Training		5.50		
	Runs/Full Court Scrimmages		12.50		In the spring, the NCAA allows a player 8 hours of "coach supervised activities" allocated among 5 days per week and divided as:
	Individual/Small Group Practice Sessions (Including Individual Shooting Practice)		5.00		· 2 hours on-court instruction. (May be used by coach for scrimmages, small group or individual practices.)
	Meetings with Coaches (Including Video Review)		2.25		· 6 hours off-court activities divided among weight training, plyometrics, meetings with coaches and video reviews.
	Total Hours Per-Week (Mar - May)		25.25	25.25	
5	The 'Big' In-Season Weeks (Dec - Mar)	Dec - Mar			In season, the NCAA allows 6 days of formal practices and games per-week, with one "day off." The NCAA allows a total number of "counted/supervised" hours of practices, games and meetings per-week of 20 hours, not to exceed 4 hours per day. The NCAA time regulations that apply to the formal games and practices do not include factors such as voluntary individual practice sessions and travel/shower/change times.
5a	In Season Practice Time				
	Formal Practices		17.00		
	Individual Practice Sessoins (Including) Official "Day Off")		4.75		
	Review Video		1.50		
	Team Meeting and Individual Meetings with coaches		2.00		
	Sub-Total Season Practice Time (Dec - Mar)		25.25	25.25	
5b	Games		13.33		Based on two games a week, one home and one away game.
	Sub-Total Games (Dec - Mar)		13.33	13.33	
5c	Travel Time				In-Season Weekly Total Before Travel Time is Added = 38 hrs & 35 mins/wk
	If Travel by bus		8.00 - 15.00		In-Season Weekly Total if Travel by Bus = 46 hrs & 35 mins/wk to 53 hrs & 35 mins/wk
	If Travel by Plane (assuming no delays)		9.00		In-Season Weekly Total if Travel by Plane (assuming no delays) = 47 hrs & 35 mins/wk
	Sub-Total Travel Time (Dec - Mar)			15.00	
5	Maximum Total for In-Season Weeks (Dec - Mar)			53.58	

36

Chapter 37

FINAL VERSE

"Nimble thought can jump both sea and land."
—Shakespeare

At various points in this book, I have emphasized the importance of critical thinking—the ability to look at issues from all sides and to analyze competing ideas. My final verse addresses how thousands of coaches from a past generation—unskilled in critical thinking—misused words intended for the cast-iron reality of professional football, and directed the words to impressionable teenagers.

37

Lombardi's Muted Plea

In the summer
Of his Crusade
The absolute Ruler
Roared to his
True Believing Knights:
"Winning isn't everything,
it's the only thing."

To his dismay,
The message flew
From the war room
And appeared
Laminated
On desktops
And walls
Of high school coaches
Charged with shaping
The principles
Of callow youth.

In his late winter
Softened by perspective
Weakened by cancer
The uncertain Ruler whispered
"I wish I had never said
The damn thing.
I intended it to be
About excellence,
Not to trample
Human morality and values."

He left the world
Knowing – and ruing
That the whisper
Had been drowned out
By the roar.

37

My final point: Critical thinking is an essential component of good parenting and mentoring, and a quality we must cultivate in our children.

SECTION X

APPENDIX

HOW THE NCAA DEFINES
COUNTABLE ATHLETIC ACTIVITIES

According to the NCAA manual, Division I and Division II student-athletes may not participate in countable athletically related activities for more than:

In-Season:
- 4 hours per day
- 20 hours per week

Out-of-Season:
- 8 hours per week

The following is a partial list of NCAA "countable" athletically related activities:
- Practices (not more than 4 hours per day).
- Athletic meetings with a coach initiated or required by a coach
- Competition (and associated activities, regardless of their length, count as only three hours).
- Required weight-training and conditioning activities.
- Participation outside the regular season in individual skill-related instructional activities with a member of the coaching staff.

The following is a partial list of NCAA "non-countable" athletically related activities:
- Compliance meetings.
- Meetings with a coach initiated by the student-athlete (as long as no countable activities occur).
- Voluntary weight-training not conducted by a coach or staff member.
- Voluntary sport-related activities.
- Traveling to and from the site of competition (as long as no countable activities occur).

- Training room activities.
- Rehabilitation activities and medical examinations.
- Recruiting activities.

*This information was taken from the NCAA website.

SAMPLE NCAA RECRUITING CALENDAR

The following will provide you with a good overview of what is and is not permissible in recruiting, as of the publication date of this book.

Sample Football Calendar
NCAA Division I Football Recruiting Calendar
August 1, 2007 - July 31, 2008
(See NCAA Division I Bylaw 30.11.3 for football calendar formula)
The dates in this calendar reflect the application of Bylaw 30.11 at the time of publication of this manual but are subject to change per Constitution 5.2.3.1 or if certain dates (e.g., National Letter of Intent signing dates) are altered.

(a) August 1 through November 24, 2007, [except for (1) and (2) below]:   Quiet Period

    (1) In Football Bowl Subdivision, six days during the months of September, October and through November 24, 2007, selected at the discretion of the institution (an authorized off-campus recruiter may visit a particular educational institution only once during this evaluation period):   Evaluation Period

    (2) In NCAA Football Championship Subdivision, 42 evaluation days (see Bylaw 13.02.9) during the months of September, October and November, (not to exceed a period of 42 days) selected at the discretion of the institution and designated in writing in the office of the director of athletics; authorized off-campus recruiters shall not visit a prospective student-athlete's educational institution on more than one calendar day during this period.   Evaluation Period

(b) November 25, 2007, through February 2, 2008, [except for (1) though (6) below]. Six in-person off-campus contacts per prospective student-athlete shall be permitted during this time period with not more than one permitted in any one calendar week (Sunday through Saturday) or partial calendar week: Contact Period

432

(1) December 16, 2007:	Quiet Period
(2) December 17, 2007, through January 1, 2008:*	Dead Period
(3) January 2-3, 2008:*	Dead Period

*Institutional staff members may have contact with a prospective student- athlete who has been admitted for mid-year enrollment, provided the prospect has signed a National Letter of Intent or other offer of admission and/or financial aid to attend the institution and is required to be on campus to attend institutional orientation sessions for all students.

(4) January 4-6, 2008:	Quiet Period
(5) January 7-10, 2008:	Dead Period
(6) January 11-12, 2008:	Quiet Period
(c) February 3, 2008:	Quiet Period
(d) February 4-7, 2008:	Dead Period
(e) February 8 through April 14, 2008:	Quiet Period
(f) April 15 through May 31, 2008, [except for (g) below]:	Evaluation Period

Four weeks (excluding Memorial Day and Sundays) selected at the discretion of the member institution and designated in writing in the office of the director of athletics [as provided in (1) below]:

(1) An authorized off-campus recruiter may use one evaluation to assess the prospective student-athlete's athletics ability and one evaluation to assess the prospective student-athlete's academic qualifications during this evaluation period). If an institution's coaching staff member conducts both an athletics and an academic evaluation of the prospective student-athlete on the same day during this evaluation period, the institution shall be charged with the use of an academics evaluation only and shall be permitted to conduct a second athletics evaluation of the prospective student-athlete on a separate day during this evaluation period.

(g) Those days in April/May not designated above for evaluation opportunities:	Quiet Period
(h) June 1 through July 31, 2008:	Quiet Period

Overwhelmed?

At least now you understand why the NCAA needs all of its television money! Who would want to figure out all of these rules if they weren't being well paid?!

38

SAMPLE "SEASONAL" SCHEDULES
IN COLLEGE SPORTS

The following examples were taken from phone surveys with athletic department members of each listed school, as well as a review of the schedules of each school in the sport in question. These examples illustrate the official use of traditional and non-traditional seasons in some Division I and Division III schools in a recent year. These "official" seasons do not illustrate how athletes spend their time out-of-season or during vacations, which are often occupied with intense "voluntary" activities. The following information was in effect as of the publication date of the book.

Football

Division I-A Scholarship

Penn State (Member of the Big Ten)

Traditional Season:

Days/Weeks: Approximately 15 weeks which includes 29 pre-first semester (August) practices, i.e. practices that take place before classes begin.

Number of games: 12

Non-Traditional Spring Season:

Days/weeks: 15 spring season practices that must take place within 29 days. These spring practices still fall within the 20 hours per week, 4 hours per day NCAA sport season rule.

Number of non-traditional season games: Unlike most other sports, football teams are only allowed intrasquad games in the non-traditional season.

Division I-AA Scholarship

University of Rhode Island (Member of the Atlantic 10 Conference)

Division I-AA programs such as URI follow the same "time" rules as Division I-A schools such as Penn State. The only difference is that the Division I-AA post-season games are played in early- or mid-December, before most Division I-A bowl games.

Division III Non-Scholarship

Tufts University (Member of the NESCAC)

Traditional Season:

Days/Weeks: Approximately 12 weeks, which includes 23 pre-first semester (August) practice opportunities.

Number of games: 8 *

Non-Traditional Season:

Days/weeks: Tufts and other NESCAC schools do not conduct non-traditional, spring season practices.

*Tufts and other NESCAC schools are not allowed to participate in the NCAA post-season football competition. The NESCAC limits their football programs to eight regular season games. Division III Non-Scholarship

Allegheny (Member of the North Coast Athletic Conference)

Traditional Season:

Days/Weeks: Approximately 14 weeks, which includes 27 pre-first semester (August) practices.

Number of games: 10

Non-Traditional Season:

Days/weeks: A 5-week conditioning program is allowed in the North Coast Athletic Conference.

Post-Season Football Time Commitment

In Division I-A, the post-season time commitment could extend through the Bowl games, the latest of which is played in early January. In Division III, the latest a team could compete is mid-December, the finals of the Division III National Championships. Thus, if a college football team advances to a bowl game or post-season Division III, II, or I-AA competition, the football season can extend from early August through mid-December/early-January, i.e., 18-22 weeks.

Baseball

NCAA regulations allow Division I schools to play a total of 132 days of baseball, i.e., 22 weeks, and play a total of 56 games maximum. Division I baseball coaches make strategic decisions about how to use the days and games in the traditional and non-traditional seasons.

Division I Scholarship, North
UConn (Member of the Big East)

Traditional Season:

Number of days/weeks: 103 days in the spring *(about 17 weeks).*

Number of games: 55 games

Non-traditional season:

38

Days/weeks:29 days in the fall *(about 5 weeks)*.

Number of non-traditional season games: 1 game in the fall.

Division I Scholarship, South
UNC Greensboro (Member Southern Conference)

Traditional Season:

Days/Weeks: 18 weeks

Number of games: 56 games

Non-traditional season:

Days/Weeks: 4 weeks

Number of non-traditional season games: No games.

Division I Non-Scholarship
Dartmouth College (Member of the Ivy League)

Traditional Season:

Days/Weeks:Approximately 14 weeks

Games: 44-45 (20 of which are league games)

Non-Traditional Season:

Days/Weeks: 4 weeks

Games: 2 *dates*—Ivy League rules allow their teams to play a fall tournament format with 2 games each day.

Division I Non-Scholarship
Holy Cross (Member of the Patriot League)

Traditional Season:

Days/weeks: 16 weeks

Number of games: 42 games

Non-traditional season:

Days/weeks: 6 weeks

Number of non-traditional season games: 8 games

Division III Non-Scholarship

The NCAA regulations allow Division III schools to play a total of 126 days of baseball. Twenty-one weeks are divided into a traditional and non-traditional season with 40 games maximum in the traditional season and 5 games maximum in the non-traditional season. Like Division I, Division III baseball coaches make strategic decisions about how to use the days and games in the traditional and non-traditional seasons.

Emory University, Division III South
(Member of the University Athletic Association)

Traditional Season:

   Days/Weeks: 17 weeks

   Number of games:40 games

Non-Traditional Season:

   Days/weeks: 4 weeks

   Number of non-traditional season games: 5 games

California Institute of Technology, Division III West (Member of the
Southern California Intercollegiate Athletic Conference)

Traditional Season:

   Days/Weeks: 17 weeks

   Number of games: 40 games

Non-Traditional Season:

   Days/weeks: 4 weeks

   Number of non-traditional season games: 0

Bates College, Division III North (Member of the NESCAC)

Traditional Season:

   Days/Weeks: 13 weeks

   Number of games: 32 (out of a possible 34, the maximum number of
   games allowed in the NESCAC)

Non-Traditional Season:

   Days/weeks: NESCAC does not have a non-traditional season

Post-Season Time Commitment

Post-season tournaments can extend until late June in Division I and late
May in Divisions II and III.

38

THE "TIME PROFILE" OF THE DIVISION I MEN'S BASKETBALL PLAYER

The following sections illustrate a year round "time profile" for a Division I men's basketball player. The composite is based upon surveys of players, as well as interviews with and information from Division I Men's head and assistant basketball coaches.

Three important points:

1. None of the following "seasonal" schedules factor in how much, if any, time is spent in injury rehabilitation.

2. The following profile does *not* take into account the "pre-occupation with performance" factor, which is of major significance for many college athletes.

3. The following profile takes into account many NCAA "non-countable," but required activities demanded of the Division I Men's basketball player.

The Summer Weeks — An average of 32 Hours & 45 Minutes Per Week

Few Division I players take more than 1-2 weeks off from their summer basketball training regimen, and the majority follow a summer routine similar to the following:

Weight Training

- Workouts, 3 days at 90 minutes each = 4.5 hours per week.
- Additional conditioning/plyometrics activities, 3 days at 15 minutes each = 45 minutes per week.
- Round trips to facility, 3 days at 30 minutes each = 1.5 hours per week.
- Post-workout shower/change, 3 days at 30 minutes each = 1.5 hours per week.

Total time = 8 hours & 15 minutes per week

Playing in Leagues and Organized Pick-up

- Games, 4 days at 2 hours each = 8 hours per week.
- Round trips to games, 4 days at 1 hour each = 4 hours per week. (Many summer game venues involve at least 1 hour of round trip travel).
- Post-game shower/change, 4 days at 30 minutes each = 2 hours per week.

Total time = 14 hours per week

38

Individual Workouts/Shooting/Skill Development Routines/Fun Play
- Workout routines, 5 days at 90 minutes each = 7.5 hours per week.
- Shooting, pick-up games, 3-on-3, 3 days at 30 minutes each = 1 hour & 30 minutes per week.
- Individual workouts overlap with other gym/basketball activities, so no additional travel/shower/change time is factored in.

Total time = 9 hours per week

Conditioning/Jogging
- 3 days at 30 minutes each = 1.5 hours per week.
- Conditioning/Jogging overlaps other basketball/gym, workout activities, so no additional travel/shower/change time is factored in.

Total time = 1 hour & 30 minutes per week

Summer Weekly Total = 32 Hours & 45 minutes

Out-Of-Season Fall Weeks, Start Of School Through October 15
Average of 28 Hours & 30 Minutes Per Week.

The NCAA allows a player 8 hours of "coach supervised activities" allocated among 5 days per week and divided as:
- 2 hours on-court instruction. (May be used by coach for scrimmages, small group or individual practices.)
- 6 hours off-court activities divided among weight training, plyometrics, meetings with coaches and video reviews.

The 8 supervised hours are included within the total activity hours listed below. Beyond the supervised hours, player activities are "voluntary but highly recommended," and such unsupervised activities may be spread over 7 days a week.

38

Weight Training
- Workouts, 3 days at 90 minutes each = 4.5 hours per week.
- Round trip to facility, 3 days at 30 minutes each = 1.5 hours per week.
- Post-workout shower/change, 3 days at 30 minutes = 1.5 hours per week.

Total time = 7 hours & 30 minutes per week

"Runs"/Full Court Scrimmages

- Scrimmages, 5 days at 2 hours each = 10 hours per week.
- Round trips to gym, 4 days at 30 minutes each = 2 hours per week.
- Post-workout showers/changes, 4 days at 30 minutes each = 2 hours per week.
- One day of "runs" often overlaps with other basketball/gym workout activities so only 4 days of travel/shower/changes are factored in.

Total time = 14 hours per week

Individual/Small Group Practice Sessions
(Including Individual Shooting Practices)

- Practice/shooting sessions, 6 days at 45 minutes each = 4 hours & 30 minutes per week.
- These individual/small group practice/shooting sessions overlap other workout/gym activities so no additional travel/shower/change time is factored in.

Total time = 4 hours & 30 minutes per week

Meetings with Coaches

- Meetings, 3 days at 30 minutes each = 1.5 hours per week.
- No additional travel time is factored because meetings overlap with other gym activities.

Total time = 1 hour & 30 minutes per week

Reviewing Video

- Reviewing, 2 days at 30 minutes each = 1 hour per week.
- No additional travel time factored in since video review overlaps other basketball/gym workout activities.

Total time = 1 hour per week

Out-Of-Season/Fall Weekly Total = 28 Hours & 30 Minutes

Preseason Weekly Activities, October 15 To first Game — Average of 33 Hours & 30 Minutes Per Week.

Division I teams are allowed 6 days of formal preseason practice per week. The NCAA allows 20 hours of coach-supervised activities which are included within the following time totals.

Daily Practice

- Round trip to gym, 6 days at 30 minutes each = 3 hours per week.
- Pre-practice change/preparation/warm up/stretch, 6 days at 45 minutes each = 4.5 hours per week.
- Practices, 6 days at 2.5 hours each = 15 hours per week.
- Post-practice shower/change, 6 days at 30 minutes each = 3 hours per week.

Total time =25 hours & 30 minutes per week

Weight Training

- Workouts, 2 days at 1 hour each = 2 hours per week.
- Weight training overlaps with other basketball/gym workout activities, so no additional travel/shower/change time is factored in.

Total time = 2 hours per week

Individual Practice Sessions (Including Individual Shooting Practice)

- Practices sessions, 6 days at 30 minutes each = 3 hours per week.
- Individual practice/shooting sessions overlap practices and other basketball/gym workout activities, so no additional travel/shower/change time is factored in.

Total time = 3 hours per week

Team Meetings, Including Individual Meetings with Coaches

- Team meetings, meetings with coaches, 3 days at 1 hour each = 3 hours per week.
- Meetings overlap other basketball/gym workout activities, so no additional travel time is factored in.

Total time = 3 hours per week

Preseason Weekly Total = 33 Hours & 30 Minutes

38

Out-Of-Season Spring Weeks,

Mid-Late March To End Of School Year
Average of 25 Hours & 15 minutes Per Week.

Many Division I players take 1-2 weeks off after the season ends.

In the spring, the NCAA allows a player 8 hours of "coach supervised activities" allocated among 5 days per week and divided as:

- 2 hours on-court instruction. (May be used by coach for scrimmages, small group or individual practices.)
- 6 hours off-court activities divided among weight training, plyometrics, meetings with coaches and video reviews.

The 8 supervised hours are included within the total activity hours listed below. Beyond the supervised hours, player activities are "voluntary but highly recommended," and such unsupervised activities may be spread over 7 days a week.

Spring Activities Include

Weight Training
- Workouts, 3 days at 90 minutes each = 4.5 hours per week.
- Round trip to gym, 1 day at 30 minutes = 30 minutes per week.
- Post-workout shower/change, 1 day at 30 minutes = 30 minutes per week.
- Sessions overlap other gym activities, so only 1 day of travel, shower, and change time is factored in.

Total time = 5 hours & 30 minutes per week

"Runs"/Full Court Scrimmages
- Scrimmages, 5 days at 90 minutes each = 7.5 hours per week.
- Round trip to gym, 5 days at 30 minutes each = 2.5 hours per week.
- Post-workout shower/change, 5 days at 30 minutes each = 2.5 hours per week.

Total time = 12 hours & 30 minutes per week

Individual/Small Group Practice Sessions
(Including Individual Shooting Practice)
- Practice sessions, 5 days at 1 hour each = 5 hours per week.
- Practice sessions overlap other gym activities, so no additional travel, shower, and change time is factored in.

Total time = 5 hours per week

Meetings with Coaches (Including Video Review)
- Meetings, 3 days at 45 minutes each = 2 hours & 15 minutes per week.

- Meeting with coaches overlaps other gym activities, so no additional travel time is factored in.

Total time = 2 hours & 15 minutes per week

Spring Out-Of-Season Weekly Total = 25 Hours & 15 minutes

The *"Big"* In-Season Weeks

The NCAA allows 6 days of formal practices and games per week, with 1 "day off." The NCAA allows a total number of "counted/supervised" hours of practices, games and meetings per week of 20 hours, not to exceed 4 hours per day. The NCAA time regulations that apply to the formal games and practices do not include factors such as voluntary individual practice sessions and travel/shower/change times. The times which follow include both counted/supervised and uncounted/unsupervised totals.

Formal Practices
- Pre-practice change/preparation/warm up/stretch, 4 days at 45 minutes each = 3 hours per week.
- Practice, 4 days at 2.5 hours each = 10 hours per week.
- Round trip to gym, 4 days at 30 minutes each = 2 hours per week.
- Post-workout shower/change, 4 days at 30 minutes each = 2 hours per week.

Total time = 17 hours per week

Individual Practice Sessions (Including Official "Day Off")
- Practice routines, 5 days at 45 minutes each = 3 hour & 45 minutes per week.
- Round trip to facility, 1 day at 30 minutes = 30 minutes per week.
- Post-workout shower/change, 1 day at 30 minutes = 30 minutes per week.
- Only 1 travel/shower/change day is factored since 4 days overlap official practice days.

Total time = 4 hours & 45 minutes per week

Reviewing Video
- Reviewing, 3 days at 30 minutes each = 1 hour & 30 minutes per week.

38

- No additional travel time factored in, since video review overlaps other gym activities.

Total time = 1 hour & 30 minutes per week

Team Meetings and Individual Meetings with Coaches

- Meetings, 4 days at 30 minutes each = 2 hours per week.
- No additional travel time factored in, since meetings overlap practices/individual workouts, etc.

Total time = 2 hours per week

In-Season Weekly Total Practice/ Meeting Time = 25 Hours & 15 minutes

Games

(Based on an average of 2 games per week — 1 home and 1 away)

The NCAA allows 28 Division I regular season games as well as a league post-season tournament and post-season NCAA and NIT play.

All Games

- Pre-game meal, 2 days at 1 hour & 15 minutes each (includes round trip to dining hall) = 2 hours & 30 minutes per week.
- Round trips to gym, 2 days at 30 minutes each = 1 hour per week.
- Pre-game dress, 2 days at 15 minutes each = 30 minutes per week.
- Pre-game team meeting with coach, 2 days at 30 minutes each = 1 hour 30 minutes per week.
- Pre-game individual warm-up and stretches, 2 days at 30 minutes each = 1 hour per week.
- Pre-game "on floor" warm-up, 2 days at 20 minutes each = 40 minutes per week.
- Games, 2 days at 2 hours 20 minutes each = 4 hours 40 minutes per week.
- Post-game team meeting with coach/media, 2 days at 30 minutes each = 1 hour per week.
- Post-game shower/change, 2 days at 30 minutes each = 1 hour per week.

Total time =13 hours & 20 minutes per week

In-Season Weekly Total Before Travel Time is Added = 38 hours & 35 Minutes Per Week

Away Game Travel Time

Travel times vary widely depending upon league geography and whether a team is traveling by bus or by air. Many of the "power programs" charter airplanes. Most teams play an average of one away game per week, although this depends on time of season.

Travel by Bus

- Pack prior to trip and unpack upon return = 1 hour per week.
- Time on bus, 2 trips (to and from one away game) at 3 hours & 30 minutes to 7 hours each = 7 to 14 hours per week.

Total time = 8 to 15 hours per week

Travel by Plane

- Pack prior to trip and unpack upon return = 1 hour per week.
- Bus to airport, 2 trips (to airport and back to school upon return) at 30 minutes each = 1 hour per week.
- Airport process – bags, security, boarding/seating, 2 x at 30 minutes each = 1 hour per week.
- Flight time, 2 flights at 2 hours each = 4 hours per week. (Flight times vary from 1 to 3½ or more hours. Average flight time used is 2 hours.)
- Bus trip from airport to game and back to airport - 2 x at 30 minutes each = 1 hour per week.
- Check in and out of hotel, including unpacking and packing, 30 minutes each = 1 hour per week.

Total time = 9 hours per week*

- 9 hours per week is a very conservative time estimate since the distance and traffic patterns to some airports require more than 30 minutes each trip to or from the airport. *The total time could easily be 11-13 hours per week, and this does not include:*
  - *Plane delays, which can be frequent*
  - *2-3 day road trips, during which 2 games are played.*

38

In-Season Total Time Per Week Before Travel
Time = 38 Hours & 35 Minutes Per Week

In-Season Total If Travel By Bus
Time = 46 Hours & 35 Minutes to
53 Hours & 35 Minutes Per Week

In-Season Total If Travel by Plane
Time= 47 Hours & 35 Minutes Per Week

If, for example, 46 hours & 35 minutes minimum per week is devoted to basketball in-season, and a minimum of 10 hours per week is devoted to class time, the Division I men's basketball player is at 56 hours & 35 minutes per week (excluding the "preoccupation") before study time. Is there any wonder that very few Division I men's basketball players undertake rigorous under-graduate study or attend graduate school?

38

NOTES

[1]Institute for International Sport/Encyclopedia of Sports Parenting Survey: youth coaches, parents of youth athletes, high school athletes, high school coaches, parents of high school athletes, college athletes, former high school and college athletes, college coaches and parents of college athletes. 2001-2004.

[2]Taken from Dr. John Sullivan's research, including the following articles:

Anshel, M. H. (1991). "A survey of elite athletes on the perceived causes of using banned drugs in sport." *Journal of Sport Behavior*, 14(4), 283-308.

Laure P., (1997) "Epidemiologic approach of doping in sport. A review." J Sports Med Phys Fitness. 1997 Sep; 37(3):218-24. Centre de Sociopharmacologie, Saint Max, France.

Mottram, D. R., (2003) *Drugs In Sport.*, Routledge Publishing.

NCAA, (2001) "NCAA study of substance use habits of college student-athletes." [Online]. Available: www.ncaa.org

NIDA (2003). "High school and youth trends" [Online]. Available www.nida.nih.gov.

Peretti-Watel, P. Guagliardo, V., Verger, P., Pruvost, J., Mignon, P., & Obadia, Y. (2003). "Sporting activity and drug use: Alcohol, cigarette and cannabis use among elite student athletes." *Addiction*, 98, 1249-1256.

[3]*Newsweek*, March 26, 2007; "Exercise and the Brain" , 38-66.

[4]Time Magazine, January 17, 2005.

[5]IS/ESP Survey, op. cit.,Chapter 6, p. 55.

[6]IS/ESP Survey, op. cit.,Chapter 17, page 163.

[7]IS/ESP Survey, op. cit.,Chapter 17, page 169.

[8]Written statement by Mr. Tom Slear for specific use in *The Encyclopedia of Sports Parenting*.

[9]IS/ESP Survey, op. cit.,Chapter 20, Page 194.

[10] "The Encyclopedia of Sports Parenting" survey of 500 American leaders, conducted in September, 2003.

[11]Taken from concepts presented in the book Jim Collins, *Good to Great*, (New York: Harper Collins, 2001).

[12]Taken from concepts presented in the book Jim Collins, *Good to Great*, (New York: Harper Collins, 2001).

38

[13]American Academy of Pediatrics. Clinical practice guidelines: treatment of the school-aged child with attention-deficit/hyperactive disorders. Pediatrics. 2001; 108:1044.

[14]Barkley, RA, Fischer M, Smallish, L. Fletcher K. The persistence of attention-deficit/hyperactivity disorder into adulthood as a function of reporting source and definitions of disorder. J Abnom Psych. 2002:111-279-289.

[15]"The Multimodal treatment of children with ADHD trial." (MTA).

[16]"Major League Baseball Union," *The New York Times*, August 24, 2004.

[17]D-I Men's Basketball Coaching Changes: 2004-2008. Yahoo Sports.com, Chapter 28, p. 328.

[4]D-I Men's Basketball Foreign Players on Scholarship in 2006, ESPN.com, Chapter 30, p. 353.

38

LISTS

38

38

38

38

INDEX

INDEX

453

INDEX

INDEX

INDEX

INDEX

"There are certain books—rare in number—that truly have a powerful, positive and widespread impact on society. The *Encyclopedia of Sports Parenting* is one such rare and extraordinary book. It is exciting to contemplate what The *Encyclopedia of Sports Parenting* will do for the American Sports culture—and American society. The book is absolutely brilliant."

—The Honorable Patrick Lynch, Attorney General, State of Rhode Island.

"A tremendous book!! Dan Doyle's scholarly, yet practical approach to the study of Sports Parenting is long overdue. His real world experience coupled with a discerning eye brings great credibility and authenticity to his work. In a society where many parents, student athletes and institutions are trending toward the extreme as it pertains to their view and practice of athletics, the *Encyclopedia of Sports Parenting* compellingly offers much needed balance and perspective. The book is brilliantly written, and a must read for parents, coaches, athletic directors and school administrators."

—Michael Welch, Headmaster, St. Johns High School (MA)

"Through a combination of tremendous wisdom, practical application, hands-on exercises and available resources, Doyle provides parents with a brilliant and flawless approach to guiding their children on the playing field and throughout life. Doyle proves that sport is an integral part of the American educational delivery system, which provides parents with a uniquely fertile ground where important seeds leading to a meaningful life can be purposefully planted, sown and cultivated. The *Encyclopedia of Sports Parenting* illustrates that the same challenges we face in the process of living our adult lives are the challenges our kids face in the microcosm of an athletic stage. No sport or parenting book ever written will have a more positive influence on society than Doyle's masterpiece."

—Mike Cleary, Executive Director,
National Association of College Athlete Directors.

"*Encyclopedia of Sports Parenting* should be on the desk of every parent. Dan Doyle shows us the way to raise our children in a sports environment so they are able to get the best sport has to give including integrity, ethical values, good health and a special understanding of the value of teamwork as it can impact diversity. This book is truly a great gift to American society."

—Richard Lapchick, Director, Institute for Diversity and Ethics in Sport,
and Chair of the DeVos Sport Business Management
Graduate Program at the University of Central Florida

"Dan Doyle's experience as a parent, coach, educator and visionary, results in a truly extraordinary book. Dan completely understands the positive values that sport can teach. I highly recommend this tremendous book to all who see sport as an important educational component in the education of youth. The *Encyclopedia of Sports Parenting* is a brilliant resource for parents, educators and young people!"

—Barbara Bausch, Head Women's Basketball Coach,
St. Mary's College of Maryland.

"Dan Doyle's *Encyclopedia of Sports Parenting* is a book about uncommon, common sense. Dan concisely addresses the benefits and challenges of competition from the

473

perspective of an educator, parent, and former coach. He has artfully translated the theory of effective teaching and parenting into actual practice. At Princeton, we refer to this approach as character- and/or values-based coaching, an expectation that is consistent with fulfilling the educational mission of our University. Fundamental skill development, or "doing things right," is only one part of the equation, and perhaps the least important part. The playing field should also be an ethical training ground where the participants learn "to do the right thing." This process can only take place if the parents/coaches themselves are positive role models — leaders who possess the requisite knowledge, values and character to impart transforming life lessons when "teachable moments" occur. Those of us in the field of athletic education owe Dan a debt of gratitude for identifying, raising and reinforcing the standards of conduct intrinsic to successful sports parenting."

—Gary Walters, Director of Athletics, Princeton University.

"When I was a kid, I systematically went to my dad with questions, and, just as systematically, instead of giving me a quick answer, he would say, "Look it up in the Encyclopedia!" Dad's advice rings true once again with the publication of Dan Doyle's *Encyclopedia of Sports Parenting*. If you're a parent with kids in sports, and you have questions, take my dad's advice, "Look it up in Dan Doyle's Encyclopedia!" You will indeed find topics from A to Z. Dan is a writer, a philosopher, a teacher, a parent, a coach, and a poet. His values laden approach to youth sports combines discussions of the practical "how to" and the thought provoking "what if." Whether it's the well-designed and thorough organization of his material, or his easy-to- read style, or his concise summary boxes to ensure that we take away the kernel message on every topic, Dan Doyle has produced a work truly worthy of the term "encyclopedic."

—Darrell J. Burnett, Ph.D., Clinical Psychologist,
Certified Sports Psychologist, specializing in Youth Sports.

Encyclopedia of Sports Parenting teems with information for all levels and interests of sports and athletics. With great insight and near-reverence for the power of sport not only to change lives, but even more importantly, to change the world, In conducting his research, Doyle plumbed the minds and expertise of hundreds of renowned and respected coaches as well as student athletes for information about the college recruiting process, the pros and cons of playing Division I or Division III sports, how and when to talk to your child's coach, sports camps, and so much more. Open to any page and you will be rewarded with advice, statistics, web information, and a host of resources for athletes, playing at all levels, in this essential sports guide for parents. *Encyclopedia of Sports Parenting* makes you feel as if you have your own personal sports consultant at your disposal, 24-7, at a fraction of a sports consultant's fee. Now that's a slam-dunk!"

—Lynn Hoffman, sports parent and acclaimed poet.

"Tying in his incredible wealth of sports knowledge with his unwavering belief in good sportsmanship, Dan Doyle has written an amazing sports bible for everyone from the parents of youngsters approaching sports for the first time, to the parents of talented Division I prospects. Along the way meticulously researched advice and

factual examples abound for everyone. As a teacher I loved the clear instructions and the ethics espoused for parents, coaches and children alike. As a parent I only wish that I could have gotten his invaluable advice twenty-five years earlier when my children went through all the issues he expands upon from good/bad coaches to parental input to sportsmanship to balancing numerous sports to, in our case, college advice for the Division III student-athlete and parent. Kudos to Dan Doyle and to this great book!"
—Linda Pearson, sports parent and educator

"Dan Doyle's *Encyclopedia of Sports Parenting* functions as a powerful 'go to' book, an invaluable lookup or reference source. Dan has been the founder of several of the most powerful organizations and movements where sports, ethics and international relations talk to one another. In a time when sports and ethics often seem to be on different planets, let alone different wavelengths, Dan's voice as an ethicist who knows more about sport than all but a handful is both needed and powerful."
—William C. Hiss, Vice President for External Affairs, Bates College

"In Dan Doyle's stunningly thorough book, his is a voice of sanity amid a bedlam of hype. He knows that what the real loss is: the loss of the multitude of other values that attention only to being the best, not ones best mind you, but THE best causes. He knows how quickly a child can have the soul-nourishing experience of sports anesthetized by even well meaning coaches, parents, schools, and sports fans. He knows what happens to our selves when we narrow the plurality of values inherent in sport not just to winning but to defeating the other. . . Dan Doyle's work is in behalf of all the good that sport can bring into our days whether we are playing or rooting for a champion or shooting hoops under a garage light in the driveway. Many voices call for reform. His voice calls for restoration, the restoration of what, after the madness of March, really matters." —Jack Ridl, acclaimed poets, and son of the late "Buzz" Ridl, legendary basketball coach at the University of Pittsburgh

"I spent more than 30 years hosting a sports talk program on a powerful radio station. Through thousand of hours many issues were debated, few were resolved. Does one learn more from a loss than a win? Should we praise a coach for "working the officials"? Is it right to retaliate? Dan Doyle dissects and examines these and many other subjects in *Encyclopedia of Sports Parenting*. This is a "must have" book for administrators, coaches and parents. The values revealed and encouraged will create a new generation of those who would restore the true meaning of sports. And best of all it's a fascinating read. This is the perfect time for this definitive work and Dan Doyle is the right person to compile it. In every way it's a grand slam!"
—Arnold Dean, former sports director, WTIC Radio, Hartford, CT

"Consider this book to be a toolbox full of practical insights, lessons, and advice for anyone participating in sports at any level. It examines the myriad questions, quandaries, decisions and dilemmas faced by student athletes, their parents and coaches, explores them deeply, and provides a solid framework to promote mutual understanding. It just makes sense. As a bonus, Dan Doyle puts ethical conduct and sportsmanship at the forefront as moral guidelines and lessons for life. No student-athlete, parent or coach should be without the wisdom in this book."
—Art Quirk, former Dartmouth College and Major League Baseball player

"Pediatrician Benjamin Spock wrote his heralded book, *Baby and Child Care*, to help parents answer questions about raising happy and healthy children. Dan Doyle has written the *Encyclopedia of Sports Parenting* for those same parents whose children are about to undertake youth sports programs. In Dan's long overdue and much needed Encyclopedia, every conceivable question a parent may have about supporting and encouraging children in their engagement in sports is addressed. For parents with children engaged in youth programs through high school athletics, *Encyclopedia of Sports Parenting* is a "must read". I have two daughters with young children. My gift to each will be Dan's book. They must have it on their book shelves."

—Edmund J. Wilson is the Associate Dean Emeritus for Master's Degree Programs & Student Affairs at Northwestern University's Kellogg School of Management, Evanston, Illinois.

"As a parent and coach, I appreciate the commitment Dan Doyle has made to synthesize an astounding array of information and to sharpen our focus on those philosophies and practices that will most positively impact our players. As someone who works with young people—many of whom are student-athletes—and supports their collegiate experience, I appreciate the consistent focus Dan maintains on the student-athlete as a young person working to develop his or her highest potential—wherever that potential may lie."

—Colleen J. Quint, Executive Director, the Mitchell Institute and Senator George J. Mitchell Scholarship Research Institute, Portland, Maine

"As a college coach, the section on college recruiting is outstanding. There is so much misinformation and misleading advice that parents don't know where to turn when sons or daughters are looking to continue their athletic careers at the college level. Dan Doyle gives us an in-depth perspective on this subject, to help parents and students avoid mistakes and understand the recruiting process. He explains the process and helps any parent or student with college aspirations understand how things work and how best to find the school that is the right fit, academically and athletically. Those looking for a high quality text on sports parenting, coaching youth sports, and the values in helping our children become people of character in life, need not look any further.

—Laura Hungerford, Head Women's Basketball Coach, Connecticut College

"*Encyclopedia of Sports Parenting* is a tremendous resource not only for parents but also coaches and administrators at all levels of amateur sports. It offers great advice and knowledge to a broad spectrum from the first-time parent to the parent who has worked in amateur athletics for many, many years such as myself. No matter what your background, experience or knowledge, this book has practical and valuable information that will help you guide your child through all levels of athletic participation in a healthy manner. This book also helps remind coaches and administrators what they should be emphasizing as they educate our young athletes. I truly believe that every youth league across the country should make this book available to its coaches and administrators and it is absolutely a must have for parents. All will benefit from this extraordinary book by Dan Doyle!"

—Chuck Mitrano, Commissioner, Empire 8 Conference

"Dan Doyle has brilliantly encapsulated all of the major issues that define the relationship that parents should have with their young athletes, and the pitfalls they often find themselves succumbing to—and the excesses we all seek to avoid. USA Volleyball is eagerly anticipating making Dan's text required reading in our junior programs as well as coaching development sessions."

—Douglas P. Beal, Chief Executive Officer, USA Volleyball

"*Encyclopedia of Sports Parenting* is a masterful effort filled with up-to-date information and resources for parents who are interested in deciphering the complex world of youth sports and beyond. I highly recommend this brilliantly written book to anyone as a helpful guide in their journey through raising a child who plays sports."

—Dr. John Sullivan, Clinical Psychologist

"Once you begin reading Dan Doyle's Guide to Sports Parenting, you'll realize that you've finally found a companion to help you put and keep the world of youth, school, and college sports in perspective! Doyle has thought of every scenario in which children and parents intersect with the world of athletics, and he provides helpful advice and perspective for each situation. You'll want to keep this valuable resource within easy grasp. You'll find yourself regularly searching for the comfort of Doyle's advice (as well as some of his literary references to athletics) as your child progresses through the world of organized sports."

—Jim Skiff, Assistant Head for Institutional Advancement,
Providence Country Day School

A touching and compelling book on issues in sports parenting and competition that we face in the 21st century. This book is filled with wisdom, inspiration and sports and social competition strategies. Dan Doyle is a true renaissance man! I recommend this book to everyone concerned about the impact of sports competition on children and their parents. *Encyclopedia of Sports Parenting* should win a Pulitzer Prize. It's the Thesaurus of sports parenting."

—Susan Summons, Miami Dade College, Associate Professor,
Head Women's Basketball Coach and acclaimed motivational speaker

"Awesome! *Encyclopedia of Sports Parenting* speaks to what is really important and valuable about participation in sports. This should be required reading for every parent whose children participate in youth sports. USA Swimming completely supports this extraordinary book."   —Chuck Wielgus, Executive Director, USA Swimming

"*Encyclopedia of Sports Parenting* is a must have roadmap for the parent who takes on the important responsibility for overseeing their child's sporting dreams, at whatever level."

—Noel Keating, former CEO, Irish Basketball Association, former Assistant Chef de
Mission Irish Olympic Team, sports parent and teacher

"Parents, read this terrific book - your child will thank you!"

—Jim Thompson, Executive Director,
Positive Coaching Alliance, Stanford University

COLOPHON

I chose the title "The Encyclopedia of Sports Parenting" because my objective with this three-volume series is to carefully address issues essential to developing a comprehensive sports parenting and coaching philosophy. While I do not employ the A-Z format of most encyclopedias, the series, which will include a Volume II of *The Encyclopedia of Sports Parenting* and *The Master Coach Manual*, scrupulously follows *The American Heritage Dictionary* definition of encyclopedia, *i.e., a comprehensive work covering numerous aspects of a particular field.*

Volume II (scheduled for publication in 2009) will provide in-depth commentary on additional issues faced by sports parents, commentary which will also be useful for the further development of a comprehensive sports parenting philosophy.

The objective of *The Master Coach Manual* (scheduled for publication in 2009) is to raise the standard of coaching and enhance the impact of coaches on society. Among other objectives, *The Master Coach Manual* will help coaches develop a coherent philosophy which they can impart to their student-athletes—a philosophy that encompasses the recognition that sport, at its best, can contribute to a positive and civil society.

The text was set in Minion. Minion is a the text face designed by Robert Slimbach (1956-) in 1989. Minion was developed during his time at Adobe and shows his preference for classical design. Slimbach is multi-talented in a very American way getting a scholarship to college in gymnastics. He has some renown as a calligrapher and a photographer. With Cochin em-dashs and Trajan display type and folios, the type compliment is classical.

The cover and text design is by Spencer Berger, Newport, Rhode Island. This book was typeset by Rhode Island Book Composition, Kingston, Rhode Island and printed by Data Reproduction, Auburn, Michigan on acid free paper.